THE LINGO

Programmer's Reference

VENTANA

THE LINGO
Programmer's
Reference

Darrel Plant & Doug Smith

Library of Congress Catalog Card Number: 97-060676

First Edition 9 8 7 6 5 4 3 2
Printed in the United States of America

Ventana Communications Group
P.O. Box 13964
Research Triangle Park, NC 27709-3964
919.544.9404
FAX 919.544.9472
http://www.vmedia.com

Ventana Communications Group is a division of International Thomson Publishing.

President
Michael E. Moran

**Vice President of
Content Development**
Karen A. Bluestein

**Director of Acquisitions and
Development**
Robert Kern

Managing Editor
Lois J. Principe

Production Manager
John Cotterman

Art Director
Marcia Webb

**Technology Operations
Manager**
Kerry L. B. Foster

Brand Manager
Jamie Jaeger Fiocco

Creative Services Manager
Diane Lennox

Acquisitions Editor
JJ Hohn

Project Editor
Judith F. Wilson

Development Editor
Michelle Corbin Nichols

Copy Editor
Marion Laird

CD-ROM Specialist
Ginny Phelps

Technical Reviewer
Rob Terrell

Desktop Publisher
Jaimie Livingston

Proofreader
Chris Riffer

Interior Designer
Patrick Berry

Cover Illustrator
Lisa Gill

About the Authors

Darrel Plant is the author of Ventana's *Shockwave! Breathe New Life Into Your Web Pages*. He is the principal at Moshofsky/Plant, in Portland, Oregon, a creative services company specializing in graphic design and production, as well as World Wide Web/network-based multimedia delivery. Plant graduated from Portland's Reed College with a degree in English Literature, and he has a certificate from the New York University Summer Institute in Book and Magazine Publishing.

Plant has worked in the bookselling and electronic prepress industries; designed, written software for, and operated a play-by-mail game company; published and edited a book review magazine; written for *WIRED*, *Step-by-Step Graphics*, *The Net*, and *Lingo User's Journal*; and run as a Democratic primary candidate for the Oregon State House of Representatives. Plant can be contacted at:

World Wide Web: www.moshplant.com
E-mail: dplant@moshplant.com

Doug Smith is an independent multimedia producer living in Yachats (pronounced yaw-hots) on the beautiful Oregon Coast. After 10 years with Idaho-based computer and chip manufacturer Micron Technology (four of these years as the leader of their Multimedia Development team), he moved back to his native state to found Arôgos Interactive. Doug's experience runs the gamut of Director-based multimedia: hard-drive presentations, floppy-disk demos, CD-ROM video, Shockwave, and intranet training. His diligence and attention to detail were put to their full use in the creation and testing of the reference sections of this book. Contact Doug at:

World Wide Web: www.arogos.com
E-mail: dugsmith@arogos.com

Acknowledgments

My greatest thanks go once again to my wife, Barbara Moshofsky, who manages to pick up all the slack left behind when I'm writing a book.

Thanks also to:

David and Sherry Rogelberg, of the Studio B Literary Agency (www.studiob.com), for the help and advice they've given.

Judy Wilson, JJ Hohn, Michelle Nichols, and everyone else at Ventana (www.vmedia.com) for making sure that everything was ready for the release date.

The Surf Trio (www.surftrio.com): Jeff Martin, Pete Weinberg, Ron Kleim, Aaron Temple, and Ramon LaMadrid—they know why.

the-guys@moshplant.com: Eric, Ptr, Brian—you got your full names in here last time, OK?

Peter Small, author of *Lingo Sorcery: The Magic of Lists, Objects and Intelligent Agents*, for ideas, and for his family's hospitality.

John Dowdell, Dorian Dowse, Scott Flowers, Marvyn Hortman, Kirk Keller, Buzz Kettles, Alan Levine, Gretchen McDowell, David Mndels, Glenn Picher, Michael Rose, Gary Rosenzweig, Terry Schussler, Alex Zavatone, and everyone else at the 1996 Macromedia International User Conference who provided inspiration and support.

Roy Pardi, Chino, and the other members of the Direct-L and ShockeR lists, whose constant chatter provides the hydrogen line static of my existence.

My parents, my relatives, and everyone who's been accidentally left out of any book acknowledgment from now unto perpetuity.

–DP

First, I want to thank Darrel Plant for the opportunity to work with him on this ambitious project. He has been gracious enough to share his time and talents to mentor me into the wild and wonderful world of book publishing.

To the team at Micron Digital Imagery: Brian Soderman, Doug Armentrout, Darren Isaacs, Ron Bearry, Susan Hamilton, Caitlin Williams, Chris Bernardi, Brian Boyd, Terry Dobler, Jason Jacopian, Michelle Waddell, Aaron Gallup, and Mark Spear. Thanks for the opportunity to cut my multimedia teeth with the best video, animation, and multimedia team in the world.

Thanks to the Direct-L community, especially Glenn Picher, John Dowdell, Alex Zavatone, and the rest of the regulars for an unending supply of answers to real-world questions.

Finally, I wish to thank the people who bring joy and color to my otherwise code-filled world: Wendy, for whom words will never fully express my love and admiration; and our dear children, Stephanie and Tiffany. You truly are my inspiration.

–DS

Contents

Jump Tables

The following jump tables will help you find the information you need if you can't find it by category. There are two tables:

- A guide to the examples in the book, which answer common "How do I. . .? Lingo questions.
- An alphabetical listing of all the entries in this book.

These jump tables supplement the categorical listings by providing an alternative method to finding a specific command, as well as a way to track down the code example that did what you need to do now.

Examples Sorted by Task

This table contains brief descriptions of the more complex examples in the book. In most cases, these examples consist of one or more handlers that can be used to accomplish a common task in Lingo. These aren't necessarily the only methods to achieve the same result, but they are in the book.

Task Description	Entry	Keyword Type	Page
Align graphics with text automatically	charPosToLoc	Function	182
Animate a sprite in a continuous loop	the number of member	Member Prop.	165
Animate the scrolling of a field	the scrollTop of member	Member Prop.	194
Check to see if computer can play CD Audio	mci	Command	111
Check to see if the digital video type can be played	the digitalVideoType of member	Member Prop.	218
Check to see whether movie is running in Shockwave	version	System Variable	117
Choose a cast based on mood	the number of castLib	Cast Prop.	145
Collision detection of a list of sprites	sprite intersects	Function	288
Convert all frame labels into a linear list	the labelList	Movie Prop.	45
Convert the names of all 8-bit members to a linear list	the depth of member	Member Prop.	153
Convert the standard date to an international date format	the date	Movie Prop.	346
Convert uppercase characters to lowercase	charToNum	Function.	477
Convert uppercase letters to lowercase	the shiftDown	Movie Prop.	71
Copy a cast member and give it a new name	duplicate member	Command	154
Create a thermometer-style status bar	the height of sprite	Sprite Prop.	273
Create list of files from directory	getNthFileNameInFolder	Function	369
Create list of unique random numbers	addAt	Command	431
Delete a range of frames in the score	deleteFrame	Command	329
Delete HTML tags from text string	delete	Command	478
Directory paths: supporting cross-platform conventions	go loop	Command	3
Display all MIAWs in order	moveToBack	Command	390
Display available Xtras	xtra	Keyword	427
Display the playback time of a digital video	framesToHMS	Function	43
Display the time before the movie goes into timeout mode	the timeoutLapsed	Movie Prop.	74
Dissolve a sprite from opaque to fully transparent	the blend of sprite	Sprite Prop.	265

Description	Function	Category	Page
Download and display a movie in a window	the fileName of window	Window Prop.	387
Download media from Internet with error checking	downloadNetThing	Command	12
Draw movie at 50% of size	the drawRect of window	Window Prop.	386
Duplicate all members of current cast into a new cast	the activeCastLib	Movie Prop.	142
Enable all custom buttons on the stage	the enabled of member	Member Prop.	155
Error checking when downloading from Internet	netError	Function	20
Estimate the data rate of the Internet connection	the ticks	Movie Prop.	350
Fade in the sound of a Shockwave Audio member	the volume of member	Member Prop.	262
Get any "chunk" of text the mouse is over with one handler	the mouseChar	Movie Prop.	92
Get the height of the tallest line in a field	lineHeight	Function	187
Get the length of a digital video member in seconds	the digitalVideoTimeScale	Movie Prop.	212
Get the most recent cue point passed	the cuePointNames of member	Member Prop.	207
Get the number of sound tracks in a digital video member	trackCount	Function	223
Get the total memory size of all cast members	the size of member	Member Prop.	175
Highlight specific word of a field	hilite	Command	482
Horizontal distance between points	abs	Function	510
Keyboard control of sprite movement	the key	Movie Prop.	63
Keyboard shortcuts with Shift, Alt/Option, and Control	the commandDown	Movie Prop.	60
Maintain movie position when window is moved	on moveWindow	Handler	391
Maintain original movie position when window is moved	the sourceRect of window	Window Prop.	395
Mouse control of sprite movement	the mouseDown	Movie Prop.	93
Move a sprite in an elliptical orbit, record the path in the score	beginRecording	Command	328
Move pictures between different Shockwave movies	the picture of member	Member Prop.	169
Normalize the display of a transition	the duration of member	Member Prop.	201
Read parameters from HTML page making into a list	externalParamName	Function	32
Send messages from Shockwave movie to browser script	on EvalScript	Handler	528
Set the alignment of text in a field with certainty	the alignment of member	Member Prop.	178
Show a scroll bar automatically when necessary	the boxType of member	Member Prop.	181
Simulate a trackpad mouse	map	Function	302
Toggle playback with pause/continue	continue	Command	2
Wait in a frame for an amount of time	delay	Command	2

Alphabetical Listing of Entries

This table is organized alphabetically by keyword. The type of keyword, and the page and chapter where it can be found, are here as well. Also listed in shorthand form is the information indicated by the icons in each entry, detailing which versions of Director the keyword can be used with, its compatibility with different platforms and the Shockwave plug-in, and whether it is URL-enhanced (can use a URL as a file path in Director 6).

Entry	Type	Restrictions[†]
	Found in Chapter	Go to Page
[ ]	Operator	D4, D5, D6
	Chapter 36: Lists Category	430
&	Operator	D4, D5, D6
	Chapter 38: Strings Category	472
&&	Operator	D4, D5, D6
	Chapter 38: Strings Category	473
( )	Operator	D4, D5, D6
	Chapter 39: Math: Operators Category	500
−	Operator	D4, D5, D6
	Chapter 39: Math: Operators Category	500
*	Operator	D4, D5, D6
	Chapter 39: Math: Operators Category	502
/	Operator	D4, D5, D6
	Chapter 39: Math: Operators Category	502
+	Operator	D4, D5, D6
	Chapter 39: Math: Operators Category	503
<	Operator	D4, D5, D6
	Chapter 39: Math: Operators Category	503
<=	Operator	D4, D5, D6
	Chapter 39: Math: Operators Category	504
<>	Operator	D4, D5, D6
	Chapter 39: Math: Operators Category	504
=	Operator	D4, D5, D6
	Chapter 39: Math: Operators Category	505
>	Operator	D4, D5, D6
	Chapter 39: Math: Operators Category	505
>=	Operator	D4, D5, D6
	Chapter 39: Math: Operators Category	506

† Restrictions Legend:

D4 Used in Director 4   **NS** Cannot be used with Shockwave

D5 Used in Director 5   **SH** Can be used with Shockwave

D6 Used in Director 6   **OBS** Obsolete in Director 6

MO Used only on the Macintosh platform   **WO** Used only on the Windows platform

URL URL-enhanced (can use a URL as a file path in Director 6)

Entry	Type	Restrictions†
	Found in Chapter	Go to Page
the bitRate of member	Member Property	D5, D6
	Chapter 21: Shockwave Audio Category	252
the bitsPerSample of member	Member Property	D6
	Chapter 21: Shockwave Audio Category	253
the blend of sprite	Sprite Property	D4, D5, D6
	Chapter 22: Sprites Category	265
the border of member	Member Property	D5, D6
	Chapter 14: Fields Category	180
the bottom of sprite	Sprite Property	D4, D5, D6
	Chapter 22: Sprites Category	266
the boxDropShadow of member	Member Property	D5, D6
	Chapter 14: Fields Category	180
the boxType of member	Member Property	D5, D6
	Chapter 14: Fields Category	181
browserName	Movie Property	D6, NS
	Chapter 4: Network: Cache Category	36
the buttonStyle	Movie Property	D4, D5, D6
	Chapter 29: Buttons Category	354
the buttonType of member	Member Property	D5, D6
	Chapter 29: Buttons Category	354
cacheDocVerify	Movie Property	D6, NS
	Chapter 4: Network: Cache Category	37
cacheSize	Movie Property	D6, NS
	Chapter 4: Network: Cache Category	38
call	Command	D6
	Chapter 33: Behaviors Category	405
callAncestor	Command	D6
	Chapter 33: Behaviors Category	406
cancelIdleLoad	Command	D5, D6
	Chapter 11: Memory Management (Idle Loading) Category	136
case	Logic	D5, D6
	Chapter 37: Code Structures & Syntax Category	454

† Restrictions Legend:

- **D4** Used in Director 4
- **D5** Used in Director 5
- **D6** Used in Director 6
- **MO** Used only on the Macintosh platform
- **URL** URL-enhanced (can use a URL as a file path in Director 6)
- **NS** Cannot be used with Shockwave
- **SH** Can be used with Shockwave
- **OBS** Obsolete in Director 6
- **WO** Used only on the Windows platform

† Restrictions Legend:

D4 Used in Director 4
D5 Used in Director 5
D6 Used in Director 6
MO Used only on the Macintosh platform
URL URL-enhanced (can use a URL as a file path in Director 6)

NS Cannot be used with Shockwave
SH Can be used with Shockwave
OBS Obsolete in Director 6
WO Used only on the Windows platform

† **Restrictions Legend:**
- **D4** Used in Director 4
- **D5** Used in Director 5
- **D6** Used in Director 6
- **MO** Used only on the Macintosh platform
- **URL** URL-enhanced (can use a URL as a file path in Director 6)
- **NS** Cannot be used with Shockwave
- **SH** Can be used with Shockwave
- **OBS** Obsolete in Director 6
- **WO** Used only on the Windows platform

Entry	Type	Restrictions†
	Found in Chapter	Go to Page
externalParamName	Function	D5, D6, SH
	Chapter 3: Network: Shockwave Category	32
externalParamValue	Function	D5, D6, SH
	Chapter 3: Network: Shockwave Category	33
FALSE	Constant	D4, D5, D6
	Chapter 41: Logic Category	520
field	Keyword	D4, D5, D6
	Chapter 42: Miscellaneous Lingo Category	531
the fileName of castLib	Cast Property	D5, D6, URL
	Chapter 12: Casts Category	143
the fileName of castLib	Cast Property	D5, D6, URL
	Chapter 31: External Files Category	367
the fileName of member	Member Property	D5, D6, URL
	Chapter 13: Cast Members Category	156
the fileName of member	Member Property	D4, D5, D6
	Chapter 31: External Files Category	368
the fileName of window	Window Property	D4, D5, D6, URL
	Chapter 32: Movie in a Window (MIAW) Category	387
the filled of member	Member Property	D5, D6
	Chapter 30: Shapes Category	360
findEmpty	Function	D5, D6
	Chapter 12: Casts Category	144
findPos	Function	D4, D5, D6
	Chapter 36: Lists Category	437
findPosNear	Function	D4, D5, D6
	Chapter 36: Lists Category	437
finishIdleLoad	Command	D5, D6
	Chapter 11: Memory Management (Idle Loading) Category	136
the fixStageSize	Movie Property	D4, D5, D6
	Chapter 5: Movie Control Category	42
float	Function	D4, D5, D6
	Chapter 40: Math: Functions Category	512

† Restrictions Legend:

D4	Used in Director 4	**NS**	Cannot be used with Shockwave
D5	Used in Director 5	**SH**	Can be used with Shockwave
D6	Used in Director 6	**OBS**	Obsolete in Director 6
MO	Used only on the Macintosh platform	**WO**	Used only on the Windows platform
URL	URL-enhanced (can use a URL as a file path in Director 6)		

Entry	Type	Restrictions[†]
	Found in Chapter	Go to Page
the frameTransition	Movie Property	D4, D5, D6
	Chapter 24: Frames Category	314
the freeBlock	Movie Property	D4, D5, D6
	Chapter 10: Memory Management Category	120
the freeBytes	Movie Property	D4, D5, D6
	Chapter 10: Memory Management Category	121
the frontWindow	Movie Property	D5, D6
	Chapter 32: Movie in a Window (MIAW) Category	388
the fullColorPermit	Movie Property	D6
	Chapter 9: Computer & Monitor Control Category	109
getaProp	Function	D4, D5, D6
	Chapter 36: Lists Category	438
getAt	Function	D4, D5, D6
	Chapter 36: Lists Category	439
getError	Function	D5, D6
	Chapter 37: Code Structures & Syntax Category	458
getErrorString	Function	D5, D6
	Chapter 37: Code Structures & Syntax Category	458
getLast	Function	D4, D5, D6
	Chapter 36: Lists Category	439
getLatestNetID	Function	D4, D5, D6, URL, SH
	Chapter 2: Network Category	14
getNetText	Command	D4, D5, D6, URL, SH
	Chapter 2: Network Category	14
getNthFileNameInFolder	Function	D4, D5, D6, NS
	Chapter 31: External Files Category	369
getOne	Function	D4, D5, D6
	Chapter 36: Lists Category	440
getPos	Function	D4, D5, D6
	Chapter 36: Lists Category	441
getPref	Function	D5, D6, SH
	Chapter 2: Network Category	16

† Restrictions Legend:

D4	Used in Director 4	**NS**	Cannot be used with Shockwave
D5	Used in Director 5	**SH**	Can be used with Shockwave
D6	Used in Director 6	**OBS**	Obsolete in Director 6
MO	Used only on the Macintosh platform	**WO**	Used only on the Windows platform
URL	URL-enhanced (can use a URL as a file path in Director 6)		

Entry	Type	Restrictions[†]
	Found in Chapter	Go to Page
the idleLoadMode	Movie Property	D5, D6
	Chapter 11: Memory Management (Idle Loading) Category	138
the idleLoadPeriod	Movie Property	D5, D6
	Chapter 11: Memory Management (Idle Loading) Category	139
the idleLoadTag	Movie Property	D5, D6
	Chapter 11: Memory Management (Idle Loading) Category	139
the idleReadChunkSize	Movie Property	D5, D6
	Chapter 11: Memory Management (Idle Loading) Category	140
if	Logic	D4, D5, D6
	Chapter 37: Code Structures & Syntax Category	460
ilk	Function	D4, D5, D6
	Chapter 36: Lists Category	442
importFileInto	Command	D5, D6, URL
	Chapter 13: Cast Members Category	159
importFileInto	Command	D4, D5, D6, URL
	Chapter 31: External Files Category	371
inflate	Command	D4, D5, D6
	Chapter 23: Rects and Points Category	300
the initialToggleState of member	member Property	D6, NS
	Chapter 13: Cast Members Category	160
the ink of sprite	Sprite Property	D4, D5, D6
	Chapter 22: Sprites Category	274
insertFrame	Command	D5, D6
	Chapter 26: Score Generation Category	331
inside	Function	D4, D5, D6
	Chapter 23: Rects and Points Category	300
installMenu	Command	D4, D5, D6, NS
	Chapter 27: Menus Category	339
integer	Function	D4, D5, D6
	Chapter 40: Math: Functions Category	514
integerP	Function	D4, D5, D6
	Chapter 40: Math: Functions Category	514

† Restrictions Legend:

D4	Used in Director 4	**NS**	Cannot be used with Shockwave
D5	Used in Director 5	**SH**	Can be used with Shockwave
D6	Used in Director 6	**OBS**	Obsolete in Director 6
MO	Used only on the Macintosh platform	**WO**	Used only on the Windows platform
URL	URL-enhanced (can use a URL as a file path in Director 6)		

Entry	Type	Restrictions[†]
	Found in Chapter	Go to Page
the lastRoll	Movie Property	D4, D5, D6
	Chapter 8: User Interaction (Mouse) Category	91
the left of sprite	Sprite Property	D4, D5, D6
	Chapter 22: Sprites Category	276
length	Function	D4, D5, D6
	Chapter 38: Strings Category	485
line	Function	D4, D5, D6
	Chapter 38: Strings Category	486
the lineCount of member	Member Property	D5, D6
	Chapter 14: Fields Category	187
lineHeight	Function	D5, D6
	Chapter 14: Fields Category	187
the lineHeight of member	Member Property	D5, D6
	Chapter 14: Fields Category	188
linePosToLocV	Function	D5, D6
	Chapter 14: Fields Category	189
the lineSize of member	Member Property	D5, D6
	Chapter 30: Shapes Category	360
the lineSize of sprite	Sprite Property	D4, D5, D6
	Chapter 22: Sprites Category	276
list	Function	D4, D5, D6
	Chapter 36: Lists Category	444
listP	Function	D4, D5, D6
	Chapter 36: Lists Category	444
the loaded of member	Member Property	D5, D6
	Chapter 10: Memory Management Category	121
the loc of sprite	Sprite Property	D4, D5, D6
	Chapter 22: Sprites Category	277
the locH of sprite	Sprite Property	D4, D5, D6
	Chapter 22: Sprites Category	277
locToCharPos	Function	D5, D6
	Chapter 14: Fields Category	189

† Restrictions Legend:

D4	Used in Director 4	**NS**	Cannot be used with Shockwave
D5	Used in Director 5	**SH**	Can be used with Shockwave
D6	Used in Director 6	**OBS**	Obsolete in Director 6
MO	Used only on the Macintosh platform	**WO**	Used only on the Windows platform
URL	URL-enhanced (can use a URL as a file path in Director 6)		

Entry	Type	Restrictions†
	Found in Chapter	Go to Page
member	Keyword	D5, D6
	Chapter 13: Cast Members Category	162
the member of sprite	Sprite Property	D6
	Chapter 22: Sprites Category	279
the memberNum of sprite	Sprite Property	D5, D6
	Chapter 22: Sprites Category	279
the memorySize	Movie Property	D4, D5, D6
	Chapter 10: Memory Management Category	123
menu	Keyword	D4, D5, D6, NS
	Chapter 27: Menus Category	340
min	Function	D4, D5, D6
	Chapter 42: Miscellaneous Lingo Category	533
mInstanceRespondsTo	Method	D4, D5, D6
	Chapter 34: Methods Category	421
mMessageList	Method	D4, D5, D6
	Chapter 34: Methods Category	421
mName	Method	D4, D5, D6
	Chapter 34: Methods Category	422
mNew	Method	D4, D5, D6
	Chapter 34: Methods Category	422
mod	Operator	D4, D5, D6
	Chapter 39: Math: Operators Category	506
the modal of window	Window Property	D4, D5, D6, NS
	Chapter 32: Movie in a Window (MIAW) Category	389
the modified of member	Member Property	D4, D5, D6
	Chapter 13: Cast Members Category	162
the mostRecentCuePoint of sprite	Sprite Property	D6
	Chapter 16: Sound: Cue Points Category	209
the mouseChar	Movie Property	D4, D5, D6
	Chapter 8: User Interaction (Mouse) Category	92
the mouseDown	Movie Property	D4, D5, D6
	Chapter 8: User Interaction (Mouse) Category	93

† Restrictions Legend:

D4	Used in Director 4	**NS**	Cannot be used with Shockwave
D5	Used in Director 5	**SH**	Can be used with Shockwave
D6	Used in Director 6	**OBS**	Obsolete in Director 6
MO	Used only on the Macintosh platform	**WO**	Used only on the Windows platform
URL	URL-enhanced (can use a URL as a file path in Director 6)		

† Restrictions Legend:

D4	Used in Director 4	**NS**	Cannot be used with Shockwave
D5	Used in Director 5	**SH**	Can be used with Shockwave
D6	Used in Director 6	**OBS**	Obsolete in Director 6
MO	Used only on the Macintosh platform	**WO**	Used only on the Windows platform
URL	URL-enhanced (can use a URL as a file path in Director 6)		

Entry	Type	Restrictions†
	Found in Chapter	Go to Page
objectP	Function	D4, D5, D6
	Chapter 33: Behaviors Category	413
offset	Function	D4, D5, D6
	Chapter 23: Rects and Points Category	303
offset	Function	D4, D5, D6
	Chapter 38: Strings Category	489
on	Keyword	D4, D5, D6
	Chapter 42: Miscellaneous Lingo Category	534
on activateWindow	Handler	D5, D6, NS
	Chapter 32: Movie in a Window (MIAW) Category	382
on alertHook	Handler	D6
	Chapter 37: Code Structures & Syntax Category	452
on alertHook	Handler	D6
	Chapter 42: Miscellaneous Lingo Category	526
on beginSprite	Handler	D6
	Chapter 25: Frames: Sprites Category	322
on closeWindow	Handler	D4, D5, D6, NS
	Chapter 32: Movie in a Window (MIAW) Category	384
on cuePassed	Handler/Behavior	D6
	Chapter 16: Sound: Cue Points Category	206
on deactivateWindow	Handler	D5, D6, NS
	Chapter 32: Movie in a Window (MIAW) Category	385
on endSprite	Handler	D6
	Chapter 25: Frames: Sprites Category	323
on enterFrame	Handler	D4, D5, D6
	Chapter 24: Frames Category	308
on EvalScript	Handler	D6, SH
	Chapter 42: Miscellaneous Lingo Category	528
on exitFrame	Handler	D4, D5, D6
	Chapter 24: Frames Category	309
on getBehaviorDescription	Handler	D6
	Chapter 33: Behaviors Category	407

† Restrictions Legend:

D4	Used in Director 4	**NS**	Cannot be used with Shockwave
D5	Used in Director 5	**SH**	Can be used with Shockwave
D6	Used in Director 6	**OBS**	Obsolete in Director 6
MO	Used only on the Macintosh platform	**WO**	Used only on the Windows platform
URL	URL-enhanced (can use a URL as a file path in Director 6)		

Entry	Type	Restrictions†
	Found in Chapter	Go to Page
on streamStatus	Handler	D6
	Chapter 2: Network Category	25
on timeout	Handler	D4, D5, D6
	Chapter 6: User Interaction (Keyboard & Timer) Category	72
on zoomWIndow	Handler	D5, D6, NS
	Chapter 32: Movie in a Window (MIAW) Category	400
open	Command	D4, D5, D6, NS
	Chapter 31: External Files Category	372
open window	Command	D4, D5, D6, NS, URL
	Chapter 32: Movie in a Window (MIAW) Category	392
openResFile	Command	D4, D5, OBS, MO
	Chapter 31: External Files Category	373
openXLib	Command	D4, D5, D6
	Chapter 31: External Files Category	373
the optionDown	Movie Property	D4, D5, D6
	Chapter 6: User Interaction (Keyboard & Timer) Category	70
or	Operator	D4, D5, D6
	Chapter 41: Logic Category	522
the pageHeight of member	Member Property	D5, D6
	Chapter 14: Fields Category	191
the palette of member	Member Property	D5, D6
	Chapter 13: Cast Members Category	167
the paletteMapping	Movie Property	D5, D6
	Chapter 5: Movie Control Category	47
the paletteRef of member	Member Property	D5, D6
	Chapter 13: Cast Members Category	168
param	Function	D4, D5, D6
	Chapter 42: Miscellaneous Lingo Category	534
the paramCount	Handler Property	D4, D5, D6
	Chapter 42: Miscellaneous Lingo Category	535
pass	Command	D4, D5, D6
	Chapter 42: Miscellaneous Lingo Category	536

† Restrictions Legend:

D4	Used in Director 4	**NS**	Cannot be used with Shockwave
D5	Used in Director 5	**SH**	Can be used with Shockwave
D6	Used in Director 6	**OBS**	Obsolete in Director 6
MO	Used only on the Macintosh platform	**WO**	Used only on the Windows platform
URL	URL-enhanced (can use a URL as a file path in Director 6)		

Entry	Type	Restrictions†
	Found in Chapter	Go to Page
the preLoad of member	Member Property	D4, D5, D6
	Chapter 10: Memory Management Category	126
preLoadBuffer member	Command	D5, D6
	Chapter 21: Shockwave Audio Category	257
the preLoadEventAbort	Movie Property	D4, D5, D6
	Chapter 10: Memory Management Category	127
preLoadMember	Command	D4, D5, D6
	Chapter 10: Memory Management Category	127
the preLoadMode of CastLib	Cast Property	D5, D6
	Chapter 10: Memory Management Category	128
the preLoadMode of castLib	Cast Property	D5, D6
	Chapter 12: Casts Category	147
preLoadMovie	Command	D5, D6, URL, NS
	Chapter 10: Memory Management Category	129
preloadNetThing	Command	D4, D5, D6, URL, SH
	Chapter 2: Network Category	24
the preLoadRAM	Movie Property	D4, D5, D6
	Chapter 10: Memory Management Category	129
the preLoadTime of member	Member Property	D5, D6
	Chapter 21: Shockwave Audio Category	258
printFrom	Command	D4, D5, D6, NS
	Chapter 9: Computer & Monitor Control Category	114
property	Keyword	D4, D5, D6
	Chapter 33: Behaviors Category	413
proxyServer	Movie Property	D6, NS
	Chapter 4: Network: Cache Category	39
the puppet of sprite	Sprite Property	D4, D5, D6
	Chapter 22: Sprites Category	281
puppetPalette	Command	D4, D5, D6
	Chapter 24: Frames Category	317
puppetSound	Command	D4, D5, D6
	Chapter 20: Sound Category	243

† Restrictions Legend:

D4	Used in Director 4	**NS**	Cannot be used with Shockwave
D5	Used in Director 5	**SH**	Can be used with Shockwave
D6	Used in Director 6	**OBS**	Obsolete in Director 6
MO	Used only on the Macintosh platform	**WO**	Used only on the Windows platform
URL	URL-enhanced (can use a URL as a file path in Director 6)		

Entry	Type	Restrictions†
	Found in Chapter	Go to Page
repeat while	Logic	D4, D5, D6
	Chapter 37: Code Structures & Syntax Category	463
repeat with	Logic	D4, D5, D6
	Chapter 37: Code Structures & Syntax Category	463
repeat with down to	Logic	D4, D5, D6
	Chapter 37: Code Structures & Syntax Category	464
repeat with in	Logic	D4, D5, D6
	Chapter 37: Code Structures & Syntax Category	465
restart	Command	D4, D5, D6, MO, NS
	Chapter 9: Computer & Monitor Control Category	115
the result	Movie Property	D4, D5, D6
	Chapter 37: Code Structures & Syntax Category	466
return	Command	D4, D5, D6
	Chapter 37: Code Structures & Syntax Category	466
RETURN	Constant	D4, D5, D6
	Chapter 38: Strings Category	492
the right of sprite	Sprite Property	D4, D5, D6
	Chapter 22: Sprites Category	283
the rightMouseDown	Movie Property	D5, D6
	Chapter 8: User Interaction (Mouse) Category	99
the rightMouseUp	Movie Property	D5, D6
	Chapter 8: User Interaction (Mouse) Category	100
rollOver	Function	D4, D5, D6
	Chapter 8: User Interaction (Mouse) Category	100
the rollOver	Movie Property	D4, D5, D6
	Chapter 8: User Interaction (Mouse) Category	101
the romanLingo	Movie Property	D4, D5, D6
	Chapter 9: Computer & Monitor Control Category	115
runMode	Movie Property	D6, SH
	Chapter 2: Network Category	24
the runMode	Movie Property	D6
	Chapter 9: Computer & Monitor Control Category	116

† Restrictions Legend:

D4	Used in Director 4	**NS**	Cannot be used with Shockwave
D5	Used in Director 5	**SH**	Can be used with Shockwave
D6	Used in Director 6	**OBS**	Obsolete in Director 6
MO	Used only on the Macintosh platform	**WO**	Used only on the Windows platform
URL	URL-enhanced (can use a URL as a file path in Director 6)		

† Restrictions Legend:

D4 Used in Director 4

D5 Used in Director 5

D6 Used in Director 6

MO Used only on the Macintosh platform

URL URL-enhanced (can use a URL as a file path in Director 6)

NS Cannot be used with Shockwave

SH Can be used with Shockwave

OBS Obsolete in Director 6

WO Used only on the Windows platform

Entry	Type	Restrictions†
	Found in Chapter	Go to Page
sound playFile	Command	D4, D5, D6, URL
	Chapter 31: External Files Category	379
sound stop	Command	D4, D5, D6
	Chapter 20: Sound Category	247
soundBusy	Function	D4, D5, D6
	Chapter 20: Sound Category	248
the soundChannel of member	Member Property	D6
	Chapter 21: Shockwave Audio Category	259
the soundEnabled	Movie Property	D4, D5, D6
	Chapter 20: Sound Category	249
the soundLevel	Movie Property	D4, D5, D6
	Chapter 20: Sound Category	249
the sourceRect of window	Window Property	D4, D5, D6
	Chapter 32: Movie in a Window (MIAW) Category	395
SPACE	Constant	D4, D5, D6
	Chapter 38: Strings Category	492
sprite	Keyword	D4, D5, D6
	Chapter 22: Sprites Category	288
sprite intersects	Function	D4, D5, D6
	Chapter 22: Sprites Category	288
sprite within	Function	D4, D5, D6
	Chapter 22: Sprites Category	289
spriteBox	Command	D4, D5, OBS
	Chapter 22: Sprites Category	290
the spriteNum of me	Object Property	D6
	Chapter 33: Behaviors Category	416
sqrt	Function	D4, D5, D6
	Chapter 40: Math: Functions Category	517
the stage	Movie Property	D4, D5, D6
	Chapter 5: Movie Control Category	50
the stageBottom	Movie Property	D4, D5, D6
	Chapter 5: Movie Control Category	50

† Restrictions Legend:

D4 Used in Director 4	**NS** Cannot be used with Shockwave
D5 Used in Director 5	**SH** Can be used with Shockwave
D6 Used in Director 6	**OBS** Obsolete in Director 6
MO Used only on the Macintosh platform	**WO** Used only on the Windows platform
URL URL-enhanced (can use a URL as a file path in Director 6)	

† Restrictions Legend:

D4 Used in Director 4	**NS** Cannot be used with Shockwave
D5 Used in Director 5	**SH** Can be used with Shockwave
D6 Used in Director 6	**OBS** Obsolete in Director 6
MO Used only on the Macintosh platform	**WO** Used only on the Windows platform
URL URL-enhanced (can use a URL as a file path in Director 6)	

Entry	Type	Restrictions†
	Found in Chapter	Go to Page
trackType	Function	D5, D6
	Chapter 19: Video Sprites Category	236
the trails of sprite	Sprite Property	D4, D5, D6
	Chapter 22: Sprites Category	293
the transitionType of member	Member Property	D5, D6, "
	Chapter 15: Transitions Category	203
TRUE	Constant	D4, D5, D6
	Chapter 41: Logic Category	523
the tweened of sprite	Sprite Property	D6
	Chapter 22: Sprites Category	293
the type of member	Member Property	D5, D6
	Chapter 13: Cast Members Category	175
the type of sprite	Sprite Property	D5, D6
	Chapter 22: Sprites Category	294
union	Function	D4, D5, D6
	Chapter 23: Rects and Points Category	306
unLoad	Command	D4, D5, D6
	Chapter 10: Memory Management Category	132
unLoadMember	Command	D5, D6
	Chapter 10: Memory Management Category	133
unLoadMovie	Command	D5, D6, URL, NS
	Chapter 10: Memory Management Category	133
updateFrame	Command	D5, D6
	Chapter 26: Score Generation Category	334
the updateLock	Movie Property	D5, D6
	Chapter 5: Movie Control Category	57
the updateLock	Movie Property	D5, D6
	Chapter 26: Score Generation Category	334
the updateMovieEnabled	Movie Property	D4, D5, D6, NS
	Chapter 5: Movie Control Category	58
updateStage	Command	D4, D5, D6
	Chapter 22: Sprites Category	295

† Restrictions Legend:

- **D4** Used in Director 4
- **D5** Used in Director 5
- **D6** Used in Director 6
- **MO** Used only on the Macintosh platform
- **URL** URL-enhanced (can use a URL as a file path in Director 6)
- **NS** Cannot be used with Shockwave
- **SH** Can be used with Shockwave
- **OBS** Obsolete in Director 6
- **WO** Used only on the Windows platform

Entry	Type	Restrictions†
	Found In Chapter	**Go to Page**
the wordWrap of member	Member Property	D5, D6
	Chapter 14: Fields Category	197
XFactoryList	Function	D4, D5, D6
	Chapter 31: External Files Category	380
xtra	Keyword	D5, D6
	Chapter 35: Xtras Category	427
zoomBox	Command	D4, D5, D6
	Chapter 15: Transitions Category	204

† Restrictions Legend:

D4 Used in Director 4
D5 Used in Director 5
D6 Used in Director 6
MO Used only on the Macintosh platform
URL URL-enhanced (can use a URL as a file path in Director 6)

NS Cannot be used with Shockwave
SH Can be used with Shockwave
OBS Obsolete in Director 6
WO Used only on the Windows platform

Introduction

*T*he *Lingo Programmer's Reference* is part of this publisher's commitment to provide programmers with the tools they need to do their jobs quickly and efficiently. As in other books in this series—beginning with *The HTML Programmer's Reference*—care has been taken to design for the professional who needs information about their subject and needs to find it in a hurry.

With *The Lingo Programmer's Reference*, we faced a different task than authors writing about HTML, JavaScript, Java, C++, or indeed any number of open standard languages. Lingo is a Macromedia creation, part of the Director multimedia authoring environment, and by writing a programmer's reference we invite comparison, not—as in the case of other languages—to numerous other references on the topic but to the official *Lingo Dictionary*, which ships with every copy of Director.

In addition, the mission of this book was to cover the latest version (6) of Director, which was released the week before we went to press. For many of the additions to the Lingo lexicon (and there are about 100 changes since Director 5), we had to determine exactly how they were supposed to work and whether they worked as advertised. We've included code samples showing how to use every Lingo construct, either in the entry's Syntax section or in the Examples section. The examples attempt to show—in the context of actual usage—not just how to *type* the command, but how to *use* it.

Each and every code example in this book has been tested by at least one of the authors.

We've also organized the book in a different manner than most other references (including the *Lingo Dictionary*). With over 650 entries in this book, including keywords, functions, properties, handlers, and more, we felt that an alphabetical listing was unwieldy. Rather than mimic the structure of other books, we've organized *The Lingo Programmer's Reference* to match the organization of the categorized Lingo menus in Director itself.

Do you want to know what functions, commands, or properties you can use with digital video? Look in Chapters 17 ("Video"), 18 ("Video Cast Members"), or 19 ("Video Sprites"). Want to know how to manipulate Shockwave audio? Check out Chapter 21 ("Shockwave Audio"). Skimming through each chapter gets you to all of the Lingo that's oriented to what you're doing now.

The commands in this book are organized by category for task-oriented people.

This book has icons identifying which of the last three versions of Director supported the command, whether it can be used with URLs in Director 6, if it's specific to use in Shockwave (or if it can't be used in Shockwave), and more.

Icons for each entry indicate new commands as well as other capabilities.

References can often be rather vague about the types of parameters that functions require, using variable names to show what the parameter represents but not the type of data that needs to be provided. With some languages, this approach works, but Lingo is very tolerant of multiple data types—except for where it isn't. The *Parameters* section for each entry specifies whether a parameter should be a string, an integer, a float, a cast member reference, whatever. We've done the same for the values stored in properties and returned by functions.

The parameters and values guides in this book tell you explicitly what types of data they require and contain.

As Director and Lingo have developed over the years, some terminology has slid around as new bits and pieces have been added. We've tried to make sure that the terms used in *The Lingo Programmer's Reference* are standardized so that when we refer to a *property,* you know that the name of the property will be preceded by the keyword *the.* A function *returns* a value. A property *contains* a value. Anything to help you remember proper syntax.

> *"A foolish consistency is the hobgoblin of little minds, adored by little statesmen and philosophers and divines." —Ralph Waldo Emerson*
> *". . . and Lingo programmers." —Darrel Plant*

Who Is This Book For?

The Lingo Programmer's Reference is intended as a supplement to the existing body of work on the language or, indeed, Macromedia Director. It is designed to be the first book you reach for when you're in the middle of a project and you can't quite remember the term you're thinking of.

It's for the person who knows Director 5 Lingo like the back of their programming hand, who doesn't want to look through other documentation to track down new commands. The icon system provides a quick guide to what's new and what it can do.

It's for the Lingo user who's familiar with the basic suite of commands but has never ventured into some of the wilder areas of Lingo, and isn't even aware of all it can do. By grouping the descriptions of similar commands together, they can read all about a specific area of Lingo without tracking down the entries elsewhere.

It's for new users who need all the help they can get to swim in a veritable sea of properties, functions, handlers, messages, operators, and other bits and pieces of Lingo jetsam.

Online Updates Keep You Current

Lingo isn't changing constantly—only about once a year. Each change brings a number of new issues to the fore. New techniques are developed that surprise even the people who developed the software, problems are discovered and/or solved, resources become available, and so on.

The changes to Lingo in Director 6 promise to be among the most influential in years, with Internet capabilities, behaviors, streaming, integration of Shockwave commands into projectors, and more—nobody knows exactly what's going to happen in the next few months. So stay in touch by pointing your browser at *http://www.vmedia.com/updates.html*.

Categories

These chapters comprise the bulk of the book, with each keyword, command, property, function, and operator in Director 6 Lingo set in a separate entry.

Each entry has icons indicating information about the entry that you can scan at a glance:

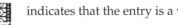 indicates that the entry is a valid Director 4 Lingo construct.

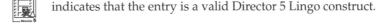 indicates that the entry is a valid Director 5 Lingo construct.

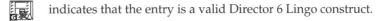 indicates that the entry is a valid Director 6 Lingo construct.

 indicates that the entry is URL Enhanced and can be used with HTTP and FTP addresses.

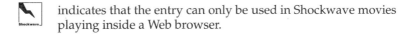 indicates that the entry can only be used in Shockwave movies playing inside a Web browser.

indicates that the entry cannot be used in Shockwave movies playing inside a Web browser.

 indicates that the entry works only on MacOS computers.

 indicates that the entry works only on Windows computers.

 indicates that the entry is still in the Categorized Lingo menus for Director 6 but should not be used.

Each entry includes a number of sections:

- **Syntax** shows how the keyword described by the entry appears in an actual line of Lingo code. Variations of the usage are shown as well.
- **Usage** describes what the entry does and how it is used, as well as explaining the types of parameters and data used in the entry.
- **Example** provides one or more examples of how to use the entry, in many cases in the context of an actual code fragment or handler, along with a specific description of what each example does.
- **Parameters** shows each variant of the entry with any accompanying parameters in italics—by type of data expected. Many of these are obvious to experienced Lingo programmers, but others may need a little explanation:

Parameter Listing	Description
boolean	Either the constants *TRUE* and *FALSE* or the integer values *1* and *0*.
chunk	A string value or part of a string determined by chunk keywords such as *word*, *char*, *line*, and so on. An example would be *line 5 to 7 of field "names."*
field	A field cast member, indicated by the use of the keyword *field* and an integer or string, as in *field 30* or *field "scores."*
float	A floating point value.
integer	An integer value.
linear list	A linear list, sometimes specifying the type of data stored in the list, such as *linear list of integer*, in which the list must contain integer values.
list	A linear or property list.
member	A member reference including the keyword *member* and an integer or string value identifying the cast member, with the optional keywords *of castLib* and another integer or string identifying the cast library of the cast member. Examples would be *member 4*, *member "joe,"* or *member "java" of castLib 4*.

➡

Parameter Listing	Description
#message	A value sent to an object or script, targeted at a handler in the object with the same name as the message but preceded by a hash, so that it is in symbol form, as in *#animate* or *#stepFrame*.
object	A child object created using the *new* command with a parent script or Xtra.
script	A script cast member, indicated by the use of the keyword *script* and an integer or string, as in *script 200* or *script "Multiplier."*
point	A value in the special Director *point* form, such as *point (100, 100)*.
property	Some value, usually an integer, string, or symbol, used as a property name in a property list or an object.
property list	A property list where each item in the list is a property and value pair.
rect	A value in the special Director *rect* form, such as *rect (100, 100, 200, 200)*.
string	A string value.
statements	One or more Lingo commands or control structures.
value	A generic value of any type, ranging from booleans to objects.
window	A reference to movie window by properties such as *the stage* and *the activeWindow*, or a direct reference including the keyword *window*, such as *window 3* or *window "control panel."*
Xobject	An open Xobject file name.

If two or more different types of values may be used in the same situation, a vertical bar (|) separates each possible data type. An example would be the first parameter variant of the *new* function in Chapter 33, "Behaviors":

```
new (script string|integer)
```

In this case, either a string value or integer value can be used to identify which script cast member will be used to create a new object.

Where the number of parameters is indeterminate, and a number of similar values can be strung together separated by commas, an ellipsis (...) has been used to indicate this fact. The second parameter variant for the *new* function reads:

```
new (script string|integer, value ...)
```

In this case, indeterminate values, separated by commas, can be strung together as in the Syntax section on the same page:

```
new (script "LineAnim", 13, 300, 20, 60)
```

- **Value**, when it appears, describes the data type stored by a property or returned by a function. The data types described are in the same format as those used in Parameters.
- **See also** points you toward other related entries.

Jump Tables

The jump tables appear after the Table of Contents and help you find the information you need if you can't find it by category. They include alphabetical listings of all the entries in this book. Along with the jump tables is an Example Guide, an index of the examples used for the entries in this book.

Additional Resources

The Lingo Programmer's Reference includes the following resources in the back of the book:

- *Appendix A: About the Companion CD-ROM*—This appendix contains information about the use of the accompanying CD-ROM, which includes a complete hyperlinked version of *The Lingo Programmer's Reference*.

- *Appendix B: Error Messages*—A list of common Lingo error messages and tips on how to avoid them.

- *Appendix C: Director 6 Techniques*—Tips on using behaviors and other changes to Lingo for Director 6.

- *Appendix D: Shockwave Reference*—Information on the use of the EMBED and OBJECT tags for adding Shockwave movies to HTML pages, and a brief guide to JavaScript objects.

- *Appendix E: Director Resources Online*—Online resources for the Director programmer.

- *Glossary*—A reference to Director-related terms in alphabetical order.

Navigation Category

1

These commands control the movement of the playback head in a movie, allowing you to move from frame to frame in the score, jump forward or backward to predefined positions, and even stop movement of the playback head entirely.

continue

Syntax `continue`

Usage The *continue* command resumes the playback of the movie after you have used the *pause* command.

Example This code fragment will toggle the playback of the movie by checking the *pauseState* and alternately continuing or pausing playback:

```
if the pauseState then
  continue
else
  pause
end if
```

See also delay, pause, pauseState

delay

Syntax `delay 30`

Usage The *delay* command stops the movie for the number of ticks you specify in the parameter (there are 60 ticks per second). No interactivity can take place during the time of the delay. Use the *delay* command in either an *enterFrame* or an *exitFrame* handler.

The *delay* command only works when the playback head is moving. This can cause problems when in Shockwave movies, although it isn't specifically disallowed. Because it stops all interactivity, you may want to use a different approach to achieve a timed-delay effect. See the examples below.

Examples This handler stops the playback of the movie, including all interactivity, for three seconds:

```
on exitFrame
  delay 60 * 3
end exitFrame
```

These handlers mimic the behavior of the *delay* command, while allowing interactivity to continue. The first script (placed in the first frame of two frames) stores the current ticks in a global variable. The next script (placed in the second frame) causes the playback head to loop in the second frame for three seconds:

```
-- script for first frame
on exitFrame
  global gDelayStartTicks
  set gDelayStartTicks = the ticks
end exitFrame

-- script for second frame
on exitFrame
  global gDelayStartTicks
  if gDelayStartTicks < 60 * 3 then
    go the frame -- loop in frame
  end if
end exitFrame
```

Parameters   delay *integer*

See also   continue, pause, the ticks

go loop

COMMAND

Syntax   go loop

Usage   The *go loop* command sends the playback head to the first marker to the left of the current frame and continues playback from there. If there are no markers to the left of the current frame, playback continues moving to the right of the current frame.

The *go loop* command is equivalent to the command *go marker(0)*.

Example   This handler sends the playback head to the first marker to the left of the current frame if the mouse button is clicked:

```
on mouseUp
  go loop
end mouseUp
```

See also   go, go marker, go next, go previous, label, marker, play

go next

Syntax   go next

Usage   The *go next* command sends the playback head to the first marker to the right of the current frame. It is equivalent to a *go marker(1)* command with the following exceptions:

- If there are no markers to the right of the current frame, the playback head moves to the first marker to the left of the current frame (like the *go loop* command).
- If there are no markers to the left of the current frame, the playback head goes to frame 1.

Example   This handler sends the playback head to the next marker to the right of the current frame if the mouse button is clicked:

```
on mouseUp
  go next
end mouseUp
```

See also   go, go loop, go marker, go previous, label, marker, play

go previous

Syntax   go previous

Usage   The *go previous* command sends the playback head to the second marker to the left of the current frame. It is equivalent to a *go marker(-1)* command. If there are no markers to the left of the current frame, playback continues moving to the right of the current frame.

Example   This handler sends the playback head to the first marker to the left of the current frame if the mouse button is clicked:

```
on mouseUp
  go previous
end mouseUp
```

See also   go, go loop, go marker, go next, label(), marker(), play

go to

Syntax
```
go to frame 30

go frame 30

go 30

go to frame "amarker"

go frame "amarker"

go "amarker"

go to movie "newmovie"

go movie "newmovie"

go to frame 30 of movie "newmovie"

go frame "amarker" of movie "newmovie"

go "amarker" of movie "newmovie"
```

Usage
The *go to* command (the *to* is optional, as is the keyword *frame*) sends the playback head to a specific frame in a movie. The frame reference must be an integer value or a string value. The default movie is the currently playing movie. The value of the movie parameter must be a string and may be a URL in Director 6.

Examples
This handler causes the playback head to loop in the current frame:

```
on exitFrame
  go to the frame
end exitFrame
```

The movie property *the frame* is an integer value. This is a very common way to handle Lingo-only "one-frame" movies, which are prevalent in Shockwave applications. Each time *go to the frame* is called, the stage is updated, objects in *the actorList* are sent a *stepFrame* message, and Lingo execution continues.

This handler loads the module1 movie, which is located in different places relative to the projector on different platforms, and begins playback from frame 1 of that movie:

```
on loadModuleOne
  if the machineType = 256 then
    -- I'm a Windows machine
    set tPath = "c:\movies\"
```

```
    else
      -- I'm a Macintosh
      set tPath = the applicationPath & "movies:"
    end if
    go to movie tPath & "module1"
end loadModuleOne
```

Notice that the filename extension isn't used when referring to the name of the movie. Director automatically resolves the extension, by looking for a .dir, .dxr, or .dcr extension in the specified directory.

If the *go to* command is called from inside a handler, the remaining commands in that handler continue to execute. If you need to stop execution of the remaining commands in a handler after going to a new movie, use the *play* command or make sure that the *go to* command is the last statement in the handler.

Parameters go *integer|string*
go movie *string*
go *integer|string* of movie *string*

See also the frame, go loop, go marker, go next, go previous, gotoNetMovie, label, marker, play

marker

FUNCTION

Syntax `set aframe = marker (-3)`

Usage The *marker* function returns the frame number of a frame with a marker, relative to the position of the playback head. The marker in the current frame is indexed with a value of 0. If no marker is in the current frame, the nearest marker to the left in the score is assigned the index value 0. Markers are indexed with negative values toward frame 1 and increasing values toward the last frame of the score. The first marker to the right of the playback head (and not in the same frame) can be found by using 1 as the parameter value for the marker function.

Examples   This line sets a variable equal to the frame number of the closest marker to the left of the current frame (or the frame number of the current frame if it contains a marker):

```
set aframe = marker(0)
```

This handler uses the *marker()* function to jump to certain marked frames when certain conditions are met:

```
on exitFrame
  -- the text file has begun to load
  -- with getNetText(). gNetID contains
  -- the latest net ID.
  global gNetID
  if netDone(gNetID) then
    go to marker(1) -- next marked frame
  else
    go to marker(-1) -- previous marked frame
end exitFrame
```

Parameters   marker (*integer*)

Value   *integer*

See also   the frame, the frameLabel, go, go loop, go marker, go next, go previous, label, the labelList, play

pause

Syntax   pause

Usage   The *pause* command stops the playback of the movie. The playback head will then stay in the current frame until a *continue, go, play,* or other similar command is executed.

Example   See "Example" under *continue* earlier in this chapter.

See also   continue, delay, pauseState

the pauseState

Syntax   `set astate = the pauseState`

Usage   *the pauseState* is a function that returns TRUE if the movie is currently paused.

Value   *boolean*

Example   This code fragment will pause the playback head if the movie is not currently paused:

`if not(the pauseState) then pause`

See also   continue, delay, pause

play

Syntax   `play frame 30`

`play 30`

`play frame "amarker"`

`play "amarker"`

`play movie "newmovie"`

`play frame "amarker" of movie "newmovie"`

`play "amarker" of movie "newmovie"`

Usage   The *play* command is similar to the *go* command, in that it causes the playback head to jump to a specific frame of a movie. However, the *play* command remembers the current frame and returns to the following frame after a *play done* command is executed or the end of the destination movie is reached. If the *play* command was not issued from a frame script, the playback head returns to the same frame instead of the next frame. In addition, unlike the *go* command, the *play* command halts the execution of the current Lingo handler and resumes upon its return.

In Shockwave, the *play* command can only be used with frame numbers and marker labels. The *GotoNetMovie* command can be used with anchors to jump to a marker label within another Shockwave movie.

Director 6 allows the use of a URL for the movie name.

Parameters

```
play integer|string
play movie string
play integer|string of movie string
```

Example

The following statements will jump to a labeled frame in another movie when it leaves the current frame. The frame can be indicated by a number or label. After encountering a *play done* command in the other movie, it will return to the current movie and begin play in the frame following the current frame:

```
on exitFrame
   play "amarker" of movie "newmovie"
end exitFrame
```

See also

go, gotoNetMovie, play done, marker

play done

COMMAND

Syntax

```
play done
```

Usage

The *play done* command causes the playback head to return to one of two possible frames, only if a *play* command was called earlier. If the *play* command was called from a frame script, the playback head will return to the frame following the *play* command. Otherwise, the playback head will return to the same frame from which the *play* command was called.

Example

This command will return to a certain frame (using the above criteria) when the mouse is clicked:

```
on mouseUp
   play done
end mouseUp
```

See also

play

Network
Category

2

This section includes most of the networking operations available in Director. They include commands for initiating and managing file transfers in projectors as well as Shockwave movies. For commands dealing with sound files on networks, see Chapter 21. Caching of documents retrieved by projectors is controlled by the commands in Chapter 4.

downloadNetThing

Syntax
```
downloadNetThing ¬
  "http://www.aserver.com/media/animage.pct", ¬
  "C:\Temp\afile.pct"
```

Usage   The *downloadNetThing* command copies a file from a server using HTTP or
FTP protocols and saves it to the local hard drive. Downloading occurs in the
background as the movie plays. Multiple simultaneous downloads are
possible but should be limited, as the combined download speed is still
restricted to the connection speed. Files retrieved from a network with
downloadNetThing are unaffected by cache commands like *cacheSize* and
cacheDocVerify.

> **Tip**
>
> *Shockwave movies cannot use the* downloadNetThing *command.*

The *downloadNetThing* command is asynchronous. Once the operation has
begun, it continues in the background while other commands execute.

Example   This example illustrates several steps for initiating a download, verifying its
status, and adding it to the current cast:

```
on downloadMedia someMedia  -- custom handler
  global gDLid  --global list of download ops
  global gPath  --global identifying this directory
  set gPath = the applicationPath  -- identify directory
  set anURL = "http://www.aserver.com/media/" & someMedia
  downloadNetThing anURL, (gPath & someMedia)
  addProp gDLid, getLatestNetID (), someMedia
  -- adds operation id and file name to download list
end downloadMedia

on checkDownloads  --custom handler
  global gDLid, gPath
  if count (gDLid) > 0 then
    repeat with i = 1 to count (gDLid)
      set anID = getPropAt (gDLid, i)
      set aFileName = getAt (gDLid, i)
      if netDone (gDLid) then  --operation completed
        deleteAt (gDLid, i)  --removes op from list
        set i = i - 1 ·--accounts for shortened list
        if netError (gDLid) = "OK" then
          --completed successfully
```

```
        importFileInto member 10, gPath & aFileName
      else  --error in downloading
        downloadMedia aFileName  --new download attempt
      end if
    end if
  end repeat
end if
end checkDownloads
```

Parameters   downloadNetThing *string, string*

See also   getLatestNetID, netAbort, netDone, netError, preloadNetThing

frameReady   FUNCTION

Syntax   set isMovieReady = frameReady ()

set isRangeReady = frameReady (20, 30)

set isFrameReady = frameReady (25)

Usage   The *frameReady* function determines if media used for the movie is currently available. Used with no parameter, the function checks for media in all of the frames of the movie. Used with a single integer value, the movie checks an individual frame. Two integer values separated by a comma indicate a range of frames to be checked. The function returns a boolean value.

Using *frameReady* makes it possible for you to check whether all of the media in a section of your movie is ready for use. The function works only with streaming movies or streaming Shockwave movies (saved with Use Media Available or Show Placeholders selected in the Modify | Movie | Playback dialog).

Example   This script will check to see if the media for the next frame of a movie is available, loop in the current frame until it's ready, and move on if it's not:

```
on exitFrame
  if not frameReady (the frame + 1) then go the frame
end exitFrame
```

Parameters   frameReady (*none|integer|integer, integer*)

Value   *boolean*

See also   the mediaReady of member

getLatestNetID

Syntax `set networkOp = getLatestNetID ()`

Usage The *getLatestNetID* function returns a unique identifier for the last network operation performed. After the first operation carried out by a movie, *getLatestNetID* returns the integer value 1, and each subsequent operation increments the result by 1. This value is used as the parameter for other network functions that test the status of operations and retrieve the results of operations.

This function must be used before another network operation is started.

Example See the example earlier in this chapter for *downloadNetThing*.

Parameters `getLatestNetID ()`

Value *integer*

See also downloadNetThing, getNetText, netAbort, netDone, netError, preloadNetThing

getNetText

Syntax `getNetText "http://www.aserver.com/index.html"`

Usage The *getNetText* command starts downloading a text file from a server. You can also use *getNetText* to send data to CGI scripts or pass statements from a Shockwave movie to be interpreted by a browser's scripting language.

The parameter can be either an absolute reference to the file or a reference that is relative to the file sending the *getNetText* command.

The data in the file is retrieved with the command *netTextResult*, after the operation is completed.

The *getNetText* command is asynchronous. Once the operation has begun, it continues in the background while other commands execute.

Examples   These statements start the process of retrieving a remote text file:

full URL

```
getNetText "http://www.nnn.com/data/text.txt"
```

relative URL

```
getNetText "../data/text.txt"
```

This statement sends parameters to a CGI program on the server. If data is returned by the CGI program, it can be retrieved with *netTextResult*:

```
set tName = "Fred Flintstone"
set tAge = "Stone"
getNetText "http://www.nnn.com/cgi-bin/" & ¬
    "prog.pl?name="& tVariable & "+age=" & tAge
```

This example shows a typical sequence of events for using *GetNetText*, *GetLatestNetID*, and *NetTextResult*:

```
-- in a frame script
on exitFrame
   global gNetOp
   getNetText "http://www.nnn.com/data/data.txt"
   set gNetOp = getLatestNetID ()
end exitFrame


--in the next frame
on exitFrame
   global gNetOp, gResult
   set opIsDone = netDone (gNetOp)
   if opIsDone then set gResult = NetTextResult ()
   else go the frame
end exitFrame
```

Parameters   getNetText *string*

See also   getLatestNetID, netAbort, netDone, netError, netTextResult, preloadNetThing

getPref

Syntax

```
set aResult = getPref ("preffile")
```

Usage

The *getPref* function returns the text contained in a Shockwave preference file written by a *setPref* command.

If the file specified by the parameter doesn't exist, then the *getPref* function returns void.

This powerful Shockwave feature allows you to store user settings that can later be recalled and used in a variety of ways. You can let the user store their own way to view your Shockwave movie, bookmark their current page so they can return later, or even control the look of HTML pages. You can even use this to let multiple Shockwave movies share common data. For Shockwave movies, the preference files are stored in the Shockwave plug-in support folder on the local hard drive. In a projector, the files are stored in a directory called "Prefs" in the same directory as the projector.

Example

This code segment uses *getPref* to retrieve the last frame the user was viewing. The frame must have been stored by the *setPref* command in a previous session:

```
if not(voidP(getPref("lastfram")) then
  go to frame(value(getPref("lastfram"))
end if
```

Parameters

```
getPref (string)
```

Value

string

See also

setPref

gotoNetMovie

Syntax

```
gotoNetMovie "newmovie.dcr"
```

Usage

The *gotoNetMovie* command will load a Shockwave movie into the browser's cache (if it isn't there already) then replace the current movie with the newly loaded movie. The parameter must be a string containing a valid HTTP URL and can be either an absolute or relative path.

Example This command will load the Web-based movie "marvel.dcr" and replace the currently playing movie in the browser window:

```
gotoNetMovie "http://www.mysite.com/marvel.dcr"
```

You could also use this relative path if the current movie is in the same directory on the server as the new movie:

```
gotoNetMovie "marvel.dcr"
```

Parameters gotoNetMovie *string*

See also gotoNetPage

gotoNetPage

COMMAND

Syntax gotoNetPage "newpage.html", "targetframe"

Usage The *gotoNetPage* command tells the browser to open a new HTML page. The first parameter is a string that contains an HTTP URL. The second parameter is an optional string that can direct the new HTML page to a particular browser frame or window. See the <FRAME> section in the HTML reference for ways to specify the frame or window.

> **Tip**
>
> *The target parameter is not functional in the Shockwave plug-in for Director 4.*

Example This statement will load the HTML page "extra.html" into the frame named "content":

```
gotoNetPage "extra.html", "content"
```

This statement will load the HTML page "extra.html" into a new browser window:

```
gotoNetPage "extra.html", "_blank"
```

Parameters gotoNetPage *string*

gotoNetPage *string, string*

See also gotoNetMovie

the mediaReady of member

CAST MEMBER PROPERTY

Syntax   `set isItReady = the mediaReady of member "afile"`

Usage   *the mediaReady of member* is a property that can be used to determine if a cast member has finished downloading from a remote location. It returns a boolean value and can only be tested.

Testing *the mediaReady of member* property of a cast member that is not being loaded from a network connection will result in a FALSE value.

Example   This example loops the movie in the current frame until the cast member with the name "background" has loaded from a remote address:

```
on exitFrame
  if not the mediaReady of member "background" then
    go the frame
  end if
end exitFrame
```

Parameters   `the mediaReady of` *member*

Value   *boolean*

See also   frameReady

netAbort

COMMAND

Syntax   `netAbort (3)`

Usage   The *netAbort* command cancels a download operation started by a Shockwave command like *getNetText*, *downloadNetThing*, or *preloadNetThing*.

The optional parameter corresponds to the network ID number of the operation. You can get the ID number by calling the *getLatestNetID* function immediately after you start the operation. If the parameter is omitted, the last network operation is the one canceled.

Example   This handler cancels the first Shockwave operation *netAbort* if the user
presses the backspace key:

```
on keyDown
  if the key = BACKSPACE then
    netAbort(1)
  end if
end keyDown
```

Parameters   netAbort (*none|integer*)

See also   downloadNetThing, getNetText, getLatestNetID, netDone, netError,
preloadNetThing

netDone
FUNCTION

Syntax   `set isItDone = netDone (3)`

Usage   The *netDone* function returns TRUE if the Shockwave operation identified by
the parameter has finished downloading. It returns FALSE otherwise.
The optional *whichNetID* parameter corresponds to the ID number of the
operation. You can get the net ID by calling the *getLatestNetID()* function
immediately after you start the download operation. If the parameter is
omitted, the last network operation is the one canceled.

Example   This handler uses the *netDone* function to decide when to display the .dcr file
that began downloading with the *preloadNetThing* command:

```
on exitFrame
  global gNetID, gMovieName
  if netDone(gNetID) then
    gotoNetMovie gMovieName
  end if
  go to the frame
end exitFrame
```

Parameters   netDone (*none|integer*)

Value   *boolean*

See also   downloadNetThing, getNetText, getLatestNetID, netDone, netError,
preloadNetThing

netError

Syntax   `set isItAnError = netError (3)`

Usage   The *netError* function returns a string that corresponds to an error that may have occurred during the Shockwave operation identified by the parameter value. If no error occurred, this function returns the "OK" string.

   The optional parameter corresponds to the ID number of the operation. You can get the net ID by calling the *getLatestNetID* function immediately after you start the download operation.

Example   This code segment adds error-checking to the *netDone* function, before it displays the downloaded text in a field:

```
global gNetID
if netDone(gNetID) then
 if netError(gNetID) = "OK" then
  put netTextResult(gNetID) into field "out"
 else
  alert "Error downloading"
 end if
end if
```

Parameters   `netError (none|integer)`

Value   *integer|string*

See also   downloadNetThing, getNetText, getLatestNetID, netDone, netError, preloadNetThing

netLastModDate

Syntax   `set isItModified = netLastModDate (3)`

Usage   The *netLastModDate* function returns a string that contains the date and time of an item retrieved by the specified network operation.

The optional parameter corresponds to the ID number of the operation. You can get the net ID by calling the *getLatestNetID* function immediately after you start the download operation. Omitting the parameter returns the modification date of the most recently completed network operation.

> ### Tip
>
> *The* netLastModDate *function, while in the specifications for Director 4 and 5, is inoperative with those versions of the plug-in.*

Example

This code segment sends the date and time the item identified by the net ID stored in gNetID was last modified to the field named "result":

```
global gNetID
put netLastModDate(gNetID) into field "result"
```

Field "result" would now contain something like the following:

```
Thu, Dec 19, 1996 9:30:14 PM GMT
```

Parameters   `netLastModDate (`*none/integer*`)`

Value   *string*

See also   downloadNetThing, getNetText, getLatestNetID, preloadNetThing

netMIME

FUNCTION

Syntax   `set whatType = netMIME (3)`

Usage   The *netMIME* function returns a string that contains the MIME type of the item retrieved with a network operation. This can help you identify what kind of data was downloaded.

The optional parameter corresponds to the ID number of the operation. You can get the network operation ID by calling the *getLatestNetID* function immediately after you start the download operation. Omitting the parameter returns the modification date of the most recently completed network operation.

Common MIME types include text/plain, text/html, image/gif, image/jpeg, and—of course—application/x-director.

> ### Tip
>
> *The* netMIME *function, while in the specifications for Director 4 and 5, is inoperative with those versions of the plug-in.*

Example   This code segment checks the MIME type of the item downloaded and identified by *gNetID*, and branches to different choices:

```
global gNetID, gItem, gResult
case netMIME(gNetID) of
"text/plain":
  put netTextResult(gNetID) into gResult
"application/x-director":
  gotoNetMovie gItem
"text/html":
  gotoNetPage gItem
end case
```

Parameters   netMIME (*none*/*integer*)

Value   *string*

See also   downloadNetThing, getNetText, getLatestNetID, preloadNetThing

netStatus

Syntax   `netStatus "I am a Shockwave movie!"`

Usage   The *netStatus* command displays a string in the status bar of the browser window this Shockwave movie is playing in. The status bar is the area (usually in the bottom left corner of the browser window) that displays information about a hyperlink the cursor is pointing to.

> **Tip**
>
> *As of this writing, the* netStatus *command did not work with the Shockwave ActiveX control in Microsoft's Internet Explorer 3.0.*

Example   This handler displays text in the browser's status bar when the user points to various objects on the screen. Notice that the *otherwise* keyword clears the status bar if the user isn't pointing to one of the designated sprite channels:

```
on exitFrame
  case rollover() of
    1: netStatus "Click here to set your options"
    2: netStatus "Click here to go back to the home page"
    3: netStatus "Click here to view a digital video"
    otherwise
      netStatus ""
  end case
end exitFrame
```

Parameters   netStatus *string*

netTextResult

FUNCTION

Syntax   `set someText = netTextResult ()`

Usage   The *netTextResult* function returns the text that was downloaded by a *getNetText* command. The text is only available after it has completely downloaded, which can be verified using the *netDone* function. The function *must* be called before another network operation has finished, or the results will be lost. No parameter is used with this function, but parentheses must be used.

Example   This code segment sends the text that was downloaded by the *getNetText()* command to the field named "out" after it has completely downloaded:

```
global gNetID
if netDone(gNetID) then
   put netTextResult() into field "out"
end if
```

Parameters   `netTextResult ()`

Value   *string*

See also   getNetText, getLatestNetID, netAbort, netDone, netError, netLastModDate, netMIME

preloadNetThing

Syntax `preloadNetThing "http://www.aserver.com/sound.swa"`

Usage The *preloadNetThing* command loads the specified item into the browser's cache for Shockwave movies or the program cache for projectors, if it hasn't been loaded there already. The parameter is a string containing a valid HTTP URL. The URL can point to any kind of Internet file, including Shockwave movies, HTML pages, text files, images, and so on. Once the item is preloaded, it will be available much faster to the browser or projector when it is needed.

When the file has downloaded, the *netDone* function will return TRUE. If no error has occurred during downloading, the *netError* function will return OK. See these functions in the reference for more information.

The URL can be either an absolute or a relative path for a Shockwave movie. It should be a fully qualified URL (beginning with "http://") when used with a projector.

The *preloadNetThing* command is asynchronous. Once called, the operation continues in the background as the movie continues playing.

Example This statement will begin the preload of the GIF image "cool.gif" into the browser's cache when executed in a Shockwave movie:

```
preloadNetThing "cool.gif"
```

Parameters `preloadNetThing string`

See also downloadNetThing, getLatestNetID, getNetText, netAbort, netDone, netError, netMIME

runMode

See the entry for the *runMode* property in Chapter 9.

setPref

Syntax   setPref "afile", "datastring"

Usage   The *setPref* command stores the contents of a string into a file, without the need of the File IO Xtra. For Shockwave movies, the file is stored in the Shockwave plug-in support directory of the local computer. With projectors, the file is saved to a folder called "Prefs," which is created in the same directory as the projector file.

You can retrieve data from preference files created with the *setPref* command by using the *getPref* function.

This feature allows you to store user settings that can later be recalled and used in a variety of ways. You can let the user store their own way to view your movie, bookmark their current position so they can return later, or even control the look of HTML pages with a Shockwave movie. You can also use this feature to let multiple Shockwave movies share common data.

Example   This code segment uses *setPref()* to store the contents of three variables in a preference file named "dugPref":

```
global gName, gStatus, gScore
setPref("dugPref", string(gName) & "," && ¬ string(gStatus)& "," && ¬
    string(gScore))
```

Parameters   setPref *string, string*

See also   getPref

on streamStatus

Syntax   on streamStatus URL, state, bytesSoFar, bytesTotal, error

Usage   The *on streamStatus* handler determines how much of an object has downloaded from a server. The handler is only called if *the tellStreamStatus* property has a value of TRUE. This handler is then called automatically, much the same as *on idle* is called.

The *on streamStatus* handler has a number of parameters, but since the handler is never called directly as the result of a statement, the parameters exist only within the handler and need not be passed to the handler. Parameters for the *on streamStatus* event handler have the following uses:

- **URL:** A string containing the network address of the data being retrieved.
- **state:** A string representing the state of the stream being downloaded. Possible values are: Connecting, Started, InProgress, Complete, and Error.
- **bytesSoFar:** An integer with the number of bytes retrieved from the network so far.
- **bytesTotal:** An integer with the total number of bytes in the stream, if known. The value may be 0 if the HTTP server does not include the Content-Length parameter in the MIME header.
- **error:** An integer containing an error code if the stream state is Error; otherwise 0.

Network streams can be initiated using Lingo commands, by linking media from a URL or by using an external cast member from a URL.

The *on streamStatus* handler should be placed in a movie script. If multiple download streams are occurring, it will be necessary to test the URL of the object to determine which stream's status is currently being reported.

Example   This statement determines the state of a streamed object and displays the URL of the object:

```
on streamStatus URL state bytesSoFar bytesTotal
  if state = "Complete" then
    put URL && "download finished"
  end if
end streamStatus
```

tellStreamStatus

MOVIE PROPERTY

Syntax   `tellStreamStatus TRUE`

Usage   This property controls stream status reporting. Setting the parameter for *tellStreamStatus* to TRUE enables the *on streamStatus* handler, which is called automatically during network operations. This property is implemented in a different manner than most other properties. It can be called as a command, with a parameter to set a value, or as a function, with empty parentheses to determine the value already set. Using *tellStreamStatus* as a function with a boolean value will also set the property.

Examples   The following lines both set the property to FALSE:

```
tellStreamStatus FALSE
put tellStreamStatus(FALSE)
```

This statement determines the status of the [stream status[handler:

```
put tellStreamStatus()
```

Parameters   `tellstreamstatus` *boolean*

`tellstreamstatus` (*boolean*)

`tellstreamstatus` ()

Value   *boolean*

Network:
Shockwave Category

3

These commands are considered specific to the playback of Shockwave movies in browsers. They allow you to access data passed to the movie from EMBED and OBJECT tags, and to save and read preferences files in the browser plug-ins folder.

The preference file commands *can* be used in standard projectors, but they are limited in the amount of data that they can write to a file. Standard file input/output routines may be preferable if you have large amounts of data to store.

externalEvent

Syntax   `externalEvent "MakeNewWindow(300,150,'windowname')"`

Usage   The *externalEvent* command allows a Shockwave movie to access a browser
script procedure, or function in the HTML page currently being viewed. This
requires a combination of an HTML page with embedded scripting commands, as well as the *externalEvent* command in the Shockwave movie.

   Because scripting languages and implementations vary between browsers, it's best to use *externalEvent* in situations where you can be reasonably
sure you can identify which browser a user is viewing the movie with.

Example   This JavaScript routine (placed in an HTML page) and Lingo script (in a
Shockwave movie embedded on the page) put a message into a text field on
the HTML page when the movie starts to play.

   This is the HTML page the movie is embedded in:

```
<HTML>
  <HEAD>
    <TITLE>Shockwave Talks To JavaScript</TITLE>
    <SCRIPT LANGUAGE="JavaScript">
      function sendMovie(param1) {
        document.Controller.Display.value = param1;
        }
    </SCRIPT>
  </HEAD>
  <BODY>
    <CENTER>
      <H3>Shockwave Talks To JavaScript</H3>
      <EMBED HEIGHT=180 WIDTH=640 SRC="shoktalk.dir"
       AutoStart=true NAME="MovieName"><P>
      <FORM NAME="Controller">
        <TEXTAREA NAME="Display" ROWS=3 COLS=80 WRAP=on>
          Display field
        </TEXTAREA>
      </FORM>
    </CENTER>
  </BODY>
</HTML>
```

   Within the embedded Shockwave movie, this script goes in a movie script:

```
on prepareMovie
  externalEvent "sendMovie('Shockwave talks to JavaScript!')"
end
```

When the page is opened in a JavaScript-capable browser and the movie has loaded the script, the words "Jshockwave talks to JavaScript" will appear in the text field of the HTML page.

Parameters   externalEvent *string*

See also   browserName, getNetText

externalParamCount

FUNCTION

Syntax   `set numParams = externalParamCount ()`

Usage   The *externalParamCount* Shockwave function returns the number of parameters passed to the Shockwave movie by the <EMBED> or <OBJECT> tag in an HTML page. For example, there are four parameters in this tag:

`<EMBED SRC="t.dcr" WIDTH=400 HEIGHT=240 sw1=5>`

Example   This handler segment builds a property list out of all of the external parameters passed by the <EMBED> or <OBJECT> tag. The resulting property list will be in the form *[#param1:value1, #param2:value2, ...]*:

```
on buildParamList
  global gParamList
  set gParamList = [:]
  set tNumOfParams = externalParamCount()
  repeat with i = 1 to tNumOfParams
    -- used "do" to convert string to symbol
    set tProp = 0
    do("set tProp=#" & externalParamName(i))
    addProp(gParamList, tProp, externalParamValue(i))
  end repeat
end buildParamList
```

After running this handler in your Shockwave movie, you can access the values of parameters quickly from the list *gParamList*, like this:

`set the foreColor of sprite 5 = sw1 of gParamList`

Parameters   externalParamCount ()

Value   *integer*

See also   externalParamName, externalParamValue

externalParamName

FUNCTION

Syntax   `set aName = externalParamName (3)`

Usage   The *externalParamName* function returns a string with the name of a parameter passed to the Shockwave movie by the <EMBED> or <OBJECT> tag in the HTML page. The value passed to the function determines which parameter by its order in the tag. If that value is greater than the number of parameters in the tag, then the function returns an empty string ("").

While the original specifications for parameters in Netscape's <EMBED> tags allowed any name for a parameter, the <OBJECT> tag developed for Microsoft Internet Explorer allows only a specific set of parameter names. See the HTML reference section for a complete list.

Example   This handler segment builds a property list out of all of the external parameters passed by the <EMBED> tag. The resulting property list will be in the form [#param:value, …]:

```
on buildParamList
  global gParamList
  set gParamList = [:]
  set tNumOfParams = externalParamCount()
  repeat with i = 1 to tNumOfParams
    -- used "do" to convert string to symbol
    set tProp = 0
    do("set tProp=#" & externalParamName(i))
    addProp(gParamList, tProp, externalParamValue(i))
  end repeat
end buildParamList
```

After running this handler in your Shockwave movie, you can access the value of parameters quickly from the list *gParamList*, like this:

```
set the foreColor of sprite 5 = sw1 of gParamList
```

Parameters   `externalParamName (`*integer*`)`

Value   *string*

See also   externalParamCount, externalParamValue

externalParamValue

Syntax
```
set aValue = externalParamValue (3)
set aValue = externalParamValue ("sw1")
```

Usage
The *externalParamValue* Shockwave function returns the value of the specified parameter passed to the Shockwave movie by the <EMBED> or <OBJECT> tag in the HTML page. The value passed to the function can be a number that refers to the position of the parameter in the tag, or it can be a string containing the name of the parameter.

The function always returns a string, even if the result appears to be a numeric value. You can convert a string to a number using the *value* function.

Example
See the Example for *externalParamName*.

Parameters
externalParamValue (*integer|string*)

Value
string

See also
externalParamCount, externalParamName

getPref

Syntax
```
set aResult = getPref ("preffile")
```

Usage
The *getPref* function returns the text contained in a Shockwave preference file written by a *setPref* command.

If the file specified by the parameter doesn't exist, then the *getPref* function returns void.

This powerful Shockwave feature allows you to store user settings that can later be recalled and used in a variety of ways. You can let the user store their own way to view your Shockwave movie, bookmark their current page so they can return later, or even control the look of HTML pages. You can even use this to let multiple Shockwave movies share common data. For Shockwave movies, the preference files are stored in the Shockwave plug-in support folder on the local hard drive. In a projector, the files are stored in a directory called "Prefs" in the same directory as the projector.

Example This code segment uses *getPref* to retrieve the last frame the user was viewing. The frame must have been stored by the *setPref* command in a previous session:

```
if not(voidP(getPref("lastfram")) then
  go to frame(value(getPref("lastfram"))
end if
```

Parameters getPref (*string*)

Value *string*

See also setPref

setPref

Syntax setPref "afile", "datastring"

Usage The *setPref* command stores the contents of a string into a file, without the need of the File IO Xtra. For Shockwave movies, the file is stored in the Shockwave plug-in support directory of the local computer. With projectors, the file is saved to a folder called "Prefs," which is created in the same directory as the projector file.

You can retrieve data from preference files created with the *setPref* command by using the *getPref* function.

This feature allows you to store user settings that can later be recalled and used in a variety of ways. You can let the user store their own way to view your movie, bookmark their current position so they can return later, or even control the look of HTML pages with a Shockwave movie. You can also use this feature to let multiple Shockwave movies share common data.

Example This code segment uses *setPref()* to store the contents of three variables in a preference file named "dugPref":

```
global gName, gStatus, gScore
setPref("dugPref", string(gName) & " , " && ¬
    string(gStatus)& " , " && string(gScore))
```

Parameters setPref *string, string*

See also getPref

Network:
Cache Category

4

These Lingo keywords control the storage of files retrieved by projectors with Network commands (see Chapter 2). Files are added to the cache until the cache size limit is reached. When the limit is reached, the first files added to the cache are purged to make room for new files.

Shockwave movies played within a browser environment use the browser's cache settings.

browserName

Syntax
```
set whereBrowser = browserName ()
browserName ¬
    "C:\PROGRA~1\NETSCAPE\NAVIGA~1\PROGRAM\NETSCAPE.EXE"
```

Usage
The *browserName* property contains the path to the computer's currently selected default browser. Unlike most properties, *browserName* is not referenced with the keyword *the* (*the browserName* is not recognized). Its value can be set and tested. Using *browserName* as a function, with parentheses, returns a string value with the current browser path; using it as a command sets the current browser to the path represented by the command's parameter.

> **Tip**
>
> the browserName *property is not available to Shockwave movies.*

Examples
This example opens the browser application from within Director:
```
open browserName ()
```

This example changes the default browser application to Microsoft Internet Explorer:
```
browsername ¬
    "C:\Program Files\Plus!\Microsoft Internet\IEXPLORE.EXE"
```

Parameters
```
browserName ()
browserName string
```

Value
```
string
```

cacheDocVerify

Syntax
```
set isItVerified = cacheDocVerify ()
cacheDocVerify #always
```

The *cacheDocVerify* property determines whether a file downloaded from a URL to the network cache is verified each time an access to the file is made (*#always*) or only one time (*#once*) during a session. Unlike most properties, *cacheDocVerify* is not referenced with the keyword *the* (*the cacheDocVerify* is not recognized). Its value can be set and tested. Using *cacheDocVerify* as a function, with parentheses, returns the current setting; using it as a command sets the value of the property.

Shockwave movies displayed in a browser are not affected by this property, using the setting for the browser instead.

Example
This example changes the verification status of a Director projector to look for updated documents every time a URL is accessed during a session:
```
CacheDocVerify #always
```

Parameters
```
cacheDocVerify ()
cacheDocVerify #always|#once
```

Value
```
#always|#once
```

See also
cacheSize, clearCache

cacheSize

Syntax
```
set howBig = cacheSize ()
```
```
cacheSize 5000
```

Usage
The *cacheSize* property can be used to determine and set the size of the cache used to store files downloaded from a URL. Unlike most properties, *cacheSize* is not referenced with the keyword *the* (*the cacheSize* is not recognized). Its value can be set and tested. Using *cacheSize* as a function, with parentheses, returns an integer containing the current setting; using it as a command sets the size of the cache. Using it as a command with an integer parameter sets the size of the cache to the integer value in K (a value of 5000 equals 5000K, or 5MB).

Shockwave movies displayed in a browser are not affected by this property, using the setting for the browser instead.

Example
This example modifies the size of the network document cache to 7.5MB (7,500K):
```
cacheSize 7500
```

Parameters
```
cacheSize ()
```
```
cacheSize integer
```

Value
```
integer
```

See also
cacheDocVerify, clearCache

clearCache

Syntax
```
clearCache
```

Usage
The *clearCache* command empties the network document cache of all files not currently in use. Normally, files are cleared in the order they have been downloaded. Shockwave movies displayed in a browser may not use this command.

Example   This handler clears the cache when the playback head leaves the current frame:

```
on exitFrame
  clearCache
end exitFrame
```

See also   cacheDocVerify, clearSize

proxyServer

MOVIE PROPERTY

Syntax   `proxyServer #http, "proxy.company.com", 1080`

`put proxyServer (#http,#port)`

`put string (proxyServer (#ftp)) into field 10`

`set proxyAddress = proxyServer (#http)`

`proxyServer #http, #stop`

Usage   The *proxyServer* property allows Director applications to use an HTTP or FTP proxy server instead of a local network file cache. Proxy servers are used for security purposes and prevent damaging files from being saved directly to the user's computer. To make use of a proxy server, one must be available on the user's network.

In command form, *proxyServer* can be used to establish or terminate FTP or HTTP proxy services for use in networked Director applications. Non-standard TCP/IP ports can be specified for use by either service.

proxyServer can also operate as a function, returning data about currrent proxy server services. It is possible to identify the proxy server's address and the port in use for the service.

It is not available to Shockwave movies in browsers—they use the proxy server available to the browser (if any).

Examples   This handler sets up an FTP proxy server when the movie begins:

```
on startMovie
  proxyServer #ftp, "proxy.school.edu", 5
end startMovie
```

This command puts an integer with the current FTP proxy server's port into the Message window. It will return the integer value –1 if there is no proxy server available:

```
put proxyServer (#ftp, #port)
```

This command puts a string with the current FTP proxy server's address into the Message window. It will return an empty string if there is no proxy server available:

```
put proxyServer (#http)
```

This command closes the current HTTP proxy server connection as the movie leaves the current frame:

```
on exitFrame
  proxyServer #http, #stop
end exitFrame
```

Parameters

```
proxyServer #http|#ftp, string, integer
```

```
proxyServer #http|#ftp, #stop
```

```
proxyServer (#http|#ftp, #port)
```

```
proxyServer (#http|#ftp)
```

Movie Control Category

5

These commands, functions, and properties are related to the display and performance of a movie.

the centerStage

Syntax `set the centerStage = TRUE`

Usage *the centerStage* is a movie property that will force the next movie played to be centered within the current stage size, even if the new movie is a different size.

> **Tip**
>
> *In Shockwave, since the stage window is held within the browser, unpredictable results occur.*

Example This only branches to the next movie if *the centerStage* has been set to TRUE:

`if the centerStage then go movie "nextmovie"`

Value *boolean*

See also the fixStageSize

the fixStageSize

Syntax `set the fixStageSize = TRUE`

Usage When *the fixStageSize* property is set to TRUE, a new movie opened with *go to movie* or *gotoNetMovie* will fill the current stage area. This is the default behavior. However, if this property is FALSE, the movie opened with *gotoNetMovie()* will play on top of the original movie and be offset by the "location" set in the Movie Properties dialog.

This second behavior makes it possible to mimic a MIAW-like behavior in Shockwave. For example, you can begin by embedding a Shockwave movie that is 400 x 240 pixels. Then set *the fixStageSize* property to FALSE and go to a Net movie that is 100 x 100 pixels but offset by 200 pixels left and 50 pixels top. This second movie will play on top of the first movie. To return to the first movie, send a *gotoNetMovie()* command from the second movie. If the first movie has a 0 x 0 offset, it will begin playing at its correct position.

Example   This code segment sets *the fixStageSize* system property to FALSE, and then opens a smaller net-based movie that will play on top of the original movie as described above:

```
set the fixStageSize = FALSE
gotoNetMovie("fakeMIAW.dcr")
```

Value   *boolean*

See also   the centerStage, the sourceRect of window

framesToHMS

FUNCTION

Syntax   `put framesToHMS (600, 24, FALSE, TRUE)`

Usage   The *framesToHMS* function converts a number of frames in a digital video to the equivalent length in hours, minutes, and seconds.

The first parameter is the number of frames; the second value is the number of frames per second. The third parameter, representing dropped frames, should usually contain FALSE, unless you are assuming 30 frames per second and working with NTSC video. The final parameter should be TRUE if you wish to display fractions of a second in the result, or FALSE for frames. The result is a string that looks like "sHH:MM:SS.FFd", which is hours, minutes, seconds, and either frames or fractional seconds. The "s" at the beginning is the sign, which can be negative "–" or positive "+". The "d" at the end of the string appears if the dropped frames parameter passed to the function was TRUE.

Example   This handler will constantly send the current time of the digital video in sprite 20 to field "howLong" while it is playing:

```
on exitFrame
  if the movieRate of sprite 20 = 1 then
    -- we're playing
    set tMovTime = the movieTime of sprite 20
    set tHMS = framesToHMS(tMovTime, ¬
        the digitalVideoTimeScale, FALSE, FALSE)
    put string(tHMS) into field "howLong"
  end if
  go to the frame
end exitFrame
```

Parameters   `framesToHMS (integer, integer, boolean, boolean)`

Value   *string*

See also   the digitalVideoTimeScale of member, the duration of member, the frameRate of member, HMStoFrames, the movieRate of sprite, the movieTime of sprite, the timeScale of member, the type of member

HMStoFrames

FUNCTION

Syntax   `put HMStoFrames (" 00:34:24.15d", 30, FALSE, TRUE)`

Usage   The *HMStoFrames* function converts a string representing a time value to the equivalent number of frames.

The string is in the format "sHH:MM:SS.FFd", which is hours, minutes, seconds, and either frames or fractional seconds. The "s" in the front is the sign, which can be negative "–" or positive "+". The "d" indicates that the digital video contains dropped frames and should be represented by a space (" ") if the video is anything but NTSC video and the rate is anything but 30 frames per second.

The second value is the number of frames per second. The third parameter should remain FALSE, unless you are using 30-frames-per-second NTSC video. The final parameter should be TRUE if you wish to display fractions of a second, or FALSE if you wish to display frames.

Example   This excerpt from the message window shows a typical use of the *HMStoFrames* function. It returns the number of frames in 10 minutes and 30 seconds of 30 frames-per-second video:

```
put HMStoFrames(" 00:10:30.00 ",30,FALSE,FALSE)
-- 18900
```

Parameters   `HMStoFrames (string, integer, boolean, boolean)`

Value   *integer*

See also   the digitalVideoTimeScale of member, the duration of member, the frameRate of member, framesToHMS(), the movieRate of sprite, the movieTime of sprite, the timeScale of member, the type of member

the labelList

Syntax   set amarker = line 3 of the labelList

Usage   *the labelList* is a property that contains a single string value with the text of all of the frame labels in the current movie. Each frame label is separated by a RETURN character, on a separate line.

Example   This Lingo function will convert *the labelList* to an actual linear list:

```
on makeLabelListAList
  set tReturnList = []
  set tNumOfLabels = the number of lines ¬
    of the labelList-1 -- ignore extra return
  repeat with tLabel = 1 to tNumOfLabels
    add tReturnList, line tLabel of the labelList
  end repeat
  return tReturnList
end makeLabelListAList
```

   Then you can use a statement like this:

```
put makeLabelListAList()
-- ["start", "break"]
```

Value   *string*

See also   go, go loop, go marker, go next, go previous, label, marker, play

the lastFrame

Syntax   put the lastFrame

Usage   *the lastFrame* is a property that contains the number of the last frame in the movie. You can test but not set this property with Lingo.

Example   This statement sets the variable *tFramesLeft* to the number of frames remaining to play in the movie:

```
set tFramesLeft = the lastFrame - the frame
```

Value   *integer*

See also   the frame

the movieName

MOVIE PROPERTY

Syntax   `set thisMovie = the movieName`

Usage   The properties *the movie* and *the movieName* both refer to the name of the current movie. When in Shockwave playback, these functions return the name of the movie as it was renamed by the browser for storage in its cache, not the name as it was stored on the server.

Example   This code segment looks in *the movieName* property for the string ".dcr", and sets a global variable accordingly:

```
global gShockFlag
if the movieName contains ".dcr" then
  -- I've been afterburned
  set gShockFlag = TRUE
else
  set gShockFlag = FALSE
end if
```

The above code could be done this way more efficiently:

```
global gShockFlag
set gShockFlag = the movieName contains ".dcr"
```

Value   *string*

See also   the moviePath, the pathName

the paletteMapping

Syntax   `set the paletteMapping = TRUE`

Usage   The movie property *the paletteMapping* determines if the movie is allowed to remap the colors of cast members with different palettes than the movie. The default value is FALSE. You can test and set this property with Lingo.

       When this property is FALSE, setting *the palette of member* or *the paletteRef of member* properties to something other than the movie palette has no effect.

Example   This statement lets the movie remap the color palette of cast members to something other than the movie palette:

`set the paletteMapping = TRUE`

Value   *boolean*

See also   the palette of member, the paletteRef of member

on prepareMovie

Syntax   `on prepareMovie`

Usage   A *prepareMovie* message is the first message sent to the movie. The handler will be executed before the first frame is drawn on the screen, and before any other Lingo is executed. It is an ideal place to determine which platform or run mode the movie is playing in.

Example   This handler assigns an internal cast to the variable *gCast* if the movie is playing in the Shockwave environment; otherwise it assigns an external cast called "bigger.cxt", presumably with larger-sized cast members, to cast library 2, an external cast of the movie. The movie then uses cast library 1 or cast library 2 throughout the rest of the movie, depending on the mode it's running in:

```
on prepareMovie
  global gCast
  if the runMode = "Plugin" then
    set gCast = 1
  else
    set aCast = "http://www.surftrio.com/casts/bigger.cxt"
    set the filename of castLib 2 = aCast
    set gCast = 2
  else if
end
```

Parameters

```
on prepare
  statements
end
```

See also   on startMovie

saveMovie

Syntax   `saveMovie "revisedmovie"`

Usage   The *saveMovie* command saves the currently opened movie to the file path specified by the parameter. This enables changes that have been made to the score, fields, scripts, and so on, to be retained from session to session. Only files in the editable Director format can be saved—protected and compressed (Shockwave) files cannot use this command. Files can only be saved to a local drive; this command does not support URLs for the file path.

Parameter   `saveMovie string`

the score

Syntax   `set the score = the media of member "aLoop"`

Usage   *the score* is a property that contains the score data associated with the current movie. Scores different from that described in the Score window can be stored as film loop cast members. You can test and set this property with Lingo.

Example   This code segment replaces the current score with a film loop, but stores the old score in a global variable so it can be used later:

```
global gScore
set gScore = the score
set the score = the media of member "filmloop"
```

Then, you can use a code segment like this to restore the score:

```
global gScore
set the score = gScore
```

Value   the media of member *boolean/string*

See also   the media of member, the scoreSelection, the type of member

the *scoreSelection*

MOVIE PROPERTY

Syntax   `set aSelectionList = the scoreSelection`

Usage   *the scoreSelection* is a property that contains a list of sublists. Each sublist contains one of the areas currently selected in the score. Each sublist has four values, which are *startSprite, endSprite, startFrame, endFrame.* You can test and set this property with Lingo.

This property can be useful when you wish to build custom Lingo score-generation tools.

These numbers correspond to the nonsprite channels in the score:

  0   script channel

 -1   sound channel 2

 -2   sound channel 1

 -3   transition channel

 -4   palette channel

 -5   tempo channel.

Example   This statement in the Message window shows that three areas are selected in the score. They include the script channel and sprites 6, 12, and 13 in frames 5 through 10.

```
put the scoreSelection
-- [[0,0,5,10], [6,6,5,10], [12,13,5,10]]
```

Value   *list of [integer, integer, integer, integer]*

the stage

Syntax   `tell the stage to boogie`

Usage   *the stage* is a property that contains a reference to the main movie being played. It can be used as an object reference but cannot be set. Combined with the *tell* command, it is used to send commands from MIAWs to the main movie.

Example   Here are some examples of *commands* you can use with *the stage* property:

```
put the drawRect of the stage
-- rect(0, 0, 320, 280)
put the rect of the stage
-- rect(16, 52, 336, 332)
put the sourceRect of the stage
-- rect(16, 52, 336, 332)
```

Value   (*the stage*)

See also   the visible of window

the stageBottom

Syntax   `set whereBottom = the stageBottom`

Usage   *the stageBottom* is a property that contains a value indicating the position of the bottom edge of the stage window on the screen. For a movie 480 pixels tall, centered on an 800- x 600-pixel screen, the value of *the stageBottom* would be 540 (480 + (600 – 480) / 2). In Shockwave movies played within a Web browser, the value is simply the vertical dimension of the stage.

This property can only be tested, not set.

Example   This statement sets the variable *tHeight* to the height of the stage:

```
set tHeight = the stageBottom - the stageTop
```

Value   *integer*

See also   the stageLeft, the stageRight, the stageTop

the stageColor

MOVIE PROPERTY

Syntax `set whatColor = the stageColor`

Usage *the stageColor* is a property that determines the color of the movie's background. You can test and set this property with Lingo.

The value of this property corresponds to the index value of the color in the current palette, regardless of the color depth of the monitor. You can find the index value of a color in the palette by clicking on the corresponding position in Director's Color Palette window.

Example This statement will set the stage color to the value specified by the parameter "sw2" that was passed to the Shockwave movie by the browser:

`set the stageColor = value(externalParamValue("sw2"))`

Value *integer*

See also the backColor of member, the backColor of sprite, the foreColor of member, the foreColor of sprite

the stageLeft

MOVIE PROPERTY

Syntax `set whereLeft = the stageLeft`

Usage *the stageLeft* is a property that contains a value indicating the position of the left edge of the Stage window on the screen. For a movie 640 pixels wide, centered on an 800- x 600-pixel screen, the value of *the stageLeft* would be 80 ((800 – 640) / 2). In Shockwave movies played within a Web browser, the value is 0.

This property can only be tested, not set.

Example See *the stageRight*.

Value *integer*

See also the stageBottom, the stageRight, the stageTop

the stageRight

Syntax   `set whereRight = the stageRight`

Usage   *the stageRight* is a property that contains a value indicating the position of the right edge of the stage window on the screen. For a movie 640 pixels wide, centered on an 800- x 600-pixel screen, the value of *the stageRight* would be 720 (640 + (800 – 640) / 2). In Shockwave movies played within a Web browser, the value is the width of the stage as defined in the Movie Properties dialog.

   This property can only be tested, not set.

Example   This statement sets the variable *tWidth* to the width of the stage:

`set tWidth = the stageRight - the stageLeft`

Value   *integer*

See also   the stageBottom, the stageLeft, the stageTop

the stageTop

Syntax   `set whereTop = the stageTop`

Usage   *the stageTop* is a property that contains a value indicating the position of the top of the stage window on the screen. For a movie 480 pixels tall, centered on an 800- x 600-pixel screen, the value of *the stageBottom* would be 540 (480 + (600 – 480) / 2). In Shockwave movies played within a Web browser, the value is simply the vertical dimension of the stage.

   This property can only be tested, not set.

Example   See *the stageBottom*.

Value   *integer*

See also   the stageBottom, the stageLeft, the stageRight

on startMovie

HANDLER

Syntax   on startmovie

Usage   A *startMovie* message is the first message sent to a movie as it starts to play. Statements placed in the *on startMovie* handler will be executed before any other action is taken in the movie. It is typically used to initialize global variables and other functions to prepare the movie for play. It must be placed in a movie script.

Example   This handler clears all global variables from memory, then calls a custom handler to initialize puppet sprites for this movie:

```
on startMovie
  clearGlobals
  initPuppets
end
```

Parameters
```
on startMovie
    statements
end
```

See also   on stopMovie

on stopMovie

HANDLER

Syntax   on stopmovie

Usage   A *stopMovie* message is sent when the current movie is told to quit. Statements placed in the *on stopMovie* handler execute as the last action taken in the movie. *on stopMovie* is typically used to clear global variables, shut down Xtras, and so on. It must be placed in a movie script.

Example   This handler clears all global variables from memory, then calls a custom handler to turn off puppet sprites for this movie:

```
on startMovie
  clearGlobals
  deletePuppets
end
```

Parameters
```
on stopMovie
    statements
end
```

See also   on stopMovie

the switchColorDepth

Syntax   `set the switchColorDepth = TRUE`

Usage   *the switchColorDepth* is a MacOS-specific property that determines whether the next movie automatically changes the monitor's color depth on its own. This property has no effect on Windows machines or in Shockwave movies on any platform.

   If you need to change the monitor depth for the current movie, use the movie property *the colorDepth*.

Example   These statements test to see if a machine is running under Windows and set *the switchColorDepth* property to TRUE if it is not already:

```
case the machineType of
  256: nothing
  otherwise
    set the switchColorDepth = TRUE
end case
```

Value   *boolean*

See also   the colorDepth

the trace

Syntax
```
set the trace = TRUE
```

Usage
the trace is a property that is used in the authoring mode to control the function that displays messages in Director's Message Window. It has no purpose in the final version of a movie. A sample trace segment looks like the following:

```
== Movie: C:\Work\DS0397.dir Frame: 1 Script: Main Movie Utilities
   Handler: startMovie
--> initMIAW
== Script: Main Movie Utilities Handler: initMIAW
--> set the title of window  "DS0397.dir"  to "Director Solutions
   DIRzine - Launch Issue March 1997"
--> updateStage
--> end  initMIAW
== Script: Main Movie Utilities Handler: startMovie
--> end
== Script: 4 Handler: exitFrame
--> go the frame
--> end
--> go the frame
--> end
```

Each object referred to—movie, frame, script, handler, and so on—is set off with a ":" character before its name or cast member number. The first object in a series is preceded by "==". Each line of code is preceded by "-->".

Controlling *the trace* property from Lingo enables you to turn on tracing for a specific portion of your movie, eliminating trace statements for portions of the movie under observation that are already debugged, and keeping the amount of data in the Message window to a minimum.

Statements containing the trace should be commented out or removed entirely before creating projectors, protecting movies, or compressing movies.

Example
This code fragment turns on tracing before the *complicatedStuff* handler begins its action, then turns it off immediately after the handler is finished. Only the call to *complicatedStuff* and its own statements (plus any handlers it may call itself) will be traced:

```
set the trace = TRUE
complicatedStuff
set the trace = FALSE
```

Value
boolean

See also
the traceLoad, the traceLogFile

the traceLoad

Syntax   `set the traceLoad = 2`

Usage   *the traceLoad* is a property which contains a number that controls the amount of information displayed about cast members when they are loaded into memory. The possible values are:

    0   Display no information

    1   Display cast members' names

    2   Display cast members' names, number of the current frame, movie name, and file seek offset.

The most detailed result is in the following form:

```
Loaded cast 1   frame=1   movie=DS0397.dir   seekOffset=154998
```

The first two values are the cast member number and the frame number; the third is the movie's name, and the last is the number of bytes the read head of the disk drive had to travel to get to the beginning of the data for the cast member from the last cast member. This is useful for determining the organization of a movie's cast on a disk as well as being useful for determining how networked movies and external files are being loaded.

> **Tip**
>
> *By rearranging the cast members to reduce the* seekOffset *values, cast member loading can be sped up to make the movie run faster.*

You can test and set this property with Lingo. Since the code generated by the property is sent to the Message window, this is only useful in the Director authoring environment.

Example   This handler initiates detailed tracing of cast member loading as the playback head leaves a frame:

```
on exitFrame
  set the traceLoad = TRUE
end
```

Value   0|1|2

See also   the trace, the traceLogFile

the traceLogFile

MOVIE PROPERTY

Syntax   `set the traceLogFile = "Mac HD:Work:tracer.txt"`

Usage   *the traceLogFile* is a property that defines a file and path where any messages or tracing information sent by the program or to the Message window is duplicated. The log file can be closed by setting the property to EMPTY.

You can test and set this property with Lingo. Since the text saved to the file mirrors that sent to the Message window, this is only useful in the Director authoring environment.

Example   This Lingo sequence begins writing Message window data to the file "dirlog.txt" in the directory where the movie is located, turns tracing on, executes a handler that will have its execution traced, then turns tracing off and closes the trace file.

```
set the traceLogFile = "dirlog.txt"
set the trace = TRUE
doaComplicatedThing
set the trace = FALSE
set the traceLogFile = EMPTY
```

Value   *string*

See also   the trace, the traceLoad

the updateLock

MOVIE PROPERTY

Syntax   `set the updateLock = TRUE`

Usage   *the updateLock* is a property that determines whether the stage will be updated during score recording. You can test and set this property with Lingo.

When *the updateLock* property is TRUE, the stage display is unchanged even while the score is being modified by Lingo during score recording. You can use this property to hide score changes from the user.

Example   This code segment freezes the display on the stage while another frame is updated:

```
set tCurrFrame = the frame
beginRecording
 set the updateLock = TRUE
 go to frame 10
 set the memberNum of sprite 10 = ¬
  the number of member "box"
 set the loc of sprite 10 = point(100,100)
 updateFrame
 go to frame tCurrFrame
 set the updateLock = FALSE
endRecording
```

Value   *boolean*

See also   beginRecording, clearFrame, deleteFrame, duplicateFrame, endRecording,
the score, the scoreSelection, updateFrame

the updateMovieEnabled

MOVIE PROPERTY

Syntax   `set the updateMovieEnabled = TRUE`

Usage   *the updateMovieEnabled* is a property that controls whether changes made to
the current movie are to be automatically saved before navigating to another
movie. You can test and set this property with Lingo.

> ### Tip
>
> *You cannot save changes made to a Shockwave movie or a protected
> movie.*

Example   This code would cause the current movie to be saved with any changes
made to it during the current session before it displays the "Made With
Macromedia" movie:

```
on stopMovie
  set the updateMovieEnabled = TRUE
  go "MWM"
end
```

Value   *boolean*

See also   saveMovie

User Interaction (Key-board & Timer) Category

6

These Lingo keywords are related to keyboard events and timing mechanisms built into Director. Several mouse-related items appear here as well, mostly having to do with when mouse events happened.

the commandDown

MOVIE PROPERTY

Syntax   `set isCommandDown = the commandDown`

Usage   *the commandDown* is a property that returns TRUE when the Command key on a Macintosh or the Ctrl key on a Windows machine is pressed. This is useful when used with *the key* property, to let you define special keyboard options.

Example   This handler uses the case structure to make special events happen when various key combinations are pressed:

```
on keyDown
  set tKey = the key
  case TRUE of
   (the commandDown AND tKey = "A"):
    go to frame "cA"
   (the optionDown AND tKey = "A"):
    go to frame "oA"
   (the shiftDown AND tKey = "A"):
    go to frame "sA"
   (the controlDown AND tKey = "A"):
    go to frame "tA"
  end case
end keyDown
```

Value   *boolean*

See also   the controlDown, the key, the keyCode, on keyDown, on keyUp, the optionDown, the shiftDown

the controlDown

MOVIE PROPERTY

Syntax   `set isControlDown = the controlDown`

Usage   *the controlDown* is a property that returns TRUE when the Command key on a Macintosh or the Ctrl key on a Windows machine is pressed. This is useful when used with *the key* property, to let you define special keyboard options.

Example   See *the commandDown*.

Value   *boolean*

See also   the commandDown, the key, the keyCode, on keyDown, on keyUp, the
optionDown, the shiftDown

cursor

COMMAND

Syntax   cursor 0

cursor [50]

cursor [32, 40]

Usage   The *cursor* command changes the appearance of the cursor. It only affects the
cursor when it is pointing anywhere over a movie. If the user drags outside
the movie, the system takes control of the cursor's appearance.

Use the first form of this command when you want to use a built-in
cursor. These cursors are:

0	Normal cursor operation
–1	Arrow cursor
1	I-beam cursor
2	Crosshair cursor
3	Crossbar cursor
4	Wait cursor (watch on Mac, hourglass on Windows)
200	Blank cursor

Use the *cursor* command with a list of one or two integers when you want
to use cast members as a custom cursor. The cast members used must be 1-bit
bitmap members, and should be 16 x 16 pixels. If the bitmap is larger than 16 x
16 pixels, Director will crop it to fit that size, starting from the upper left corner
of the bitmap. The bitmap's registration point is the cursor's active point. The
first item in the list is the image you want to use as the cursor. The second item
in the list is an optional mask. When used, it allows you to determine how the
cursor interacts with background elements. Black pixels in the mask will affect
the pixels in the cursor with the Reverse ink; white pixels in the mask affect the
cursor pixels with the Copy ink.

Example   This segment of a behavior script modifies the cursor to display a browser-style hand when it rolls over a hyperlinked button, then back to the default cursor when it rolls off:

```
property  standardCursor, alternateCursor
on mouseEnter me
  cursor [the number of member "hand", ¬
    the number of member "handmask"]
end
on mouseLeave me
  cursor standardCursor
end
```

Parameters   cursor -1|0|1|2|3|4|200

cursor [*integer*]

cursor [*integer, integer*]

See also   the cursor of sprite

the cursor of sprite

Syntax   set the cursor of sprite 4 = 0

set the cursor of sprite aLinkSprite = [50]

set the cursor of sprite 120 = [32, 40]

Usage   *the cursor of sprite* property behaves similarly to the *cursor* command above, using either a built-in cursor number or custom 1-bit member in the cast. However, the cursor is only changed when it is pointing at the specified sprite, if it has its *cursor of sprite* property set. You can remove a custom sprite cursor by setting its *cursor of sprite* property to 0. The built-in cursor values are the same as those for the *cursor* command.

Example   This script modifies the cursor property of a sprite to display a browser-style hand when it rolls over a hyperlinked button.

```
set the cursor of sprite 20 = [the number of member "hand", ¬
  the number of member "handmask"]
```

Parameters the cursor of sprite *integer*

Value -1|0|1|2|3|4|200|[*integer*]|[*integer, integer*]

See also cursor

the exitLock

MOVIE PROPERTY

Syntax set the exitLock = TRUE

Usage When *the exitLock* property is TRUE, the user is blocked from quitting the Director projector by using any typical key combination like Ctrl | Command + period, Ctrl | Command + Q, Ctrl | Command + W, or Esc. Its default value is FALSE.

In Shockwave, any of the above key combinations (or the *quit* keyword) will stop the playback of the Shockwave movie, making it completely inactive until reloaded by the browser. Setting *the exitLock* property to TRUE can prevent this unfortunate situation.

If *the exitLock* is TRUE, the only way to quit a projector (or make a Shockwave movie inactive) is to send the *quit* command with Lingo.

Value *boolean*

See also quit

the key

MOVIE PROPERTY

Syntax set whatKey = the key

Usage The property *the key* contains a string representing the character of the last key that was pressed. If you need to know the ASCII value of the last key that was pressed, use the *charToNum* function.

You can use *the key* property in key event handlers to determine which action to take.

In a Shockwave movie, the movie must be active in order for it to receive key events. Modifier keys like Shift, Command/Ctrl, and Option/Alt are not recorded by *the key*. The movie becomes active with either a mouse click or by including the parameter TEXTFOCUS=ONSTART in the <EMBED> tag, like this:

```
<EMBED SRC=my.dcr WIDTH=240 HEIGHT=240, TEXTFOCUS=ONSTART>
```

Example   This handler uses the *on keyDown* handler and *the case* logical structure with *the key* function to move a sprite around the screen:

```
on keyDown
 case the key of
  "i":set the loc of sprite 8 = ¬
    the loc of sprite 8 + point(0,-2)
  "j":set the loc of sprite 8 = ¬
    the loc of sprite 8 + point(-2,0)
  "k":set the loc of sprite 8 = ¬
    the loc of sprite 8 + point(2,0)
  "m":set the loc of sprite 8 = ¬
    the loc of sprite 8 + point(0,2)
 end case
end keyDown
```

Value   *string*

See also   BACKSPACE, charToNum, the commandDown, the controlDown, ENTER, the keyCode, on keyDown, on keyUp, numToChar, the optionDown, RETURN, the shiftDown, TAB

the keyCode

MOVIE PROPERTY

Syntax   `set whatCode = the keyCode`

Usage   The movie property *the keyCode* contains a numeric (not ASCII) value of the last key that was pressed. This can be useful for working with keys that don't return a string character, such as arrow keys. Modifier keys like Shift, Command/Ctrl, and Option/Alt are not recorded by *the keyCode*, nor do they affect the value of other keys pressed (i.e., pressing the "A" key always yields the same value, even if the Shift key is held down).

Example   This handler uses the *on keyUp* handler and *the case* structure with *the keyCode* function to move a sprite around the screen using *the keyCode* value of the arrow keys after the key has been pressed and released:

```
on keyUp
 case the keyCode of
  126: set the loc of sprite 8 = ¬
   the loc of sprite 8 + point(0,-2) - up arrow
  123: set the loc of sprite 8 = ¬
   the loc of sprite 8 + point(-2,0) - left arrow
  124: set the loc of sprite 8 = ¬
   the loc of sprite 8 + point(2,0) - right arrow
  125: set the loc of sprite 8 = ¬
   the loc of sprite 8 + point(0,2) - down arrow
 end case
end
```

Value   *integer*

See also   BACKSPACE, charToNum, the commandDown, the controlDown, ENTER, the key, on keyDown, on keyUp, numToChar, the optionDown, RETURN, the shiftDown, TAB

on keyDown   HANDLER

Syntax   on keyDown

on keyDown me

Usage   A *keyDown* message is sent when one of the keys on the keyboard is pressed. Statements placed in an *on keyDown* handler are executed when the message is received by the object the handler is attached to. The first object to inter-cept the message will prevent other objects from executing their own *keyDown* handlers.

The precedence order for objects is: the behavior or sprite script of the selected editable field sprite (if there is one), the cast script of the selected editable field sprite, the current frame script, and the movie. The *keyDownScript* actually receives the message first but will not prevent the message from passing on to the other objects.

Modifier keys like Shift, Command/Ctrl, and Option/Alt do not trigger *on keyDown*.

The keyword *me* is used in the handler when the *on keyDown* handler is used in a behavior.

Example   See the Example for *the key*:

Parameters ```
on keyDown none/me
    statements
end
```

See also    on idle, the key, the keyCode, the keyDownScript, the keyPressed, on keyUp, the keyUpScript

# the keyDownScript

<span style="float:right">**MOVIE PROPERTY**</span>

Syntax      `set the keyDownScript = "if the key = RETURN then quit"`

Usage       *the keyDownScript* is a property that contains a string with a default command to be executed when a key is pressed. This command can be a simple Lingo statement or a handler name. By default, *the keyDownScript* is an empty string. To clear *the keyDownScript*, set it to EMPTY.

            *the keyDownScript* is the first object the movie sends a *keyDown* message to. The message then passes on to the appropriate objects containing *on keyDown* handlers (see above).

            Modifier keys like Shift, Command/Ctrl, and Option/Alt do not trigger *the keyDownScript*.

Example     This statement causes all *keyDown* events to be sent to the handler "doKeys":

            `set the keyDownScript = "doKeys"`

Value       *string*

See also    on idle, the key, the keyCode, on keyDown, the keyPressed, the keyUp, the keyUpScript
```

the keyPressed

Syntax `set aKey = the keyPressed`

Usage *the keyPressed* is a property that contains the last key that was pressed, as a string. It is much the same as the *key* function, but it works within repeat loops. Other key events are not received while a repeat loop is processing, for increased performance.

> **Tip**
>
> *If you use a repeat loop to wait for a key event, you can tie up valuable processor time the browser and other applications will need. It is typically better to use an* on keyDown *handler or the* keyDownScript *property to receive key events, and loop in an* exitFrame *handler with a* "go to the frame" *statement.*

Modifier keys like Shift, Command/Ctrl, and Option/Alt are not recorded by *the keyPressed*.

You can test but not set this property with Lingo.

Example This code segment waits until any key is pressed, then exits the repeat loop:

```
repeat while TRUE -- repeats forever
  if the keyPressed <> EMPTY then exit repeat
  -- do lingo here
  -- but don't use this technique
  -- very often, since it ties up
  -- valuable processor time!
end repeat
```

Value *string*

See also BACKSPACE, charToNum, the commandDown, the controlDown, ENTER, the key, on keyDown, on keyUp, numToChar, the optionDown, RETURN, the shiftDown, TAB

on keyUp

Syntax
```
on keyUp
on keyUp me
```

Usage
A *keyUp* message is sent when one of the keys on the keyboard is pressed and then released. Statements placed in an *on keyUp* handler are executed when the message is received by the object the handler is attached to. The first object to intercept the message will prevent other objects from executing their own *keyDown* handlers. The precedence order for objects is: the behavior or sprite script of the selected editable field sprite (if there is one), the cast script of the selected editable field sprite, the current frame script, and the movie. The *keyUpScript* actually receives the message first but will not prevent the message from passing on to the other objects.

The keyword *me* is used in the handler when the *on keyUp* handler is used in a behavior.

Example
See the Examples for *the keyCode*:

Parameters
```
on keyUp none/me
    statements
end
```

See also
on idle, the key, the keyCode, on keyDown, the keyDownScript, the keyPressed, the keyUpScript

the keyUpScript

Syntax
```
set the keyUpScript = "if the key = BACKSPACE then doDelete"
```

Usage
the keyUpScript is a property that contains a string with a default command to be executed when a key is pressed. This Lingo can be a simple statement or a handler name. By default, *the keyUpScript* is an empty string. To clear *the keyUpScript*, set it to EMPTY.

The *keyUpScript* is the first object the movie sends a *keyUp* message to. The message then passes on to the appropriate objects containing *on keyUp* handlers (see above).

Example This statement causes all *keyUp* events to be sent to the handler "doKeys":

```
set the keyUpScript = "doKeys"
```

Value *string*

See also on idle, the key, the keyCode, on keyDown, the keyDownScript, the keyPressed, the keyUp

the lastEvent

MOVIE PROPERTY

Syntax `set howLong = the lastEvent`

Usage *the lastEvent* is a property that returns the time in ticks (1 tick = 1/60 of a second) since the most recent cursor movement, mouse click, or key press occurred. This is, in effect, the lowest of the three values associated with *lastKey*, *lastRoll*, and *lastClick*. Continuous cursor movement or a key held down will also affect *lastEvent*, while holding a mouse button down will not. Releasing a mouse button never affects *lastEvent*, nor does releasing a key or events such as *mouseWithin*. The *starttimer* command sets this property to 0.

The *lastEvent* property is not updated while the movie is within a *repeat* loop. Modifier keys like Shift, Command/Ctrl, and Option/Alt do not affect *lastEvent*.

Example This handler automatically goes to a frame labeled "waiting" if it has been more than one minute since the mouse was moved, clicked, or a key was pressed or held down:

```
on exitFrame
  if the lastEvent > 60*60 then
    go to frame "waiting"
  else
    go to the frame
  end if
end exitFrame
```

Value *integer*

See also the lastClick, the lastKey, the lastRoll, startTimer

the lastKey

Syntax   `set whenKeyDown = the lastKey`

Usage   *the lastKey* is a property that returns a value in ticks since the last key on the keyboard was pressed and released. It is not updated within repeat loops. Holding a key down continually resets the value until it is released. The *starttimer* command sets this property to 0.

   Modifier keys like Shift, Command/Ctrl, and Option/Alt do not affect *the lastKey*.

Example This handler automatically goes to a frame labeled "waiting" if it has been more than one minute since a key was pressed:

```
on exitFrame
  if the lastKey > 60*60 then
    go to frame "waiting"
  else
    go to the frame
  end if
end exitFrame
```

Value   *integer*

See also the lastClick, the lastEvent, the lastRoll, startTimer

the optionDown

Syntax   `set isOptDown = the optionDown`

Usage   *the optionDown* is a property that returns TRUE when the Option key on a Macintosh, or the Alt key on a Windows machine, is being pressed. This is useful when used with *the key* function, to let you define special keyboard options. Note that unlike the Command/Ctrl key, the Option key actually modifies some values returned by *the key* property.

Example   See the Example for *the commandDown*.

Value   *boolean*

See also   the commandDown, the controlDown, the key, the keyCode, on keyDown, on keyUp, the shiftDown

the shiftDown

MOVIE PROPERTY

Syntax   `set upperCase = the shiftDown`

Usage   *the shiftDown* is a property that indicates that the Shift key is being pressed on the keyboard. Note that unlike the Command/Ctrl key, the Option key actually modifies some values returned by *the key* property.

Example   This handler tests for a character between A and Z and adds only the lowercase version to a field:

```
on keyDown
  set isShifted = the shiftDown
  set aKey = the key
  if aKey > "a" and aKey < "z" then
    --true for all characters of the alphabet
    if isShifted then
      set aKey = numToChar (charToNum (aKey) + 32)
      --shifts ASCII value of character to lowercase
    end if
    put aKey after field "textfield"
  end if
end
```

Value   *boolean*

See also   the commandDown, the controlDown, the key, the keyCode, on keyDown, on keyUp, the optionDown, the shiftDown

starttimer

Syntax   `starttimer`

Usage   The *starttimer* command resets the counters for the properties *the timer, the lastClick, the lastEvent, the lastKey,* and *the lastRoll.*

Example   This handler resets *the timer* property to 0, then waits for three seconds (180 ticks) before moving on to the next frame.

```
on exitFrame
  starttimer
  repeat while the timer < 180
    nothing
  end repeat
end
```

See also   the lastClick, the lastEvent, the lastKey, the lastRoll, on timeOut, the ticks, the timeoutKeyDown, the timeoutLapsed, the timeoutLength, the timeoutMouse, the timeoutPlay, the timeoutScript, the timer

on timeout

Syntax   `on timeout`

Usage   The *on timeout* handler is called when the number of ticks specified by *the timeoutLength* property has elapsed without any event being generated by the keyboard or mouse. Place this handler in a movie script. The default value for *the timeoutLength* is three minutes (180 seconds or 10800 ticks).

Use the *timeout* handler when the entire movie should use the same script to handle timeouts. If the *timeout* script will change periodically, use *the timeoutScript* property.

Example   This portion of a movie script sets *the timeoutLength* to 10 seconds, and uses the *timeout* handler to turn off puppeted sprites, dispose of global variables, and go to a new movie:

```
on startmovie
  set the timeoutLength = 600
end
on timeout
  repeat with i = 1 to 120
    if the puppet of sprite i then puppetsprite i, FALSE
  end repeat
  clearGlobals
  go movie "waiting"
end
```

Parameters

```
on timeout
  statements
end
```

See also   on enterFrame, on exitFrame, on idle, on keyDown, on keyUp, on mouseDown, on mouseUp, on startMovie, on stepFrame, on startMovie, the timeoutKeyDown, the timeoutLapsed, the timeoutMouse, the timeoutPlay, the timeoutScript

the timeoutKeyDown

MOVIE PROPERTY

Syntax   `set the timeoutKeyDown = TRUE`

Usage   *the timeoutKeyDown* is a property that determines whether keyboard events affect the counter that triggers the *on timeout* handler and *the timeoutScript*. If the property is TRUE (its default value), the *timeoutLapsed* property will be set to 0 when a key is pressed and as long as it is held down. This property can be set and tested.

Modifier keys like Shift, Command/Ctrl, and Option/Alt do not affect *the timeoutKeyDown*.

Value   *boolean*

See also   the lastClick, the lastEvent, the lastKey, the lastRoll, on timeout, the timeoutKeyDown, the timeoutLapsed, the timeoutLength, the timeoutMouse, the timeoutPlay, the timeoutScript

the timeoutLapsed

Syntax   `set aTimer = the timeoutLapsed`

Usage   *the timeoutLapsed* is a property that contains a value equal to the number of ticks elapsed since the last event capable of resetting it (determined by *the timeoutkeyDown, the timeoutMouse,* and *the timeoutPlay* properties).

When the value of *the timeoutLapsed* is greater than that of *the timeoutLength*, a *timeout* message will be generated. This property can be tested but not set.

Example   This handler tests *the timeoutLapsed* and displays a message indicating the amount of time remaining before the movie responds to a *timeout* event:

```
on exitFrame
  global gMessageSprite
  if the timeoutLapsed > (60 * 60) then
    --over 1 minute has elapsed since the last event
    set secondsRemaining = (the timeoutLength - ¬
      the timeoutLapsed) / 60
    set aMessage = "seconds before entering idle mode."
    put string (secondsRemaining) && aMessage ¬
      into field "messages"
    set the memberNum of sprite gMessageSprite = ¬
      the number of member "messages"
    set the visible of sprite gMessageSprite = TRUE
  end if
end
```

Value   *integer*

See also   the lastClick, the lastEvent, the lastKey, the lastRoll, on timeout, the timeoutKeyDown, the timeoutLength, the timeoutMouse, the timeoutPlay, the timeoutScript

the timeoutLength

MOVIE PROPERTY

Syntax `set the timeoutLength = 1500`

Usage *the timeoutLength* is a property that determines the amount of time in ticks that will elapse after the last event before the movie generates a *timeout* message. The default value for *the timeoutLength* is three minutes (180 seconds or 10800 ticks). When the value of *the timeoutLapsed* is greater than that of *the timeoutLength*, a *timeout* message will be generated. This property can be tested and set.

No action will be taken if *the timeoutScript* is EMPTY and there is no *on timeout* handler.

Example See the Examples for *on timeout* and *the timeoutLapsed*.

Value *integer*

See also the lastClick, the lastEvent, the lastKey, the lastRoll, on timeout, the timeoutKeyDown, the timeoutLapsed, the timeoutMouse, the timeoutPlay, the timeoutScript

the timeoutMouse

MOVIE PROPERTY

Syntax `set the timeoutMouse = TRUE`

Usage *the timeoutMouse* is a property that determines whether mouse events affect the counter that triggers the *on timeout* handler and *the timeoutScript*. If the property is TRUE (its default value), *the timeoutLapsed* property will be set to 0 when a mouse key is pressed and as long as it is held down. This property can be set and tested.

Value *boolean*

See also the lastClick, the lastEvent, the lastKey, the lastRoll, on timeout, the timeoutKeyDown, the timeoutLapsed, the timeoutLength, the timeoutPlay, the timeoutScript

the timeoutPlay

Syntax   `set the timeoutPlay = TRUE`

Usage   *the timeoutPlay* property determines whether halting a movie using the *pause* command affects the counter that triggers the *on timeout* handler and *the timeoutScript*. If the property is TRUE (its default value is FALSE), *the timeoutLapsed* property will be set to 0 as long as the playback head is moving. This property can be set and tested.

Example   A movie containing the following code fragment will generate a *timeout* message after the period specified by *the timeoutLength* property has elapsed if no events occur:

```
set the timeoutPlay = TRUE
pause
```

Value   *boolean*

See also   the lastClick, the lastEvent, the lastKey, the lastRoll, on timeout, the timeoutKeyDown, the timeoutLapsed, the timeoutLength, the timeoutMouse, the timeoutScript

the timeoutScript

Syntax   `set the timeoutScript = "go 1000"`

Usage   *the timeoutScript* property contains a string with a default command to be executed when a *timeout* message is generated. This string can be a simple statement or a handler name. *the timeoutScript* property takes precedence over the *on timeout* handler. By default, *the timeoutScript* is an empty string. To clear *the timeoutScript*, set it to EMPTY.

Example This portion of a movie script sets *the timeoutLength* to 10 seconds, and uses *the timeoutScript* to turn off puppeted sprites, dispose of global variables, and go to a new movie:

```
on startmovie
  set the timeoutLength = 600
  set the timeoutScript = "finishMovie"
end
on finishMovie
  repeat with i = 1 to 120
    if the puppet of sprite i then puppetsprite i, FALSE
  end repeat
  clearGlobals
  go movie "waiting"
end
```

Value *string*

See also the lastClick, the lastEvent, the lastKey, the lastRoll, on timeout, the timeoutKeyDown, the timeoutLapsed, the timeoutLength, the timeoutMouse, the timeoutPlay, the timeoutScript

the timer

MOVIE PROPERTY

Syntax `set elapsed = the timer`

Usage *the timer* property is an internal clock that can be tested and reset to determine elapsed time since the movie started playing or a *starttimer* command was executed. It can be tested but not set.

Example See the Example for *starttimer*.

Value *integer*

See also starttimer, the ticks

User Interaction (Mouse Events) Category

7

These handlers all relate to actions and movements of the cursor in a movie. As the mouse and cursor are moved, the cursor's position is constantly compared to items on the stage, and events are generated when it is moved over or off of sprites. Pressing the mouse button generates events, and there are handlers for them as well.

on mouseDown

Syntax   on mouseDown

on mouseDown me

Usage   A *mouseDown* message is sent when a button on the mouse is pressed. The
message will first be sent to *the mouseDownScript*. After that, *mouseDown*
handlers will be notified in this order: the sprite script or behavior of the
sprite identified by *the clickOn* property, the cast member script of the cast
member used for the sprite, the frame script for the current frame, and
finally the movie script. Once a *mouseDown* handler has intercepted the
message, it is not passed on unless specifically told to do so with the *pass*
command.

Shockwave movies have typically used the *mouseDown* message for
button triggers due to some unreliability with receiving *mouseUp* messages
from browsers in earlier versions of the plug-ins.

Example   This *on mouseDown* handler will cause a sprite to follow the mouse cursor as
long as the mouse button is being pressed:

```
on mouseDown
  repeat while the mouseDown
    set the loc of sprite 10 = ¬
      point(the mouseH, the mouseV)
    updateStage
  end repeat
end mouseDown
```

Parameters   on mouseDown *none*/me
statements
end

See also   the mouseH, the mouseV, on mouseDown, on mouseUp, the
mouseDownScript, the mouseUpScript, rollOver, the stillDown

on mouseUp

Syntax on mouseUp

on mouseUp me

Usage A *mouseUp* message is sent when a button on the mouse has been pressed and released. The message will first be sent to *the mouseUpScript*. After that, *on mouseUp* handlers will be notified in this order: the sprite script or behavior of the topmost sprite underneath the cursor at the time the button is released, the cast member script of the cast member used for the sprite, the frame script for the current frame, and finally the movie script. Once an *on mouseUp* handler has intercepted the message, it is not passed on unless specifically told to do so with the *pass* command.

Example Use of the *on mouseUp* handler to trigger button actions allows users to roll off of buttons they've begun to select if they've made a mistaken selection. This frame script handler checks to see that the mouse is still over the sprite it clicked on before taking any action:

```
on mouseUp
  set clickedSprite = the clickOn
  set currentSprite = the rollover
  if currentSprite = clickedSprite then doSomething
end
```

Parameters on mouseUp *none*/me
  statements
end

See also the mouseH, the mouseV, on mouseDown, the mouseUp, the mouseDownScript, the mouseUpScript, on mouseUpOutSide, rollOver, the stillDown

on mouseUpOutSide

Syntax   on mouseUpOutside me

Usage   The *mouseUpOutSide* message is sent to a sprite when a click occurs on a sprite but the mouse button is released when the cursor is no longer over the sprite. The handler should be placed in a behavior script attached to a sprite.

Example   This behavior handler resets the current sprite to its original cast member value when the mouse button is released outside of the sprite's bounding box (this example does not include the *getPropertyDescriptionList* handler for the behavior):

```
property originalMember
on mouseUpOutSide me
    set the memberNum of sprite the spritenum of me = ¬
    the originalMember of me
end
```

Parameters
```
on mouseUpOutSide me
    statements
end
```

See also   on mouseDown, the mouseDown, the mouseDownScript, on mouseUp, the mouseUp, the mouseUpScript

on mouseWithin

Syntax   on mouseWithin

on mouseWithin me

Usage   This handler can be attached to a sprite or a cast member. When the cursor is over a sprite with *on mouseWithin* in its sprite script, behavior, or the script of its cast member, the movie will send *mouseWithin* messages as often as possible.

The handler can be used with or without the parameter *me* in a sprite behavior. If used in a cast member script, the *me* parameter should not be used.

If the matte ink effect is used with a 1-bit bitmap sprite, a *mouseWithin* message is sent when the cursor is over a nontransparent pixel of the spite. Otherwise, the *mouseWithin* message is sent whenever the cursor is within the rect of the sprite.

Example This behavior puts the channel number of the sprite into the message window while the cursor is over the sprite:

```
on mouseWithin me
  put the spritenum of me
end
```

Parameters
```
on mouseWithin
  statements
end
```
```
on mouseWithin
  statements
end
```

See also on mouseDown, the mouseDown, the mouseDownScript, on mouseUp, the mouseUp, the mouseUpScript

on rightMouseDown

HANDLER

Syntax `on rightMouseDown`

`on rightMouseDown me`

Usage A *rightMouseDown* message is sent when the right button on the mouse is pressed. The *on rightMouseDown* handlers will be notified in this order: the sprite script or behavior of the sprite identified by *the clickOn* property, the cast member script of the cast member used for the sprite, the frame script for the current frame, and finally the movie script. Once an *on rightMouseDown* handler has intercepted the message, it is not passed on unless specifically told to do so with the *pass* command.

On MacOS computers, if the *emulateMultiButtonMouse* property is set to TRUE, pressing the mouse button and the Control key simultaneously will generate a *rightMouseDown* message.

Example | This *on rightMouseDown* handler from a movie script identifies the sprite that was clicked and chooses an action based on that sprite:

```
on rightMouseDown
  global gExit, gHelp, gCredits
  set whichSprite = the clickOn
  case whichSprite of
    gExit: quitMovie
    gHelp: showHelp
    gCredits: showCredits
  end case
end
```

Parameters
```
on rightMouseDown none/me
  statements
end
```

See also | the mouseH, the mouseV, on mouseDown, on mouseUp, the mouseDownScript, the mouseUpScript, the rightMouseDown, the rightMouseUp, on rightMouseUp, rollOver, the stillDown

on rightMouseUp

HANDLER

Syntax
```
on rightMouseUp

on rightMouseUp me
```

Usage | An *on rightMouseUp* message is sent when the right button on the mouse has been pressed and released. The *on mouseUp* handlers will be notified in this order: the sprite script or behavior of the topmost sprite underneath the cursor at the time the button is released, the cast member script of the cast member used for the sprite, the frame script for the current frame, and finally the movie script. Once an *on rightMouseUp* handler has intercepted the message, it is not passed on unless specifically told to do so with the *pass* command.

On MacOS computers, if the *emulateMultiButtonMouse* property is set to TRUE, releasing the mouse button while the Control key is held down will generate a *rightMouseUp* message.

Example   This sprite behavior hides the sprite when the right mouse button is released over the sprite, if it was the sprite originally clicked on:

```
on rightMouseUp me
  set clickedSprite = the clickOn
  set currentSprite = the rollover
  if currentSprite = clickedSprite then
    set the visible of sprite the spriteNum of me = FALSE
  end if
end
```

Parameters   on rightMouseUp *none*/me
               statements
             end

See also   the mouseH, the mouseV, on mouseDown, the mouseUp, the mouseDownScript, the mouseUpScript, on mouseUpOutSide, the rightMouseDown, on rightMouseDown, the rightMouseUp, rollOver, the stillDown

User Interaction [Mouse] Category

8

These Lingo keywords are related to movement and actions of the mouse and cursor. These properties and commands allow you to discover the location of the cursor, determine the exact position of clicks, and test the state of the buttons on the mouse.

the clickLoc

Syntax   `set aLoc = the clickLoc`

Usage   The property *the clickLoc* contains a point value that contains the stage coordinates of the last mouse click. Point values are in the form *point (150,245)*, and have *locH* and *locV* properties. *the clickLoc* property is only updated when the mouse button is initially clicked, not if the button is held down and the mouse is moved.

Example   This handler moves sprite 1 to the position where the mouse was clicked, if it is puppeted:

```
on mouseDown
  set the loc of sprite 1 = the clickLoc
  updateStage
end mouseDown
```

Value   *point*

See also   the clickOn, the mouseCast, the mouseChar, on mouseDown, the mouseDown, the mouseDownScript, the mouseH, the mouseItem, the mouseLine, the mouseUp, the mouseUpScript, the mouseV, the mouseWord, rollOver, the stillDown

the clickOn

Syntax   `set whichActiveSprite = the clickOn`

Usage   *the clickOn* is a property that contains the sprite number of the last active sprite the user clicked, or 0 if the last click was not on an active sprite. An active sprite is one with a sprite script attached to it, even if the script consists of just a comment marker.

You can use this property to handle a group of similar clickable objects with the same handler in a movie script, rather than attaching the same handler in each of several buttons.

> **Tip**
>
> *Director 6 behaviors do not count as sprite scripts. Clicking on a sprite with only a behavior attached will result in a* clickOn *value of 0.*

Example This handler, when placed in a movie script, uses *the clickOn* to determine which action to take:

```
on mouseDown
  set tSprite = the clickOn
  puppetSound "mapClickSound"
  case tSprite of
   1:zoom(#Portland)
   2:zoom(#Salem)
   3:zoom(#Eugene)
   4:zoom(#Albany)
   5:zoom(#Yachats)
   otherwise
    pass
  end case
end mouseDown
```

Value *integer*

See also the clickLoc, the mouseCast, the mouseChar, on mouseDown, the mouseDown, the mouseDownScript, the mouseH, the mouseItem, the mouseLine, the mouseUp, the mouseUpScript, the mouseV, the mouseWord, rollOver, the stillDown

the doubleClick

MOVIE PROPERTY

Syntax `set isItDoubleClicked = the doubleClick`

Usage *the doubleClick* is a property that is TRUE if the last two clicks were within the computer's parameters for a double click. The parameter value that determines this is set by the computer's system software.

Example   This sprite script sends the HTML page "special.htm" to the frame called "content" if the user double-clicks on the sprite:

```
on mouseDown
  if the doubleClick then
    gotoNetPage "special.htm", "content"
  end if
end
```

Value   *boolean*

See also   the clickOn, on mouseDown, the mouseDownScript, on mouseUp, the mouseUpScript

the emulateMultiButtonMouse   MOVIE PROPERTY

Syntax   `set the emulateMultiButtonMouse = TRUE`

Usage   *the emulateMultiButtonMouse* is a property that allows Director movies running on MacOS systems to be functionally equivalent to Windows systems with two-button mice. When the property is set to TRUE, a combination of the control button being pressed and a mouse click on a MacOS system will generate the same response as a right-button click on a Windows system (i.e., testing for *the rightMouseDown*, or *the rightMouseUp* properties will yield TRUE; *rightMouseDown* and *rightMouseUp* handlers will be called).

This property can be tested and set. It has no effect on Windows machines.

Example   This movie script tests for a Windows machine on startup. If it detects a non-Windows machine, it begins multibutton emulation. A *rightMouseUp* handler in the movie script calls a routine that presents the user with a menu.

```
on startmovie
  if not (the machineType = 256) then
    set the emulateMultiButtonMouse = TRUE
  else
    set the emulateMultiButtonMouse = FALSE
  end if
end
on rightMouseUp
  bringUpMenu
end
```

Value   *boolean*

See also   the keyPressed, the rightMouseDown, on rightMouseDown, the rightMouseUp, on rightMouseUp

the lastClick

Syntax   `set howLong = the lastClick`

Usage   *the lastClick* is a property that contains the time in ticks since a mouse button was clicked. There are 60 ticks per second. This property can be tested but not set, although the *starttimer* command resets this property to 0.

Example   This handler automatically goes to a frame labeled "waiting" if it has been more than one minute since the last mouse click:

```
on exitFrame
 if the lastClick > 60*60 then
  go to frame "waiting"
 else
  go to the frame
 end if
end exitFrame
```

Value   *integer*

See also   the lastEvent, the lastKey, the lastRoll, starttimer

the lastRoll

Syntax   `set aRollTime = the lastRoll`

Usage   *the lastRoll* is a property that contains the time in ticks since the mouse was last moved. There are 60 ticks per second. This property can be tested but not set, although the *starttimer* command resets this property to 0.

Example This handler automatically goes to a frame labeled "waiting" if it has been more than one minute since the mouse was moved:

```
on exitFrame
  if the lastRoll > 60*60 then
    go to frame "waiting"
  else
    go to the frame
  end if
end exitFrame
```

Value *integer*

See also the lastClick, the lastEvent, the lastKey, starttimer

the mouseChar

MOVIE PROPERTY

Syntax `set whichChar = the mouseChar`

Usage *the mouseChar* is a property that contains the position of the character the cursor is currently over, if the cursor is over a character in a field cast member. If the cursor is not over a character in a field cast member, this property value is –1.

Example This Lingo function combines *the mouseChar, the mouseLine, the mouseItem,* and *the mouseWord* properties into one useful handler. It makes it easy to obtain any text chunk that the mouse cursor is above:

```
on getMouseText myChunkSymbol
  -- myChunkSymbol should be
  -- #char, #item, #line, or #word
  set tCst = the mouseMember
  if tCst < 1 then exit
  if the type of member tCst <> #field then exit
  case myChunkSymbol of
    #char: return(char the mouseChar of field tCst)
    #line: return(line the mouseLine of field tCst)
    #item: return(item the mouseItem of field tCst)
    #word: return(word the mouseWord of field tCst)
  end case
end getMouseText
```

Value   *integer*

See also   char, chars, contains, field, item, the itemDelimiter, the last, length, line, member, the mouseItem, the mouseLine, the mouseMember, the mouseWord, the number of chars, the number of items, the number of lines, the number of words, offset, starts, stringP, string, value, word

the mouseDown

MOVIE PROPERTY

Syntax   `set isItDown = the mouseDown`

Usage   The property *the mouseDown* returns TRUE if the mouse button is currently being pressed, or FALSE otherwise.

Example   This *on mouseDown* handler will cause a sprite to follow the mouse cursor as long as the mouse button is being pressed:

```
on mouseDown
 repeat while the mouseDown
  set the loc of sprite 10 = point(the mouseH, the mouseV)
  updateStage
 end repeat
end mouseDown
```

Value   *boolean*

See also   the mouseH, the mouseV, on mouseDown, the mouseUp, on mouseUp, the mouseDownScript, the mouseUpScript, rollOver(), the stillDown

the mouseDownScript

MOVIE PROPERTY

Syntax   `set the mouseDownScript = "doAClick"`

Usage   *the mouseDownScript* is a property that contains the Lingo that will be executed when the mouse button is pressed. This command can be a Lingo statement or a handler name. By default, *the mouseDownScript* contains an empty string. To clear *the mouseDownScript*, set it to EMPTY.

the mouseDownScript is the first object to receive a *mouseDown* message when the mouse button is pressed. It is then passed to the objects listed in the Usage section of the entry for the *mouseDown* handler.

Example   This statement causes all *mouseDown* messages to be sent to the handler "doMouse":

```
set the mouseDownScript = "doMouse"
```

Value   *string*

See also   dontPassEvent, the keyDownScript, the keyUpScript, the mouseDown, the mouseH, the mouseUp, the mouseV, on mouseDown, on mouseUp

the mouseH

MOVIE PROPERTY

Syntax   `set hPosition = the mouseH`

Usage   *the mouseH* is a property that returns the horizontal position of the cursor. You can test but not set *the mouseH* property. The value is relative to the upper left corner of the movie and will return values even when the cursor is no longer over the stage.

Example   This *on mouseDown* handler will make a sprite to follow the mouse cursor as long as the mouse button is being pressed:

```
on mouseDown
  repeat while the mouseDown
    set the loc of sprite 10 = point(the mouseH, the mouseV)
    updateStage
  end repeat
end mouseDown
```

Value   *integer*

See also   the mouseDown, the mouseUp, on mouseDown, on mouseUp, rollOver

the mouseItem

MOVIE PROPERTY

Syntax `set whichItem = the mouseItem`

Usage *the mouseItem* is a property that contains the index number of the item the cursor is currently over, if the cursor is over an item in a field cast member. If the cursor is not over an item in a field cast member, this property value is –1. The items in the field are set apart by the character contained in the movie property *the itemDelimiter*.

Example See the Example for *the mouseChar*.

Value *integer*

See also char, chars, contains, field, item, the itemDelimiter, the last, length, line, member, the mouseChar, the mouseLine, the mouseMember, the mouseWord, the number of chars, the number of items, the number of lines, the number of words, offset, starts, stringP, string, value, word

the mouseLine

MOVIE PROPERTY

Syntax `set whichLine = the mouseLine`

Usage *the mouseLine* is a property that contains the number of the line of text the cursor is currently over, if the cursor is over a line in a field cast member. If the cursor is not over a line in a field cast member, this property value is –1. The number of lines is affected by the size of the text in the field and the font used.

Example See the Example for *the mouseChar*.

Value *integer*

See also char, chars, contains, field, item, the itemDelimiter, the last, length, line, member, the mouseChar, the mouseItem, the mouseMember, the mouseWord, the number of chars, the number of items, the number of lines, the number of words, offset, starts, stringP, string, value, word

the mouseMember

MOVIE PROPERTY

Syntax
```
set whichMember = the mouseMember
```

Usage
the mouseMember is a property that contains a reference to the topmost cast member the cursor is currently over. When the mouse cursor is not over a cast member, the property's value is <Void>. The reference is in the format *(member 1 of castLib 1)*.

Example
This function uses *the mouseCast* function, as an alternative to constantly checking the *rollOver* function, to execute a command if the user points to a cast member named "target":
```
if the name of member ¬
    max(1,(the mouseCast)) = "target" then
  doTargetFunction(rollover())
end if
```

Value
member

See also
the memberNum of sprite, the mouseChar, the mouseItem, the mouseLine, the mouseWord, the number of member, the name of member, rollOver

the mouseUp

MOVIE PROPERTY

Syntax
```
set isItUp = the mouseUp
```

Usage
The property *the mouseUp* returns TRUE if the mouse button is not pressed, or FALSE otherwise.

Example
This handler will set a puppeted sprite back to its original cast member (stored in the global variable gNormal) when the mouse is released:

```
on exitFrame
  global gButton, gNormal
  if the mouseUp then
    set the memberNum of sprite gButton = gNormal
  else
    set the memberNum of sprite gButton = gNormal + 1
  end if
end
```

Value   *boolean*

See also the mouseH, the mouseV, the mouseDown, on mouseDown, on mouseUp, the mouseDownScript, on mouseUpOutSide, the mouseUpScript, rollOver, the stillDown

the mouseUpScript

MOVIE PROPERTY

Syntax   set the mouseUpScript = "go 50"

Usage   *the mouseUpScript* is a property that contains the Lingo statement that will be executed when the mouse button is released. This value can be a single statement or a handler name. By default, *the mouseUpScript* contains an empty string. To reset *the mouseUpScript,* set it to EMPTY.

the mouseUpScript is the first object to receive a *mouseUp* message when the mouse button is released. It is then passed to the objects listed in the usage of *the mouseUp* handler.

Example This segment from a movie script causes all *mouseUp* messages to be sent to *findButton*. The *findButton handler* matches the current position of the cursor with the sprite that was originally clicked (the sprite needs to have a dummy script attached to it; see the *clickOn* property description), then determines an action based on that information:

```
on startMovie
  set the mouseUpScript = "findButton"
end
on findButton
  set whereClicked = the clickOn  --clicked active sprite
  set whereUp = the rollover  --current mouse location
```

```
          if whereUp = whereClicked then
            case whereUp of
              13: exitProgram
              14: showHelp
              15: showCredits
            end case
          end if
        end
```

Value   *string*

See also   dontPassEvent, the keyDownScript, the mouseDown, the mouseDownScript, the mouseH, the mouseUp, the mouseV, on mouseDown, on mouseUp

the mouseV

MOVIE PROPERTY

Syntax   `set vPosition = the mouseV`

Usage   *the mouseV* is a property that returns the vertical position of the cursor. You can test but not set *the mouseV* property. The value is relative to the upper left corner of the movie; it will return values even when the cursor is no longer over the stage.

Example   See the Example for *the mouseH* property.

Value   *integer*

See also   the mouseDown, the mouseUp, on mouseDown, on mouseUp, rollOver

the mouseWord

MOVIE PROPERTY

Syntax   `set whichWord = the mouseWord`

Usage   *the mouseWord* is a property that contains the index number of the word the cursor is currently over, if the cursor is over a word in a field cast member. If the cursor is not over a word in a field cast member, this property value is –1.

Example   See the Example for *the mouseChar.*

Value   *integer*

See also   char, chars, contains, field, item, the itemDelimiter, the last, length, line,
member, the mouseChar, the mouseItem, the mouseLine, the mouseMember,
the number of chars, the number of items, the number of lines, the number of
words, offset, starts, stringP, string, value, word

the rightMouseDown

MOVIE PROPERTY

Syntax   `set isItDown = the rightMouseDown`

Usage   The property *the rightMouseDown* returns TRUE if the right mouse button is
currently being pressed on a multibutton mouse, or FALSE otherwise. On
MacOS computers, if *the emulateMultiButtonMouse* property is set to TRUE,
pressing the mouse button and the control key simultaneously will generate
a *rightMouseDown* message.

Example   This movie script handler executes a command that displays a pop-up menu
specific to a cast member used as a sprite when the right mouse button is
pressed; it takes another action if the left mouse button was pressed:

```
on mouseDown
  if the rightMouseDown then showPopUp (the mouseMember)
  else doAction (the mouseMember)
end
```

Value   *boolean*

See also   the mouseH, the mouseV, on mouseDown, the mouseUp, on mouseUp, the
mouseDownScript, the mouseUpScript, on rightMouseDown, the
rightMouseUp, on rightMouseUp, rollover, the stillDown

the rightMouseUp

MOVIE PROPERTY

Syntax   `set isItUp = the rightMouseUp`

Usage   The property *the rightMouseUp* is TRUE if the mouse button is not pressed, or
FALSE if the mouse button is currently down.
          On MacOS computers, if *the emulateMultiButtonMouse* property is set to
TRUE, releasing the mouse button while the control key is held down will
generate a *rightMouseUp* message.

Example   This handler will hide a sprite when the right mouse is not being held down:

```
on exitFrame
  if the rightMouseUp then
    set the visible of sprite popUpMenu = FALSE
  end if
end
```

Value   *boolean*

See also the mouseH, the mouseV, the mouseDown, on mouseDown, on mouseUp,
the mouseDownScript, on mouseUpOutSide, the mouseUpScript, the
rightMouseDown, on rightMouseDown, on rightMouseUp, rollOver, the
stillDown

rollOver

FUNCTION

Syntax   `set isItOver = rollover (6)`

Usage   The *rollOver* function, with a parameter indicating a sprite channel, returns a
boolean value revealing whether the cursor is currently over the sprite. Note
that this may result in slightly different results than *the rollOver* property,
when sprites are layered over one another. The *rollOver* function returns a
TRUE value even when the sprite it's evaluating is not the topmost sprite as
indicated by *the rollOver* property.

Example   These statements create a list of all the sprites that the cursor is currently over:

```
set rolloverList = []
repeat with i = 1 to 120
  if rollover (i) then add rolloverList, i
end repeat
```

Parameter   rollover (*integer*)

Value   *boolean*

See also   the rollOver

the rollOver

MOVIE PROPERTY

Syntax   `set whatover = the rollover`

Usage   *the rollOver* is a property that contains a value for the topmost sprite that the cursor is over. Note that this may result in slightly different results than the *rollOver* function, when sprites are layered over one another.

Example   See the Example for *the mouseUp* property.

Value   *integer*

See also   rollOver

the *stillDown*

Syntax   `set isItDown = the stillDown`

Usage   *the stillDown* is a property that returns a boolean value based on a mouse button being pressed down. It cannot be tested within repeat loops and has largely been superseded by *the mouseDown* property, which can be tested in repeat loops.

Example   This frame script loops in the current frame as long as a mouse button is pressed:

```
on exitFrame
  if the stillDown then go the frame
end
```

Value   *boolean*

See also   the mouseDown

Computer & Monitor Control Category

9

These Lingo keywords provide and affect information about the computer a movie is playing on. This category of Lingo keywords is useful in determining specifics about how the movie will be played back, for deciding which movies and media will be used, and so on.

beep

Syntax   beep

Usage   The *beep* command makes the speaker beep the number of times specified by its parameter, or once if no parameter value is used.

Example   This statement will cause the system to beep when a network operation is complete:

```
if netDone() then beep
```

Parameters   beep *none/integer*

See also   the beepOn

the beepOn

Syntax   set the beepOn = TRUE

Usage   If *the beepOn* property is TRUE, then a beep is generated when the user clicks the mouse on a sprite with no script attached to it (i.e., the clickOn = 0).

Value   *boolean*

See also   beep

the colorDepth

MOVIE PROPERTY

Syntax `set howDeep = the colorDepth`

Usage The system property *the colorDepth* stores the number of bits used for each pixel of the computer's monitor (or the highest-value setting for a monitor the stage appears on, if there is more than one). This property can be tested in all movies. MacOS monitors can have their color depth setting changed by setting *the colorDepth* to a new value. Most Windows machines must restart the operating system to change color depth for the monitor and hence this property cannot be set under Windows. You can test but not set this property in a Shockwave movie.

The value of *the colorDepth* corresponds to the number of bits used to store each pixel's color information in memory. Typically, the less memory that's needed to store image data, the faster the execution of the program. Director 6 allows you to sidestep the issue of restarting the computer to reset the monitor color depth by using *the fullColorPermit* property to limit the size of the offscreen drawing buffer.

This chart shows the number of colors available for each valid value of *the colorDepth* and the equivalent setting in the Monitor Control Panel for MacOS and Windows computers.

1	Black-and-white
2	4 colors
4	16 colors
8	256 colors
16	32,768 colors (Thousands I High Color)
24	16,777,216 colors (True Color on Windows)
32	16,777,216 colors (Millions on the MacOS)

Due to a discrepancy in the way the two operating systems address the issue of monitor color depth, the MacOS and Windows versions of Director use different values to refer to the same setting.

In the world outside of Director, 24-bit color is known interchangeably as 32-bit color (the additional 8 bits are typically used for an alpha channel mask in other applications).

Setting *the colorDepth* to an invalid value or if the setting cannot be changed will not affect the value.

Examples   This handler checks *the colorDepth* and chooses an appropriate graphic to display:

```
on pickGraphic
  case the colorDepth of
    4:return(the number of member "4-bit")
    8:return(the number of member "8-bit")
    16:return(the number of member "16-bit")
    24, 32:return(the number of member "24-bit")
  end case
end pickGraphic
```

Then, this statement can be used to set the graphic of a puppeted sprite to the one that will look the best at each possible *colorDepth*:

```
set the memberNum of sprite 1 = pickGraphic()
```

This handler checks the color depth of the monitor, sets it to 8 bits if possible, and displays an alert if not. It takes advantage of the fact that the property won't be modified if the monitor's depth can't be changed:

```
on setEightBits
  set the colorDepth = 8  --changes setting if possible
  if the colorDepth <> 8 then  --tests if setting's changed
    alert "This movie must be viewed in 256-colors"
    quit
  end if
end
```

Value   1|2|4|8|16|24|32

See also   the fullColorPermit, switchColorDepth

the colorQD

MOVIE PROPERTY

This property, used to test the playback computer for the ability to display color, is now obsolete.

the cpuHogTicks

MOVIE PROPERTY

Syntax   `set the cpuHogTicks = 5`

Usage   *the cpuHogTicks* property is a MacOS-specific movie property that determines how often the movie allows other processes running on the computer to gain access to the CPU. Setting the value to a higher number dedicates more CPU time to the Director movie. The value of *the cpuHogTicks* corresponds to the number of ticks (1/60 of a second) between each interrupt of the movie. The default value is 20.

> ### Tip
>
> *Because network operations, mouse movement, and keyboard response are actually background processes, high values for this property can cause problems when your movie is dependent on those services.*

Value   *integer*

the desktopRectList

MOVIE PROPERTY

Syntax   `set firstMonitor = getAt (the desktopRectList, 1)`

Usage   *the desktopRectList* property is a linear list of rect values containing the coordinates of each of the monitors attached to the computer viewing the movie. A single-monitor machine might have a *desktopRectList* property with the value [rect(0, 0, 1024, 768)]. Each additional monitor's coordinates are relative to the first monitor in the list. A secondary 640- x 480-pixel monitor set to the left of the monitor in the above example, and aligned at the top, would modify *the desktopRectList* property to read [rect(0, 0, 1024, 768), rect(-640, 0, 0, 480)].

Example
These statements create a rect variable that encompasses all of the monitors attached to the computer:

```
set monitors = the desktopRectList
set howMany = count (monitors)
set allMonitors = rect(0, 0, 0, 0)
repeat with i = 1 to howMany
  set allMonitors = union (allMonitors, ¬
    getAt (monitors, i))
end repeat
```

Value
linear list of rects

See also
the drawRect of window, the rect of window, the stageBottom, the stageLeft, the stageRight, the stageTop

the floatPrecision

MOVIE PROPERTY

Syntax
`set the floatPrecision = 3`

Usage
the floatPrecision is a property that determines how many decimal places are displayed when a floating point (decimal) value is displayed. The property doesn't affect float values or computation, only their display.

> **Tip**
>
> *The number of significant digits of any float value in Director is limited to 15, and although you can set the property to large values, calculations beyond that point are unreliable.*

Float values are truncated, not rounded, by *the floatPrecision* property.

Example
This Message window session shows how *the floatPrecision* value affects display of a float value.

```
set the floatPrecision = 2
set aFloat = 1.315
put aFloat
-- 1.31
```

```
set the floatPrecision = 3
put aFloat
-- 1.315
```

Value   *integer*

See also   float, floatP

the fullColorPermit

Syntax   `set the fullColorPermit = TRUE`

Usage   *the fullColorPermit* is a new Director 6 property that enables faster playback of 8-bit (256-color) movies on machines with monitors set to 16-bit or 24-bit color. Windows machines have typically had to restart the operating system to change color depth and gain playback speed. This property controls the off-screen drawing buffer where each frame of a Director movie is prepared before being displayed.

If *the fullColorPermit* is TRUE, each pixel of the drawing buffer is drawn with the same number of bytes as the monitor. If *the fullColorPermit* is FALSE, each pixel of the drawing buffer is drawn as 8-bit color, regardless of the monitor setting. In either case, once an *updateStage* message is generated by either the movement of the playback head or a command, the buffer is displayed onscreen at the color depth of the monitor.

Example   This handler attempts to set the color depth of the screen to 8 bits for optimum performance, then uses an 8-bit offscreen drawing buffer as the next best option.

```
on setEightBits
  set the colorDepth = 8  --changes setting if possible
  if the colorDepth <> 8 then  --tests it setting's changed
    set the fullColorPermit = FALSE
  end if
end
```

Value   *boolean*

See also   the colorDepth

the machineType

Syntax   `set whatmachine = the machineType`

Usage   *the machineType* is a property that returns a value originally identifying which MacOS system the movie is running on. All Windows machines return the value 256. As some MacOS machines return values higher than 256, it's not safe to assume that testing for a value less than 256 will identify MacOS machines.

> ### Tip
>
> *Macromedia does not recommend using* the machineType *to make assumptions about system capabilities on MacOS machines.*

Example   This movie script tests for a Windows machine on startup. If it detects a non-Windows machine, it begins multibutton emulation.

```
on startmovie
  if the machineType = 256 then
    set the emulateMultiButtonMouse = FALSE
  else
    set the emulateMultiButtonMouse = TRUE
  end if
end
```

Value   *boolean*

See also   the emulateMultiButtonMouse, the platform

the maxInteger

Syntax
```
if aNumber > the maxinteger then ¬
    set aNumber = the maxinteger
```

Usage   *the maxInteger* is a property that contains the largest integer value that can be used by the current system. This is typically just over 2 billion (and 10 significant digits). Larger numbers, and numbers with up to 15 significant digits, can be represented with floating-point numbers.

Example   This command puts *the maxInteger* into the Message window:

```
put the maxinteger
-- 2147483647
```

Value   *boolean*

See also   float, integer

mci

Syntax   mci "pause cdaudio"

Usage   The *mci* command provides a way to communicate directly with Windows system multimedia extensions, by sending Media Control Interface (MCI) commands. The parameter must be a valid MCI command string.

   MCI commands can be used to control a number of different media devices, including Midi and Wave sound file players, audio CD players, video disc players, and so on.

> ### Tip
>
> *For a good reference on the use of the* mci *Lingo command, see Geoff Choo's reference to MCI on his Web site:* http://sunflower.singnet.com.sg/~henryzhu.

You can derive the results from MCI commands that operate as functions to return data about files and performance by testing the movie property *the result*. Values returned from MCI commands are returned as strings.

Example These commands check for the capability to play CD audio, test to see if a CD is present, assign an alias to the CD, and test the number of tracks on the CD.

```
mci "capability cdaudio can play"
if the result = "true" then
  mci "status cdaudio media present"
  if the result = "true" then
    mci "open cdaudio alias pyvl"
    mci "status pyvl number of tracks"
    set numTracks = value (the result)
  end if
end if
```

Parameters mci *string*

Value *string*

the multiSound

MOVIE PROPERTY

Syntax `set twoSounds = the multiSound`

Usage *the multiSound* is a property that contains TRUE if the current computer can play more than one sound channel at a time.

Example This code segment allows a mouse-click sound to play in sound channel 2, in addition to the loop that is currently playing in sound channel 1, only if *the multiSound* property is TRUE:

`if the multiSound then puppetSound "mouse click", 2`

Value *boolean*

See also puppetSound, soundBusy, the soundEnabled, the soundLevel, sound close, sound fadeIn, sound fadeOut, sound playFile, sound stop, the volume of sound

pasteClipBoardInto

Syntax   `pasteClipBoardInto member 20 of castLib 3`

Usage   The *pasteClipBoardInto* command copies the contents of the clipboard to the designated cast member. The command creates a new cast member if none already exists, or replaces the content and type of an existing cast member. This command is not available in Shockwave movies.

Parameters   `pasteClipBoardInto` *member*

See also   copyToClipBoard

the platform

Syntax   `set whichPlatform = the platform`

Usage   *the platform* is a property that contains a string that gives you information about the platform the movie is playing on. More precisely, *the platform* tells you which platform the projector, authoring environment, or browser was created for, regardless of the computer's actual operating system. You can test but not set this property with Lingo.

For example, if you create a projector for 68K Macintosh only, *the platform* property will contain "Macintosh, 68K", even if the projector is currently running on a Power Macintosh.

Another example: If you create a .dcr movie and play it back in a 16-bit version of Netscape while running on Windows 95, *the platform* will contain "Windows, 16", even though you are running in a 32-bit Windows environment.

Value   The possible values of *the platform* property are:

Value	Platform
"Macintosh,68k"	Original 68K Macintosh
"Macintosh,PowerPC"	PPC Macintosh
"Windows,16"	Windows 3.1 or earlier
"Windows,32"	Windows 95 or WinNT

Example   This code segment provides a way to do different things depending on the value of *the platform* property:

```
case the platform of
  "Windows,16":
    -- do something for Windows 3.1
  "Windows,32":
    -- do something for Windows 95 or NT
  "Macintosh,68K":
    -- do something for Macintosh 68K
  "Macintosh,PowerPC":
    -- do something for Power Macintosh
end case
```

Value   "Macintosh,68k"|"Macintosh,PowerPC"|"Windows,16"|"Windows,32"

See also   the machineType, the movie, the multiSound, version

printFrom

COMMAND

Syntax   printFrom "Menu", 50, 25

Usage   The *printFrom* command prints the sprites on the stage beginning with the frame in the score represented by the first parameter value to the frame represented by the second parameter, at the percentage of full size represented by the third parameter.

The parameters for the frame values may be either integer values (or functions, like *label*, that return integers) or frame labels. The *size* parameter can be 25, 50, or 100 percent.

Value   printFrom *integer/string*, *integer/string*, 100|50|25

quit

Syntax   `quit`

Usage   The *quit* command shuts down the movie's projector or exits Director if in authoring mode. It has no effect in Shockwave movies.

Example   This handler quits the projector when the user presses Command/Ctrl-Q:

```
on keyDown
  if the key = "q" and the commandDown then quit
end
```

See also   restart, shutDown

restart

Syntax   `restart`

Usage   The *restart* command quits all programs and restarts a MacOS computer. It has no effect on Windows machines or in Shockwave movies on either platform.

See also   quit, shutDown

the romanLingo

Syntax   `set the romanLingo = TRUE`

Usage   *the romanLingo* is a property that is TRUE when Lingo is set to use a single-byte code interpreter. This is the faster method, and is typically used in most systems. However, in operating systems such as Japanese versions, which use double-byte character sets, Lingo may need to use a double-byte interpreter.

If you use any double-byte characters in your Lingo, you'll need to set this property to FALSE. Otherwise, you should set it to TRUE to cause your Lingo to execute faster on any platform and operating system.

Example   This handler is passed a parameter that sets *the romanLingo* property and branches to the appropriate movie after setting the property:

```
on selectMovie whichLanguage
  case whichLanguage of
    #english:
      set the romanLingo = TRUE
      play movie "English"
    #nihongo:
      set the romanLingo = FALSE
      play movie "Japanese"
  end case
end
```

Value   *boolean*

the runMode

MOVIE PROPERTY

Syntax   `set whatMode = the runMode`

Usage   *the runMode* is a property that contains a string value with information about the environment the movie is playing in.

    the runMode has three possible values: "Author" (if the movie is being played in Director), "Projector" (if the movie is played as or from a projector), and "Plugin" (if the movie is played with the Shockwave plug-in inside a browser.

    Uses for *the runMode* abound, from restricting browser scripting functions so they only execute in Shockwave movies, to making sure that some scripts only execute in the authoring mode.

Example   This handler executes a *replaceWithFiles* handler only if the *replace* handler is called from within the Director authoring environment:

```
on replace
  if the runMode = "Author" then replaceWithFiles
end
```

See also   the version

shutDown

COMMAND

Syntax   `shutDown`

Usage   The *shutDown* command quits all programs and turns off a MacOS computer. It has no effect on Windows machines or in Shockwave movies on either platform.

See also   quit, restart

version

SYSTEM VARIABLE

Syntax   `set isItShockwave = version contains "net"`

Usage   The *version* variable contains a string that is the version of Director or Shockwave that the movie is currently playing in. It is very useful when you need to determine whether your movie is playing in Shockwave, so you know whether Net-Lingo commands are available.

You can test but not set this variable with Lingo. The form the string takes is "6.0 net".

If the movie is currently playing in a Shockwave plug-in, the *version* variable will always contain the word *net*, regardless of the version.

Example   This code segment uses the *version* variable to determine whether to use a Net Lingo command:

```
if version contains "net" then
  -- we're playing in Shockwave
  getNetText("file.htm")
else
  -- not Shockwave, use FileIO
  set tFileReader = new(xtra "fileio")
  openFile(tFileReader, "file.txt",0)
  -- etcetera
end if
```

Value   *string*

See also   the machineType, the platform, the runMode

Memory Management Category

These Lingo keywords control the way data for the movie is loaded into RAM for playback, and they allow you to test available RAM.

frameReady

Usage See the *frameReady* listing in Chapter 2.

the freeBlock

Syntax `set howMuchFree = the freeBlock`

Usage *the freeBlock* is a property that contains the size (in bytes) of the largest contiguous chunk of RAM available to the movie. Since cast members are loaded into contiguous blocks, it is important to know how much RAM is available, particularly when working with large images or audio files.

Example You can use *the freeBlock* function to determine which of a pair of available Shockwave movies to load, under different memory conditions:

```
if the freeBlock < 3 * 1024 then
  -- load the smaller movie
  gotoNetMovie "small.dcr"
else
  -- load the bigger movie
  gotoNetMovie "big.dcr"
end if
```

Value *integer*

See also the freeBytes, the memorySize, the movieFileSize, preLoadMovie, preLoadNetThing, ramNeeded, unLoadMovie

the freeBytes

MOVIE PROPERTY

MOVIE PROPERTY

Syntax   `set totalFreeK = the freeBytes / 1024`

Usage   *the freeBytes* is a property that contains the size (in bytes) of the total amount of free RAM. This may or may not be contiguous free space.

    You may be able to make some basic assumptions about the computer's ability to play your movie based on a combination of the properties *the freeBytes* and *the colorDepth*, and your knowledge about the size of your cast members.

Example   This statement sends the number of free bytes to the message window, in megabytes:

```
put the freeBytes/(1024*1024) && "MB"
-- 20 MB
```

Value   *integer*

See also   the freeBlock, the memorySize, the movieFileSize, preLoadMovie, preLoadNetThing, ramNeeded, unLoadMovie

the loaded of member

MEMBER PROPERTY

Syntax   `set isItLoaded = the loaded of member 45`

Usage   *the loaded of member* property is TRUE if the cast member specified by the parameter is currently loaded into RAM. It returns FALSE otherwise. You can test but not set this property with Lingo.

    This property only indicates if the member has been loaded into memory from disk. If cast members have been downloaded using network commands or if they are part of a large cast, they are not necessarily available in RAM and may cause hesitation if a portion of the movie containing the cast member is played back.

To test whether a cast member is available on the hard disk (as opposed to being in RAM), test *the mediaReady of member* property.

You can't use this property to test the results of the Shockwave command *preLoadNetThing*. If you want to see if a net-based file has finished loading, use the *netDone* function.

Example This code segment waits for the cast member *bigOne* to load into memory before going to the next frame:

```
if not(the loaded of member "bigOne") then
  go to the frame
else
  go to the frame + 1
end if
```

Parameters the loaded of *member*

Value *boolean*

See also the mediaReady of member, netDone, preLoad, preLoadMember, preLoadNetThing

the mediaReady of member   MEMBER PROPERTY

Syntax set isItLocal = the mediaReady of member "background"

Usage *the mediaReady of member* property is TRUE if the data for the specified cast member is resident on the local hard drive. This is useful for movies being streamed from networks, to determine if portions of the casts have been completely downloaded.

This command does for individual cast members what the *frameReady* function does for all of the media used in individual frames or a range of frames. If your streaming movies are largely Lingo-driven (meaning the cast members used may not be used anywhere in the score), *the mediaReady of member* property allows you to check on the status of streaming cast members.

Example   This behavior handler replaces the placeholder cast member being used in a streaming movie with the cast member identified by *realmember*, once *realmember* has fully downloaded.

```
property realmember, spritenum
on prepareframe me
  if the mediaReady of member the realmember of me then
    set the member of sprite the spritenum of me = ¬
      member the realmember of me
  end if
end
```

Parameters   the mediaReady of *member*

Value   *boolean*

See also   downloadNetThing, frameReady, the loaded of member, netDone, preLoad, preLoadMember, preLoadNetThing

the memorySize

Syntax   `set totalMemory = the memorySize`

Usage   *the memorySize* is a property that contains the total amount of memory available to the movie—whether used or free—in bytes.

Example   This function handler returns the total amount of memory used by the movie:

```
on memoryUsed
  return (the memorySize - the freeBytes)
end
```

Value   *integer*

See also   the freeBlock, the freeBytes, the movieFileSize, preLoadMovie, preLoadNetThing, ramNeeded, unLoadMovie

the movieFileFreeSize

MOVIE PROPERTY

Syntax   `set wastedBytes = the movieFileFreeSize`

Usage   *the movieFileFreeSize* is a property that returns the number of wasted bytes in the current movie file. The normal movie development process—deletion and editing of cast members, changes to the score, etc.—will create portions of a file that are unused. You can use the Save And Compact command from the File menu in Director if *the movieFileFreeSize* returns something greater than 0 in the authoring environment.

  Wasted space in the file will affect storage requirements and may impact media loading time during playback.

Example   See the Example for *the movieFileSize*.

Value   *integer*

See also   the freeBlock, the freeBytes, the movieFileSize

the movieFileSize

MOVIE PROPERTY

Syntax   `set movieSize = the movieFileSize`

Usage   *the movieFileSize* is a property that contains the size of the current movie file, in bytes.

Example   This example of a handler used during authoring alerts the Director author that 5 percent or more of the movie file is wasted space, and that a Save And Compact operation should be performed.

```
on checkWaste
  if (the movieFileFreeSize * 100 / ¬
    the movieFileSize) >= 5 then ¬
      alert "Too much wasted space! Save and Compact!"
  end if
end
```

Value   *integer*

See also   the freeBlock, the freeBytes, the movieFileFreeSize

preLoad

Syntax   preLoad

preLoad marker (2)

preLoad 30, label "end"

Usage   The *preLoad* command loads cast members in a range of frames into RAM.

If you don't specify any parameters, *preLoad* will attempt to load all of the cast members from the current frame through the end of the score. If you include one parameter, *preLoad* will attempt to load all of the cast members from the current frame to the frame specified. If you include two parameters, *preLoad* attempts to load all of the cast members in that range of frames.

Cast members must appear in the score as sprites, sounds, transitions, etc., in order to be loaded by the *preLoad* command. Cast members that will appear on the stage only through the use of Lingo must be loaded with *preLoadMember*. Which cast member frames are loaded depends on available RAM.

You can find the last frame actually loaded with the *preLoad* command by testing *the result* property immediately after the command is issued. This value will represent the last frame in which there are cast members assigned places in the score; if there is no cast member occupying the last frame specified by the parameters, the value of *the result* will not equal the parameter.

Example   These statements attempt to load the cast members in the frames between the marker labeled "start" and the marker labeled "end" then test to see which frame was the last to be loaded into memory.

```
preLoad "start", "end"
if label ("end") <> the result then
   alert "Not enough RAM to preLoad this section"
end if
```

Parameters   preLoad

preLoad *integer|string*

preLoad *integer|string*, *integer|string*

Value   *integer*

See also   label, marker, netDone, preLoadBuffer, [preLoadMember], preLoadEventAbort, preLoadNetThing, the preLoadTime of member, unLoad, unLoadMember

the preLoad of member

MEMBER PROPERTY

Syntax   `set the preLoad of member "avideo" = TRUE`

Usage   *the preLoad of member* property is TRUE if a digital video cast member is allowed to be preloaded into memory. The default value is FALSE. Loading entire digital video files into memory can delete other needed cast members from RAM.

You can test and set this property with Lingo.

A digital video can only be played from a Shockwave movie if it is located in the Shockwave plug-in support directory.

Example   This example checks a sequence of cast members for digital video sprites that can be preloaded, and loads those that can be:

```
on loadMembers aStart, anEnd
  repeat with i = aStart to anEnd
    if the type of member i = #digitalVideo then
      if the preLoad of member i then
        preLoad member i
      end if
    end if
  end repeat
end
```

Parameters   `the preLoad of` *member*

Value   *boolean*

See also   the controller of member, the digitalVideoType of member, the directToStage of member, the quickTimePresent, the videoForWindowsPresent

the preLoadEventAbort

MOVIE PROPERTY

Syntax   `set the preLoadEventAbort = TRUE`

Usage   *the preLoadEventAbort* is a property that controls whether preloading of cast members is canceled when the user clicks a mouse button or presses a key. The default value for this property is FALSE, which continues the preloading of members, regardless of user actions, until all specified cast members have been loaded or memory is full. Only then will the movie respond to user actions.

the preLoadEventAbort property should be set to TRUE if, for instance, the user can skip over a section of the movie using a number of cast members that are being preloaded for fast playback.

Value   *boolean*

See also   preLoad, preLoadMember, unLoad, unLoadMember

preLoadMember

COMMAND

Syntax   `preLoadMember "blue box", "yellow box"`

Usage   The *preLoadMember* command loads cast members in a range of cast positions into RAM.

If you don't specify any parameters, *preLoadMember* will attempt to load all of the cast members for the movie. If you include one parameter, *preLoadMember* will attempt to load the specified cast member. If you include two parameters, *preLoadMember* attempts to load all of the cast members between and including the specified cast member.

Cast members that will appear on the stage only through the use of Lingo must be loaded with *preLoadMember*. If cast members appear in the score, they may be loaded into RAM with the *preLoad* command.

Cast members in the specified range will be loaded into RAM until all cast members are loaded or all available RAM is full.

You can determine *the memberNum* property of the last cast member actually loaded with the *preLoadMember* command by testing *the result* property immediately after the command is issued.

Example　These statements attempt to load the cast members from position 4 to position 25, then test to see which cast member was the last to be loaded into memory.

```
preLoadMember 4, 25
if the result < 25 then
  alert "Not enough RAM to preLoad these cast members"
end if
```

Parameters　`preLoadMember integer|string`

Value　`integer`

See also　label, marker, netDone, preLoad, preLoadBuffer, preLoadEventAbort, preLoadNetThing, the preLoadTime of member, unLoad, unLoadMember

the preLoadMode of CastLib

CAST PROPERTY

Syntax　`set the preLoadMode of castLib "Internal"`

Usage　*the preLoadMode of castLib* is a property that controls default preloading for all of the members of the specified cast. The possible values are:

　　0　When Needed
　　1　Before Frame One
　　2　After Frame One.

This property performs the same functions as the "Preload" selector in the Cast Properties dialog box.

　　In general, it is better to set this property to 0 and control the preloading of members with Lingo. This gives you more precise control over memory management. The other options give the user a longer wait after loading your movie, which makes your movie seem slower.

Parameters　`the preLoadMode of castLib integer|string`

Value　`0|1|2`

See also　preLoad, the preLoad of member, preLoadMember

preLoadMovie

COMMAND

Syntax   preLoadMovie ¬
       "http://www.moshplant.com/direct-or/bezier/bezier.dir"

Usage   The *preLoadMovie* command loads cast members from the first frame of a movie's score into memory, or as much as it can load until memory is full. You can use this command to load part of another movie before playing it with the *play* or *go to movie* commands, making the transition between the movies more seamless.

> ### Tip
>
> *This command does not work within the Shockwave plug-in, but it is network-aware and can be used with a URL as a parameter.*

Parameters   preLoadMovie *string*

See also   go to, gotoNetMovie, play

the preLoadRAM

MOVIE PROPERTY

Syntax   set the preLoadRAM = 102400

Usage   *the preLoadRAM* is a property that controls the amount of RAM (in kilobytes) available to preload digital video cast members. The default value is 0, which lets digital video cast members use all available RAM for preloading. You can test and set this property with Lingo.

       Since digital video cast members can be quite large, it may be necessary to limit the amount of memory available to them, in order to prevent them from pushing other cast members out of memory when they're loaded.

Example This command sets the RAM available to preload digital video cast members to 50 kilobytes:

```
set the preLoadRAM = 50 * 1024
```

Value *integer*

See also preLoad, preLoadMember, preLoadEventAbort, preLoadNetThing, the preLoadTime of member, unLoad, unLoadMember

the purgePriority of member
MEMBER PROPERTY

Syntax set the purgePriority of member "background" = 0

Usage *the purgePriority of member* is a property that gives you control over the automatic purging of cast members from RAM. The possible values are:

0 Never purge
1 Purge last
2 Purge next
3 Purge normal.

The default value is 3. You can test and set this property with Lingo.

This property can be useful when cast members used throughout your movie would need to be continually reloaded from disk if they were purged from RAM. It also enables you to schedule cast members that are used only once for instant disposal after they have been used.

Tip

If you use this property, it's advisable to take some precautions to prevent memory from becoming full of priority 0 (Never Purge) cast members. You can always use the purge *command to manually purge any cast member from memory.*

Cast members with a purge priority of 2 will always be the first to be purged from memory when RAM is needed for new cast members. Priority 3 cast members will be purged if there are no priority 2 members in RAM. Priority 1 cast members will be purged if there are no priority 2 or 3 cast members.

Parameters the purgePriority of member *integer|string*

Value 0|1|2|3

See also preLoad, preLoadMember, unLoad, unLoadMember

ramNeeded

FUNCTION

Syntax `set howMuchRAM = ramNeeded ("LOOP", 50)`

Usage The *ramNeeded* function allows you to determine how much RAM is required to load cast members from a range of frames in the score. Specifying two frame numbers or labels as parameters for the function returns the number of bytes needed to store the cast members for all of the frames specified.

Example This example checks the amount of RAM available, compares it to the amount of RAM needed for frames 200 to 300 of the movie, and calls a purge routine if necessary before loading the cast members in the score from frame 200 to 300:

```
set availableRAM = the freeBytes
set sectionNeeds = ramNeeded (200, 300)
if availableRAM < sectionNeeds then purgeStuff
-- purgeStuff is a custom purge routine
preLoad 200, 300
```

Value *integer*

See also the freeBlock, the freeBytes, preLoad, preLoadMember, the size of member, unLoad, unLoadMember

unLoad

Syntax
```
unLoad
```
```
unLoad 30
```
```
unLoad "start", "sequence 1"
```

Usage
The *unLoad* command removes the cast members that are in the specified frame or range of frames from memory.

If you don't specify any frame numbers, *unLoad* will remove all cast members in all frames from memory, except for the cast members used in the current frame. If you use a single parameter, *unLoad* will remove the cast members used in that frame from memory. If you use a range of frames as the parameters, *unLoad* will remove all of the cast members used in those frames from memory.

Example
This handler unloads all of the cast members from the beginning of the movie to the frame previous to the current frame if the amount of available RAM falls below 50K:

```
on exitFrame
  if the freeBytes < 50K then
    unLoad 1, the frame - 1
  end if
end
```

Parameters
```
unLoad
```
```
unLoad integer|string
```
```
unLoad integer|string, integer|string
```

See also
label, marker, netDone, preLoad, preLoadBuffer, preLoadMember, preLoadEventAbort, preLoadNetThing, the preLoadTime of member, unLoadMember

unLoadMember

Syntax   unLoadMember 25

Usage   The *unLoadMember* command removes the specified cast members from memory.

    If you don't specify any frame numbers, *unLoadMember* will remove all cast members from memory, except for the cast members currently in use as sprites. If you include a single parameter, *unLoadMember* will remove that cast member from memory. If you include a range of cast members, *unLoadMember* will remove all of those cast members from memory.

Example   This command removes five cast members from RAM:

    unLoadMember 20, 24

Parameters   unLoadMember

    unLoadMember *integer|string*

    unLoadMember *integer|string*, *integer|string*

See also   label, marker, netDone, preLoad, preLoadMember, preLoadBuffer, preLoadEventAbort, preLoadNetThing, the preLoadTime of member, unLoad

unLoadMovie

Syntax   unLoadMovie "http://www.aserver.com/amovie.dcr"

Usage   The *unLoadMovie* command removes a movie from RAM, unless it is the currently playing movie.

    Movies can be loaded as the result of MIAW operations, *go to movie* commands, *preLoadMovie* commands, and so on, and may remain in memory until RAM is needed for other movies or cast members.

    Movies preloaded from URLs are not erased from the network cache by the *unLoadMovie* command; they are merely removed from RAM.

    The *unLoadMovie* command does not work in Shockwave.

Parameters   unLoadMovie *string*

See also   preLoadMovie

Memory Management (Idle Loading) Category

11

These Lingo keywords control how Director movies load cast members into RAM during idle CPU cycles. Idle loading is an option that became available in Director 5, and allows a movie to continue playing while cast member data is loaded from disks or networks. Idle loading operates in conjunction with the standard memory management Lingo in Chapter 10.

cancelIdleLoad

Syntax   `cancelIdleLoad 2`

Usage   The *cancelIdleLoad* command stops the preloading of a group of cast members queued for preloading. It is only effective when idle loading is enabled (using *idleLoadMode*), and when there are cast members waiting to be loaded.

     The parameter for the command refers to an arbitrary value assigned to a batch of cast members with the *idleLoadTag* command.

Parameters   `cancelIdleLoad` *integer*

See also   finishIdleLoad, the idleHandlerPeriod, idleLoadDone, the idleLoadMode, the idleLoadPeriod, the idleLoadTag, the idleReadChunkSize

finishIdleLoad

Syntax   `finishIdleLoad 2`

Usage   The *finishIdleLoad* command forces the completion of preloading for a group of cast members queued for preloading. It is only effective when idle loading is enabled (using *idleLoadMode*), and when there are cast members waiting to be loaded.

     The parameter for the command refers to an arbitrary value assigned to a batch of cast members with the *idleLoadTag* command.

Parameters   `browserName` *integer*

See also   cancelIdleLoad, the idleHandlerPeriod, idleLoadDone, the idleLoadMode, the idleLoadPeriod, the idleLoadTag, the idleReadChunkSize

the idleHandlerPeriod

MOVIE PROPERTY

Syntax   `set the idleHandlerPeriod = 0`

Usage   The *idleHandlerPeriod* property controls the number of ticks between *idle* messages, which affects the frequency with which an *idle* handler will be executed. The default is 0, which causes the *idle* message to be sent as frequently as possible.

There are 60 ticks per second.

Example   This statement causes the idle message to be sent no more than three times per second (other movie actions may slow processing between *idle* messages):

`set the idleHandlerPeriod = 20`

Value   *integer*

See also   on idle

idleLoadDone

FUNCTION

Syntax   `set isItDone = idleLoadDone (2)`

Usage   The *idleLoadDone* function returns TRUE if Director has loaded all of the cast members that have been tagged with an *idleLoadTag* command.

Example   This handler waits until all of the tagged cast members have been loaded before going to the next frame:

```
on exitFrame
  global gTag
  if idleLoadDone(gTag) then
    go to the frame + 1
  else
    go to the frame
  end if
end exitFrame
```

Parameters   `idleLoadDone (`*integer*`)`

Value   *boolean*

See also   cancelIdleLoad, finishIdleLoad, the idleHandlerPeriod, the idleLoadMode, the idleLoadPeriod, the idleLoadTag, the idleReadChunkSize

the idleLoadMode

MOVIE PROPERTY

Syntax   `set the idleLoadMode = 3`

Usage   *the idleLoadMode* is a property that controls whether and how idle loading of cast members is handled by a movie. There are four possible values:

      0   No idle loading

      1   Idle loading happens between frames

      2   Idle loading happens during idle events

      3   Idle loading happens as frequently as possible

    Idle loading, if it is enabled (*the idleLoadMode <> 0*) lets the movie load cast members specified by *preLoad* commands while other events are happening. If idle loading is not enabled (*the idleLoadMode = 0*), the movie waits for all cast members specified by a *preLoad* command to be loaded before moving on to the next task.

Value   0|1|2|3

See also   cancelIdleLoad, finishIdleLoad, the idleHandlerPeriod, the idleLoadDone, the idleLoadPeriod, the idleLoadTag, the idleReadChunkSize

the idleLoadPeriod

MOVIE PROPERTY

Syntax   `set the idleLoadPeriod = 0`

Usage   *the idleLoadPeriod* is a property that contains the number of ticks Director waits between trying to load cast members in the preload queue, giving other idle events time to operate. The default value is 0, which allows idle loading to happen as frequently as possible. There are 60 ticks per second.

Example   This statement will cause a tenth of a second pause between idle loading of cast members:

`set the idleLoadPeriod = 6`

Value   *integer*

See also   cancelIdleLoad, finishIdleLoad, the idleHandlerPeriod, the idleLoadDone, the idleLoadMode, the idleLoadTag, the idleReadChunkSize

the idleLoadTag

MOVIE PROPERTY

Syntax   `set the idleLoadTag = 3`

Usage   *the idleLoadTag* is a property that creates an arbitrary reference to the cast members currently queued for idle loading. It's used by the *cancelIdleLoad* and *finishIdleLoad* commands, and the *IdleLoadDone* function to refer to the cast members currently in the queue.
　　　　The number you choose for the reference is arbitrary and has no effect on performance.

Example   This example loads a range of cast members into the preload queue and creates a reference to them using the *idleLoadTag* property:

```
 preLoadMember "background", "exit button"
set the idleLoadTag = 3
```

Value   *integer*

See also   cancelIdleLoad, finishIdleLoad, the idleHandlerPeriod, the idleLoadDone, the idleLoadPeriod, the idleReadChunkSize

the idleReadChunkSize

Syntax   `set the idleReadChunkSize = 100000`

Usage   *the idleReadChunkSize* is a property that determines the maximum number of bytes Director attempts to load during each idle loading session. The default is 32, 768 (32K) bytes.

Value   *integer*

See also   cancelIdleLoad, finishIdleLoad, the idleHandlerPeriod, the idleLoadDone, the idleLoadPeriod, the idleLoadTag, the idleReadChunkSize

Casts Category

12

These keywords, properties, and commands relate to the use and management of multiple cast libraries. Casts are where everything from text to Lingo scripts to graphics to references for external media files are stored.

the activeCastLib

Syntax   `set thisCast = the activeCastLib`

Usage   *the activeCastLib* is a property that contains an identifier for the last cast library that was brought to the front, that was opened, or in which a selection was made. It is usually employed in authoring mode as a part of the tools used to help automate the authoring process.

The property can be tested but not set.

Example   This authoring handler duplicates all cast members from cast library 1 to the same positions in the currently selected cast:

```
on dupeMembers
  repeat with i = 1 to the number of members of castlib 1
    duplicate member i of castlib 1, ¬
      member i of castlib the activeCastLib
  end repeat
end
```

Value   *integer*

See also   the fileName of castLib, the name of castLib, the number of castLib, the number of members of castLib

castLib

Syntax   `castLib "Internal"`

Usage   The *castLib* keyword is used in conjunction with the *member* keyword to refer to a specific cast in movies with multiple cast libraries (a feature added in Director 5). The parameter for *castLib* can be either an index number reference to the cast or the name of the cast.

If a cast member is referred to without a cast library being specified, and there is any ambiguity about which library the member belongs to, cast library 1 (the cast named "Internal" by default) is used.

Parameters   `castLib` *`integer|string`*

See also   the fileName of castLib, member, the name of castLib, the number of castLib, the number of members of castLib, the preLoadMode of castLib, save castLib, the selection of castLib

the fileName of castLib
CAST PROPERTY

Syntax   `set whichCast = the fileName of castLib 3`

Usage   *the fileName of castLib* is a property that contains the filename of a specified cast library. If the cast library is internal, it returns EMPTY. If the cast library is external, a string value with the filename is returned.

In a Shockwave movie, external casts must be located in the plug-in support directory. You can include an empty placeholder cast in a Shockwave movie, then link to any external cast with Lingo by setting this property, provided that the external cast is located in the Shockwave plug-in support directory.

You can test or set this property with Lingo (although modifying the property is only possible for external casts). Changing the property's value changes which file is used to provide cast members for the library.

> ### Tip
> *Linking to remote locations with a URL is possible, but downloading the file to a local drive with* downloadNetThing *before accessing the file with* the fileName of castLib *is recommended due to performance considerations.*

Example   This statement sets *the fileName of castLib* property to the file "extLink.cst." If used in a projector, the default location for the file would be the directory where the projector is located. If used in a Shockwave movie, the file would need to be located in the plug-in support directory:

`set the fileName of castLib "ext" = "extLink.cst"`

Parameters   `the fileName of castLib` *`integer|string`*

Value   *`string`*

See also   the applicationPath, the pathName

findEmpty

Syntax
```
set nextEmptyMember = ¬
    findEmpty (member "joe" of castLib "Internal")
```

Usage
The *findEmpty* function returns the number of the first empty cast member space that is on or after *castmemberNumber*.

Example
This statement sends the number of the first empty cast member space after number 100 to the message window:

```
put findEmpty (member 100)
-- 100
```

In this case, member 100 itself is empty.

Parameters
```
findEmpty (member integer|string)
```
```
findEmpty (member integer|string of castLib integer|string)
```

Value
integer

See also
new

the name of castLib

Syntax
```
set whatName = the name of castLib 1
```

Usage
the name of castLib is a property that contains the name of the cast library specified by the parameter. *the name of castLib* property merely changes one way to refer to the cast library, it does not change any data within the cast itself. You can test and set this property with Lingo.

Example
This example changes the name of the cast library named "Internal":

```
set the name of castLib "Internal" = "Main"
```

Parameters   the name of castLib *integer/string*

Value   *string*

See also   the castLibNum of sprite, the fileName of castLib, the memberNum of sprite, the name of castLib, the number of castLibs, the number of members, the number of members of castLib, the preLoadMode of castLib

the number of castLib

CAST PROPERTY

Syntax   `set whatCast = the number of castLib "backgrounds"`

Usage   *the number of castLib* is a property that contains a reference to the specified cast library. The integer value of the property for each of the cast libraries represents the order in which the library was created or linked to the current movie.

Example   This code segment sets a global variable to the numeric reference for a cast determined by the *gGallery* variable:

```
global gGallery, gCurrCast

on setMood
  case gGallery of
    #printmaking: set whichGall = "G1"
    #digitalart: set whichGall = "G2"
    #painting: set whichGall = "G3"
    #sculpture: set whichGall = "G4"
  end case
  set gCurrCast = the number of castLib whichGall
end setMood
```

Parameters   the number of castLib *integer/string*

Value   *integer*

See also   the castLibNum of sprite, the fileName of castLib, the memberNum of sprite, the number of castLib, the number of castLibs, the number of members, the number of members of castLib, the preLoadMode of castLib

the number of castLibs

Syntax   `set howManyLibs = the number of castLibs`

Usage   *the number of castLibs* is a property that contains the quantity of internal and external cast libraries in use by the movie.

Example This example contains a function handler that verifies the validity of the cast library number specified by an operation:

```
set the memberNum of sprite 6 = ¬
   the number of member 5 of castLib verifyCast (6)
--
on verifyCast aCast
  if aCast > the number of casLibs then return 1
  else return aCast
end
```

Value   *integer*

the number of members of castLib

Syntax   `set howMany = the number of members of castLib 3`

Usage   *the number of members of castLib* is a property that indicates the last occupied position in a cast library, even if there are open positions in the library. If you need to find open internal positions within the library, use the *findEmpty* function.

Example This handler determines if there are empty cast positions in the library, returning the boolean value TRUE if there are no empty positions:

```
on collapsedCast aCast
  return findempty (member 1 of castLib aCast) = ¬
     the number of members of castLib aCast
end collapsedCast
```

Parameters the number of members of castLib *integer|string*

Value *integer*

See also the castLibNum of sprite, the fileName of castLib, the memberNum of sprite, the number of castLib, the number of castLibs, the number of castLib, the preLoadMode of castLib, the selection of castLib

the preLoadMode of castLib

CAST PROPERTY

Syntax `set the preLoadMode of castLib 3 = 2`

Usage *the preLoadMode of castLib* is a property containing a value that sets the specified cast library's preload mode. The possible values are: **0** - When Needed, **1** - Before Frame One, **2** - After Frame One. This has the same effect as the "Preload" selector in the Cast Properties dialog box.

> ### Tip
>
> *In general, it is better to set this property to 0 and control the preloading of members with Lingo. This gives you more precise control over memory management. The other options give the user a longer wait after loading your movie, which makes your movie seem slower.*

Parameters the preLoadMode of castLib *integer|string*

Value 0|1|2

See also preLoad, preLoadMember

save castLib

Syntax   `save castLib "bitmaps", "C:\Project\bitmaps.cst"`

Usage   The *save castLib* command saves a cast library to an external file, and reassigns the cast library to that file. Used with only one parameter, the *save castLib* command saves a modified cast over the existing external cast file. An optional second parameter can be used to specify a new filename and path.

> **Tip**
>
> *While it is possible to save an internal cast library to an external file, this will cause errors. This command will not work in Shockwave or with protected or compressed cast libraries.*

Parameters   `save castLib string`

`save castLib string, string`

See also   saveMovie

the selection of castLib

Syntax   `set the selection of castLib "Internal" = [[1, 6]]`

Usage   *the selection of castLib* is a property that controls which cast members are currently selected. It stores these as a list of sublists, with each sublist containing a pair of numbers indicating the first and last cast members in a series.

You can test and set this property with Lingo. However, it only works in the Director authoring environment.

Example   This statement selects the cast members from number 4 to number 9, and from number 12 to number 16 in castLib "photos":

```
set the selection of castLib "photos" = [[4, 9], [12, 16]]
```

Parameters   the selection of castLib *integer/string*

Value   *linear list of* [*integer, integer*]

See also   the scoreSelection

Cast Members Category

13

These commands and properties affect properties related to cast members.

the backColor of member

MEMBER PROPERTY

Syntax   `set the backColor of member "data field" = 5`

Usage   The property *the backColor of member* contains the background color assigned to a cast member of the type *#field* or *#button*. Bitmap cast members do not have this property and should be colorized with *the backColor of sprite* property.

    the backColor of member, unlike *the backColor of sprite*, actually modifies the cast member.

    In Director Version 4, this command was *the backColor of cast*.

    The value of this property corresponds to the index value of a color in the current color palette, in color depth settings between 1 bit and 8 bits. You can see the index value of a color in the palette by clicking on the color in Director's Color Palette window.

    In higher-bit color settings, this property returns a number between 0 and 32767 (16-bit) or 16777216 (24/32-bit).

Example   This statement sets the background color of a field or button cast member to the color of the stage:

`set the backColor of member "explanation" = the stageColor`

Parameters   `the backColor of` *member*

Value   *integer*

See also   the foreColor of member, the stageColor

the behavesLikeToggle of member

MEMBER PROPERTY

Syntax   `set the behavesLikeToggle of member "exit" = FALSE`

Usage   *the behavesLikeToggle of member* property controls the toggle action of *#btned* cast members, which are created with the Custom Button command from the Insert | Control menu. Clicking on a toggled button changes its appearance, and it remains that way until clicked on again. Untoggled buttons may change appearance when clicked, but they return to their unclicked state when the mouse is released.

Parameters   the behavesLikeToggle of *member*

Value   *boolean*

See also   the behavesLikeToggle of sprite, the enabled of member, the enabled of sprite, the initialToggleState of member, the labelString of member, setButtonImageFromCastMember

the castLibNum of member

MEMBER PROPERTY

Syntax   set whatCast = the castLibNum of member "home"

Usage   *the castLibNum of member* is a property that contains the index number of the cast library containing the specified cast member. It can be tested but not set.

Parameters   the castLibNum of *member*

Value   *integer*

See also   the castLibNum of sprite

the depth of member

MEMBER PROPERTY

Syntax   set howDeep = the depth of member "background"

Usage   The value of *the depth of member* property is determined by the number of bits used to store data for each pixel of a bitmap image. You cannot set the bit depth of the image with this property; it can only be tested. Values for *the depth of member* vary when the image is in 24/32-bit color: on MacOS systems the value is 32, on Windows systems the value is 24.

Example   This handler creates a list of the 8-bit (256-color) bitmap members and stores
them in a list:

```
on getEightBit
  global gEightBitList
  set gEightBitList = []
  set tHowMany = the number of members
  repeat with tCast = 1 to tHowMany
    if the type of member tCast = #bitmap then
      if the depth of member tCast = 8 then
        add gEightBitList, the name of member tCast
      end if
    end if
  end repeat
end getEightBit
```

Parameters   the depth of *member*

Value   1|2|4|8|16|32 *(MacOS)*

1|2|4|8|16|24 *(Windows)*

See also   the colorDepth, the switchColorDepth, the type of member

duplicate member   COMMAND

Syntax   duplicate member "cannonbeach", 3

Usage   The *duplicate member* command makes a copy of the cast member specified
by the first parameter and places it in a position specified by the second
parameter. If no second parameter is used, the new cast member will be
placed in the first open cast location in the same cast.
    When a cast member is copied into an already occupied cast position, the
cast member occupying that position is eliminated.

Example   This Lingo handler lets you make a copy of the cast member *myMem* and
gives it the name *myName*.

```
on copyMember myMem, myName
  set tMemberType = the type of member myMem
  set tNewPos = new(tMemberType)
  duplicate member myMem, tNewPos
  set the name of member tNewPos = myName
end copyMember
```

This command copies the "cannonbeach" cast member into the position occupied by the cast member named "yachats," eliminating "yachats." The new cast member will also be named "cannonbeach."

```
duplicate member "cannonbeach", "yachats"
```

This command copies the "background" cast member from cast library 1 into position 1 of cast library 2.

```
duplicate member "background" of castLib 1, ¬
    member 1 of castLib 2
```

Parameters
```
duplicate member
```
```
duplicate member, member
```

See also   erase member, move member, new

the enabled of member

MEMBER PROPERTY

Syntax   `set the enabled of member "exit button" = TRUE`

Usage   *the enabled of member* is a property that controls whether *#btned* cast members respond to mouse activities. If this property is TRUE, the button responds to rollovers and clicks. If the property is set to FALSE, the image designated for the disabled state of the button is displayed.

Custom button cast members are created with the Custom Button command from the Insert | Control menu.

Example   This handler enables all *#btned* cast members on the stage as the playback head leaves the frame:

```
on exitFrame
  repeat with i = 1 to 120
    if the type of sprite i = 16
      --sprite is not empty
      set aMember = the memberNum of sprite i
      set aCast = the castLibNum of sprite i
      if the type of member amember ¬
        of castLib aCast = #btned then
        set the enabled of member aMember of ¬
          castLib aCast = TRUE
      end if
    end if
  end repeat
end exitFrame
```

Parameters   `set the enabled of `*`member`*

Value   *`boolean`*

See also   the behavesLikeToggle of member, the behavesLikeToggle of sprite, the enabled of sprite, the initialToggleState of member, the labelString of member, setButtonImageFromCastMember

erase member

Syntax   `erase member 3 of castLib 2`

Usage   The *erase member* command deletes a cast member specified by name or position from a cast library.

Examples   This statement removes cast member 2 from the default cast:

`erase member 2`

This statement removes cast member "dv" from cast library 2:

`erase member "dv" of castLib 2`

Parameters   `erase `*`member`*

See also   duplicate member, move member, new

the fileName of member

Syntax   `set the fileName of member "picture" = "picture2.pct"`

Usage   *the fileName of member* is a property that contains the name of the file in use by a linked cast member (one in which the media is stored outside of the cast). You can change the file the cast member is linked to by modifying the value of the property.

It is convenient to change *the filename of member* with Lingo, to update media "on the fly."

> **Tip**
>
> *It is possible to use a URL for the filename of member property, but it is recommended that you download the file to a local drive with* downloadNetThing *instead.*

For projectors, filenames without directory information assume the file is in the same directory as the projector. In Shockwave movies, the file referred to by filename must be located in the Shockwave plug-in support folder and URLs should not be used.

Example   This statement sets the filename of the digital video member "dv" to "shocker.mov," which is currently located in the Shockwave plug-in support folder:

```
set the fileName of member "dv" = "shocker.mov"
```

Parameters   `the fileName of` *member*

Value   *string*

See also   the applicationPath, the media of member, the pathName, the picture of member

the foreColor of member

MEMBER PROPERTY

Syntax   `set the foreColor of member "data field" = 47`

Usage   The property *the foreColor of member* contains the color assigned to the text of a cast member of the type *#field* or *#button*. Bitmap cast members do not have this property and should be colorized with *the backColor of sprite* property.

   the foreColor of member, unlike *the foreColor of sprite*, actually modifies the cast member.

   In Director Version 4, this command was *the foreColor of cast*.

   The value of this property corresponds to the index value of a color in the current color palette, in color depth settings between 1 bit and 8 bits. You can see the index value of a color in the palette by clicking on the color in Director's Color Palette window.

   In higher-bit color settings, this property returns a number between 0 and 32767 (16-bit) or 16777216 (24/32-bit).

Example
This statement sets the text in the field member "region" to the third color in the current color palette (remember, palette entries start with 0):

```
set the foreColor of member "region" = 2
```

This statement sets the color of the third line in the field "region" to the sixth entry in the current color palette:

```
set the foreColor of line 3 of member "region" = 5
```

Parameters
the foreColor of *member*

Value
integer

See also
the foreColor of member, the stageColor

the height of member

MEMBER PROPERTY

Syntax
set the height of member 2 = 20

Usage
the height of member is a property that contains the height of a cast member, in pixels. You can test but not set this property with Lingo.
For field and text cast members, this value is determined by the number of lines of text in the cast member, how the text wraps from line to line, and the spacing between each line of text. Other cast members such as bitmaps and digital video simply derive the sprite from the height of the original image. Director movies imported as cast members, palettes, transitions, and sounds all have *height of member* values of 0.

Example
This code segment calculates the number of pixels that a slider will need to move along the height of a vertical scroll bar built for the field cast member "bar":

```
set tBarHeight = the height of member "bar"
set tNumOfLins = the lineCount of member "txt"
set tScrollIncrement = tBarHeight/tNumOfLins
```

Parameters
the height of *member*

Value
integer

See also
the height of sprite, rect, the rect of member, the rect of sprite, the regPoint of member, spriteBox, the width of member, the width of sprite

importFileInto

Syntax
```
importFileInto member "safari" of castLib "albums", ¬
    "http://www.surftrio.com/albums/safari.gif"
```

Usage
The *importFileInto* command imports the content of a file (specified by the second parameter) into a cast member position (specified by the first parameter). The media from the file then becomes a part of one of the movie's casts.

> **Tip**
>
> *Typically, this command is used to bring linked content into the cast before delivering a finished project. At run time, use of this command can be problematic, due to memory overhead associated with the command. Setting* the filename of member *property will give better results at run time.*

As with all linked media in Shockwave delivery, you must place a file in the plug-in support folder before a Shockwave movie can use *importFileInto*. Any other path to a drive on the local system will be rejected.

> **Tip**
>
> *Director 6 supports the use of URLs for the filename of the cast member, but it is recommended that you use the* downloadNetThing *command to copy the file from its remote location to a local address before using* importFileInto.

Example
This command will import the sound "safari.wav" into the next new cast member:
```
importFileInto new(#sound),"test.wav"
```

Parameters
```
importFileInto integer|string, string
importFileInto member, string
```

See also
downloadNetThing, the fileName of member, new

the initialToggleState of member

Syntax   `set the initialToggleState of member "show" = FALSE`

Usage   *the initialToggleState of member* is a property that determines whether a cast member of the *#btned* is set to its toggled or untoggled state when it first appears. If the property is FALSE, the default image is used; if the property is TRUE, the toggled image is used. The default value is FALSE.

Parameters   `the initialToggleState of` *member*

Value   *boolean*

See also   the behavesLikeToggle of member, the behavesLikeToggle of sprite, the enabled of member, the enabled of sprite, the labelString of member, setButtonImageFromCastMember

the labelString of member

Syntax   `set the name of member 3 = the labelString of member 3`

Usage   *the labelString of member* is a property that contains the text displayed in *#btned* cast members created with the Custom Button Editor. This is largely useful during authoring, as it can only be tested with Lingo. To modify the text, you must use the Custom Button Editor.

Parameters   `the labelString of` *member*

Value   *string*

See also   the behavesLikeToggle of member, the behavesLikeToggle of sprite, the enabled of member, the enabled of sprite, the labelString of member, setButtonImageFromCastMember

the media of member

Syntax   `set the media of member 3 = the media of member 2`

Usage   *the media of member* is a property containing the actual data that makes up the cast member. You can use this property to copy the contents of cast members to other cast members, cast libraries, and even different movies with Lingo.

> **Tip**
>
> *You can even store* the media of member *in a global variable or as a property of a parent script. Global variables can be passed between movies—even Shockwave movies.*

Examples   This statement stores *the media of member* "picture" in the global variable *gPicture*:

`set gPicture = the media of member "picture"`

This statement duplicates *the media of cast member 2* into a new cast member:

```
set the media of new (the type of member 2) = ¬
    the media of member 2
```

Parameters   `the media of` *member*

Value   *media*

See also   the fileName of member, the picture of member, the type of member

member

Syntax   `member 5`

`member "background"`

`member "smith" of castLib "jones"`

Usage   The *member* keyword is used to denote a specific cast member in commands, functions, and other Lingo constructs.

While the use of *member* is optional in many cases where cast members are referred to, some Lingo properties, commands, and functions require it. Generally, the examples in this book opt to drop it where unnecessary, in order to highlight the cases in which it is essential.

Cast members can be specified by either the cast position number or the name of the cast member. Additionally, a cast library can be addressed by incorporating the *castLib* keyword. If the *member* reference is ambiguous (for instance, there are multiple cast members with the same name or number) and no cast library is specified, cast library 1 is assumed to be the library the cast member is in.

Parameters   `member integer/string`

`member integer/string of castLib integer/string`

the modified of member

Syntax   `set isItMod = the modified of member 5`

Usage   *the modified of member* is a property that contains TRUE if the specified cast member has been changed in any way since the current movie has been open. You can test but not set this property with Lingo.

Example   This code segment resets the text of the field cast member "user text" if it has been changed during the current session:

```
if the modified of member "user text" then
  set the text of member "user text" = ¬
    the text of member "save text"
end if
```

Parameters   the modified of *member*

Value   *boolean*

move member

COMMAND

Syntax   `move member 3 of castLib 1, "back"`

Usage   The *move member* command moves a cast member to a different position within the current cast, or even a different cast library. If a destination is not specified, then the cast member will be moved to the first open location within the current library. The original position is left empty.

     If you move a member currently used as a sprite, the sprite will continue to refer to the original cast member's location, which would become empty after the *move* command. If you use cast names rather than numbers in your development, then this shouldn't affect your Lingo scripts. It will affect items appearing on the stage, however.

     If you move a cast member to a slot in the cast that is already used by another cast member, that cast member will be deleted and replaced.

Examples   This statement moves the cast member named "image" to the next open cast slot in the current castLib:

```
move member "image"
```

     This statement moves the cast member named "image" to a certain slot in a different cast library:

```
move member "image", member 3 of castLib 2
```

Parameters   move   *member*

move   *member, member*

See also   duplicate member, erase member, new

the name of member

Syntax   `set the name of member "A4" = "A5"`

Usage   *the name of member* is a property that contains the name of the specified cast member. You can test and set this property with Lingo.

> ### Tip
>
> *In general, it is useful to refer to a cast member by its name rather than its number. As you reorganize your cast during development, the names of cast members remain the same, whereas the numbers will change with the position of the cast member.*

Examples   Because the processing of string data used for cast member names during playback may slow movies down, one practice is to create a set of global variables that are initialized at the start of the movie, referring to the name of the member (for flexibility during authoring) but containing the member number reference (for speed during playback). This handler returns the member number:

```
on getMemberNumber whichMember
  return the number of whichmember
end
```

In a *startMovie* handler, calls to *getMemberNumber* would look like this:

```
set gBackgroundMember = getMemberNumber ("background")
```

Parameters   the name of *member*

Value   *string*

See also   the memberNum of sprite, the mouseChar, the mouseCast, the mouseItem, the mouseLine, the mouseWord, the number of member, the name of member, rollOver

new

Syntax `new #richtext`

Usage This version of the *new* command creates a new cast member, of the type specified. The type can be a symbol representing any of the cast member types: *#bitmap, #button, #digitalVideo, #field, #filmLoop, #movie, #picture, #richText, #script, #shape, #sound, #SWA, #palette,* and *#transition.*

After a *new* command, *the result* property contains a reference to the new cast member.

If you use only the cast member type parameter, the new cast member will be created in cast library 1. You may also use a second parameter to specify a cast member position and/or cast library.

Example This statement uses the *new* command with *importFileInto* to create a new *#bitmap* member and import a file in one step:

`importFileInto new #bitmap ,"picture.bmp"`

Parameters `new symbol`

`new symbol, member`

`new symbol, castLib integer|string`

See also the type of member

the number of member

Syntax `set aMember = the number of member 5 of castLib 3`

Usage *the number of member* is a property that contains a unique identification number for the specified cast member. It's commonly used in conjunction with *the memberNum of sprite* property to change the appearance of a sprite on the stage.

This property's value is equal to the cast position for cast members in cast library 1. Values for members in other cast libraries can be derived from the formula:

(65536 * cast library number) + (cast member position)

Thus, cast member 1 of cast library 2 will have a *number of member* value of 131073 ((65536 * 2) + 1), and cast library 3's members start with 186609.

If the specified cast member doesn't exist, *the number of member* property will be –1.

Example

This example animates a sprite by setting up a list of cast member numbers as a global variable (*gAnimation*), then rotating through those cast members in an *exitFrame* handler:

```
global gAnimation, gAnimSprite, gCel

on startMovie
  set cities = ["Vancouver", "Seattle", "Spokane"]
  set gAnimation = []
  repeat with i to count (cities)
    set city = getAt (cities, i)
    add gAnimation, the number of member city
  end repeat
  set gAnimSprite = 1
  puppetSprite gAmimSprite, TRUE
  set gCel = 0
  set the memberNum of sprite gAnimSprite = ¬
    getAt (gAnimation, gCel + 1)
end

on exitFrame
  set gCel = (gCel + 1) mod 3
  set the memberNum of sprite gAnimSprite = ¬
    getAt (gAnimation, gCel + 1)
end
```

Parameters

```
the number of member
```

Value

```
integer
```

See also

the memberNum of sprite

the palette of member

MEMBER PROPERTY

Syntax   `set the palette of member "background" = -101`

Usage   *the palette of member* is a property that determines the palette assigned to a bitmap cast member. You can test and set this property with Lingo.

   If the palette has been imported as a cast member, the value of this property will be equal to the palette's *number of member* property. If the cast member uses one of Director's built-in palettes, then *the palette of member* contains a negative value corresponding to a particular palette. You can work with the built-in palettes more directly by using *the paletteRef of member* property.

   Changing the palette assigned to a bitmap cast member from Lingo does not change the data contained in the bitmap image; it merely changes the way it's displayed. Unlike the Transform Bitmap process, no remapping of colors to the new palette takes place.

Example   This code segment sets the palette of the member "photo" to a different palette depending on *the machineType* property:

```
if the machineType = 256 then
  -- we're on Windows
  set the palette of member "photo" = "NetW"
else
  set the palette of member "photo" = "NetM"
end if
```

Parameters   the palette of *member*

Value   *integer*

See also   the paletteMapping, the paletteRef of member

the paletteRef of member

MEMBER PROPERTY

Syntax   `set whichPal = the paletteRef of member "background"`

Usage   *the paletteRef of member* is a property that contains a nonnumeric reference to the palette assigned to a bitmap cast member. If the cast member uses a custom palette, this property contains the cast position of that palette, in the following form:

`(member 4 of castLib 3)`

If a built-in palette is used for the cast member, *the paletteRef of member* contains a symbol value. You can test and set this property with Lingo.

The built-in palette reference values are *#systemMac*, *#systemWin*, *#rainbow*, *#grayscale*, *#pastels*, *#vivid*, *#NTSC*, *#metallic*, and *#systemWinDir4*.

Example   This code segment sets the palette reference of the member "a1" to a different palette depending on *the machineType* property:

```
if the machineType = 256 then
  -- we're on Windows
  set the paletteRef of member "a1" = #systemWin
else
  set the paletteRef of member "a1" = #systemMac
end if
```

Parameters   `the paletteRef of` *member*

Value   *symbol* | *integer*

See also   the palette of member, the paletteMapping

the picture of member

Syntax   `set anImage = the picture of member "background"`

Usage   *the picture of member* is a property that contains the data for the image being
used by a *#bitmap*, *#richText*, or *#picture* cast member. You can copy this data
to variables, other cast members, parent script properties, or other movies
(by using global variables).

 You cannot directly access or modify the data contained in *the picture of
member* property.

Examples   These Lingo functions allow you to store pictures in a global property list,
and to retrieve them. When you navigate to other movies with commands
like *gotoNetMovie*, you can retrieve pictures that were previously loaded in
other movies. Instructions about how to use these handlers follow them:

```
------------------------
on addPicture myCastName
  -- adds picture to global
  -- property list gPictureList
  -- you can retrieve it by using
  -- retrievePicture
  -- myCastName must be a valid
  -- cast member name
if the number of member myCastName < 1 then exit
global gPictureList
  if not(listP(gPictureList)) then
    set gPictureList = [:]
  end if
if the type of member myCastName = #bitmap OR ¬
    the type of member myCastName = #picture then
    -- OK to add picture
set tPictureData = ¬
      [#picture: the picture of member myCastName, ¬
      #type: the type of member myCastName]
addProp gPictureList, myCastName, tPictureData
  end if
end addPicture
```

```
------------------------
on retrievePicture myCastName
  -- retrieves picture from
  -- global property list gPictureList
  -- and deletes it afterwards.
  -- myCastName must be the valid
  -- cast member name
  -- which was used in the addPicture handler.
global gPictureList
set tPictureData = getaProp(gPictureList, myCastName)
  if voidP(tPictureData) then exit
  if pictureP(the picture of tPictureData) then
    -- valid picture
    set tNewMemberNum = new(the type of tPictureData)
    set the name of member tNewMemberNum = myCastName
    set the picture of member tNewMemberNum = ¬
      the picture of tPictureData
  deleteProp gPictureList, myCastName
end if
end retrievePicture
------------------------
```

You can use these handlers to store pictures in global variables, navigate to other movies, and place these pictures in the cast for use there. This is one method to share data between movies.

1. Copy these scripts to any movie script in any movie you wish to add or retrieve pictures.

2. Add a picture—for example, a bitmap named "button1"—using a command like this:

   ```
   addPicture("button1")
   ```

   The picture and its type will be added to a global property list named gPictureList.

3. Next, navigate to the next movie with a command like *gotoNetMovie*:

   ```
   "myMovie.dcr"
   ```

4. To make this picture available in the cast of the new movie, use this command (use the same cast name as before):

   ```
   retrievePicture("button1")
   ```

> **Tip**
>
> *Don't use the* **clearGlobals** *command in the new movie; otherwise, the global list that holds your picture will be deleted.*

Parameters	the picture of *member*
Value	*picture*
See also	the fileName of member, the media of member, the type of member

the rect of member

MEMBER PROPERTY

Syntax	set howBig = the rect of member 4
Usage	*the rect of member* is a property that contains the rectangular coordinates of the specified cast member. You can test but not set this property with Lingo.

Cast member types *#bitmap*, *#button*, *#digitalVideo*, *#field*, *#movie*, *#picture*, *#richText*, and *#shape* members have a *rect of member* property. Attempts to access the property for other cast member types will yield a value of:

rect(0, 0, 0, 0)

the rect of member property itself has the usual *rect* properties: *left*, *top*, *right*, and *bottom*. The *left* and *top* values are always 0. So it is possible to determine the width of a cast member by referring to *the right of the rect of member* property.

Example	This example opens the browser application from within Director:

open browserName ()

Parameters	the rect of *member*
Value	*rect*
See also	the height of sprite, the height of member, inflate, rect, the rect of sprite, the regPoint of member, spriteBox, the width of member, the width of sprite

the regPoint of member

Syntax   `set the regPoint of member 5 = point (-40, 35)`

Usage   *the regPoint of member* is a property that contains the registration point of a cast member. The property contains a *point* value. The location of the registration point determines the reference point for drawing a sprite on the screen (*the loc of sprite* property) when the cast member is placed on the stage.

The value of this property represents the amount that the upper left corner of the bounding rectangle for all of the pixels in a bitmap is offset from the registration point. It is possible for the registration point of a *#bitmap* to lie outside the bounding rectangle, although the default value is the center of the image.

You can test this property for all cast members and set this property for *#bitmap* cast members.

Example   When a single *#bitmap* cast member is used for several different sprites on the stage, it is possible to animate them all by modifying the cast member's *regPoint* property instead of changing *the loc* property for each sprite.

This segment animates all of the sprites using the cast member "jitter" by modifying *the regPoint* property of the cast member. Each of the instances of the cast member on the stage will move in unison while the mouse is held down:

```
repeat while the stillDown
  set oldReg = the regPoint of member "jitter"
  set newReg = oldReg + ¬
    point (random (7) - 4, random (7) - 4)
  set the regPoint of member "jitter" = newReg
end repeat
```

Parameters   `the regPoint of` *member*

Value   *point*

See also   the loc of sprite, the locH of sprite, the locV of sprite, the rect of member

the scriptsEnabled of member

MEMBER PROPERTY

Syntax set the scriptsEnabled of member "control panel" = TRUE

Usage *the scriptsEnabled of member* property is TRUE if the specified *#movie* cast member can execute its own Lingo scripts. The default is FALSE.
You can test and set this property with Lingo.

> ### Tip
>
> *Testing for this property with any cast member type other than #movie will result in an error.*

Parameters the scriptsEnabled of member *integer|string* ¬
{of castLib *integer|string*}

Value *boolean*

See also the type of member

the scriptText of member

MEMBER PROPERTY

Syntax set aScript = the scriptText of member

Usage *the scriptText of member* is a property that contains the content of a script assigned to a cast member. It enables you to create and make changes to scripts using the string-handling capabilities of Lingo.
All Lingo script text is compiled and removed from a file when it is protected, made into a projector, or saved as a Shockwave movie. Testing the property in those situations will not yield a usable result, but new values for the property can be set and then tested.

Example This handler attaches a *mouseUp* handler to the cast member *whatMember* that moves the playback head to the frame represented by *whatFrame*:

```
on setButton whatMember, whatFrame
  set the scripttext of member whatMember = ¬
    "on mouseUp" & RETURN & "  go" & string (whatFrame) ¬
    & RETURN & "end"
end
```

Parameters the scriptText of *member*

Value *string*

the scriptType of member

MEMBER PROPERTY

Syntax `set the scriptType of member 4 = #score`

Usage *the scriptType of member* is a property that determines the kind of script a *#script* cast member is, whether *#movie*, *#score*, or *#parent*. You can test and set this property with Lingo.

This property is used in the authoring mode. Changing the type of a script is rarely useful during playback.

Example This handler, useful only in the Director authoring environment, goes through the entire cast, looks for the *property* keyword in the *scriptText* of each script cast member, then sets that script to be a parent script:

```
on makeParent
  set tMems = the number of members
  repeat with tCast = 1 to tMems
    if the type of member tCast = #script then
      if the scriptText of member tCast ¬
        contains (RETURN & "property") then
          set the scriptType of member tCast = #parent
      end if
    end if
  end repeat
end makeParent
```

Parameters the scriptType of *member*

Value #parent|#score|#movie

See also the scriptText of member, the type of member

the size of member

MEMBER PROPERTY

Syntax   `set howBig = the size of member "background"`

Usage   *the size of member* is a property that contains the size, in bytes, of the cast member.

Example   This handler returns the sum of the size of all of the cast members:

```
on getAllMemSize
  set tReturnSize = 0
  set tMems = the number of members
  repeat with tCurrMem = 1 to tMems
    set tSize = the size of member tCurrMem
    set tReturnSize = tReturnSize + tSize
  end repeat
  return tReturnSize
end getAllMemSize
```

Parameters   `the size of` *`member`*

Value   *`integer`*

See also   the freeBlock, the freeBytes, ramNeeded, preload, preloadMember, unload, unloadMember

the type of member

MEMBER PROPERTY

Syntax   `set whatKind = the type of member 4`

Usage   *the type of member* property indicates what kind of media is stored in a cast member. Prior to Director Version 5, this property was called *castType*. You can test but not set this property with Lingo.

The possible built-in cast member types are *#bitmap, #btned, #button, #digitalVideo, #empty, #field, #filmLoop, #movie, #ole, #palette, #picture, #richText, #script, #shape, #sound, #SWA,* and *#transition.* Cast members created by Asset Xtras can have custom types.

Example   This code segment checks to see if the type of the cast member "audio" is the type #SWA, which refers to Shockwave audio, and sets one of its properties if it is #SWA:

```
if the type of member 18 = #SWA then
  set the URL of member 18 = "safari.swa"
end if
```

Parameters   the type of *member*

Value   *symbol*

the width of member

MEMBER PROPERTY

Syntax   `set howWide = the width of member "background"`

Usage   *the width of member* is a property that contains the width of a cast member in pixels. You can test but not set this property with Lingo.

Example   This code segment restores the width of puppeted sprite 10 to its original size, as contained in its cast member:

```
set the width of sprite 10 = ¬
  the width of member (the memberNum of sprite 10)
```

Parameters   the width of *member*

Value   *integer*

See also   the height of member, the height of sprite, rect, the rect of member, the rect of sprite, the regPoint of member, spriteBox, the width of sprite

Fields Category

These Lingo properties, functions, and commands are related to the manipulation of field cast members (of the type *#field*) and the text they contain. Most of the properties relating to the actual text in the cast member can use the keyword *field* interchangeably with *member*.

the alignment of member

MEMBER PROPERTY

Syntax `set the alignment of member "header" = "center"`

Usage *the alignment of member* is a property that allows you to check or set the horizontal position of text within a field. The possible values for this property are the strings "left", "center", or "right." The parameter can be either the number or the name of the field cast member.

   The field cast member must not be empty; if it is empty *the alignment of member* property has no effect. This is typical with any property of a field, including *the font of member, the fontSize of member,* etc.

> ### Tip
>
> *This command is incorrectly called "the align of member" in Version 5 of Macromedia's Lingo Dictionary.*

Example This handler sets the alignment of a field. If the field is empty, it puts a space into the field so that the alignment will take effect.

```
on setFieldAlignment myField, myAlign
  -- myAlignment must be "left" ,
  -- "center", or "right"
  if the type of member myField ¬
    <> #field then exit
  if not("leftcenterright" contains ¬
    myAlign) then exit
  if length(myField) = 0 then ¬
    put " " into member myField
  set the alignment of member ¬
    myField = myAlign
end setFieldAlignment
```

Parameters `the alignment of` *member*

     `the alignment of` *field*

Value `"left"|"center"|"right"`

See also the dropShadow of member, the font of member, the fontSize of member, the fontStyle of member, the lineHeight of member, the text of member

the autoTab of member

MEMBER PROPERTY

Syntax   `set the autoTab of member 4 = TRUE`

Usage   When *the autoTab of member* property of a *field* member is set to TRUE, the
user can jump to the next editable field by pressing the Tab key.

   The tab order of editable fields on the stage is determined by their order
in the score, not by their order in the cast or their placement on the stage. For
example, you might have three field members stored in sprite channels 2, 4,
and 5. If *the autoTab of member* is TRUE for the field in sprite 2, and you press
the Tab key while in that field, the cursor will jump to the field in sprite 4, if
that field is editable.

Example   This authoring handler will set *the autoTab of member* of all editable field cast
members to TRUE:

```
on tabEditFields
  repeat with i = 1 to the number of castLibs
    repeat with j = 1 to the number of members of ¬
      castLib i
      if the type of member j of casLib i = #field then
        if the editable of member j of ¬
          castLib i = TRUE then
          set the autoTab of member j of castLib i = TRUE
        end if
      end if
    end repeat
  end repeat
end
```

Parameters   `the autoTab of member` *integer|string {of castLib integer|string}*

Value   *boolean*

See also   the border of member, the boxDropShadow of member, the boxType of
member, the editable of member, the margin of member

the border of member

MEMBER PROPERTY

Syntax   `set the border of member "trap" of castLib 3 = 5`

Usage   *the border of member* is a property that contains the thickness (in pixels) of a border around a field cast member. It can be tested and set by Lingo.
   Unlike shape cast members, the borders of fields cannot be modified at the sprite level.

Example   This statement will place a 2-pixel border around the field cast member named "country":

`set the border of member "country" = 2`

Parameters   `the border of` *member*

Value   *integer*

See also   the border of member, the boxDropShadow of member, the boxType of member, the editable of member, the margin of member

the boxDropShadow of member

MEMBER PROPERTY

Syntax   `set the boxDropShadow of member "tom" = 5`

Usage   *the boxDropShadow of member* is a property that contains the size in pixels of the drop shadow that is added to the outside rectangle of *field*. You can test and set this property with Lingo. If you wish to change the drop shadow of the text contained in a *field* cast member, use *the dropShadow of member* property.

Example   This code segment will set *the boxDropShadow* of the field member in sprite channel 5 to 3 pixels, if it really is a *field* member:

```
set tMember = the memberNum of sprite 5
if the type of member tMember = #field then
  set the boxDropShadow of member tMember = 3
end if
```

Parameters the boxDropShadow of *member*

Value *integer*

See also the autoTab of member, the border of member, the boxType of member, the dropShadow of member, the editable of member, the margin of member

the boxType of member

MEMBER PROPERTY

Syntax set the boxType of member "results" = #fixed

Usage *the boxType of member* is a property that contains the main field type of a *field* cast member. These values correspond to those in the field member dialog box; they are *#adjust*, *#fixed*, *#limit*, and *#scroll*. You can test and set this property with Lingo.

The field reacts to this property in the following ways based on the value:

#adjust Automatically modifies the vertical height of the field member to match the number of lines of text. It does not modify the width. Text wraps.

#fixed Does not modify the width or height. Extra characters are not displayed. Text wraps.

#limit Does not modify the width or height. Prevents characters from being entered when the line length exceeds the width of the field.

#scroll Adds a scroll bar to the right side of the field (does not affect *the width of member* property). Text wraps.

The *member* keyword is not interchangeable with *field* when used with *the boxType of member*.

Example This handler checks the height of a field sprite, checks it against the height of a member, and sets it to a scrolling field if there is more text than the sprite can display; otherwise, it sets it to a fixed-size field:

```
on exitFrame
  set whatMember = the member of sprite 6
  if the type of whatMember = #field then
    set howMuchText = the height of whatMember
    set howHighSprite = the height of sprite 6
    if howMuchText > howHighSprite then
      set whatType = #scroll
```

```
        else
          set whatType = #fixed
        end if
        set the boxType of whatType = whatType
      end if
    end
```

Parameters   the boxType of *member*

Value   #adjust|#fixed|#limit|#scroll

See also   the autoTab of member, the border of member, the boxType of member, the
dropShadow of member, the editable of member, the margin of member

charPosToLoc

FUNCTION

Syntax   set whereAt = charPosToLoc (member "possibilities", 203)

Usage   The *charPosToLoc* function returns the distance (in pixels) from *the loc* of a
field member (its upper left corner) to the bottom left corner of a character
within that field. It returns this as a point value. The first parameter of the
function must be a reference to a field cast member; the second is an integer
containing the position of the character within the field.

This information can be very helpful when you need to coordinate the
placement of graphics with some text in a field. For example, you might
want to place a pointing finger icon at a certain word within a field. With the
charPosToLoc function, you can easily do this.

The height of a sprite does not affect this function. Because the calculations are performed on the cast member, *charPosToLoc* will function in
exactly the same fashion even if not all of the characters in the field are
visible on the stage.

Examples   This Lingo function uses the *charPosToLoc* function to return the location of a
certain word within a field:

```
on getWordLoc myField, myWord, myFieldSprite
  set tPoint = the loc of sprite myFieldSprite
  set tOffset = offset(myWord, field myField)
  if tOffset > 0 then
    set tCharLoc = charPosToLoc(member myField, tOffset)
    set tPoint = tPoint + tCharLoc
  end if
  return tPoint
end getWordLoc
```

You can use this function to set *the loc* of a sprite, with a pointer that would point to the certain word, like this:

```
set the loc of sprite 11 = getWordLoc("prose", "woof", 2)
```

Parameters   charPosToLoc (*member*, *integer*)

Value   *point*

See also   lineHeight, linePosToLocV, locToCharPos, locVToLinePos

the dropShadow of member

MEMBER PROPERTY

Syntax   `set the dropShadow of member "ominous" = 3`

Usage   *the dropShadow of member* is a property that contains the size (in pixels) of the drop shadow applied to the text of a field cast member. If you want to add a drop shadow to the exterior of a field, use *the boxDropShadow of member* property.

Example   This code segment will set the drop shadow of the text in the field member of sprite channel 9 to 2 pixels, if it really is a *field* member:

```
set tMember = the memberNum of sprite 9
if the type of member tMember = #field then
  set the dropShadow of member tMember = 2
end if
```

Parameters   the dropShadow of *member*

Value   *integer*

See also   the autoTab of member, the border of member, the boxType of member, the boxDropShadow of member, the editable of member, the margin of member

the editable of member

Syntax   `set the editable of field = FALSE`

Usage   *the editable of member* is a property that contains TRUE if a field cast member is editable while the movie is running, and FALSE if it is not. You can test or set this property with Lingo.

Example   This *exitFrame* handler waits until the text that began to load with a *getNetText* command is loaded, then stores that text in a field "shopping list" and makes that field editable:

```
on exitFrame
  global gLastNetID, gDone
  -- gDone is set to 0 at getNetText time,
  -- and makes this run only once.
  if netDone(gLastNetID) AND not(gDone) then
    put netTextResult(gLastNetID) into ¬
      field "shopping list"
    set the editable of member ¬
      "shopping List" = TRUE
    set gDone = TRUE
  end if
  go to the frame
end exitFrame
```

Parameters   `the editable of member integer|string {of ¬`
`      castLib integer|string}`

Value   `boolean`

See also   the autoTab of member, the border of member, the boxType of member, the boxDropShadow of member, the dropShadow of member, the margin of member, the wordWrap of member

the font of member

MEMBER PROPERTY

Syntax `set the font of member 4 = "Helvetica"`

Usage *the font of member* is a property that determines the typeface the *field* cast member uses to display the text contained in it. It does not affect *#richText* cast members.

You can test and set this property with Lingo. If you set it, it affects all of the text in the field. When tested, it returns only the font of the first character of the field (other characters may be set to different fonts).

Parameters `the font of member`

`the font of field`

Value *string*

See also the alignment of member, the dropShadow of member, the fontSize of member, the fontStyle of member, the foreColor of member, the lineHeight of member, the text of member

the fontSize of member

MEMBER PROPERTY

Syntax `set the fontSize of member 3 = 12`

Usage *the fontSize of member* is a property that controls the default size of the text in a *field* cast member. You can test and set this property with Lingo.

Example This statement sets the size of the text of a field named "region" to 24 points:

`set the fontSize of member "region" = 24`

Parameters the fontSize of member *integer|string {of castLib integer|string}*

the fontSize of *field*

Value *integer*

See also the alignment of member, the dropShadow of member, the font of member, the fontStyle of member, the foreColor of member, the lineHeight of member, the text of member

the fontStyle of member
MEMBER PROPERTY

Syntax set the fontStyle of member 2 = "bold,condense"

Usage *the fontStyle of member* is a property that contains the style of the text in a field cast member. You can test and set this property with Lingo.

The value of the property is a string. Possible styles include *"plain"*, *"bold"*, *"italic"*, *"underline"*, *"shadow"*, *"outline"*, *"condense"*, and *"extend"*. The style *"plain"* will remove all styles applied.

Stringing several font styles together, separated by commas, allows multiple styles to be applied. Multiple styles can also be added by subsequent *set* statements.

Examples This statement removes all of the font styles applied to the text in a field named "region" to 24 points:

set the fontStyle of member "region" = "plain"

This statement sets the style of the field "region" to bold and underlined:

set the fontStyle of member "region" = "bold, underline"

These statements perform the same function as the single statement above:

set the fontStyle of member "region" = "underline"
set the fontStyle of member "region" = "bold"

Parameters the fontStyle of *member*

the fontStyle of *field*

Value *string*

See also the alignment of member, the dropShadow of member, the font of member, the fontSize of member, the foreColor of member, the lineHeight of member, the text of member

the lineCount of member

MEMBER PROPERTY

Syntax `set howManyLines = the lineCount of member 3`

Usage *the lineCount of member* is a property that returns the number of lines in a field, as determined by the word-wrap of the field on the stage, not the number of RETURN characters. This can be useful for custom scrolling routines, where you need to make sure a specific portion of text in a text field is onscreen at a particular time.

Example This code segment calculates the number of pixels a slider will need to move along the height of a vertical scroll bar:

```
set tBarHeight = the height of member "bar"
set tNumOfLins = the lineCount of member "txt"
set tScrollIncrement = tBarHeight/tNumOfLins
```

Parameters `the lineCount of` *member*

Value *integer*

See also charPosToLoc, lineHeight, the lineHeight of member, linePosToLocV, locToCharPos, the pageHeight of member, scrollByLine, scrollByPage, the scrollTop of member, the wordWrap of member

lineHeight

FUNCTION

Syntax `set howHigh = lineHeight (member 5, 1)`

Usage The *lineHeight* function finds the pixel height of a specific line in a *field* cast member. While you can test the default height and set the height of all of the lines in a field with *the lineHeight of member* property, line height will vary from line to line in fields with mixed font sizes. The *lineHeight* function gives you the ability to test line heights on an individual basis.

Example This function returns the maximum line height in a *field* cast member:

```
on maxLineHeight whatField
  if the type of whatField <> # field then return -1
  else
    set heightList = []
    repeat with i = 1 to the lineCount of whatField
      add heightList, lineHeight (whatField, i)
    end repeat
    return max (heightList)
  end if
end
```

Parameters   lineHeight (*member*, *integer*)

Value   *integer*

See also   charPosToLoc, the lineCount of member, the lineHeight of member,
linePosToLocV, locToCharPos, the pageHeight of member, scrollByLine,
scrollByPage, the scrollTop of member, the wordWrap of member

the lineHeight of member

MEMBER PROPERTY

Syntax   set the lineHeight of member "address" = 19

Usage   *the lineHeight of member* is a property that controls the amount of space
between lines of text (in pixels) of a *field* cast member. You can test and set
this property with Lingo.

Example   This statement sets the *lineHeight* of the field named "result" to 1 ½ times the
size of the font in that field:

```
set the lineHeight of member "result" = ¬
  the fontSize of member "result" * 1.5
```

Parameters   the lineHeight of *member*

the lineHeight of *field*

Value   *integer*

See also   charPosToLoc, the lineCount of member, lineHeight, linePosToLocV,
locToCharPos, the pageHeight of member, scrollByLine, scrollByPage, the
scrollTop of member, the wordWrap of member

linePosToLocV

FUNCTION

Syntax   set howFarDown = linePosToLocV (member 3, 6)

Usage   The *linePosToLocV* function returns the distance (in pixels) from the top of a *field* cast member to the top of the specified line within that field. It returns this value as an integer.

This function is essentially the sum of the heights of all of the lines preceding the specified line.

Example   This code segment sets *the locV of sprite 8* to the vertical middle of the third line in the field "result". Notice that we add *the locV* of the sprite the field is in to *the linePosToLocV* value to get the actual vertical location of the line:

```
set tFLocV = the locV of sprite 2
--the sprite using the field "result"
set tLLocV = linePosToLocV(member "result",3)
--distance from top of cast member to line 3
set tLineMid= lineHeight(member "result",3)/2
--half of height of line 3
set tLineLocV = tFLocV + tLLocV + tLineMid
--combination of sprite location, line location,
--and line height
set the locV of sprite 8 = tLineLocV
```

Parameters   linePosToLocV (*member*, *integer*)

Value   *integer*

See also   charPosToLoc, lineHeight, locToCharPos, locVToLinePos

locToCharPos

FUNCTION

Syntax   set whatChar = locToCharPos (member "menu", point (35, 200))

Usage   The *locToCharPos* function returns the index number of the character in the field closest to the specified point value. The point is relative to the upper left corner of the cast member, not a stage coordinate.

Example

This code segment uses the *locToCharPos* function to see if sprite 8 is closest to an asterisk (*) character. The field "user text" is used for sprite 2. Notice that its *loc* property is subtracted from *the loc of sprite 8* to make the point value work with this function:

```
if char locToCharPos (member "user text", ¬
   the loc of sprite 8 - the loc of sprite 2) ¬
   of field "user text" = "*" then
      doFoundIt
end if
```

Parameters

locToCharPos (*member*, *point*)

Value

integer

See also

charPosToLoc, lineHeight, linePosToLocV, locVToLinePos

locVToLinePos

FUNCTION

Syntax

```
set whatLine = locVToLinePos (member "menu", 240)
```

Usage

The *locVToLinePos* function returns a reference number to the line of a *field* cast member closest to a vertical coordinate (in pixels). The vertical coordinate is relative to the top of the cast member.

Example

This statement returns the contents of the line in the field "user text" closest to sprite 8. The field "user text" is in sprite 2. Its locV is subtracted from *the locV of sprite 8* to determine the vertical offset:

```
return locVToLinePos(member " user text", ¬
   the locV of sprite 8 - the locV of sprite 2)
```

Parameters

locVToLinePos (*member*, *integer*)

Value

integer

See also

charPosToLoc, lineHeight, linePosToLoc, locToCharPos

the margin of member

Syntax   `set`

Usage   *the margin of member* is a property that determines the size, in pixels, of the space between the edges of the text as it appears in a *field* cast member and the edges of a sprite using the cast member. The space between the left edge of the sprite and the left edge of the text will be equal to the value of this property, as will the right edges of the sprite and text. The space between top and bottom edges of the sprite and text will be roughly half the value of *the margin of member* property. You can test and set this property with Lingo.

Example   This statement sets the margin of the field named "data" to 2 pixels:

`set the margin of member "data" = 2`

Parameters   `the margin of `*`member`*

Value   *`integer`*

See also   the autoTab of member, the border of member, the boxType of member, the boxDropShadow of member, the dropShadow of member

the pageHeight of member

Syntax   `set howHigh = the pageHeight of member "constitution"`

Usage   *the pageHeight of member* is a property that contains the vertical size in pixels of the visible portion of a *field* cast member. You can test but not set this property with Lingo.

Example   This code segment sets the height of a custom scroll bar graphic in sprite 7 to the same height as the field member in sprite 2. It also places that scroll bar exactly to the right of the field:

```
set tFieldSprite = 2
set tVsiz = the pageHeight of member ¬
   (the memberNum of sprite tFieldSprite)
set tBarSprite = 7
set tBarWidth  = ¬
the width of sprite tBarSprite
set tBarRect = rect(the right of sprite tFieldSprite, ¬
   the top of sprite tFieldSprite, ¬
   the right of sprite tFieldSprite + tBarWidth, ¬
   the top of sprite tFieldSprite + tVsiz)
puppetSprite(tBarSprite, TRUE)
set the stretch of sprite tBarSprite = TRUE
set the rect of sprite tBarSprite = tBarRect
```

Parameters   the pageHeight of *member*

Value   *integer*

See also   charPosToLoc, the lineCount of member, lineHeight, the lineHeight of member, linePosToLocV, locToCharPos, scrollByLine, scrollByPage, the scrollTop of member, the wordWrap of member

scrollByLine

COMMAND

Syntax   `scrollByLine member "menu", 3`

Usage   The *scrollByLine* command makes a *field* cast member scroll by the specified number of lines. The number of lines can be positive or negative.
The *field* cast member must be either a scrolling or fixed-size field type.

Examples   This command scrolls the text in field "result" down by 1 line:

`scrollByLine member "result", 1`

This command scrolls the text in field "result" up by 1 line:

`scrollByLine member "result", -1`

Parameters   `scrollByLine member, integer`

See also   the boxType of member, charPosToLoc, the lineCount of member, lineHeight, the lineHeight of member, linePosToLocV, locToCharPos, scrollByPage, the pageHeight of member, the scrollTop of member, the wordWrap of member

scrollByPage

COMMAND

Syntax   `scrollByPage member "menu", 2`

Usage   The *scrollByPage* command scrolls a *field* cast member to scroll the number of pages specified by the second parameter. The number of pages can be positive or negative.

A "page" in this case is the amount of text that fits in the displayed field area, and is dependent on the sprite height.

The *field* cast member must be either a scrolling or fixed-size field.

Examples   This command scrolls the text in field "result" down by 1 page:

`scrollByPage member "result", 1`

This command scrolls the text in field "result" up by 1 page:

`scrollByPage member "result", -1`

Parameters   `scrollByPage member, integer`

See also   the boxType of member, charPosToLoc, the lineCount of member, lineHeight, the lineHeight of member, linePosToLocV, locToCharPos, scrollByLine, the pageHeight of member, the scrollTop of member, the wordWrap of member

the scrollTop of member

Syntax `set the scrollTop of member "data" = 0`

Usage *the scrollTop of member* property controls the visible portion of a *field*. Its value (in pixels) corresponds to the portion of the cast member scrolled off the top of the sprite. It gives you fine control over the scrolling of text in a *field* (of *#scroll* or *#fixed* types) or *#richText* cast members.

Example This code segment scrolls the *field* cast member "credits" 288 pixels over a period of about 4.5 seconds:

```
starttimer
set the scrollTop of member "credits" = 0
--resets any scrolling of the cast member
repeat while the timer < 288
  set the scrollTop of member "credits" = the timer
end repeat
set the scrollTop of member "credits" = 288
--in case the timer never reached 288
```

Parameters the scrollTop of *member*

Value *integer*

See also the boxType of member, charPosToLoc, the lineCount of member, lineHeight, the lineHeight of member, linePosToLocV, locToCharPos, scrollByLine, scrollByPage, the pageHeight of member, the wordWrap of member

the selection

Syntax `set whatsSelected = the selection`

Usage *the selection* is a property that contains the string that is currently selected in an editable field. You can test but not set this property with Lingo. If no selection is made, the value of the property is 0.

Example   If any string is selected in an editable field, then this statement will put it into the variable *tString*:

```
if the selection <> 0 then
  set tString = the selection
end if
```

Parameters   the selection

Value   *string*| 0

See also   the selEnd, the selStart

the selEnd

MOVIE PROPERTY

Syntax   set the selEnd = 4

Usage   *the selEnd* is a property that determines the last character of the selection in an editable *field* cast member. You can test and set this property from Lingo.

> ### Tip
>
> *This is a difficult property to test by typing commands into the Message window, because bringing the Message window to the front deselects the cast member.*

Example   This example puts *the selStart*, *the selEnd*, and *the selection* into the Message window each time the *exitFrame* handler is called:

```
on exitFrame
  put the selStart, the selEnd, the selection
end
```

Parameters   the selEnd

Value   *integer*

See also   the selection, the selStart

the selStart of member

Syntax   `set the selStart = 0`

Usage   *the selStart* is a property that determines the first character of the selection in an editable *field* cast member. You can test and set this property from Lingo.

> ### Tip
>
> *This is a difficult property to test by typing commands into the Message window, because bringing the Message window to the front deselects the cast member.*

Example   See the Example for *the selEnd*.

Parameters   `the selStart`

Value   *integer*

See also   the selection, the selEnd

the text of member

Syntax   `set the text of member "city" = "Portland"`

Usage   *the text of member* is a property that contains the text stored in the *field* cast member. You can test and set this property with Lingo. You can also access the text by referring to the member as "field" instead.

Example These two statements are equivalent:

```
put "Shock" into the text of member "display"
put "Shock" into field "display"
```

Parameters `the text of member`

Value *string*

See also the alignment of member, the dropShadow of member, the font of member, the fontSize of member, the fontStyle of member, the foreColor of member, the lineHeight of member

the wordWrap of member

MEMBER PROPERTY

Syntax `set the wordWrap of member 3 = FALSE`

Usage *the wordWrap of member* is a property that is TRUE when the specified field is set to wrap the words within the field, and FALSE otherwise. You can test and set this property with Lingo.

Setting *the wordWrap of member* to FALSE will cause long lines of text to be partially hidden from the viewer. Because there is no horizontal scrolling mechanism, the only way to see the ends of the cropped lines is to set *the wordWrap of member* to TRUE.

the lineCount of member property of a field contains the number of lines formed by the words wrapping within that field.

Parameters `the wordWrap of member`

Value *boolean*

See also the autoTab of member, the border of member, the boxType of member, the boxDropShadow of member, the dropShadow of member, the editable of member, the lineCount of member

Transitions
Category

These Lingo keywords control transition cast members. Transitions can be
controlled by Lingo, but not while the transition is in progress.

the changeArea of member

Syntax
```
set the changeArea of member "checkerboard" = TRUE
```

Usage
the changeArea of member is a property that contains a TRUE or FALSE value that corresponds to the Affects radio buttons in the Frame Properties: Transition dialog box. If *the changeArea of member* is TRUE, the transition is applied only to the area of the stage where sprites have moved, disappeared, or appeared between updates. If it is FALSE, the transition applies to the entire stage. You can test and set this property with Lingo.

the changeArea of member property does not affect the look of some transitions. The Affects buttons in the Frame Properties: Transition dialog are disabled for transitions such as dissolves and wipes, where no difference is discernible.

Example
This example sets all of the transition cast members in cast library 1 to affect the entire stage:

```
repeat with i = 1 to the number of members of castLib 1
  if the type of member i = #transition then
    set the changeArea of member i = FALSE
  end if
end repeat
```

Parameters
```
the changeArea of member
```

Value
```
boolean
```

See also
the chunkSize of member, the duration of member, the transitionType of member

the chunkSize of member

Syntax   `set the chunkSize of member "wipe" = 1`

Usage   *the chunkSize of member* is a property that determines how smooth a transition appears, and corresponds to the Smoothness slider bar in the Frame Properties: Transition dialog box. *the chunkSize* is a value from 1 to 128 pixels; it affects the number of steps making up the transition. A smaller value will be smoother, with smaller steps and, therefore, a slower transition.

Parameters   `the chunkSize of` *member*

Value   *integer*

See also   the changeArea of member, the duration of member, the transitionType of member

the duration of member

Syntax   `set howLong = the duration of member "trans"`

Usage   *the duration of member* is a property that contains a value representing the length of time of a digital video (*#digitalVideo*), a transition (*#transition*), or a Shockwave audio (*#SWA*) cast member.

   For a transition, the value is equal to the transition's desired length in milliseconds and is represented in the Frame Properties: Transition dialog by the Duration slider. If the processor cannot process the data for the transition in the desired time, the transition will occur more slowly.

While the number of steps in a transition animation is controlled by *the chunkSize* property, the time between each of those steps is a derivative of *chunkSize* and *duration*. For example, a transition that travels 640 pixels (such as a Wipe Left on a standard-size stage), with a *chunkSize* of 4 and a *duration* of 4000, needs to take 160 steps or chunks (640 pixels/4 pixels per chunk) in 4 seconds (transition *duration* values are in milliseconds). That's 40 stage updates per second, and it probably won't happen on time except on faster computers. Either a longer *duration* or a larger *chunkSize* should be specified.

Example   This handler finds transition cast members and modifies the *chunkSize* parameter to a value determined by the *duration* and a target stage update speed of about 15 frames per second (assuming all transitions are equal to the stage width):

```
on normalizeTransitions
  set stageWidth = the right of the rect of the stage - ¬
    the left of the rect of the stage
  repeat with i = 1 to the number of castLibs
    repeat with j = 1 to ¬
      the number of members of castLib i
      set aMember = the number of member j of castLib i
      if the type of member aMember = #transition then
        set howLong = the duration of member aMember
        set numChunks = howLong / 67
        --1000 (milliseconds/second) / 15 (frames/second)
        --yields 66-2/3 milliseconds/frame. 67ms is
        --slightly more than is needed to sustain 15fps
        set idealChunkSize = stageWidth / numChunks
        if idealChunkSize < 1 then set idealChunkSize = 1
        if idealChunkSize > 128 then ¬
          set idealChunkSize = 128
        set the chunkSize of member aMember = ¬
          idealChunkSize
      end if
    end repeat
  end repeat
end exitFrame
```

Parameters   the duration of *member*

Value   *integer*

See also   the changeArea of member, the chunkSize of member, the transitionType of member

the transitionType of member

MEMBER PROPERTY

Syntax   `set the transitionType of member "tran14" = 15`

Usage   *the transitionType of member* is a property that contains a numeric identifier for the transition assigned to the transition cast member. The possible values are listed under the *puppetTransition* command in Chapter 24. You can test and set this property with Lingo.

Example   This handler sets *the transitionType* property of the transition cast member to the number contained in the parameter *myType*, if it really is a transition member:

```
on changeTransition myMember, myType
   if the type of member myMember = #transition then
     set the transitionType of member myMember = myType
   end if
end changeTransition
```

Parameters   `the transitionType of` *member*

Value   *integer*

See also   the changeArea of member, the chunkSize of member, the duration of member, the frameTransition, puppetTransition, zoomBox

zoomBox

Syntax   zoomBox 5, 7

zoomBox 6, 4, 10

Usage   The *zoomBox* command is a special transition that animates a dotted rect-angle similar to the zooming window effect on the MacOS. The rectangle starts at the size and position of the sprite specified by the first parameter, and finishes at the size and position of the sprite specified by the second parameter. The optional third parameter indicates the number of ticks to wait between each animation. If omitted, the 15 steps of the animation happen as quickly as the computer can draw them. The movie must be playing to view the *zoomBox* effect—typing it into the Message window with the movie stopped will not work.

There are two options available for setup of the *zoomBox* command. If both of the sprites appear in the same frame of the score when the command is executed, they will be drawn on the stage, and the effect will be drawn over them. If the destination sprite (second parameter) is in the frame after the *zoomBox* command is executed, the effect will take place and the sprite will be drawn on the next stage update.

The playback head does not move during a zoom effect.

Example   This statement causes a zoom effect to be displayed between sprites 15 and 20, with a period of 2 ticks between each animation of the zoom effect:

zoomBox 15, 20, 2

Parameters   zoomBox *integer*, *integer*

zoomBox *integer*, *integer*, *integer*

See also   the changeArea of member, the chunkSize of member, the duration of member, the frameTransition, puppetTransition, the transitionType of member

Sound:
Cue Points Category

These Lingo keywords give you access to information about cue points embedded in AIFF, Shockwave audio, or QuickTime files. You can add cue points to files with Macromedia's SoundEdit 16 on the MacOS. To access cue points on Windows machines, QuickTime 2.5 or later needs to be installed.

on cuePassed

Syntax

```
on cuePassed channelID, cueIndex, cueName

on cuePassed me, channelID, cueIndex, cueName
```

Usage

The *cuePassed* handler is used with sound and video that has cue points embedded in it in order to determine when key points of the media have been reached, and to extract text information from the cue point names.

This handler can be placed in movie, behavior, frame, cast, and sprite scripts. Any nonkeyword identifiers can be used for the handler's parameters (*channelID, cueIndex,* and *cueName* in the Syntax description above). The handler is not called explicitly by other scripts: *cuePassed* events are automatically generated when a sound, Shockwave audio, or QuickTime digital video with cue points embedded reaches one of the cue points.

If the *cuePassed* handler is used in movie or cast scripts, it's used without the *me* parameter. If the handler is placed in a behavior, frame, or sprite script, the *me* parameter is used.

Inside the handler, the values of the parameters provide the following information (again, referring to the parameter names used above, although these need not be the parameter identifiers you use):

- **me**: If used, contains an object reference to the object in which the current cue point was found.

- **channelID**: The channel in which the sound, SWA, or QuickTime cast members containing the cue appears. For sounds, this value will be a symbol in the form *#Sound1, #Sound2,* and so on. For SWA or QuickTime cast members, the value will be the channel number the cast member appears in.

- **cueIndex**: Indicates which cue point has been passed, as counted from the first cue point in the cast member.

- **cueName**: Contains the text of the label associated with the cue point.

Example

When placed in a frame script this handler will put the values extracted from cue points of a sound in sound channel 1 in the Message window:

```
on cuePassed me, whatChannel, whatIndex, whatText
  if whatChannel = #Sound1 then
    put whatChannel, whatIndex, whatText
  end if
end
```

Parameters
```
on cuePassed parameter, parameter, parameter
   statements
end
```

```
on cuePassed me, parameter, parameter, parameter
   statements
end
```

Values *symbol|integer, integer, string*

See also the cuePointNames of member, the cuePointTimes of member, isPastCuePoint, the mostRecentCuePoint of sprite

the cuePointNames of member   MEMBER PROPERTY

Syntax `set cueList = the cuePointNames of member 121 of castLib 1`

Usage *the cuePointNames of member* is a property that lists the items containing the labels of all cue points in the sound, Shockwave audio, or QuickTime cast member. This list can be used to modify rich text (in authoring mode) or field (in both authoring and playback mode) cast members with the contents of the list. The values of this list cannot be modified.

Example This function returns the text label of the most recent cue point label in a sprite:
```
on getLatestCueName whatSprite
   set whatCue = the mostRecentCuePoint of ¬
     sprite whatSprite
   set whatMember = the member of sprite whatSprite
   return getAt (the cuePointNames of member ¬
     whatMember, whatCue)
end
```

Parameters the cuePointNames of *member*

Value *list of string*

See also cuePassed, the cuePointTimes of member, isPastCuePoint, the mostRecentCuePoint of sprite

the cuePointTimes of member

MEMBER PROPERTY

Syntax   `set whatTimes = the cuePointTimes of member "soundtrack"`

Usage   *the cuePointTimes of member* is a property that contains a list with the times at which the cue points of a cast member are placed, in milliseconds. The values in this list cannot be modified.

Example   This function determines the number of cue points in a cast member by counting the number of cue point times:

```
on countCues aMember
  return count (the cuePointTimes of member aMember)
end
```

Parameters   the cuePointTimes of *member*

Value   *list of integers*

See also   cuePassed, the cuePointNames of member, isPastCuePoint, the mostRecentCuePoint of sprite

isPastCuePoint

FUNCTION

Syntax   `set isPassed = isPastCuePoint (sound 2, "chorus")`

Usage   The *isPastCuePoint* function determines if a cue point has been passed in the cast member of a specific sprite or sound channel. The first parameter indicates the channel of the score containing the cast member; the second parameter can be a cue point's index number or name.

The value returned by *isPastCuePoint* is 0 if the cue point has not been reached. If the cue point has been reached, the value will be 1 or greater. The value may be greater than 1 if there are multiple cue points with the same name in the cast member, and more than one has been been reached. Repeat loops do not affect this value (i.e., looping past the same cue point multiple times does not increase the returned value).

Example   isPastCuePoint moves the playback head to the frame labeled "help" when the cue point named "help" of a cast member in sprite 3 is reached:

```
on exitFrame
  if isPastCuePoint (3, "help") then go "help"
  else go the frame
end
```

Parameters   isPastCuePoint (*integer, integer/string*)

isPastCuePoint (sound *integer, integer/string*)

Value   *integer*

See also   cuePassed, the cuePointNames of member, the cuePointTimes of member, the mostRecentCuePoint of sprite

the mostRecentCuePoint of sprite   SPRITE PROPERTY

Syntax   `set whatCue = the mostRecentCuePoint of sprite 4`

Usage   *the mostRecentCuePoint of sprite* is a property that contains the index number of the last cue point passed during the playback of a Shockwave audio or QuickTime cast member placed in the score as a sprite.

Example   This example holds the playback in the current frame until the third cue point of the cast member in sprite channel 4 is reached:

```
on exitFrame
  if the mostRecentCuePoint of sprite 4 < 3 then
    go the frame
  end if
end
```

Parameters   the mostRecentCuePoint of sprite *integer*

Value   *integer*

See also   cuePassed, the cuePointNames of member, the cuePointTimes of member, isPastCuePoint

Video
Category

17

These Lingo properties provide information about the overall playback of digital video on the computer.

the digitalVideoTimeScale

MOVIE PROPERTY

Syntax `set the digitalVideoTimeScale = 100`

Usage *the digitalVideoTimeScale* is a system property that controls the units the system uses to measure time in digital video cast members. The value of the property sets the number of units per second used when working with digital video. The default value is 60, with each unit being equal to 1/60 of a second, or 1 tick.

> **Tip**
>
> *This is an* inverse *relationship. The lower the value of* the digitalVideoTimeScale, *the fewer units per second (and the less exact) your information about the digital video will be.*

You can use this property in combination with *the duration of member* property to determine the length of a digital video cast member. You can also set this property to different values to control the resolution of *the movieTime of sprite* property.

Example This handler returns the length of time, in seconds, of the digital video member *myDVMember*:

```
on howManySeconds myDVMember
  if the type of member myDVMember = #digitalVideo then
    set tSaveScale = the digitalVideoTimeScale
    set the digitalVideoTimeScale = 1
    set tTimeInSeconds = the duration of member myDVMember
    set the digitalVideoTimeScale = tSaveScale
    --resets property to original value
    return tTimeInSeconds
  else
    return 0
  end if
end howManySeconds
```

Value *integer*

See also the digitalVideoType of member, the duration of member, the frameRate of member, the movieRate of sprite, the movieTime of sprite, the timeScale of member

the quickTimePresent

MOVIE PROPERTY

Syntax   `set playQT = the quickTimePresent`

Usage   *the quickTimePresent* is a property that is TRUE when QuickTime is installed and available on the current system. It is FALSE otherwise. You can test but not set this property with Lingo.

Example   This code segment uses *the quickTimePresent* property to determine whether to play a digital video clip:

```
if the quickTimePresent then
  set the fileName of member "dv" = "clp.mov"
  -- The DV sprite is # 10
  set the memberNum of sprite 10  = ¬
      the number of member "dv"
  set the movieRate of sprite 10  = 1
end if
```

Value   *boolean*

See also   the controller of member, the digitalVideoType of member, the directToStage of member, the pausedAtStart of member, the quickTimePresent, the videoForWindowsPresent

the videoForWindowsPresent

MOVIE PROPERTY

Syntax   `set playAVI = the videoForWindowsPresent`

Usage   *the videoForWindowsPresent* is a property that is TRUE when Video for Windows is installed and available on the current system. It is FALSE otherwise. You can test but not set this property with Lingo.

Example   This code segment uses *the quickTimePresent* and *the videoForWindowsPresent* properties to determine which digital video clip (if any) to play. It assumes that both QuickTime and AVI file versions of the same digital video clip are present, differing only in format and file extension:

```
set vid = ""
if the quickTimePresent then set vid = "mov"
else if the videoForWindowsPresent then set vid = "avi"
if vid <> "" then
  set the fileName of member "dv" = "intro." & vid
  set the movieRate of sprite 10 = 1
  --sprite 10 uses member "dv"
end if
```

Value   *boolean*

See also   the controller of member, the digitalVideoType of member, the quickTimePresent

Video Cast Members Category

These Lingo properties and functions control cast members of the type *#digitalVideo*. Digital video cast members can be incorporated into Shockwave movies by placing them into the Shockwave support folder in the browser's plug-ins directory.

the center of member

MEMBER PROPERTY

Syntax `set isCentered = the center of member "aVideo"`

Usage *the center of member* is a property that contains a TRUE or FALSE value, corresponding to the check box labeled "center" in the Digital Video Cast Member Properties dialog box. When TRUE, the cropping rectangle of a digital video will be centered on the cast member rather than aligned with the upper left corner.

This property is used only if *the crop of member* property of the cast member is TRUE.

Example This code segment causes the digital video "chicken" to be cropped in the center only if its crop property is TRUE:

```
if the crop of member "chicken" = TRUE then
  set the center of member "chicken" = TRUE
end if
```

Parameters `the center of` *member*

Value *boolean*

See also the crop of member

the controller of member

MEMBER PROPERTY

Syntax `set isControlled = the controller of member "aVideo"`

Usage If *the controller of member* property is TRUE, the playback controls of a QuickTime digital video member are displayed.

This property only applies to QuickTime digital video. It does not affect Video for Windows movies.

The QuickTime digital video member must be playing in *directToStage* mode for the controller to be displayed.

Example   This code segment checks to see if the digital video member "cool" is a
          QuickTime movie, and displays its controller if it is:

```
if the digitalVideoType of member "cool" = ¬
    #quickTime then
  set the directToStage of member "cool" = ¬
    TRUE
  set the controller of member "cool" = TRUE
end if
```

Parameters   the controller of *member*

Value   *boolean*

See also   the digitalVideoType of member, the directToStage of member, the
           quickTimePresent, the videoForWindowsPresent

the crop of member

MEMBER PROPERTY

Syntax   `set isCropped = the crop of member "aVideo"`

Usage   *the crop of member* is a property that is a TRUE or FALSE value, correspond-
        ing to the radio buttons labeled Framing in the Digital Video Cast Member
        Properties dialog. If the size of a digital video sprite is smaller than the video
        itself, it will be cropped to the sprite's size if the property is TRUE, or scaled
        to fit the size of the sprite if the property is FALSE.

Example   This code segment causes the digital video "chicken" to be cropped in the
          center only if its crop property is TRUE:

```
if the crop of member "chicken" = TRUE then
  set the center of member "chicken" = TRUE
end if
```

Parameters   the crop of *member*

Value   *boolean*

See also   the center of member

the digitalVideoType of member

MEMBER PROPERTY

Syntax set whatType = the digitalVideoType of member "aVideo"

Usage *the digitalVideoType of member* is a property that contains information about the format of a digital video cast member. The two possible values are *#quickTime* and *#videoForWindows*. You can only test this property with Lingo.

Example This handler uses *the digitalVideoType of member* property along with *the quickTimePresent* and *the videoForWindowsPresent* to determine whether the movie *myDVMember* can be played:

```
on canIPlayDV myDVMember
  if the type of member myDVMember = #digitalVideo then
    if the digitalVideoType of member myDVMember = #quickTime AND ¬
      the quickTimePresent then
        return(TRUE)
    else if the digitalVideoType of member myDVMember = ¬
      #videoForWindows AND the videoForWindowsPresent then ¬
      return(TRUE)
    else
        return(FALSE)
    end if
  else
    return(FALSE)
  end if
end canIPlayDV
```

Parameters the digitalVideoType of *member*

Value #quickTime|#videoForWindows

See also the digitalVideoTimeScale of member, the duration of member, the frameRate of member, the movieRate of sprite, the movieTime of sprite, the timeScale of member, the type of member

the directToStage of member

MEMBER PROPERTY

Syntax `set isDirect = the directToStage of member "aVideo"`

Usage *the directToStage of member* property is TRUE if the digital video cast member will play in front of all other sprites on the stage, regardless of what sprite channel it's in. If the property is FALSE, other sprites can be layered on top of the digital video sprite.

Note: This property has no effect on Windows systems, as digital videos always play direct to stage in the Windows environment.

You can test and set this property with Lingo on the MacOS.

Example This code segment allows other sprites to appear on top of the digital video member "dv", only if the computer is a Macintosh:

```
if not(the machineType = 256) then
  -- I'm not a PC
  set the directToStage of member "dv" = FALSE
end if
```

Parameters `the directToStage of *member*`

Value *boolean*

See also the controller of member, the digitalVideoType of member, the quickTimePresent, the videoForWindowsPresent

the duration of member

MEMBER PROPERTY

Syntax `set howLong = the duration of member "trans"`

Usage *the duration of member* is a property that contains a value representing the length of time of either a digital video (#*digitalVideo*), a transition (#*transition*), or a Shockwave audio (#*SWA*) cast member.

If the cast member is a digital video cast member, the duration value is equal to the length of the movie in the units determined by the *digitalVideoTimeScale* property. If *the digitalVideoTimeScale* is set to 60, the play time of the movie is reported in ticks (1/60 of a second). If the time scale is set to 1000, the length of the movie is reported in milliseconds (1/1000 of a second).

You may test but not set this value for a digital video cast member.

Example
This *exitFrame* handler writes the percentage of completion of the digital video member in sprite 20 to a field named "howLong":

```
on exitFrame
  if the movieRate of sprite 20 = 1 then
    -- we're playing
    set tDVTime = float(the movieTime of ¬
      sprite 20)
    set tDuration = float(the duration of ¬
      member (the memberNum of sprite 20))
    set tPerc = integer(tDVTime*100/tDuration)
    if tPerc mod 5 = 0 then
      -- only update every 5%
      put string(tPerc) & "%" into ¬
        field "howLong"
    end if
  end if
  go to the frame
end exitFrame
```

Parameters
the duration of *membert*

Value
integer

See also
the digitalVideoTimeScale, the digitalVideoType of member, the frameRate of member, the movieRate of sprite, the movieTime of sprite, the timeScale of member

the frameRate of member

MEMBER PROPERTY

Syntax
set howFast = the frameRate of member 1

Usage
the frameRate of member is a property that contains the number of frames per second of a digital video cast member in its Digital Video Cast Member Properties dialog box.

This property, in conjunction with the *directToStage* property and the Video pop-up menu in the Digital Video Cast Member Properties dialog can play the movie back as fast as the computer can display the frames on the screen.

> **Note**
>
> *Results from the use of this command are, however, unpredictable and may not work in all situations.*

Parameters the frameRate of *member*

Value *integer*

See also the digitalVideoTimeScale, the digitalVideoType of member, the duration of member, the movieRate of sprite, the movieTime of sprite, the timeScale of member

the loop of member

MEMBER PROPERTY

Syntax set isLooped = the loop of member "aVideo"

Usage When *the loop of member* property is TRUE, the sound or digital video member will start playing from its beginning each time the video ends. If the property is FALSE, the movie simply ends. It has the same effect as selecting the Loop button in the Digital Video Cast Member Properties dialog box. You can test or set this property with Lingo.

Example This statement sets the loop of the digital video cast member in sprite 8 to TRUE:

set the loop of member (the memberNum of sprite 8) = TRUE

Parameters the loop of *member*

Value *boolean*

See also the sound of member, the video of member, the volume of sound

the pausedAtStart of member

MEMBER PROPERTY

Syntax   `set startsPaused = the pausedAtStart of memeber 1`

Usage   If *the pausedAtStart of member* property is TRUE, a digital video will not
automatically begin playing when it appears on the stage as a sprite. In this
case, you must send a command like *set the movieRate of sprite n = 1* to make
the movie start playing.

The default value is FALSE, which causes the digital video to begin
playing as soon as it appears.

This property has the same effect as setting the Paused button in the
Digital Video Cast Member Properties dialog.

You can test and set this property with Lingo.

Example This statement causes the digital video "dv" to be paused when it is available on the stage:

`set the pausedAtStart of member "dv" = TRUE`

Parameters `the pausedAtStart of` *member*

Value   *boolean*

See also the controller of member, the digitalVideoType of member, the directToStage
of member, the quickTimePresent, the videoForWindowsPresent

the sound of member

MEMBER PROPERTY

Syntax   `set isSoundOn = the sound of member 4`

Usage   *the sound of member* property is TRUE if the digital video or movie cast
member is set to play its sound, and FALSE otherwise. You can test and set
this property with Lingo.

This property has the same effect as setting the Sound button in the
Digital Video Cast Member Properties dialog.

Example   This statement enables the sound in the digital video clip "doodle":

    `set the sound of member "doodle" = TRUE`

Parameters   the sound of *member*

Value   *boolean*

See also   the fileName of member, the video of member

the timeScale of member   MEMBER PROPERTY

Syntax   `set whatScale = the timeScale of member "intro.mov"`

Usage   *the timeScale of member* is a property that contains the number of time units
per second that the digital video cast member was based on when it was
created. You can test but not set this property with Lingo.
    This property is independent of *the digitalVideoTimeScale* system property.
the movieTime of sprite property uses *the digitalVideoTimeScale* rather than *the
timeScale of member* to calculate the digital video's current time.

Parameters   the timeScale of *member*

Value   *integer*

See also   the digitalVideoTimeScale, the digitalVideoType of member, the duration of
member, the frameRate of member, the movieRate of sprite, the movieTime
of sprite

trackCount   FUNCTION

Syntax   `set numTracks = trackCount (member 3 of castLib 2)`

Usage   The *trackCount* function contains the number of tracks in the digital video
member *digitalVideoMember*. You can test but not set this function with Lingo.

Example   This handler returns a list that contains the track numbers of all of the sound channels in the digital video cast member *myDVMember* using *the trackCount* function:

```
on getSoundTracks myDVMember
  set tSoundTracks = []
  if the type of member myDVMember <> ¬
    #digitalVideo then return 0
  set tTracks = trackCount(member myDVMember)
  repeat with i = 1 to tTracks
    if trackType(member myDVMember, i) = #sound then
      add tSoundTracks, i
    end if
  end repeat
  return tSoundTracks
end getSoundTracks
```

Parameters   trackCount (*member*)

Value   *integer*

See also   setTrackEnabled, trackEnabled, trackStartTime, trackStopTime, trackText, trackType

trackStartTime   FUNCTION

Syntax   set whatTime = trackStartTime (member "aVideo", 2)

Usage   *trackStartTime* is a function that specifies the amount of time between the beginning of a digital video sprite and the start of data for a specific track. The time is measured in the same units as *the digitalVideoTimeScale* property.

Example   This function determines the playing time of a particular track:

```
on trackPlayTime aMember, aTrack
  set whenStart = trackStartTime (member "aVideo", aTrack)
  set whenStop = trackStopTime (member "aVideo", aTrack)
  return whenStop - whenStart
end
```

Parameters   trackStartTime (*member*, *integer*)

Value   *integer*

See also   the digitalVideoTimeScale, setTrackEnabled, trackCount, trackEnabled, trackText, trackType

trackStopTime

FUNCTION

Syntax   `set whatTime = trackStopTime (member "aVideo", 2)`

Usage   The trackStopTime function specifies the amount of time between the beginning of a digital video sprite and the end of data for a specific track. The time is measured in the same units as *the digitalVideoTimeScale* property.

Example   See the Example for *trackStartTime*.

Parameters   `trackStopTime (`*member*`, `*integer*`)`

Value   *integer*

See also   the digitalVideoTimeScale, setTrackEnabled, trackCount, trackEnabled, trackText, trackType

trackType

FUNCTION

Syntax   `set aType = trackType (member 4 of castLib 3, 4)`

Usage   The *trackType* function returns a symbol value that allows you to determine the type of media contained in the specified track of a digital video cast member.

Most standard digital video cast members have a video track as track 1 and an audio track as track 2. Many other types of media can be embedded into QuickTime video, including text, MIDI, and so on, and it's often necessary to determine which is which.

Example : This statement puts the symbol identifying what type of media is contained in track 1 of the digital video sprite "anarchy.mov" into the Message window:

```
put trackType(member "anarchy.mov", 1)
```

Parameters : trackType (*member*, *integer*)

Value : *symbol*

See also : setTrackEnabled, trackCount, trackEnabled, trackStartTime, trackStopTime, trackText

the video of member

MEMBER PROPERTY

Syntax : `set showVideo = the video of member "Judy"`

Usage : *the video of member* is a property that controls the display of the video tracks of a digital video cast member. If TRUE, the video will be displayed; if FALSE, only the audio components will play.

This property has the same effect as setting the Video button in the Digital Video Cast Member Properties dialog.

Example : This handler toggles the display of the video in the digital video clip "Bella":

```
on mouseUp
  set the video of member "Bella" = ¬
    not(the video of member "Bella")
end mouseUp
```

Parameters : `the video of` *member*

Value : *boolean*

See also : the fileName of member, the sound of member

Video Sprites Category

19

These Lingo keywords control the appearance of digital video on the stage.

the movieRate of sprite

SPRITE PROPERTY

Syntax
```
set the movieRate of sprite gDV = .75
```

Usage
the movieRate of sprite is a property that determines the speed at which a digital video sprite plays. Common values include **1** - normal playback, **0** - stopped, **-1** - playing at normal speed in reverse. Other variations are possible, including floating-point values. A value of **0.5** plays the movie at 1/2 speed.

You can test and set this property with Lingo.

If the digital video sprite is not set to loop, and plays through to the end, its *movieRate of sprite* property changes to 0, stopping the movie.

Example
This handler, when attached to a digital video sprite, causes a pause/play action:

```
on mouseDown
  if the movieRate of sprite ¬
    (the clickOn) = 1 then
    set the movieRate of sprite ¬
      (the clickOn) = 0
  else
    set the movieRate of sprite ¬
      (the clickOn) = 1
  end if
end mouseDown
```

Parameters
`the movieRate of sprite` *integer*

Value
float

See also
the digitalVideoTimeScale of member, the duration of member, the frameRate of member, framesToHMS, HMStoFrames, the movieTime of sprite, the timeScale of member, the type of member

the movieTime of sprite

SPRITE PROPERTY

Syntax   `set the movieTime of sprite gDV = 0`

Usage   *the movieTime of sprite* is a property that determines what part of the current digital video is displayed on the stage. The units used by this value are determined by *the digitalVideoTimeScale*. If *the digitalVideoTimeScale* is 60 (its default value), *the movieTime of sprite* contains the position within the digital video in ticks.

You can test and set this property with Lingo.

Example   This *exitFrame* handler causes the digital video member in sprite 20 to loop between the 5-second and 15-second point in the movie. *the digitalVideoTimeScale* is set to 60 units, so there are 60 *movieTime* units per second:

```
on exitFrame
  if the movieRate of sprite 20 = 0 OR ¬
  the movieTime of sprite 20 >= 15 * 60 then
  set the movieTime of sprite 20 = 5 * 60
  set the movieRate of sprite 20 = 1
  end if
  go to the frame
end exitFrame
```

Parameters   `the movieRate of sprite` *integer*

Value   *integer*

See also   the digitalVideoTimeScale, the digitalVideoType of member, the duration of member, the frameRate of member, the movieRate of sprite, the timeScale of member

setTrackEnabled

COMMAND

Syntax   setTrackEnabled (sprite gDV, 2, FALSE)

Usage   The *setTrackEnabled* command lets you control playback of tracks in a digital
            video. Setting the property to FALSE disables the track during playback.
                Tracks are enabled and disabled at the sprite level. It is possible to use the
            same digital video cast member for two different sprites and have different
            tracks of each enabled or disabled.

Example   This example disables all *#sound* tracks for digital video sprite *gDV*:

```
repeat with i = 1 to trackCount (sprite gDV)
  if trackType (sprite gDV, i) = #sound then ¬
    setTrackEnabled (sprite gDV, i, FALSE)
end repeat
```

Parameters setTrackEnabled (sprite *integer*, *integer*, *boolean*)

See also   trackCount, trackEnabled, trackNextKeyTime, trackNextSampleTime,
            trackPreviousKeyTime, trackPreviousSampleTime, trackStartTime,
            trackStopTime, trackText, trackType

trackCount

FUNCTION

Syntax   set howMany = trackCount (sprite 5)

Usage   See *trackCount* in Chapter 18.

Parameters trackCount (sprite *integer*)

Value   *integer*

See also   setTrackEnabled, trackEnabled, trackNextKeyTime, trackNextSampleTime,
            trackPreviousKeyTime, trackPreviousSampleTime, trackStartTime,
            trackStopTime, trackText, trackType

trackEnabled

FUNCTION

Syntax   `set isEnabled = trackEnabled (sprite gDV, 2)`

Usage   The *trackEnabled* function returns TRUE if the specified track of a digital video sprite is enabled to play. If you wish to enable or disable a digital video track, use the *setTrackEnabled* command.

Example   This code segment tests and enables all of the tracks of digital video sprite *gDV*:

```
repeat with i = 1 to trackCount (gDV)
  if not trackEnabled (sprite gDV, i) then ¬
     setTrackEnabled (sprite gDV, i, TRUE)
end repeat
```

Parameters   `trackEnabled (sprite integer, integer)`

Value   *integer*

See also   setTrackEnabled, trackCount, trackStartTime, trackStopTime, trackText, trackType

trackNextKeyTime

FUNCTION

Syntax   `set nextKeyAt = trackNextKeyTime (sprite 1, 3)`

Usage   The *trackNextKeyTime* function returns a value showing where the next key frame of a specific track in a digital video appears. The value is expressed in units determined by the value of the movie property *the digitalVideoTimeScale,* and is relative to the beginning of the movie. The key frame sampled is the first one following the current position of the digital video, as determined by *the movieTime of sprite* property.

Example   This example determines the number of milliseconds remaining until the
next key frame in track 1 of sprite *gDV*:

```
on exitFrame
  set the digitalVideoTimeScale = 1000
  --sets time units to 1/1000 of a second
  set timeToNextKey = trackNextKeyTime (sprite gDV, 1) - ¬
    the movietime of sprite gDV
  put timeToNextKey into field "milliseconds"
end
```

Parameters   trackNextKeyTime (sprite *integer*, *string*)

Value   *integer*

See also   digitalVideoTimeScale, setTrackEnabled, trackCount, trackEnabled,
trackNextSampleTime, trackPreviousKeyTime, trackPreviousSampleTime,
trackStartTime, trackStopTime, trackText, trackType

trackNextSampleTime

FUNCTION

Syntax   set nextFrame = trackNextSampleTime (sprite 2, 1)

Usage   The *trackNextSampleTime* function returns a value indicating the position in
the movie of the next sample of the specified track in a movie. For a video
track, each frame is a sample. An audio track will have thousands of samples
per second. A text track may have only one or two samples during the length
of the movie. Essentially, each time the track changes, a new sample is
generated.

The value returned is relative to the beginning of the movie and is
expressed in units determined by *the digitalVideoTimeScale* property. The
sample reported is the one immediately following the position of the portion
of the movie being played, as expressed by *the movieTime*.

Example   This example displays the sampling times of the media in track 1 of sprite
gDV:

```
on exitFrame
  set the digitalVideoTimeScale = 1000
  --sets time units to 1/1000 of a second
put trackNextSampleTime (sprite gDV, 1) into ¬
  field "milliseconds"
end
```

For a 10-frame-per-second digital video, with *the digitalVideoTimeScale* set to 1000, the above script displays values in the sequence 100, 200, 300, etc.

Parameters
```
trackNextSampleTime (sprite integer, integer)
```

Value *integer*

See also digitalVideoTimeScale, setTrackEnabled, trackCount, trackEnabled, trackNextKeyTime, trackPreviousKeyTime, trackPreviousSampleTime, trackStartTime, trackStopTime, trackText, trackType

trackPreviousKeyTime
FUNCTION

Syntax
```
set lastKeyAt = trackNextKeyTime (sprite 1, 3)
```

Usage The *trackPreviousKeyTime* function returns a value showing where the last key frame of a specific track in a digital video appeared. The value is expressed in units determined by the value of the movie property *the digitalVideoTimeScale*. It is relative to the beginning of the movie. The key frame sampled is the current frame or the one immediately preceding the current position of the digital video, as determined by *the movieTime of sprite* property.

Example This example determines the number of milliseconds elapsed since the last key frame in track 1 of sprite *gDV*:

```
on exitFrame
  set the digitalVideoTimeScale = 1000
  --sets time units to 1/1000 of a second
  set timeFromLastKey = the movietime of sprite gDV - ¬
    trackPreviousKeyTime (sprite gDV, 1)
  put timeFromLastKey Into field "milliseconds"
end
```

Parameters
```
timeFromLastKey (sprite integer, string)
```

Value *integer*

See also digitalVideoTimeScale, setTrackEnabled, trackCount, trackEnabled, trackNextKeyTime, trackNextSampleTime, trackPreviousSampleTime, trackStartTime, trackStopTime, trackText, trackType

trackPreviousSampleTime

Syntax   `set lastFrame = trackPreviousSampleTime (sprite 2, 1)`

Usage   The *trackPreviousSampleTime* function returns a value indicating the position
          in the movie of the last sample of the specified track. The value returned is
          relative to the beginning of the movie, and is expressed in units determined
          by *the digitalVideoTimeScale* property. The sample reported is the one immedi-
          ately preceding the position of the portion of the movie being played, as
          expressed by *the movieTime*.

Example   This example displays the sampling times of the media in track 1 of sprite
          gDV:

```
on exitFrame
  set the digitalVideoTimeScale = 1000
  --sets time units to 1/1000 of a second
put trackNextSampleTime (sprite gDV, 1) into ¬
  field "milliseconds"
end
```

          For a 10-frame-per-second digital video, with *the digitalVideoTimeScale* set
          to 1000, the above script displays values in the sequence 100, 200, 300, and
          so on.

Parameters `trackNextSampleTime (sprite integer, integer)`

Value   *integer*

See also   digitalVideoTimeScale, setTrackEnabled, trackCount, trackEnabled,
          trackNextKeyTime, trackPreviousKeyTime, trackPreviousSampleTime,
          trackStartTime, trackStopTime, trackText, trackType

trackStartTime

FUNCTION

Syntax   set whatTime = trackStartTime (sprite gDV, 1)

Usage   This function operates on sprites in the same manner it operated for cast members. See Chapter 18.

Parameters   trackStartTime (sprite *integer*, *integer*)

Value   *integer*

See also   the digitalVideoTimeScale, setTrackEnabled, trackCount, trackEnabled, trackText, trackType

trackStopTime

FUNCTION

Syntax   set whatTime = trackStopTime (sprite gDV, 1)

Usage   This function operates on sprites in the same manner it operated for cast members. See Chapter 18.

Parameters   trackStopTime (sprite *integer*, *integer*)

Value   *integer*

See also   the digitalVideoTimeScale, setTrackEnabled, trackCount, trackEnabled, trackText, trackType

trackText

FUNCTION

Syntax
: `set videoText = trackText (sprite 3, 2)`

Usage
: The *trackText* function returns the text in the specified track of the digital video sprite if the track is a text track. You can test but not set this property with Lingo.

Example
: This statement puts the text contained in track 3 of the digital video sprite 13 into field "dvtxt":

`put trackText (sprite 10, 3) into field "dvtxt"`

Parameters
: `trackText (sprite *integer*, *string*)`

Value
: `*string*`

See also
: setTrackEnabled, trackCount, trackEnabled, trackStartTime, trackStopTime, trackType

trackType

FUNCTION

Syntax
: `set whatType (sprite 2, 4)`

Usage
: The *trackType* function works for sprites as it does for cast members. See the entry in Chapter 18.

Parameters
: `trackType (sprite *integer*, *string*)`

Value
: `#video|#sound|#text|#music`

See also
: setTrackEnabled, trackCount, trackEnabled, trackStartTime, trackStopTime, trackText

the volume of sprite

SPRITE PROPERTY

Syntax   `set the volume of sprite gDV = 128`

Usage   *the volume of sprite* is a property that contains a number from 0 (no sound) to 255 (maximum), which controls the volume of the sound in a digital video sprite. You can test and set this property with Lingo.

While this property gives you fine control over the volume of sound in a digital video cast member, it is still limited by *the soundLevel* system property, which controls the overall sound output from Director.

Example   This statement makes the sound in the digital video clip in sprite 25 play as loud as possible:

`set the volume of sprite 25 = 255`

Parameters   `the volume of sprite` *integer*

Value   *integer*

See also   the fileName of member, the sound of member, the soundLevel, the video of member

Sound
Category

These Lingo keywords determine capabilities and control of sounds in Director movies.

beep

See entry for *beep* in Chapter 9.

the beepOn

See entry for *the beepOn* in Chapter 9.

the channelCount of member

Syntax
```
set howMany = the channelCount of member "soundtrack"
```

Usage   *the channelCount of member* is a property that determines if the specified sound cast member is monaural or stereo.

This property does not work properly with Shockwave audio. You should use *the numChannels of member* property when testing the number of channels of an SWA cast member.

Example   This function tests whether a sound cast member is of the type #*sound* or #*SWA,* then uses the appropriate property to determine the number of sound channels:

```
on findChannels aSound
  set aType = the type of member aSound
  case aType of
    #sound: return the channelCount of member aSound
    #SWA: return the numChannels of member aSound
  end case
end
```

Parameters   the channelCount of *member*

Value   1|2

See also   the numChannels of member

the currentTime of sprite

SPRITE PROPERTY

Syntax `set howMuchPlayed = the currentTime of sprite gSWA`

Usage *the currentTime of sprite* is a property that reveals how much of a sound sprite (such as a Shockwave audio) or QuickTime digital video sprite has played. The value is in milliseconds. Unlike *the movieTime of sprite*, this value cannot be set to change the portion of the digital video or sound that is being played.

Example This handler displays how much of sound sprite *gSWA* remains to be played:

```
on exitFrame
  set howLong = integer (the duration of member ¬
    (the memberNum of sprite gSWA) * 1000)
  --duration of SWA member is a float in seconds
  --we convert to integer value of milliseconds
  set hmLeft = howLong - the currentTime of sprite gSWA
  put string (hmLeft) && "seconds left" into field "left"
end
```

Parameters `the currentTime of sprite` *integer*

Value *integer*

See also the digitalVideoTimeScale, the duration of member, the duration of sprite, the movieTime of sprite, the percentPlayed of member

the duration of member

MEMBER PROPERTY

Syntax `set howLong = the duration of member "background"`

Usage *the duration of member* is a property that contains a value representing the length of time of either a digital video (*#digitalVideo*), a transition (*#transition*), or a Shockwave audio (*#SWA*) cast member.

If the cast member is a Shockwave audio cast member, *the duration of member* property is its total play time in seconds, reported as a floating-point number. The property is only available after the Shockwave audio has been buffered in RAM (see the example below).

You may test but not set this value for a Shockwave audio cast member.

Example
This code segment demonstrates the steps that need to take place before *the duration of member* property returns anything other than 0. These steps may have other commands between them, but this is the minimum sequence that must be carried out:

```
set the URL of member "science" = "science.swa"
-- this can also be set before the movie is saved, in the
-- SWA Cast Member Properties dialog (press the Options
-- button in the Xtra Cast Member Properties dialog
preloadBuffer member "science"
-- wait for the buffer to take place
set playLength = the duration of member "science"
```

Parameters
the duration of *member*

Value
float

See also
the digitalVideoTimeScale, the digitalVideoType of member, the frameRate of member, the movieRate of sprite, the movieTime of sprite, the timeScale of member.

the multiSound

MOVIE PROPERTY

Syntax
`set isMulti = the multiSound`

Usage
the multiSound is a property that is TRUE if the current computer can play more than one sound channel at a time.

Example
This code segment allows a mouse-click sound to play in sound channel 2, in addition to the loop that is currently playing in sound channel 1, only if *the multiSound* property is TRUE:

```
if the multiSound then
    puppetSound 2, "mouse click"
end if
```

Value   *boolean*

See also puppetSound, soundBusy, the soundEnabled, the soundLevel, sound close, sound fadeIn, sound fadeOut, sound playFile, sound stop, the volume of sound

puppetSound

COMMAND

Syntax   puppetSound "science"

puppetsound FALSE

puppetSound 3, member 1 of castLib 2

puppetsound 3, FALSE

Usage   The *puppetSound* command gives you control of the sound channels with Lingo. On most computers, you are able to control up to four channels with *puppetSound*: the two that appear in the score as well as two others. It is possible to control more than four sound channels on some computers.

You may specify the audio cast member by its name or member reference. An optional parameter allows you to specify which sound channel to use for playback. (Sounds imported as linked media always play in sound channel 1, even if assigned to another channel.)

> **Tip**
>
> *To stop playback of a puppeted sound and return control of sound channels to the score, use the value 0 or FALSE instead of an audio cast member.*

Example   This command plays the sound in the cast member named "click" in sound channel 2:

puppetSound 2, "click"

Parameters puppetSound *member|string*

puppetSound *integer, member|string*

See also the sampleRate of member, the sampleSize of member, sound fadeIn, sound fadeOut, sound playFile, sound stop

the sampleRate of member

Syntax   `set rate = the sampleRate of member "soundtrack"`

Usage   *the sampleRate of member* is a property that contains information about the sampling rate of the data in a sound cast member. The usual values for this property are even divisors of the audio CD sampling rate 44,100 samples per second. This property can only be tested.

Parameters   `the sampleRate of` *member*

Value   `44100|22050|11025` (*other rates may be in use with MacOS sounds*)

See also   the bitRate of member, the duration of member, the sampleSize of member

the sampleSize of member

Syntax   `set howDeep = the sampleSize of member "soundtrack"`

Usage   *the sampleSize of member* is a property that reveals the number of bits used to sample a sound wave for each sampling point of a cast member of the type *#sound*. This property can only be tested.

Parameters   `the sampleSize of` *member*

Value   `8|16`

See also   the bitRate of member, the duration of member, the sampleRate of member

sound close

COMMAND

Syntax	`sound close 2`
Usage	The *sound close* command stops the sound playing in the specified sound channel.
Example	This command stops the sound that was playing in sound channel 2 and closes the channel:
	`sound close 2`
Parameters	`sound close 1|2`
See also	puppetSound, sound fadeIn, sound fadeOut, sound playFile, sound stop, soundBusy, soundEnabled, soundLevel, the volume of sound

sound fadeIn

COMMAND

Syntax	`sound fadeIn 4`
	`sound fadeIn 2, 15`
Usage	The *sound fadeIn* command fades a sound in the specified channel from silence to full volume (as determined by *the volume of sound*) over a period of time. The default fade period is equal to the time equivalent of 15 frames, as determined by the movie's current tempo (i.e., a movie with a tempo of 15 will have a default fade period of 1 second; a tempo of 30 results in a 1/2-second fade, etc.).
	The optional second parameter allows you to specify a fade period, in ticks. This command does not work on puppeted sounds or Shockwave audio.

Tip

A sound fadeIn command is typically placed in a frame script of the frame that precedes the frame in which the sound appears in the score. If you want to fade in a sound beginning in frame 10, place your sound fadeIn script in the script for frame 9.

Example This statement causes the sound in sound channel 2 to fade in over a period of 2 seconds:

```
on exitFrame
  sound fadeIn 2, 2 * 60
end exitFrame
```

Parameters sound fadeIn *integer*

sound fadeIn *integer*, *integer*

See also puppetSound, sound close, sound fadeOut, sound playFile, sound stop, soundBusy, soundEnabled, soundLevel, the volume of sound

sound fadeOut

COMMAND

Syntax sound fadeOut 2

sound fadeOut 2, 15

Usage The *sound fadeOut* command fades a sound in the specified channel from its current volume to silence over a period of time. The default fade period is equal to the time equivalent of 15 frames, as determined by the movie's current tempo (i.e., a movie with a tempo of 15 will have a default fade period of 1 second; a tempo of 30 results in a 1/2-second fade, etc.).

The optional second parameter allows you to specify a fade period, in ticks.

This command does not work on puppeted sounds or Shockwave audio.

Example This statement causes the sound in sound channel 2 to fade in over a period of 8 seconds:

```
on exitFrame
  sound fadeOut 2, 8 * 60
end exitFrame
```

Parameters sound fadeOut *integer*

sound fadeOut *integer*, *integer*

See also puppetSound, sound close, sound fadeIn, sound playFile, sound stop, soundBusy, soundEnabled, soundLevel, the volume of sound

sound playFile
COMMAND

Syntax   `sound playFile "soundtrack.aif"`

`sound playFile 4, "http://www.surftrio.com/soundtrack.wav"`

Usage   The *sound playFile* command plays an AIFF or WAV sound file in a sound channel. If no sound channel is specified, the sound plays in sound channel 1. The file path parameter must contain the full name of the file, including any extension.

While it is possible for *sound playFile* to play a sound from a URL address, it is recommended that you download the sound to a local directory before play begins.

This command does not work with internal sound cast members or Shockwave audio files. Use the *puppetSound* command to play internal sounds, and use the *play member* command to play SWA files.

Shockwave movies can access external sound files in the plug-in support directory with the *sound playfile* command.

Example   This command plays the file "talk.wav," which is located in the same folder as the movie, or in the plug-in support folder if played from a Shockwave movie. The sound plays in sound channel 1:

`sound playFile 1, "talk.wav"`

Parameters   `sound playfile string`

`sound playfile integer, string`

See also   puppetSound, sound close, sound fadeIn, sound fadeOut, sound stop, soundBusy, soundEnabled, soundLevel, the volume of sound

sound stop
COMMAND

Syntax   `sound stop 4`

Usage   The *sound stop* command makes the sound in the specified channel stop playing.

This command can stop internal sounds played using the *puppetSound* command, as well as SWA files, but it is recommended that you use the *puppetSound 0* and *stop member* commands instead.

Example   This handler checks to see if a sound channel is busy and stops the sound if it is:

```
on stopChannel whatChannel
  if soundBusy (whatChannel) then sound stop whatChannel
end
```

Parameters   sound stop *integer*

See also   puppetSound, sound close, sound fadeIn, sound fadeOut, sound playFile, soundBusy, soundEnabled, soundLevel, the volume of sound

soundBusy

FUNCTION

Syntax   set isBusy = soundBusy (4)

Usage   The *soundBusy* function returns TRUE if a sound is currently playing in the specified sound channel, and FALSE otherwise.

Example   This handler waits for sound channel 1 to become available, then plays another sound:

```
on exitFrame
  if soundBusy(1) then
    go to the frame
  else
    puppetSound "opera"
    go to the frame + 1
  end if
end exitFrame
```

Parameters   soundBusy (*integer*)

Value   *boolean*

See also   puppetSound, sound close, sound fadeIn, sound fadeOut, sound playFile, sound stop, soundEnabled, soundLevel, the volume of sound

the soundEnabled

MOVIE PROPERTY

Syntax
set the soundEnabled = FALSE

Usage
the soundEnabled is a property that is TRUE if the sound is turned on, and FALSE if it is turned off. You can test and set this property with Lingo. This property does not affect the value of any volume-setting properties such as *the soundLevel* and *the volume of sound*.

Setting this property to FALSE will stop all sound playback in the movie. Sounds will not resume playing simply by setting *the soundEnabled* to TRUE.

Example
This handler toggles the sound on or off when the sprite it's attached to is clicked:

```
on mouseUp
  set the soundEnabled = not(the soundEnabled)
end mouseUp
```

Value
boolean

See also
puppetSound, sound close, sound fadeIn, sound fadeOut, sound playFile, sound stop, soundBusy, soundLevel, the volume of sound

the soundLevel

MOVIE PROPERTY

Syntax
set the soundLevel = 4

Usage
the soundLevel is a property which contains a value that determines the volume of all sound playing through the computer's speaker. The value can be from 0 (no sound) to 7 (loudest). It can be used to simultaneously alter all playing sounds.

Example
This statement sets the system volume to the maximum level:

```
set the soundLevel = 7
```

Value
0|1|2|3|4|5|6|7

See also
puppetSound, sound close, sound fadeIn, sound fadeOut, sound playFile, sound stop, soundBusy, soundEnabled, the volume of sound

the volume of sound

Syntax set the volume of sound = 128

Usage *the volume of sound* is a property that contains a number from 0 (no sound) to 255 (loudest), representing the volume of the sound in the specified channel. You can test and set this property with Lingo.

While this property gives you fine control over the volume of sound in a sound channel, it is limited by *the soundLevel* system property, which controls the overall sound output from Director.

Digital video sprite volume is modified by *the volume of sprite* property. Shockwave audio sound volume should be controlled with *the volume of member* property.

Example This statement sets the volume of the sound in channel 2 to the maximum volume:

set the volume of sound 2 = 255

Parameters the volume of sound *integer*

Value *integer*

See also puppetSound, sound close, sound fadeIn, sound fadeOut, sound playFile, sound stop, soundBusy, soundEnabled, the volume of sprite

Shockwave Audio Category

21

These commands and properties operate on streaming Shockwave Audio (SWA) cast members.

the bitRate of member

MEMBER PROPERTY

Syntax
```
set howFast = the bitRate of member "soundtrack"
```

Usage
the bitRate of member is a property that represents the data transfer rate needed to sustain the Shockwave audio file associated with a #*SWA* type of cast member. You can test but not set this property with Lingo. Possible values are 8000, 16000, 24000, 32000, 48000, 56000, 64000, 80000, 112000, 128000, and 160000.

> ### Tip
>
> *The settings for SWA files represent* bits per second. *Most operations and file size measurements in Director are in* kilobytes (1K = 1024 bytes = 8192 bits). *The size of an SWA file compressed the maximum amount (bitRate of member = 8000) will be roughly 1K for every second of playback time. A three-minute streaming audio file will be about 180K at maximum compression.*

Example
This statement sends the *bitRate* to a field called "bit rate":
```
put the bitRate of member "swa" into field "bit rate"
```

Parameters
```
the bitRate of member
```

Value
```
integer
```

See also
the duration of member, getError, getErrorString, preLoadTime, preLoadBuffer, pause, the percentStreamed of member, the percentPlayed of member, play(member swaMember), the state of member, stop, the URL of member

the bitsPerSample of member

MEMBER PROPERTY

Syntax	`set howDeep = the bitsPerSample of member "soundtrack"`
Usage	*the bitsPerSample of member* is a property that reveals information about the quality of the Shockwave Audio file associated with the specified cast member. This property can only be tested, and only after the SWA file has been preloaded or begun play.
Parameters	`the bitsPerSample of` *member*
Value	`8|16`
See also	the bitRate of member, the duration of member, getError, getErrorString, pause member, the percentStreamed of member, playmember, [preLoadTime], [preLoadBuffer], the state of member, stop member, the URL of member

the copyrightInfo of member

MEMBER PROPERTY

Syntax	`set whatCop = the copyrightInfo of member "soundtrack"`
Usage	*the copyrightInfo of member* is a property that contains a string with information about the Shockwave audio file associated with the specified member. The string can be embedded into the sound file with Macromedia's SoundEdit Pro.
Parameters	`the copyrightInfo of` *member*
Value	*string*
See also	the bitRate of member, the duration of member, getError, getErrorString, pause member, the percentStreamed of member, playmember, preLoadTime, preLoadBuffer, the state of member, stop member, the URL of member

the numChannels of member

Syntax `set howManyChannels = the numChannels of member "soundtrack"`

Usage *the numChannels of member* is a property that contains information about whether a Shockwave audio file is monophonic (1) or stereo (2). This property can only be tested, and only after the SWA file has been preloaded or has begun to play.

Parameters `the numChannels of` *member*

Value `1|2`

See also the bitRate of member, the duration of member, getError, getErrorString, pause member, the percentStreamed of member, playmember, preLoadTime, preLoadBuffer, the state of member, stop member, the URL of member

pause member

Syntax `pause member "soundtrack"`

Usage The *pause member* command pauses the Shockwave audio (SWA) file associated with the specified cast member.

Before you can issue the *pause member* command, you must assign a valid SWA file to the cast member by setting *the URL of member* property.

Parameters `pause` *member*

See also the bitRate of member, the duration of member, getError, getErrorString, play member, the percentStreamed of member, the percentPlayed of member, preLoadTime, preLoadBuffer, the state of member, stop member, the URL of member

the percentPlayed of member

Syntax   `set howMuchLeft = 100 - the percentPlayed of member "bark"`

Usage   *the percentPlayed of member* is a property that contains a floating-point value representing the percentage of the sound file that has played. You can test but not set this property with Lingo.

　　　　If the value of *the percentPlayed of member* property gets too close to *the percentStreamed of member*, then the sound will stop playing until more of the file is streamed. This can happen if the network connection is too slow.

Example   This *exitFrame* handler displays a status message if the sound is close to cutting out. It is useful for developers who wish to test SWA playback:

```
on exitFrame
  if the state of member "swa" = 3 then
    -- we're playing
    if the percentStreamed of member "swa" <= ¬
      (the percentPlayed of member "swa" + 0.2) then
      put "sound cutout" into field "status"
    else
      put "playing" into field "status"
    end if
  end if
  go to the frame
end exitFrame
```

Parameters   `the percentPlayed of` *member*

Value   *float*

See also   the bitRate of member, the duration of member, getError, getErrorString, pause member, the percentStreamed of member, playmember, preLoadTime, preLoadBuffer, the state of member, stop member, the URL of member

the percentStreamed of member

MEMBER PROPERTY

Syntax   set howMuchReceived = the percentStreamed of member 16

Usage   *the percentStreamed of member* is a property that contains a value representing how much of a streaming Shockwave audio file has been received. This amount is a percentage, shown as a floating-point value. You can test but not set this property with Lingo.

Example   This statement displays the streamed percentage of the Shockwave audio file referenced by the cast member "swa":

    put the percentStreamed of member "swa" into ¬
       field "percent streamed"

Parameters   the percentStreamed of *member*

Value   *float*

See also   the bitRate of member, the duration of member, getError, getErrorString, pause member, the percentPlayed of member, play member, preLoadTime, preLoadBuffer, the state of member, stop member, the URL of member

play member

COMMAND

Syntax   play member "soundtrack"

Usage   The *play member* command begins playback of a Shockwave audio (SWA) file associated with a cast member's *URL* property. It also resumes playback of a file that has been momentarily stopped with the *pause member* command.

    Before you can issue the *play member* command, you must assign a valid SWA file to the cast member by setting *the URL of member* property.

Example   This code segment plays the SWA file in member "swa", after its *URL* has
been set and *the preLoadTime* has been set to 10 seconds.

```
set the URL of member "swa" = "forcal.swa"
set the preLoadTime of member "swa" = 10
play member "swa"
```

Parameters   play *member*

See also   the bitRate of member, the duration of member, getError, getErrorString,
pause member, the percentStreamed of member, the percentPlayed of
member, preLoadTime, preLoadBuffer, the state of member, stop member,
the URL of member

preLoadBuffer member   COMMAND

Syntax   preLoadBuffer member "soundtrack"

Usage   The *preLoadBuffer member* command loads a portion of a Shockwave audio
file associated with the specified cast member into memory. The number of
seconds to be preloaded is controlled by *the preLoadTime of member* property.
   Before you can issue the *preLoadBuffer member* command, you must assign
a valid SWA file to the cast member *whichSWAMember* by setting *the URL of
member* property.

Example   This code segment preloads the first five seconds of the SWA file
"soundtrack.swa":

```
set the URL of member "swa" = ¬
  "http://www.surftrio.com/soundtrack.swa"
set the preLoadTime of member "swa" = 5
preLoadBuffer member "swa"
```

Parameters   preLoadBuffer *member*

See also   the bitRate of member, the duration of member, getError, getErrorString,
pause member, the percentStreamed of member, the percentPlayed of
member, play member, preLoadTime, the state of member, stop member, the
URL of member

the preLoadTime of member

MEMBER PROPERTY

Syntax   `set the preLoadTime of member "soundtrack" = 4`

Usage   *the preLoadTime of member* is a property that determines how many seconds of a Shockwave audio file will be loaded from a URL before play begins, or the amount that will load with the *preLoadBuffer* command.

Example See the example for *preLoadBuffer*.

Parameters   `the preLoadTime of member`

Value   *integer*

See also the bitRate of member, the duration of member, getError, getErrorString, pause member, the percentStreamed of member, the percentPlayed of member, play member, preLoadBuffer, the state of member, stop member, the URL of member

the sampleRate of member

MEMBER PROPERTY

Syntax   `set rate = the sampleRate of member "soundtrack"`

Usage   *the sampleRate of member* is a property that contains information about the sampling rate of the data in a Shockwave audio file. The usual values for this property are even divisors of the audio CD sampling rate: 44100 samples per second. This property can only be tested, and only after the SWA file has been preloaded or has begun to play.

Parameters   `the sampleRate of member`

Value   `44100|22050|11025`

See also the bitRate of member, the duration of member, getError, getErrorString, pause member, the percentStreamed of member, play member, preLoadTime, preLoadBuffer, the state of member, stop member, the URL of member

the soundChannel of member

MEMBER PROPERTY

Syntax `set whatChannel = the soundChannel of member "soundtrack"`

Usage *the soundChannel of member* is a property that determines the sound channel a Shockwave audio file will play back in. The number of sound channels each computer can support varies from machine to machine. MacOS systems can support up to eight simultaneous sound channels, and most Windows systems can support four, although newer models may support more.

Setting *the soundChannel of member* to 0 assigns the sound to the highest-numbered available sound channel when it begins playing.

Parameters `the soundChannel of` *member*

Value *integer*

See also the bitRate of member, the duration of member, getError, getErrorString, pause member, the percentStreamed of member, play member, preLoadTime, preLoadBuffer, the state of member, stop member, the URL of member

the state of member

MEMBER PROPERTY

Syntax `set whatsHappeningSWA = the state of member "soundtrack"`

Usage *the state of member* is a property that contains a value representing the current state of the Shockwave audio file associated with a *#SWA* cast member. You can test but not set this property with Lingo.

The following values are the various states of a Shockwave audio file:

- **0**   Stopped
- **1**   preloading
- **2**   preloading complete
- **3**   Playing
- **4**   Paused
- **5**   Done
- **9**   Error
- **10** Insufficient CPU.

Examples   This handler implements a pause/play toggle button for a SWA file:

```
on mouseUp
  if the state of member "swa" = 3 then
    pause member "swa"
  else
    play member "swa"
  end if
end mouseUp
```

Parameters   `the state of` *member*

Value   `0|1|2|3|4|5|9|10`

See also   the bitRate of member, the duration of member, getError, getErrorString, preLoadTime, preLoadBuffer, pause(member swaMember), the percentStreamed of member, the percentPlayed of member, play(member swaMember), stop(member swaMember), the URL of member

stop member   COMMAND

Syntax   `stop member "soundtrack"`

Usage   The *stop member* command stops playback of a Shockwave audio file associated with the specified cast member. If you want the SWA file to stop playing but not return to the beginning, use the *pause member* command.

Parameters   `stop` *member*

See also   the bitRate of member, the duration of member, getError, getErrorString, pause member, the percentStreamed of member, the percentPlayed of member, play member, preLoadTime, preLoadBuffer, the state of member, the URL of member

the streamName of member

MEMBER PROPERTY

the streamName of member property is interchangable with *the URL of member* property (see next entry).

the URL of member

MEMBER PROPERTY

Syntax
```
set the URL of member "swa" = ¬
    "http://www.surftrio.com/safari.swa"
```

Usage
the URL of member is a property that contains the Internet path and filename of the Shockwave audio file associated with the cast member.

The URL can be either an absolute or relative path to the SWA file. The SWA file itself may be located on a server or, if the projector or Shockwave movie is running from the user's hard drive, a local drive.

Examples
This statement sets the URL of the SWA cast member "swa" to a certain .swa file using an absolute reference:

```
set the URL of member "swa" = ¬
    "http://www.surftrio.com/safari.swa"
```

This statement sets the URL of the SWA cast member "swa" to a relative reference, assuming the file is in the same directory as the movie using this statement:

```
set the url of member "swa" = "song.swa"
```

Parameters
the URL of *member*

Value
string

See also
the bitRate of member, the duration of member, getError, getErrorString, pause member, the percentStreamed of member, the percentPlayed of member, play member, preLoadTime, the state of member, stop member

the volume of member

MEMBER PROPERTY

Syntax
```
set the volume of member "swa" = 255
```

Usage
the volume of member is a property that controls the volume of a Shockwave audio sound. Possible values range from 0 (minimum) to 255 (maximum).

Example
This example fades in an SWA sound over a period of five seconds.
```
on fadeInSWA
  starttimer
  repeat while the timer < 300
    set the volume of member "soundtrack" = ¬
      the timer / 300
  end repeat
  set the volume of member "soundtrack" = 255
end fadeInSWA
```

Parameters
the volume of *member*

Value
integer

See also
the bitRate of member, the duration of member, getError, getErrorString, pause member, the percentStreamed of member, the percentPlayed of member, play member, preLoadTime, the state of member, stop member

Sprites Category

These Lingo keywords control the action and display of sprites on the stage.

the backColor of sprite

Syntax   `set the backColor of sprite 120 = 10`

Usage   The property *the backColor of sprite* determines the background color of a specific sprite.

You can set *the backColor of sprite* for *#bitmap* or *#shape* cast members. This sprite property doesn't affect *#field* or *#button* cast members: for these you must use *the backColor of member*.

The value of this property corresponds to the index value of a color in the current color palette, regardless of the color depth of the monitor. You can set the index value of a color in the palette by clicking on the color in Director's Color Palette window.

The color referenced by the value of *the backColor of sprite* will be displayed in place of the white pixels of a 1-bit bitmap cast member or a shape cast member. This value is also used to determine transparency when the ink of the sprite is set to Background Transparent (you're not limited to white).

The color specified by this property will be the transparent color of an 8-bit bitmap cast member with an *ink* property of Background Transparent. The default value is 0 (white).

Example   This statement will set *the backColor of sprite* 40 to the value specified by the parameter "sw1", which was passed to a Shockwave movie by the browser:

```
set the backColor of sprite 40 = ¬
    value (externalParamValue("sw1"))
```

Parameters   `the backcolor of sprite` *integer*

Value   *integer*

See also   the backColor of member, the foreColor of member, the foreColor of sprite, the ink of sprite, the puppet of sprite, the stageColor

the behavesLikeToggle of sprite

SPRITE PROPERTY

Syntax `set the behavesLikeToggle of sprite 20 = FALSE`

Usage *the behavesLikeToggle of sprite* is a property that controls the toggle action of sprites using #btned cast members, created with the Custom Button command from the Insert | Control menu. Clicking on a toggled button changes its appearance, and it remains that way until clicked on again. Untoggled buttons may change appearance when clicked but return to their unclicked state when the mouse is released.

Parameters `the behavesLikeToggle of sprite` *integer*

Value *boolean*

See also the behavesLikeToggle of member, the enabled of member, the enabled of sprite, the initialToggleState of member, the isToggle of sprite, the labelString of member, setButtonImageFromCastMember

the blend of sprite

SPRITE PROPERTY

Syntax `set the blend of sprite 4 = 75`

Usage The property *the blend of sprite* changes the transparency of a sprite using the Blend ink. The value of the property is equivalent to the Blend percentage value in the Sprite Properties dialog box. A value of 0 makes the sprite completely transparent, while a value of 100 makes it completely opaque.

> **Tip**
>
> *Director mixes the colors for each pixel in the sprite with the pixel behind the sprite, then finds the nearest equivalent in the current color palette, regardless of the movie's color depth. Your results will vary depending on the bit depth of the graphics and the monitor.*

Example   This code segment blends a fully opaque sprite to transparency in the course of two seconds:

```
on blendSprite aSprite
  set the ink of sprite aSprite = 32
  set howLong = 120
  set startTime = the ticks
  set endTime = the ticks + howLong
  repeat while the ticks < endTime
    set the blend of sprite aSprite = ¬
      (endTime - the ticks) * 100 / howLong
    updatestage
  end repeat
  set the blend of sprite aSprite = 0
  updatestage
end
```

Parameters   `the blend of sprite` *integer*

Value   *integer*

See also   the ink of sprite, the puppet of sprite, the trails of sprite, the visible of sprite

the bottom of sprite

SPRITE PROPERTY

Syntax   `set whereBottom = the bottom of sprite 3`

Usage   *the bottom of sprite* is a property that contains the position, in pixels, of the lower edge of the bounding rectangle of a sprite. The value is relative to the upper edge of the stage. It cannot be set directly, but the sprite property *the rect of sprite* can be used to set it.

Example   This statement sets the variable *tSpace* to the number of pixels between the bottom of sprite 15 and the bottom of the stage:

```
set tSpace = (the stageBottom - the stageTop) ¬
  - the bottom of sprite 15
```

Parameters   the bottom of sprite *integer*

Value   *integer*

See also   the height of sprite, the left of sprite, the loc of sprite, the locH of sprite, the locV of sprite, the rect of sprite, the right of sprite, the top of sprite, the width of sprite

the castLibNum of sprite

SPRITE PROPERTY

Syntax
```
set the castLibNum of sprite 2 = ¬
    (the castLibNum of sprite 2) + 1
```

Usage   The property *the castLibNum of sprite* determines the cast library of the cast member assigned to a sprite. You can test and set this property with Lingo.

If you set the *castLibNum* of a sprite, the cast member number assigned to that sprite stays the same. This is useful if you use Director's multiple cast feature to place different versions of the same graphic in the same position within different cast libraries.

Example   In this example, the "up" state of a button is in cast library 1, cast member 5. The "down" state of that same button is in cast library 2, cast member 5. We then use *the castLibNum of sprite* property to easily change the button from "up" to "down."

```
set the castLibNum of sprite 3 = 2
```

Parameters   the castLibNum of sprite *integer*

Value   *integer*

See also   the fileName of castLib, the memberNum of sprite, the name of castLib, the number of castLibs, the number of members, the number of members of castLib, the preloadMode of castLib

the castNum of sprite

This Lingo property is obsolete and should not be used in Director 6. See the listing for *the memberNum of sprite* property in this section.

constrainH

Syntax   set constrained = constrainH (4, the locH of sprite 5)

Usage   The *constrainH* function compares the left and right edge values of a sprite's *rect* property to an integer. If the integer value is less than the value of the left side of the *rect*, the returned value is equal to that of the left side. If the integer value is greater than that of the right side of the rect, the right side value is returned. Otherwise, the original integer value is returned.

   The function's value is always within the range of values delineated by the horizontal coordinates of the sprite specified by the first parameter. The function is often used to restrict movement of one sprite to the area bounded by another.

Example   This sprite script, when attached to sprite 2, moves the sprite to follow the mouse, keeping its *loc* property value constrained within the edges of sprite 1:

```
on mouseDown
 repeat while the mouseDown
  set the locH of sprite 2 = constrainH (1, the mouseH)
  set the locV of sprite 2 = constrainV (1, the mouseV) updateStage
 end repeat
end mouseDown
```

Parameters   constrainH (*integer, integer*)

Value   *string*

See also   constrainV, the constraint of sprite, the left of sprite, the right of sprite

the constraint of sprite

SPRITE PROPERTY

Syntax `set the constraint of sprite 4 = 1`

Usage The value of *the constraint of sprite* property determines the channel of the sprite that restricts the movement of one sprite to the size of another sprite. In other words, the *loc* property values for the sprite for which this property is set will stay within the *rect* of the sprite number referred to by this property. If *the constraint of sprite* is 0, the sprite is not constrained.

This property only constrains the *loc* value of the sprite. Depending on the position of *the loc* within the sprite, some parts of the sprite will be able to be dragged outside of the constraining sprite's *rect*.

Example This statement sets the constraint of sprite 2 to sprite 1, which makes it impossible to drag the *loc* of sprite 2 outside the bounds of sprite 1:

`set the constraint of sprite 2 = 1`

Parameters `the constraint of sprite` *integer*

Value *integer*

See also constrainH, constrainV, the locH, the locV

constrainV

FUNCTION

Syntax `set constrained = constrainV (4, the locV of sprite 5)`

Usage The *constrainV* function compares the top and bottom edge values of a sprite's *rect* property to an integer. If the integer value is less than the value of the top side of the *rect*, the returned value is equal to that of the top side. If the integer value is greater than that of the bottom side of the *rect*, the bottom side value is returned. Otherwise, the original integer value is returned.

The function's value is always within the range of values delineated by the vertical coordinates of the sprite specified by the first parameter. The function is often used to restrict movement of one sprite to the area bounded by another.

Example   See the Example for *the constrainH of sprite.*

Parameters   constrainV (*integer*, *integer*)

Value   *string*

See also   constrainH, the constraint of sprite, the left of sprite, the right of sprite

the currentSpriteNum

MOVIE PROPERTY

Syntax   set aSprite = the currentSpriteNum

Usage   *the currentSpriteNum* is a property that indicates which sprite generated the last event. In many ways, its use resembles that of *the clickOn* property, except that *the currentSpriteNum* is set by *mouseEnter*, *mouseLeave*, and other events, not just *mouseDown.*

Example   This sprite script calls a handler, passing the value of the sprite rolled over as a parameter:

```
on mouseEnter
  doButton the currentSpriteNum
end
```

Value   *integer*

See also   the clickOn, the spriteNum of me

the cursor of sprite

SPRITE PROPERTY

Syntax   set the cursor of sprite 12 = 4

set the cursor of sprite 1 = [131073]

set the cursor of sprite 5 = ¬
    [member 1 of castLib 2, member 6 of castLib 1]

Usage   *the cursor of sprite* property behaves very much like the *cursor* command. Its value can be an integer reference to a built-in cursor, a one-item list with a reference to a 1-bit bitmap cast member, or a two-item list with a reference to a 1-bit cursor bitmap and a 1-bit cursor mask bitmap. With *the cursor of sprite*, the mouse cursor is changed only when the hot point of the cursor intersects the *rect* of the sprite or nontransparent pixels of the sprite if the ink is set to Matte.

You can remove a custom sprite cursor by setting its *cursor of sprite* property to 0.

Examples   This statement makes the mouse cursor change to the built-in crosshair cursor whenever the user points to sprite 3:

```
set the cursor of sprite 3 = 2
```

This statement sets the cursor to a custom "hand" whenever the user points to sprite 3:

```
set the cursor of sprite 3 = ¬
  [the number of member "hand", ¬
   the number of member "handMask"]
```

Parameters   the cursor of sprite *integer*

Value   *integer*|[*integer*]/[*integer, integer*]

See also   cursor

the editable of sprite

Syntax   `set the editable of sprite 12 = FALSE`

Usage   At the sprite level, *the editable of sprite* property controls the ability to modify field cast members during playback, just as *the editable of member* property does at the cast member level. With this property it is possible to have multiple instances of the field on the stage with only one of them editable. See *the editable of member* in Chapter 14.

Parameters   the editable of sprite *integer*

Value   *boolean*

See also   the autoTab of member, the border of member, the boxType of member, the boxDropShadow of member, the dropShadow of member, the margin of member, the wordWrap of member

the enabled of sprite

SPRITE PROPERTY

Syntax   set the enabled of sprite 30 = TRUE

Usage   *the enabled of sprite* is a property that controls whether *#btned* cast members
         used as sprites respond to mouse events. If this property is TRUE, the button
         responds to rollovers and clicks. If the property is set to FALSE, the image
         designated for the disabled state of the button is displayed.
            Custom button cast members are created with the Custom Button com-
         mand from the Insert | Control menu.

Example This handler disables the *#btned* cast member sprite in channel 15:

         set the enabled of sprite 15 = FALSE

Parameters set the enabled of sprite *integer*

Value   *boolean*

See also the behavesLikeToggle of member, the behavesLikeToggle of sprite, the
         enabled of member, the initialToggleState of member, the labelString of
         member, setButtonImageFromCastMember

the foreColor of sprite

SPRITE PROPERTY

Syntax   set the foreColor of sprite 120 = 3

Usage   The property *the foreColor of sprite* determines the foreground color of a
         specific sprite.
            You can set *the foreColor of sprite* for *#bitmap* or *#shape* cast members. This
         sprite property doesn't affect *#field* or *#button* cast members: for these you
         must use *the foreColor of member*.
            The value of this property corresponds to the index value of a color in the
         current color palette, regardless of the color depth of the monitor. You can
         see the index value of a color in the palette by clicking on the color in the
         Director's Color Palette window.
            The color referenced by the value of *foreColor* will be displayed in place of
         the black pixels of a 1-bit bitmap cast member or a shape cast member.

Example   This statement will set the *foreColor* of sprite 20 to the color in palette position 204:

```
set the foreColor of sprite 20 = 204
```

Parameters   the forecolor of sprite *integer*

Value   *integer*

See also   the backColor of member, the backColor of sprite, the foreColor of member, the ink of sprite, the puppet of sprite, the stageColor

the height of sprite

SPRITE PROPERTY

Syntax   `set the height of sprite 3 = 40`

Usage   *the height of sprite* is a property that contains the vertical size of sprite *whichSprite* in pixels. You can test and set this property with Lingo.

> **Tip**
>
> *You must set the stretch of sprite property to TRUE before you set the height of a sprite that contains a bitmap cast member.*

Example   This handler makes a "thermometer" effect by setting the height of a sprite that contains a shape cast member:

```
on setThermometer myValue, myMax
   -- myValue is the current value,
   -- myMax is the highest value which
   -- can be displayed by this thermometer
   global gThermSprite, gMaxHeight
   -- gThermSprite is the sprite which has
   -- the shape member in it
   -- gMaxHeight is the maximum height of
   -- gThermSprite in pixels
   set tPercent = float(myValue)/float(myMax)
   set tHeight = tPercent * gMaxHeight
   set the height of sprite gThermSprite = integer(tHeight)
end setThermometer
```

Parameters   the height of sprite *integer*

Value   *integer*

See also   the height of member, rect, the rect of member, the rect of sprite, the regPoint of member, spriteBox, the width of member, the width of sprite

the ink of sprite

SPRITE PROPERTY

Syntax   set the ink of sprite 3 = 35

Usage   *the ink of sprite* is a property that contains a number indicating the ink used to draw a sprite on the stage. You can test and set this property with Lingo.
The available ink effects are:

0	Copy
1	Transparent
2	Reverse
3	Ghost
4	Not copy
5	Not transparent
6	Not reverse
7	Not ghost
8	Matte
9	Mask
32	Blend
33	Add pin
34	Add
35	Subtract pin
36	Background transparent
37	Lightest
38	Subtract
39	Darkest

Example   This statement causes sprite 3 to use the Background Transparent ink for
display:

```
set the ink of sprite 3 = 36
```

Parameters   `the ink of sprite integer`

Value   0|1|2|3|4|5|6|7|8|9|32|33|34|35|36|37|38|39

See also   the backColor of member, the backColor of sprite, the foreColor of member,
the foreColor of sprite, the moveableSprite of sprite, the puppet of sprite, the
stageColor

the isToggle of sprite

SPRITE PROPERTY

Syntax   `set the isToggle of sprite 2 = TRUE`

Usage   *the isToggle of sprite* is a property that controls sprites using cast members of
the *#btned* type, created with the Custom Button editor. If this property is
TRUE, the button is in its toggled state. If it is FALSE, it is untoggled. Only
buttons with a *behavesLikeToggle of sprite* property value of TRUE can be
toggled.

Example   This example sets the button in sprite channel 3 to its untoggled state:

```
set the isToggle of sprite 3 = FALSE
```

Parameters   `the isToggle of sprite integer`

Value   `boolean`

See also   the behavesLikeToggle of member, the behavesLikeToggle of sprite, the
enabled of member, the enabled of sprite, the initialToggleState of member,
the labelString of member, setButtonImageFromCastMember

the left of sprite

Syntax `set whereLeft = the left of sprite 3`

Usage *the left of sprite* is a property that contains the position, in pixels, of the left edge of a sprite. It cannot be set directly, but the sprite property *the rect of sprite* can be used to set it.

Example This statement sets the variable *tSpace* to the number of pixels between the left of sprite 10 and the left of the stage:

`set tSpace = the left of sprite 10`

Parameters `the left of sprite` *integer*

Value *integer*

See also the bottom of sprite, the height of sprite, the loc of sprite, the locH of sprite, the locV of sprite, the rect of sprite, the right of sprite, the top of sprite, the width of sprite

the lineSize of sprite

Syntax `set the lineSize of sprite 12 = 0`

Usage *the lineSize of sprite* is a property that contains the thickness, in pixels, of the line bordering the shape cast member in a sprite. You can test and set this property with Lingo.
  The maximum value is 14.

Example This statement sets the *lineSize* of the shape member in sprite 25 to 5 points, if it really is a #shape member:

```
if the type of member (the memberNum of sprite 25) = ¬
  #shape then
  set the lineSize of sprite 25 = 5
end if
```

Parameters   `the lineSize of sprite` *integer*

Value   *integer*

See also   the lineSize of member

the loc of sprite

SPRITE PROPERTY

Syntax   `set whereSprite = the loc of sprite 6`

Usage   *the loc of sprite* is a property that contains a point value, which represents the stage coordinates of a sprite's registration point. You can test and set this property with Lingo.

Example   This statement sets the *loc* of sprite 6 to a certain point:

`set the loc of sprite 6 = point(100,50)`

Parameters   `browserName` *integer*

Value   *point*

See also   the bottom of sprite, the height of sprite, the left of sprite, the locH of sprite, the locV of sprite, the rect of sprite, the right of sprite, the top of sprite, the width of sprite

the locH of sprite

SPRITE PROPERTY

Syntax   `set the locH of sprite 5 = 35`

Usage   *the locH of sprite* is a property that contains the horizontal screen coordinate of a sprite's registration point, or *loc*. You can test and set this property with Lingo.

Example   This statement sets the *locH* of sprite 7 to the same values as *the mouseH*, which is the horizontal coordinate of the mouse cursor.

```
set the locH of sprite 7 = the mouseH
```

Parameters   the locH of sprite *integer*

Value   *integer*

See also   the bottom of sprite, the height of sprite, the left of sprite, the loc of sprite, the locV of sprite, the rect of sprite, the right of sprite, the top of sprite, the width of sprite

the locV of sprite

SPRITE PROPERTY

Syntax   set the locV of sprite 4 = 203

Usage   *the locV of sprite* is a property that contains the horizontal screen coordinate of a sprite's registration point, or *loc*. You can test and set this property with Lingo.

Example   This statement sets the *locV* of sprite 7 to the same values as the *mouseV*, which is the vertical coordinate of the mouse cursor.

```
set the locV of sprite 7 = the mouseV
```

Parameters   the locV of sprite *integer*

Value   *integer*

See also   the bottom of sprite, the height of sprite, the left of sprite, the loc of sprite, the locH of sprite, the rect of sprite, the right of sprite, the top of sprite, the width of sprite

the member of sprite

Syntax   `set the member of sprite 45 = member 4 of castLib "BG"`

Usage   *the member of sprite* is a property that contains a full reference to the cast member, including cast member number and cast library number, used by a sprite. It can be both tested and set.

The value of the property is returned in the form (member 1 of castLib 1). Values assigned to the property can be of three types: an integer representing a unique cast member number, a cast member name, or a reference to the cast member and library.

Examples   This example changes the cast member used for sprite 3 to the cast member with the number 1:

`set the member of sprite 3 = 1`

This example changes the cast member used for sprite 3 to a cast member with the name "background":

`set the member of sprite 3 = member "background"`

This example changes the cast member used for sprite 3 to cast member 4 of cast library 2:

`set the member of sprite 3 = member 4 of castLib 2`

Parameters   `the member of sprite integer`

Value   `integer|member`

See also   the castLibNum of sprite, the memberNum of sprite

the memberNum of sprite

Syntax   `set whatMember = the memberNum of sprite 20`

Usage   *the memberNum of sprite* is a property that contains the position in a cast library of the cast member currently assigned to a sprite. You can test and set this property with Lingo.

This value is not unique. Sprites using cast members in position 13 of any cast library will return the value 13 when *the memberNum of sprite* is tested.

Example   This code segment changes the memberNum of a sprite if the mouse is currently over that sprite. It assumes that the new sprite is the next one in the cast.

```
if rollover(8) then
  set the memberNum of sprite 8 = ¬
    the number of member "nextRoll"
else
  set the memberNum of sprite 8 = ¬
    the number of member "next"
end if
```

Parameters   the memberNum of sprite *integer*

Value   *integer*

See also   the castLibNum of sprite, the member of sprite

the moveableSprite of sprite

SPRITE PROPERTY

Syntax   set isMoveable = the moveableSprite of sprite 4

Usage   *the moveableSprite of sprite* is a property that is TRUE if the sprite can be moved by the user clicking and dragging on the sprite. This is the same as checking the Moveable check box for the sprite in the score. You can test and set this property with Lingo.

Example   This statement makes sprite 10 moveable:

set the moveableSprite of sprite 10 = TRUE

Parameters   the moveableSprite of sprite *integer*

Value   *boolean*

See also   the ink of sprite, the puppet of sprite, puppetSprite, the trails of sprite

the puppet of sprite

Syntax `set isPuppeted = the puppet of sprite 3`

Usage *the puppet of sprite* is a property that is TRUE if a sprite channel is under the control of Lingo instead of the score. In versions of Director before Version 6, sprites needed to be puppeted before you could change any other sprite properties with Lingo. A puppeted sprite ignores any score changes, until its *puppet of sprite* property is set back to FALSE. Setting *the puppet of sprite* property to TRUE has the same effect as using the *puppetSprite* command.

In Director 6, sprites do not need to be explicitly puppeted to be modified by Lingo commands. However, the sprite channel itself is only under the control of Lingo as long as the sprite being affected appears in the sprite channel in the score. As soon as the playback head moves to a frame where the modified sprite no longer appears, the channel is no longer under Lingo's control. Sprites puppeted using this type of *implicit* puppeting have a *puppet of sprite* value of FALSE.

You can test and set this property with Lingo.

Examples This handler puppets a list of sprites:

```
on makePuppet mySpriteList, myValue
  if not(listP(mySpriteList)) then exit
  repeat with tSprite in mySpriteList
    set the puppet of sprite ¬
           tSprite = myValue
  end repeat
end makePuppet
```

You can use this function with a statement like this, which puppets sprites 1, 6, 9, and 14:

```
makePuppet([1,6,9,14],TRUE)
```

Parameters `the puppet of sprite` *integer*

Value *boolean*

See also the backColor of sprite, the bottom of sprite, the constraint of sprite, the foreColor of sprite, the height of sprite, the ink of sprite, the left of sprite, the lineSize of sprite, the loc of sprite, the locH of sprite, the locV of sprite, the moveableSprite of sprite, puppetSprite, the rect of sprite, the right of sprite, the stretch of sprite, the top of sprite, the type of sprite, the width of sprite

puppetSprite

Syntax puppetSprite 3, TRUE

Usage The *puppetSprite* command is another way to control the value of *the puppet of sprite* property. When you make a sprite a puppet, you take control of that sprite away from the score and give it to Lingo. The puppeted sprite then ignores any changes in the score, and responds only to changes made by Lingo. By designating a sprite channel number in the first parameter, and a boolean value for the second, you can control *the puppet of sprite* property.

In Director 6, sprites do not need to be explicitly puppeted to be modified by Lingo commands. However, the sprite channel itself is under the control of Lingo only as long as the sprite being affected appears in the sprite channel in the score. As soon as the playback head moves to a frame where the modified sprite no longer appears, the channel is no longer under Lingo's control. Sprites puppeted using this type of *implicit* puppeting have a *puppet of sprite* value of FALSE.

You can test and set this property with Lingo.

Example This command returns control of sprite 12 back to the score:

puppetSprite 12, FALSE

Parameters puppetSprite *integer*, *boolean*

See also the puppet of sprite

the rect of sprite

Syntax set the rect of sprite 4 = rect (10, 50, 40, 200)

Usage *the rect of sprite* is a property that contains the coordinates of the bounding rectangle of a sprite. You can test and set this property with Lingo.

Modifying *the rect of sprite* property changes the stage coordinates and size of a sprite on the stage. For a bitmap sprite to have its size modified, it is necessary to first set *the stretch of sprite* to TRUE.

Example   This statement sets the *rect* of sprite 13 to the position and size of the *rect* created by the *loc* properties of two bitmap graphics used as sprites 11 and 12:

```
set the rect of sprite 13 = ¬
  rect(the loc of sprite 11, the loc of sprite 12)
```

Parameters   the rect of sprite *integer*

Value   *rect*

See also   the bottom of sprite, the height of sprite, the ink of sprite, the left of sprite, the loc of sprite, the locH of sprite, the locV of sprite, the puppet of sprite, the right of sprite, spriteBox, the stretch of sprite, the top of sprite, the type of sprite, the width of sprite

the right of sprite   SPRITE PROPERTY

Syntax   `set whereRight = the right of sprite 3`

Usage   *the right of sprite* is a property that contains the stage position, in pixels, of the right edge of a sprite. It cannot be set directly, but the sprite property *the rect of sprite* can be used to modify it.

Example   This statement sets the variable *tSpace* to the number of pixels between the right edge of sprite 10 and the right edge of the stage:

```
set tSpace = (the stageRight - the stageLeft) - ¬
  the right of sprite 10
```

Parameters   the right of sprite *integer*

Value   *integer*

See also   the bottom of sprite, the height of sprite, the left of sprite, the loc of sprite, the locH of sprite, the locV of sprite, the rect of sprite, the top of sprite, the width of sprite

the scoreColor of sprite

SPRITE PROPERTY

Syntax   `if the scoreColor of sprite 20 = 3 then`

Usage   *the scoreColor of sprite* is a property that determines the color of a sprite in the score. Its value indicates which of the six colors in the score color palette (at the lower left of the Score window in Director 6) is used. By colorizing sprites in the score you can organize them during authoring. Possible values are 0 to 5.

Example   This statement sets the score color of sprite 10 to a salmon color in sprite position 5:

`set the scoreColor of sprite 10 = 5`

Parameters   `the scoreColor of sprite` *integer*

Value   `0|1|2|3|4|5`

the scriptNum of sprite

SPRITE PROPERTY

Syntax   `set whatFirst = the scriptNum of sprite 3`

Usage   *the scriptNum of sprite* is a property that contains the number of the first script cast member assigned to a sprite. The value is equivalent to *the number of member* property of the cast member containing the script. You can test but not set this property with Lingo.

Director 6 enables you to attach more than one script cast member to a sprite. Sprite scripts can be accessed and manipulated by referencing *the scriptInstanceList of sprite* property (see Chapter 33).

Example   This handler builds a list of all sprites using the script in cast member position 20 as the first script assigned:

```
on findButtonScripts
  set buttonList = []
  repeat with i = 1 to 120
```

```
        if the scriptNum of sprite i = 20 then
          add buttonList, i
        end if
      end repeat
    end
```

Parameters the scriptNum of sprite *integer*

Value *integer*

See also the castLibNum of sprite, the memberNum of sprite, the number of member, the scriptInstanceList of sprite

sendAllSprites

COMMAND

Syntax sendAllSprites #moveTo, 20, 10

Usage The *sendAllSprites* command lets you send a custom event with arguments to all of the other sprites on the stage. This enables you to do things like triggering sprite behaviors with a button that sends one message to any number of well-behaved sprites.

The first parameter for the *sendAllSprites* command is a symbol value representing the name of the message you want to sent to the sprites. All following parameters are arguments passed to the handler.

Example In a movie with a number of sprites containing the following behavior handler:

```
on jump me, howHigh
  set the locV of sprite the spriteNum of me = howHigh
end
```

and a button containing the handler:

```
on mouseUp
  sendAllSprites #jump, 10
end
```

pressing the button would make all of the sprites with the *jump* handler set their *locV* value to 10. On the next update of the stage, all of the sprites would appear near the top of the stage. Notice that a value is not passed by the *sendAllSprites* command for the *me* parameter, and that it's necessary to reference the sprite's number with *the spriteNum of me* property.

Parameters   sendAllSprites *symbol*

sendAllSprites *symbol, value*

sendAllSprites *symbol, value, . . .*

See also   sendSprite

sendSprite

Syntax   sendSprite 1, #moveTo, 20, 10

Usage   The *sendSprite* command lets you send a custom event with arguments to a specific sprite on the stage. This command works similarly to the *sendAllSprites* command, but only for one sprite.

The first parameter for the *sendSprite* command is an integer referencing the sprite channel where the message will be sent. The second is a symbol value representing the name of the message you want sent to the sprites. All following parameters are arguments passed to the handler.

Example   In a movie with a number of sprites containing the following behavior handler:

```
on jump me, howHigh
  set the locV of sprite the spriteNum of me = howHigh
end
```

executing the command

```
sendSprite 4, #jump, 10
```

would send the message *jump* to the sprite in channel 4, setting its vertical location value to 10 and moving it near the top of the stage on the next screen update.

Parameters   sendSprite *integer, symbol*

sendSprite *integer, symbol, value*

sendSprite *integer, symbol, value, . . .*

See also   sendAllSprites

setButtonImageFromCastmember

COMMAND

Syntax   `setButtonImageFromCastMember member 2, "imageNormal", ¬`
         `member 4 of castLib 2`

Usage   The *setButtonImageFromCastmember* command allows you to modify the bitmap cast members used for various states of a Custom Button cast member of the type *#btned*. The first parameter specifies which *#btned* cast member is to be modified; the second is a string that identifies the state of the button to be modified; the last is the bitmap cast member assigned to the button's state.

There are eight possible states: four are used for standard push buttons, and four extras are used for toggle buttons. The strings used to identify them are:

```
"imageNormal"  "imageToggledNormal"
"imagePressed" "imageToggledPressed"
"imageRollOver" "imageToggledRollOver"
"imageDisabled" "imageToggledDisabled"
```

Example   This authoring script assigns a series of cast members to the various states of a custom button cast member:

```
on buttonSetUp whatButton, startSprite
  if the type of member whatButton = #btned then
    setButtonImageFromCastMember member whatButton, ¬
      "imageNormal", member startSprite
    setButtonImageFromCastMember member whatButton, ¬
      "imagePressed", member startSprite + 1
    setButtonImageFromCastMember member whatButton, ¬
      " imageRollOver ", member startSprite + 2
    setButtonImageFromCastMember member whatButton, ¬
      "imageDisabled", member startSprite + 3
    if the behavesLikeToggle of member whatButton then
      setButtonImageFromCastMember member whatButton, ¬
        "imageToggledNormal", member startSprite + 4
      setButtonImageFromCastMember member whatButton, ¬
        "imageToggledPressed", member startSprite + 5
      setButtonImageFromCastMember member whatButton, ¬
        "imageToggledRollOver", member startSprite + 6
      setButtonImageFromCastMember member whatButton, ¬
        "imageToggledDisabled", member startSprite + 7
    end if
  end if
end
```

Parameters   setButtonImageFromCastMember *member*, *string*, *member*

See also   the behavesLikeToggle of member, the behavesLikeToggle of sprite, the initialToggleState of member, the isToggle of sprite, putImageIntoCastMember

sprite

KEYWORD

Syntax   sprite 4

Usage   The *sprite* keyword identifies a specific channel in the score and any cast member placed there for display on the stage. It is used in most references to sprites in handlers, although some, such as *sendSprite*, utilize just an integer value.

Parameters   sprite *integer*

sprite intersects

FUNCTION

Syntax   set isIntersect = sprite 5 intersects 3

Usage   The *sprite intersects* function returns TRUE if the bounding rectangles of two sprites overlap. If both sprites use the matte ink type, then the border defined by the nonwhite pixels of each sprite is used rather than the bounding rectangles.

Examples   This handler makes it easy to check for the collision of several sprites. You can give it a linear list of any number of sprites, and it will efficiently check for the intersection of them all and return the first pair of sprites that are touching:

```
on collisionCheck mySpriteList
  set tNumOfSprites = count(mySpriteList)
  repeat with tIndex = 1 to tNumOfSprites - 1
    set tSpriteOne = getAt(mySpriteList, tIndex)
    repeat with tIndex2 = min(tIndex+1,tNumOfSprites) ¬
      to tNumOfSprites
      set tSpriteTwo = getAt(mySpriteList, tIndex2)
```

```
      if sprite tSpriteOne intersects tSpriteTwo then
        return([tSpriteOne, tSpriteTwo])
      end if
    end repeat
  end repeat
end collisionCheck
```

Then, you can do something simple like this, by putting collisionCheck in an exitFrame handler to send the list of touching sprites to the message window:

```
on exitFrame
  put collisionCheck ([6,9,10,14,18,20])
  go to the frame
end exitFrame
```

Parameters   sprite *integer* intersects *integer*

Value   *boolean*

See also   the loc of sprite, the rect of sprite, sprite within, spriteBox

sprite within

FUNCTION

Syntax   `set isWithin = sprite 5 within 4`

Usage   The *sprite within* function returns TRUE if the bounding rectangle of the first sprite is completely inside the bounding rectangle of the second sprite; otherwise, it returns FALSE. If both sprites use the matte ink type, then the border defined by the nontransparent pixels of each sprite is used rather than the bounding rectangles.

Example   This *exitFrame* handler checks to see if the user has dragged sprite 13 within the bounds of sprite 12. If so, *exitFrame* goes to another frame:

```
on exitFrame
  if sprite 13 within sprite 12 then
    go to frame "success"
  else
    go to the frame
  end if
end exitFrame
```

Parameters	sprite *integer* within *integer*
Value	*boolean*
See also	the loc of sprite, the rect of sprite, sprite intersects, spriteBox

spriteBox

COMMAND

The *spriteBox* command is used to modify the position and size of a sprite on the stage. See *the rect of sprite* property.

the startTime of sprite

SPRITE PROPERTY

Syntax set the startTime of sprite 3 = 300

Usage *the startTime of sprite* is a property that determines the starting playback position in a digital video sprite. The time units referenced by the property are determined by the value of *the digitalVideoTimeScale*. Modifying *the digitalVideoTimeScale* alters *the startTime of sprite* property to the new unit measure.

This property and its counterpart *the stopTime of sprite* enable you to use segments of one digital video sprite for different portions of your movie.

Example This handler sets the *startTime* and *stopTime* of a digital video sprite to a value in seconds, regardless of *the digitalVideoTimeScale*. When the sprite begins playing, it begins at the position specified by *videoIn* (in seconds) and plays to *videoOut* (also in seconds):

```
on setPlayTime whatSprite, videoIn, videoOut
  set oldTimeScale = the digitalVideoTimeScale
  set the digitalVideoTimeScale = 1
  set the startTime of sprite whatSprite = videoIn
  set the stopTime of sprite whatSprite = videoOut
  set the digitalVideoTimeScale = oldTimeScale
end
```

Parameters `the startTime of sprite` *integer*

Value *integer*

See also the digitalVideoTimeScale, the stopTime of sprite

the stopTime of sprite

SPRITE PROPERTY

Syntax `set the stopTime of sprite 3 = 500`

Usage *the stopTime of sprite* is a property that determines the final playback position in a digital video sprite. The time units referenced by the property are determined by the value of *the digitalVideoTimeScale*. Modifying *the digitalVideoTimeScale* alters *the stopTime of sprite* property to the new unit measure.

This property and its counterpart *the startTime of sprite* enable you to use segments of one digital video sprite for different portions of your movie.

Example See *the startTime of sprite*.

Parameters `the stopTime of sprite` *integer*

Value *integer*

See also the digitalVideoTimeScale, the startTime of sprite

the stretch of sprite

SPRITE PROPERTY

Syntax `set the stretch of sprite 3 = TRUE`

Usage *the stretch of sprite* is a property that is TRUE if a sprite has been modified from its original size and/or its size can be modified with Lingo. Shapes, field, and button cast members may always have their sizes modified with Lingo, but other types of sprites must have their *stretch* property set to TRUE before their size can be modified by setting *the rect of sprite* property.

You can test and set this property with Lingo.

If you want a stretched sprite to return to its original size, set *the stretch of sprite* to FALSE.

Example This code segment stretches the bitmap sprite 15 to 300 pixels by 200 pixels, and butts it against the top and left side of the stage:

```
set the stretch of sprite 15 = TRUE
set the rect of sprite 15 = rect (0, 0, 300, 200)
```

Parameters the stretch of sprite *integer*

Value *boolean*

See also the bottom of sprite, the height of sprite, the ink of sprite, the left of sprite, the loc of sprite, the locH of sprite, the locV of sprite, the puppet of sprite, the rect of sprite, the right of sprite, the top of sprite, the type of sprite, the width of sprite

the top of sprite

SPRITE PROPERTY

Syntax `set whereTop = the top of sprite 3`

Usage *the top of sprite* is a property that contains the position, in pixels, of the top edge of the bounding rectangle of a sprite. The value is relative to the upper edge of the stage. It cannot be set directly, but the sprite property *the rect of sprite* can be used to modify it.

Example This statement sets the variable *tSpace* to the number of pixels between the top of sprite 15 and the bottom of the stage:

```
set tSpace = (the stageBottom - the stageTop) ¬
   - the top of sprite 15
```

Parameters the top of sprite *integer*

Value *integer*

See also the bottom of sprite, the height of sprite, the left of sprite, the loc of sprite, the locH of sprite, the locV of sprite, the rect of sprite, the right of sprite, the width of sprite

the trails of sprite

SPRITE PROPERTY

Syntax   `set the trails of sprite 4 = FALSE`

Usage   *the trails of sprite* is a property that is TRUE if the sprite will leave an image of itself behind when it is moved. This is the same as checking the Trails check box for the sprite in the score. You can test and set this property with Lingo.

Trails are useful when you need to give the impression of more than the maximum number of sprite channels, or when you need to create mock-drawing applications.

Trails are erased when another sprite moves over the trails, when a transition is executed, or when a window opens then closes over the stage.

Example   This statement causes sprite 10 to leave trails behind when it is moved around the stage:

`set the trails of sprite 10 = TRUE`

Parameters   `the trails of sprite` *integer*

Value   *boolean*

See also   the ink of sprite, the moveableSprite of sprite, the puppet of sprite, puppetSprite, the visible of sprite

the tweened of sprite

SPRITE PROPERTY

Syntax   `set the tweened of sprite 4 = TRUE`

Usage   *the tweened of sprite* is a property that is used during score recording to specify whether each frame of a sprite is considered a key frame, or if only the first frame of a sprite instance is a key frame and subsequent frames are *tweened* (in-betweened) from that key frame.

Example   This example will cause the sprite being recorded into sprite channel 5 to have key frames for each frame recorded:

```
set the tweened of sprite 5 = FALSE
```

Parameters   the tweened of sprite *integer*

Value   *boolean*

the type of sprite

SPRITE PROPERTY

Syntax   `set`

Usage   *the type of sprite* is a property that contains 0 if the sprite is empty, and 16 if it is not. You can test this property with Lingo and set it to 0 during a score recording session to clear a sprite.

Prior to Director 5, this property was more descriptive. However, with the advent of score recording, it became limited to providing a way to clear the sprite channel. If you want to know what kind of media is contained in a certain sprite, use a statement like this:

```
put the type of sprite member (the member of sprite 1)
```

Example   This handler permanently removes the contents of sprite *mySprite* in the current frame:

```
on clearSprite mySprite
   beginRecording
      set the type of sprite mySprite = 0
   endRecording
end clearSprite
```

Parameters   the type of sprite *integer*

Value   0|16

See also   the ink of sprite, the loc of sprite, the puppet of sprite, the rect of sprite, the stretch of sprite

updateStage

Syntax `updateStage`

Usage The *updateStage* command causes any changes to the stage made by Lingo to be displayed immediately, rather than waiting until the playback head moves to display stage changes. It is useful for making changes happen in the middle of Lingo handlers, in repeat loops, or while the movie is paused.

Example This handler causes the shape cast member in sprite 15 to turn red (color # 6 in the System-Win palette) while the mouse is pointing to it, using *updateStage* to make the change occur immediately:

```
on idle
  if rollover(15) then
    set the foreColor of sprite 15 = 6
    updateStage
  else
    set the foreColor of sprite 15 = 3
    updateStage
  end if
end idle
```

See also go, play, the puppet of sprite, puppetSprite

the visible of sprite

Syntax `set the visible of sprite 3 = FALSE`

Usage *the visible of sprite* is a property that is TRUE when the sprite in the score will be drawn on the stage, and FALSE when it will not be drawn. You can test and set this property with Lingo.

Example   This handler makes sprite 1 visible if the *loc* of sprite 15 is inside of the rectangle created by sprite 1:

```
on exitFrame
  if inside(the loc of sprite 15, ¬
      the rect of sprite 1) then
    set the visible of sprite 1 = TRUE
  else
    set the visible of sprite 1 = FALSE
  end if
end exitFrame
```

Parameters   the visible of sprite *integer*

Value   *boolean*

See also   the ink of sprite, the moveableSprite of sprite, the puppet of sprite, puppetSprite, the trails of sprite

the width of sprite

SPRITE PROPERTY

Syntax   `set the width of sprite 5 = 150`

Usage   *the width of sprite* is a sprite property that contains the horizontal size of a sprite in pixels. You can test and set this property with Lingo.

You must set *the stretch of sprite* property to TRUE before you set the width of most sprite types.

If the playback head is not moving, you must use the *updateStage* command to see any changes on the stage.

Example
This handler makes a "thermometer" effect by setting the width of a sprite that contains a shape cast member:

```
on setThermometer myValue, myMax
    -- myValue is the current value,
    -- myMax is the highest value which
    -- can be displayed by this thermometer
    global gThermSprite, gMaxWidth
    -- gThermSprite is the sprite which has
    -- the shape member in it
    -- gMaxWidth is the maximum width of
    -- gThermSprite in pixels
    set tPercent = float(myValue)/float(myMax)
    set tWidth = tPercent * gMaxWidth
    set the width of sprite gThermSprite = integer(tWidth)
end setThermometer
```

Parameters
the width of sprite *integer*

Value
integer

See also
the height of member, the height of sprite, rect, the rect of member, the rect of sprite, the regPoint of member, spriteBox, the width of member

Rects and Points Category

These commands and functions operate on two of the special data types available to you in Director, *rects* and *points*.

inflate

Syntax   `set aRect = inflate (rect (35, 43, 168, 99), 20, 10)`

Usage   The *inflate* function returns a *rect* value that is *rect* modified by a width value and a height value. The width is added or subtracted from both sides; the height modifier affects both top and bottom. This function makes it easy to increase or decrease the *rect* of an object by an equal amount on all sides.

     The example above would yield the same result as:

```
set aRect = ¬
    rect (35, 43, 168, 99) + rect (-20, -10, 20, 10)
```

Examples   These statements from the message window show the operation of this function:

```
put the rect of sprite 8
-- rect(300, 50, 380, 130)
put inflate(the rect of sprite 8, 20,30)
-- rect(280, 20, 400, 160)
set the rect of sprite 8 = ¬
    inflate (the rect of sprite 8, 20, 30)
```

Parameters   `inflate (rect, integer, integer)`

Value   *rect*

See also   the height of sprite, the height of member, inside, map, point, rect, the rect of member, the rect of sprite, the regPoint of member, spriteBox, union, the width of member, the width of sprite

inside

Syntax   `set isInside = inside (point (123, 250), ¬`
                 `rect (95, 100, 300, 260))`

Usage   The *inside* function returns TRUE if the point specified by the first parameter is within the rectangle specified by the second. It returns FALSE otherwise.

Example   This statement executes a custom handler if the mouse cursor is within the bounds defined by the *rect* of sprite 8:

```
if inside(point(the mouseH, the mouseV), ¬
    the rect of sprite 8) then doRollover 8
```

Parameters   inside (*point*, *rect*)

Value   *boolean*

See also   inflate, map, the mouseH, the mouseV, point, rect, union

intersect

FUNCTION

Syntax
```
set interRect = intersect (rect (30, 30, 50, 50), ¬
    rect (40, 40, 60, 60))
```

Usage   The *intersect* function returns a *rect* value, which is the rectangle formed by the overlapping portions of the two specified rectangles. If the rectangles do not intersect, then this function returns *rect (0, 0, 0, 0)*.

Example   This code segment sets the rect of sprite 8 to the intersection of sprite 6 and sprite 7:

```
set tSixR = the rect of sprite 6
set tSevR = the rect of sprite 7
set tIntersectRect = intersect(tSixR, tSevR)
set the rect of sprite 8 = tIntersectRect
```

Parameters   intersect (*rect*, *rect*)

Value   *rect*

See also   rect, the rect of member, the rect of sprite, the regPoint of member, sprite ... intersects, spriteBox, the width of member, the width of sprite

map

Syntax
```
set relativePoint = map (point (30, 20), ¬
   rect (0, 0, 50, 30), rect (0, 0, 50, 30))
```
```
set relativeRect = map (rect (190, 150, 200, 175), ¬
   rect (184, 135, 321, 225), rect (160, 157, 672, 467))
```

Usage
The *map* function compares a point or rectangle value (first parameter) to a rectangle (second parameter), and returns a point or rectangle that is in the same relationship to another rectangle (third parameter).

This function allows you to set up something that works similarly to a trackpad, where moving a sprite across a small rectangle (the trackpad) can modify the movement of an object on a large rectangle (the screen).

Example
This handler simulates a trackpad by comparing the mouse position to a small sprite (in channel 13), and moving a sprite in channel 14 across the entire stage.
```
on exitFrame
set mouseLoc = point (the mouseH, the mouseV)
  set trackPad = the rect of sprite 13
  set fullStage = offset (the rect of the stage, ¬
  - the stageLeft, - the stageTop)
  set the loc of sprite 14 = ¬
    map (mouseLoc, trackPad, fullStage)
  go the frame
end
```

Parameters
map (*point/rect*, *rect*, *rect*)

Value
point/rect

See also
inflate, inside, point, rect, union

offset

Syntax   `set target = offset (the rect of sprite 4, 10, -20)`

Usage   This *offset* function returns a *rect* representing a *rect* value with its coordinates modified by a horizontal and vertical value. Left and right properties of the *rect* are modified by the same value, as are top and bottom properties.

This function makes it easy to move a *rect* by a certain amount. However, it is often easier to move a sprite by changing its *loc of sprite property*, rather than its *rect of sprite* property.

Example   See the Example for *map*, on the preceding page.

Parameters   `offset (`*rect, integer, integer*`)`

Value   *rect*

See also   the height of sprite, the height of member, inflate, rect, the rect of member, the rect of sprite, the regPoint of member, spriteBox, the width of member, the width of sprite

point

Syntax   `set aPoint = point (100, 233)`

Usage   The *point* function returns a special linear list type (in the form Director uses to identify coordinates for sprites on the stage) consisting of two integer values. The potential values for points are not limited to the size of the stage, however.

A value of the *#point* type has two items, which, although the list is not a property list, can be referred to with the properties *the locH* and *the locV*, corresponding to the horizontal component and vertical component of the point value.

Points can be treated as vectors, and you can perform many types of vector-style arithmetic on them: adding, subtracting, multiplying, and dividing. In most instances, the result is another point value.

To determine if a value is a point, you can test it with the *ilk* function.

Examples This example assigns a point value with a horizontal coordinate of 33 and a vertical coordinate of 67 to the variable *aPoint*:

```
set aPoint = point (33, 67)
```

If you then type *put aPoint* in the Message window, the result will be:

```
-- point(33, 67)
```

Typing *put the locH of aPoint* in the Message window results in:

```
-- 33
```

To determine the type of value of *aPoint*, type *put ilk (aPoint)* in the Message window:

```
-- #point
```

Vector math can be simulated with points. Points can be added, subtracted, multiplied, and divided by points and integers. Even floats can be used, but care needs to be taken to convert the coordinates to integers before assigning the value to a sprite. The following are examples from the Message window using *aPoint* above:

```
put aPoint + point (2, 3)
-- point(35, 70)
put aPoint + 3
-- point(36, 70)
put aPoint - point (3, 7)
-- point(30, 60)
put aPoint - 7
-- point(26, 60)
put aPoint * point (2, 3)
-- point(66, 201)
put aPoint * 3
-- point(99, 201)
put aPoint / point (3, 2)
-- point(11, 33)
put aPoint / 2
-- point(16, 33)
```

Notice that in the final example, the values are rounded down to integers.

Parameters point (*integer*, *integer*)

Value *point*

See also ilk, inside, map, rect

rect

Syntax `set aRect = rect (35, 24, 320, 129)`

Usage The *rect* function returns a special linear list type (in the form Director uses to identify coordinates for rectangular areas on the stage) consisting of four integer values. The potential values for rects are not limited to the coordinates on the stage, however.

A value of the *#rect* type has four items, which, although the list is not a property list, can be referred to by the properties *the left, the top, the right*, and *the bottom* (corresponding to the horizontal and vertical component of the top left and bottom right corners of a rectangle).

Rect values may also be used with mathematical operators: added, subtracted, multiplied, and divided, although this is generally less useful than with points.

Since a *rect* value is actually composed of two points, it's possible to create a *rect* value from two *point* values, using two point values instead of four integer values as the parameters for the function. (You cannot mix a point value and two integers to form a *rect*.)

To determine if a value is a *rect*, you can test it with the *ilk* function.

Examples This example assigns a *rect* value with an upper left corner coordinate of 22, 67 and a lower right coordinate of 244, 179 to the variable *aRect*:

`set aRect = rect (33, 67, 244, 179)`

This statement returns the same result, using two points instead of four integers:

`set aRect = rect (point (33, 67), point (244 179))`

If you then type *put aRect* in the Message window, the result will be:

`-- rect (33, 67, 244, 179)`

Typing *put the bottom of aRect* in the Message window results in:

`-- 179`

To determine the type of value of *aPoint*, type *put ilk (aRect)* in the Message window:

`-- #rect`

*Rect*s can be scaled, transformed, and modified in other ways, by arithmetic, using other *rect*s and integers. Examples from the Message window use *aRect* above:

```
put aRect + rect (7, 3, 6, 1)
-- rect(40, 70, 250, 180)
put arect + 3
```

```
-- rect(36, 70, 247, 182)
put aRect * rect (2, 3, 4, 5)
-- rect(66, 201, 976, 895)
put aPoint * 3
-- rect(99, 201, 732, 537)
```

Parameters   rect (*integer*, *integer*, *integer*, *integer*)

Value   *rect*

See also   inflate, inside, intersect, map, offset, point, the rect of member, the rect of sprite, the rect of window, union

union

FUNCTION

Syntax   `set aBigRect = union rect`

Usage   The *union* function returns a rect value that is the smallest rectangle to completely surround the two rect values *rect1* and *rect2*.

Example   This handler turns the mouse cursor into a "hand" if it is within the *rect* formed by sprites 5 and 6:

```
on idle
  set mouseLoc = point(the mouseH, the mouseV)
  if inside(mouseLoc, union (the rect of sprite 5, ¬
    the rect of sprite 6)) then
    cursor [the number of member "hand", ¬
      the number of member "handMask"]
  else
    -- reset cursor
    cursor 0
  end if
end idle
```

Parameters   union (*rect*, *rect*)

Value   *rect*

See also   inflate, inside, map, point, rect

Frames Category

These Lingo keywords refer to individual frames in the score of a movie.

on enterFrame

HANDLER

Syntax   `on enterFrame`

Usage   This handler is triggered by the *enterFrame* message, sent when the playback head enters a new frame. The handler can be placed into a sprite, frame, behavior, or movie script. In earlier versions of Director, the *enterFrame* message is only sent to frame or movie scripts.

Handlers placed in frame scripts and frame behaviors intercept the message before it reaches movie scripts, unless the *pass* command is used. For sprites, multiple *enterFrame* handlers in behaviors execute in the order that the behaviors appear in the *spriteInstanceList*.

The *enterFrame* message occurs between the *prepareFrame* and *exitFrame* messages. An *enterFrame* handler in the movie script will execute in every frame of the movie. An *enterFrame* handler attached to a sprite will execute in every frame in which the sprite appears. *enterFrame* handlers in frame scripts will execute only for the frames in which they appear.

Changes to sprites made in *enterFrame* handlers will not be seen before the *exitFrame* message unless an *updateStage* command is executed.

> ### Tip
>
> *For scripts that should execute before the sprite is drawn, the* prepareFrame *handler is recommended.*

Example   This handler resets *the timer* as the playback head enters the frame:

```
on enterFrame
    startTimer
end
```

Parameters
```
on enterFrame
    statements
end
```

See also   on exitFrame, on prepareFrame, on stepFrame, on stepMovie

on exitFrame
HANDLER

Syntax   `on exitFrame`

Usage   The *exitFrame* handler is triggered by the last message sent before the playback head leaves a frame in the score. The handler can be placed into a sprite, frame, behavior, or movie script, and is typically used to perform most of the frame-based tasks of a movie.

Handlers placed in frame scripts and frame behaviors intercept the message before it reaches movie scripts, unless the *pass* command is used. For sprites, multiple *exitFrame* handlers in behaviors execute in the order that the behaviors appear in the *spriteInstanceList*.

An *exitFrame* handler in the movie script will execute in every frame of the movie. An *exitFrame* handler attached to a sprite will execute in every frame in which the sprite appears. *exitFrame* handlers in frame scripts will execute only for the frames in which they appear.

Example   This handler keeps the playback head within the same frame until the value of *the timer* is greater than or equal to 400:

```
on exitFrame
  if the timer < 400 then go the frame
end
```

Parameters
```
on exitFrame
    statements
end
```

See also   on enterFrame, on prepareFrame, on stepFrame, on stepMovie

the frame

Syntax	`set thisFrame = the frame`
Usage	*the frame* is a property that indicates the frame the playback head currently occupies. It can be tested but not set.
Example	See the Example for *on exitFrame*.
Parameters	`the frame`
Value	*integer*
See also	label, marker

the frameLabel

Syntax	`set whatlabel = the frameLabel`
Usage	*the frameLabel* is a property that contains the label attached to the current frame. If there is no label, *the frameLabel* property contains 0. You can test this property with Lingo, but you can only set it during a score recording session.
Example	This code segment checks *the frameLabel*, and jumps to a different frame if it finds the frame labeled "done":

```
if the frameLabel = "done" then
  go to frame "start"
else
  go to the frame + 1
end if
```

Parameters	`the frameLabel`
Value	`0`|*string*
See also	beginRecording, endRecording, the frame, the framePalette, the frameScript, the frameSound1, the frameSound2, the frameTempo, frameTransition

the framePalette

MOVIE PROPERTY

Syntax   `set whatpalette = the framePalette`

Usage   *the framePalette* is a property that contains the index number of the current palette. While this is usually the palette assigned to the current frame, if the palette has been modified with *puppetPalette* or through the use of the Palette window in authoring mode, the current display palette is the value stored in *the framePalette*. You can test this property with Lingo, but you can only set it during a score recording session.

If the current palette is one of the built-in ones, it isn't stored in the cast. Therefore, *the framePalette* would contain a negative number from the following list:

System-Mac	-1
Rainbow	-2
Grayscale	-3
Pastel	-4
Vivid	-5
NTSC	-6
Metallic	-7
System -Win (Dir 4)	-101
System-Win	-102

If you wish to control the palette with Lingo more dynamically, use the *puppetPalette* command.

Example   This code segment permanently changes the palette number of the current frame using score recording:

```
beginRecording
  set the framePalette = the number of member "Netscape"
endRecording
```

Parameters   `the framepalette`

Value   *integer*

See also   the frame, the frameLabel, the frameScript, the frameSound1, the frameSound2, the frameTempo, frameTransition, puppetPalette

the frameScript

Syntax   `set the frameScript = 15`

Usage   *the frameScript* is a property that contains the cast number of the script that is attached to the current frame. You can test this property with Lingo, but you can only set it during a score recording session.

　　　　　If there is no script attached to the current frame, then *the frameScript* property is 0. The value of *the frameScript* is equivalent to *the number of member* property for the script.

Examples   This code segment permanently changes the script number of the current frame using score recording:

```
beginRecording
    set the frameScript = the number of member "waitLoop"
endRecording
```

　　　　　If only one cast member with the name *"waitLoop"* exists, then this code segment performs the same task:

```
beginRecording
    set the frameScript = member "waitLoop"
endRecording
```

Parameters   `the frameScript`

Value   *integer*

See also   the frame, the frameLabel, the framePalette, the frameSound1, the frameSound2, the frameTempo, frameTransition

the frameSound1

Syntax   `set the frameSound1 = member "soundtrack"`

Usage   *the frameSound1* is a property that contains the cast number of the sound in sound channel 1 of the current frame. You can test this property with Lingo, but you can only set it during a score recording session.

If there is no sound attached to the associated sound channel, then *the frameSound1* property contains 0.

If you wish to control the sound with Lingo more dynamically, use the *puppetSound* command.

Example   This code segment permanently changes the sound of channel 1 in the current frame using score recording:

```
beginRecording
  set the frameSound1 = the number of member "loopGroov"
endRecording
```

Parameters   the frameSound1

Value   *integer*

See also   the frame, the frameLabel, the framePalette, the frameSound2, the frameTempo, frameTransition, puppetSound

the frameSound2

MOVIE PROPERTY

Syntax   set the frameSound2 = member "soundtrack"

Usage   *the frameSound2* is a property that contains the cast number of the sound in sound channel 2 of the current frame. You can test this property with Lingo, but you can only set it during a score recording session.

If there is no sound attached to the associated sound channel, then *the frameSound2* property contains 0.

If you wish to control the sound with Lingo more dynamically, use the *puppetSound* command.

Example   See the Example for *the frameSound1*.

Parameters   the frameSound2

Value   *integer*

See also   the frame, the frameLabel, the framePalette, the frameSound1, the frameTempo, frameTransition, puppetSound

the frameTempo

MOVIE PROPERTY

Syntax set whatTempo = the frameTempo

Usage *the frameTempo* is a property that contains the tempo assigned to the current frame. You can test this property with Lingo, but you can only set it during a score recording session.

This property only indicates the most recent frame rate setting, not Tempo channel settings that pause the playback head for any reason.

If you wish to control the tempo with Lingo more dynamically, use the *puppetTempo* command.

Example This code segment permanently changes the palette number of the current frame using score recording:

```
beginRecording
    set the frameTempo = 30
endRecording
```

Parameters the frameTempo

Value *integer*

See also the frame, the frameLabel, the framePalette, the frameScript, the frameSound1, the frameSound2, the frameTempo, frameTransition, puppetTempo

the frameTransition

MOVIE PROPERTY

Syntax set the frameTransition = member 30 of castLib 2

Usage *the frameTransition* is a property that contains the cast number of the transition assigned to the current frame. If there is no transition in the current frame, *the frameTransition* contains 0. You can test this property with Lingo, but you can only set it during a score recording session.

If you wish to control the transition with Lingo more dynamically, use the *puppetTransition* command.

Example This code segment permanently changes the cast number of the transition of the current frame using score recording:

```
beginRecording
    set the frameTransition = ¬
        the number of member "checkerFast"
endRecording
```

Parameters the frameTransition

Value *integer*

See also the frame, the frameLabel, the framePalette, the frameScript, the frameSound1, the frameSound2, the frameTempo, frameTransition, puppetTempo

label

Syntax set whatFrame = label ("main")

Usage The *label* function returns the frame number of the frame marker with the specified label. If no frame is marked with the label, then the function returns 0.

Use of the *label* and *marker* functions is functionally identical, and integers can be used as parameters with *label* to find relative marker positions (see the entry for *marker*, on the following page).

Example This function is TRUE if the current frame is labeled "menu":

```
on checkLabel
    if the frame = label ("menu")
end
```

Parameters label (*string*)

Value *integer*

See also go, go loop, go marker, go next, go previous, the labelList, marker, play

marker

FUNCTION

Syntax   `set whatFrame = marker (3)`

Usage   The *marker* function returns the frame number of a marker relative to the position of the playback head.

The marker in the same frame as the playback head is assigned an index value of 0. If no marker is in the same frame as the playback head, the first marker to the left of the playback head (toward frame 1) is assigned the index value of 0. Markers are indexed with increasing integer values in frames after the playback head and increasing negative values toward frame 1.

> **Tip**
>
> *An exception to the standard operation of the* marker *function is when the playback head is in a frame before the first marker. Any index value below 2 will return the frame of the first marker in this instance.*

The *label* and *marker* functions are functionally identical, and strings can be used as parameters with *marker* to find positions of specific marker labels (see the entry for *label*, on the preceding page).

Examples   This function returns the frame number of the current frame if it is *marker* or the first marked frame before the current frame:

`marker(0)`

This handler uses the *marker* function to jump to marked frames when specific conditions are met:

```
on exitFrame
  -- a text file has begun to load
  -- with getNetText. gNetID contains
  -- the latest net ID.
  global gNetID
  if netDone(gNetID) then
    go to marker(1) -- next marked frame
  else
    go to marker(-1) -- previous marked frame
end exitFrame
```

Parameters   marker (*integer*)

Value   *integer*

See also   the frame, the frameLabel, go, go loop, go marker, go next, go previous, label, the labelList, play

puppetPalette

COMMAND

Syntax   puppetPalette "MO"
puppetPalette -1, 10

Usage   The *puppetPalette* command lets you take control of the palette channel in the score with Lingo. If you wish to return control of the palette channel to the score, use the command *puppetPalette 0*.

The first parameter is the name or number of a palette cast member. An optional speed parameter will fade in the new palette over a specific time period: a value of 1 produces the slowest fade (5 seconds), and 30 produces the fastest fade (10 ticks). This is a variance from the Macromedia documentation for this command, which specifies a maximum value of 60 for this parameter.

Macromedia documentation also specifies an optional third parameter that controls the fade over a number of frames, allowing movement on the stage while the palette change is happening; however, this appears not to actually work. If you need to do palette animation with moving sprites, use the score palette settings.

The *puppetPalette* command only works in Shockwave if you use a PALETTE=FOREGROUND setting in the EMBED tag. This isn't recommended, however, as the Shockwave movie then distorts the colors of everything else on the screen. Use with discretion.

Example   This command causes the movie palette to change over a period of time from the current one to the cast member named "vivid-Win" in the cast:

puppetPalette "vivid-Win"

Parameters   puppetPalette *integer|string*
puppetPalette *integer|string, integer*

See also   the framePalette, the palette of member, the paletteMapping, the paletteRef of member

puppetTempo

Syntax   puppetTempo 60

Usage   The *puppetTempo* command lets you take control of the movie's frame rate
with Lingo. If you wish to return control of the tempo channel back to the
score, use the command *puppetTempo 0*.

The parameter must be a number between 1 and 120, with the smaller
number specifying a slower frame rate. This command does not give you the
ability to create tempo settings that wait for sounds or videos to end, or to
wait for a specific amount of time (those types of tempo settings are easily
created with standard behaviors in Director 6, or with ordinary Lingo).

Example This command sets the frame rate of the movie to 15 frames per second:

puppetTempo 15

Parameters   puppetTempo *integer*

See also   the frameTempo

puppetTransition

Syntax   puppetTransition member 5

puppetTransition "wipe", 4

puppetTransition member 3 of castLib 2, 10, 4

puppettransition "pushup", 3, 8, TRUE

Usage   The *puppetTransition* command causes a transition to occur when the
playback head moves from the current frame to the next frame. You can
specify a transition cast member, a transition Xtra stored in a cast member,
or a built-in transition.

You can use up to three parameters with a built-in transition to specify
time period, smoothness, and whether the transition affects the entire stage
or only the changing area. The time parameter is an integer specifying the
number of ¼ seconds for the period of the transition (maximum value is
120, or 30 seconds).

The smoothness parameter determines the number of pixels that will be changed in each step of the transition, and is a value from 1 to 128 (the more pixels changed per step, the faster the transition will be). This value will override the time parameter if the desired quality of smoothness causes the transition to animate more slowly than the CPU can sustain.

The last parameter is TRUE if the transition will only affect the changing area of the stage, and FALSE if the transition will affect the entire stage.

If a cast member transition is used, the settings for time, smoothness, and changing area parameters are controlled by the properties *the duration of member*, *the chunkSize of member*, and *the changeArea of member*.

This is the list of Director's built-in transitions arranged by index number:

Index No.	Transition	Index No.	Transition
01	Wipe right	27	Random rows
02	Wipe left	28	Random columns
03	Wipe down	29	Cover down
04	Wipe up	30	Cover down, left
05	Center out, horizontal	31	Cover down, right
06	Edges in, horizontal	32	Cover left
07	Center out, vertical	33	Cover right
08	Edges in, vertical	34	Cover up
09	Center out, square	35	Cover up, left
10	Edges in, square	36	Cover up, right
11	Push left	37	Venetian blinds
12	Push right	38	Checkerboard
13	Push down	39	Strips on bottom, build left
14	Push up	40	Strips on bottom, build right
15	Reveal up	41	Strips on left, build down
16	Reveal up, right	42	Strips on left, build up
17	Reveal right	43	Strips on right, build down
18	Reveal down, right	44	Strips on right, build up
19	Reveal down	45	Strips on top, build left
20	Reveal down, left	46	Strips on top, build right
21	Reveal left	47	Zoom open
22	Reveal up, left	48	Zoom close
23	Dissolve, pixels fast *	49	Vertical blinds
24	Dissolve, boxy rectangles	50	Dissolve, bits fast *
25	Dissolve, boxy squares	51	Dissolve, pixels *
26	Dissolve, patterns	52	Dissolve, bits *

Transitions marked with an asterisk (*) in the above table will not work on monitors that are set to display 32-bit color.

If you use a transition Xtra in Shockwave, the Xtra must be located in the Shockwave plug-in support directory.

Example   This command causes the "Edges in, horizontal" transition to happen when the playback head moves to the next frame, with a duration of 10 seconds, a chunkSize of 5 pixels per second, and affecting the entire stage:

```
puppetTransition 6, 40, 5, FALSE
```

Parameters   puppetTransition *member*

puppetTransition *integer*

puppetTransition *integer*, *integer*

puppetTransition *integer*, *integer*, *integer*

puppetTransition *integer*, *integer*, *integer*, *boolean*

See also   the changeArea of member, the chunkSize of member, the duration of member, the frameTransition, the transitionType of member, zoomBox

Frames: Sprites Category

This category covers Lingo events and properties related to the appearance of sprites in the score.

on beginSprite

HANDLER

Syntax
```
on beginSprite
on beginSprite me
```

Usage
The *beginSprite* message is sent each time a different sprite or script is encountered by the playback head as it enters a frame. The message is sent to the frame script if any of the sprites are modified. Then each of the new sprites in the frame receives the message, by channel number order. Handlers for the message can be placed in frame scripts, sprite scripts, or behaviors. If the handler is used in a behavior, the *me* parameter must be used.

The *beginSprite* message is sent before the *prepareFrame* message. In the first frame of the movie, it occurs after *prepareMovie* but before the *startMovie* message or the first *prepareFrame* message.

Example
This handler from a behavior sets a property of the behavior called *normalPicture* to the number of the cast member currently in use for the sprite the behavior is attached to:

```
on beginSprite me
  set the normalPicture of me = ¬
    the member of sprite the spriteNum of me
end
```

Parameters
```
on beginSprite
  statements
end
```
```
on beginSprite me
  statements
end
```

See also
on endSprite, on enterFrame, on exitFrame

the currentSpriteNum

MOVIE PROPERTY

Syntax   `set aSprite = the currentSpriteNum`

Usage   *the currentSpriteNum* is a property that indicates which sprite generated the last event. In many ways, it is used similarly to the way the *clickOn* property is used, except that *currentSpriteNum* is set by *mouseEnter*, *mouseLeave*, and other events, not just *mouseDown*.

Example   This sprite script calls a handler, passing the value of the sprite rolled over as a parameter:

```
on mouseEnter
   doButton the currentSpriteNum
end
```

Value   *integer*

See also   the clickOn, the spriteNum of me

on endSprite

HANDLER

Syntax   `on endSprite`

   `on endSprite me`

Usage   The *endSprite* message is sent each time the playback head leaves a frame for a frame that does not contain the current frame script or sprites. The message is sent to the frame script if any of the sprites are modified. Then each of the sprites in the frame receives the message, by channel number order. Handlers for the message can be placed in frame scripts, sprite scripts, or behaviors. If the handler is used in a behavior, the *me* parameter must be used.

   The *endSprite* message is sent after the *exitFrame* message. In the first frame of the movie, it occurs after *prepareMovie* but before the *startMovie* message or the first *prepareFrame* message. An *endSprite* message is issued after the *stopMovie* handler as well.

Example   This handler from a behavior explicitly depuppets the sprite channel of the
sprite it's attached to:

```
on endSprite me
  puppetSprite the spriteNum of me, FALSE
end
```

Parameters
```
on endSprite
  statements
end
```

```
on endSprite me
  statements
end
```

See also   on beginSprite, on enterFrame, on exitFrame

on prepareFrame   HANDLER

Syntax   on prepareFrame

on prepareFrame me

Usage   The *prepareFrame* message is sent every time the playback head enters a new
frame. Commands within the *prepareFrame* handler are executed before the
contents of the frame are drawn on the stage.
   The *prepareFrame* message is sent before the *enterFrame* message.
   The *prepareFrame* handler can be used in behaviors, frame scripts, or sprite
scripts.

Example   This example hides all of the sprites in the current frame before the frame is
drawn:

```
on prepareFrame
  repeat with i = 1 to 120
    set the visible of sprite i = FALSE
  end repeat
end
```

Parameters
```
on prepareFrame
  statements
end
```

```
on prepareFrame me
  statements
end
```

See also   on enterFrame, on exitFrame, on prepareMovie

stopEvent

COMMAND

Syntax   stopEvent

Usage   The *stopEvent* command is used to prevent the current message from being passed along the message hierarchy. This is similar to the *dontPassEvent* command in earlier versions of Director.

With Director 6, however, it is possible for multiple behaviors containing the same handler to be attached to the same sprite. Depending on your needs and changing conditions during the execution of handlers, it may be necessary to stop the event before another behavior receives it.

A *mouseUp* message in Director 6 travels the following path:

> **Primary Event Handler**
> *it passes to*
> **Sprite Script or Behaviors**
> (in order of appearance in Behavior Inspector)
> *if none exists it passes to*
> **Cast Script**
> *if none exists it passes to*
> **Frame Script**
> *if none exists it passes to*
> **Movie Script**

There's no need to use the *stopEvent* command at any level past the sprite behaviors, as messages are not passed by any scripts except primary event handlers and behaviors for the same sprite unless the *pass* command is used.

User-defined events are never passed.

Example   In a behavior script, this handler determines if the behavior property *operative* is FALSE. If it is, the message is stopped, and no other behaviors attached to the sprite will receive the *mouseUp* message:

```
on mouseUp me
   if not (the operative of me) then stopEvent
end
```

Parameters   stopEvent

See also   dontPassEvent, pass

Score Generation Category

These commands and properties allow you to modify the movie's score using Lingo. This powerful feature was added in Director 5. It is largely used during authoring mode, as memory considerations can make score recording problematic during playback.

beginRecording

Syntax   `beginRecording`

Usage   The *beginRecording* command starts a score recording session. Commands issued between a *beginRecording* statement and an *endRecording* statement may affect the score and may be permanent if the affected movie is saved.

Example   This handler will create a sprite that moves around the center of the stage in an elliptical path. It uses all of the basic sprite recording commands, including *beginRecording, endRecording,* and *updateFrame.*

```
on orbitSprite mySprite, myNumberOfDivisions
  set tCenterH = (the stageRight - the stageLeft) /2
  set tCenterV = (the stageBottom - the stageTop) /2
  set tIncrement = 2.0 * pi / myNumberOfDivisions
  set tCurrDiv = 0
  set tOffSet  = 30
  beginRecording
   repeat with i = 1 to myNumberOfDivisions
     go to frame i
     set the memberNum of sprite mySprite = ¬
       the number of member "ball"
     set the ink of sprite mySprite = 8
     set tXVal = sin (tCurrDiv)
     set tYVal = cos (tCurrDiv)
     set the locH of sprite mySprite = ¬
       tCenterH + (tXVal * tOffSet * 3.0)
     set the locV of sprite mySprite = ¬
       tCenterV + (tYVal * tOffSet * 1.4)
     set tCurrDiv = tCurrDiv + tIncrement
     updateFrame
   end repeat
   go to frame myNumberOfDivisions
   set the frameScript to member "loop"
   updateFrame
  endRecording
  go to frame 1
end orbitSprite
```

To use the above handler, type something like **orbitSprite 2, 20** into the Message window, where the first parameter is the sprite number and the second is the number of frames to be recorded.

Parameters   `beginRecording`

See also   endRecording, updateFrame

clearFrame

COMMAND

Syntax   `clearFrame`

Usage   The *clearFrame* command clears the entire contents of the current frame during a score recording session.

Example   This handler goes to a frame, clears its contents, then returns to the original frame:

```
on clearAndReturn myFrameNum
  set tCurrFrame = the frame
  beginRecording
    go to frame myFrameNum
    clearFrame
    updateFrame
  endRecording
  go to frame tCurrFrame
end clearAndReturn
```

Parameters   `clearFrame`

See also   beginRecording, deleteFrame, duplicateFrame, endRecording, insertFrame, updateFrame, the updateLock, the score, the scoreSelection

deleteFrame

COMMAND

Syntax   `deleteFrame`

Usage   The *deleteFrame* command deletes the frame the playback head is in during a score recording session. All subsequent frames are moved one frame closer to the beginning of the movie. The playback head moves one frame forward after a *deleteFrame* command.

Example   This handler deletes a range of frames from *myStart* to *myEnd*:

```
on delRangeOfFrames myStart, myEnd
  beginRecording
  go to frame myStart
  repeat with tFrame = myStart to myEnd
    deleteFrame
  end repeat
  endRecording
end delRangeOfFrames
```

Parameters   deleteFrame

See also   beginRecording, clearFrame, duplicateFrame, endRecording, insertFrame, updateFrame, the updateLock, the score, the scoreSelection

duplicateFrame

COMMAND

Syntax   duplicateFrame

Usage   The *duplicateFrame* command adds a duplicate of the current frame after the current frame during a score recording session. All of the frames after the current frame are moved one frame to the right to accommodate the new frame.

This command does the same thing as the *insertFrame* command.

> **Tip**
>
> *Contrary to Macromedia documentation, the new frame does not become the current frame. The playback head does not move after a* duplicateFrame *command is executed, unless the* updateFrame *command is executed.*

Example   This code segment duplicates the current frame:

```
beginRecording
  duplicateFrame
endRecording
```

Parameters   duplicateFrame

See also   beginRecording, clearFrame, deleteFrame, endRecording, insertFrame, updateFrame, the updateLock, the score, the scoreSelection

endRecording

Syntax   endRecording

Usage   The *endRecording* command signifies the end of a score recording session. Lingo that executes between a *beginRecording* and an *endRecording* statement may make permanent changes to the score. After the *endRecording* command is executed, sprites may be puppeted and changed with Lingo in the typical way.

Example   This handler permanently clears the contents of the frame *myFrameNum*. The *endRecording* statement marks the end of the score recording session:

```
on clearAndReturn myFrameNum
  set tCurrFrame = the frame
  beginRecording
    go to frame myFrameNum
    clearFrame
    updateFrame
  endRecording
  go to frame tCurrFrame
end clearAndReturn
```

Parameters   endRecording

See also   beginRecording, clearFrame, deleteFrame, duplicateFrame, insertFrame, updateFrame, the updateLock, the score, the scoreSelection

insertFrame

Syntax   insertFrame

Usage   The *insertFrame* command duplicates the current frame during a score recording session. This command does the same thing as the *duplicateFrame* command.

Example This code segment duplicates the current frame the number of times specified by the *numDupes* parameter:

```
on multipleDupe numDupes
  beginRecording
    repeat with i = 1 to numDupes
      insertFrame
    endRecording
  endRecording
end
```

Parameters insertFrame

See also beginRecording, clearFrame, deleteFrame, duplicateFrame, endRecording, updateFrame, the updateLock, the score, the scoreSelection

the score

MOVIE PROPERTY

Syntax `set the score = the media of member 4`

Usage *the score* is a property that determines which data is associated with the score of the current movie. Data for any scores that are different from the score displayed in the Score window at the time of the last saved version of the movie can be stored in film loop cast members. You can test and set this property with Lingo.

Score data can be copied from any frames of a movie and pasted into a cast member position to create a *film loop*. Film loops can contain everything from sprites to transitions and tempo settings. When a film loop is assigned to replace the score with *the score* property, the first frame of the film loop is placed in frame 1 of the score.

Examples This code segment replaces the current score with a film loop but stores the old score in a global variable so it can be used later:

```
global gScore
set gScore = the score
set the score = the media of member "filmloop"
```

Then, you can use a code segment like this to restore the score:

```
global gScore
set the score = gScore
```

Parameters   `the score`

Value   *media*

See also   the media of member, the scoreSelection, the type of member

the scoreSelection

MOVIE PROPERTY

Syntax   `set aSelectionList = the scoreSelection`

Usage   *the scoreSelection* is a property that contains a list of sublists. Each sublist contains one of the areas currently selected in the score. Each sublist has four values: [*startSprite, endSprite, startFrame, endFrame*]. You can test and set this property with Lingo.

This property can be useful when you wish to build custom Lingo score-generation tools.

These numbers correspond to the nonsprite channels in the score:

    0:   script channel

   -1:   sound channel 2

   -2:   sound channel 1

   -3:   transition channel

   -4:   palette channel

   -5:   tempo channel

Example   This statement in the Message window shows that three areas are selected in the score. They include the script channel, and sprites 6, 12, and 13 in frames 5 through 10.

```
put the scoreSelection
-- [[0,0,5,10], [6,6,5,10], [12,13,5,10]]
```

Value   *list of [integer, integer, integer, integer]*

updateFrame

Syntax
: `set`

Usage
: The *updateFrame* command causes the changes that have accumulated during a score recording session to be applied to the score. It only works during a score recording session, which consists of all of the commands between the *beginRecording* and the *endRecording* commands.
  Without the *updateFrame* command, changes to the score are not displayed until the *endRecording* command is executed.

Example
: See the Example for *beginRecording*.

Parameters
: `updateFrame`

See also
: beginRecording, clearFrame, deleteFrame, duplicateFrame, endRecording, the score, the scoreSelection, the updateLock

the updateLock

Syntax
: `set the updateLock = FALSE`

Usage
: *the updateLock* is a property that is TRUE if the stage will not be updated during score recording, and FALSE if the stage is updated while recording. You can test and set this property with Lingo.
  When *the updateLock* property is TRUE, the stage display is unchanged even while the score is changed by Lingo during score recording. You can use this property to hide score changes from the user.

Example
: This code segment freezes the display on the stage while another frame is updated:

```
set tCurrFrame = the frame
beginRecording
  set the updateLock = TRUE
  go to frame 10
```

```
    set the memberNum of sprite 10 = ¬
      the number of member "box"
    set the loc of sprite 10 = point(100,100)
    updateFrame
    go to frame tCurrFrame
    set the updateLock = FALSE
endRecording
```

Parameters   the updateStage

Value   *boolean*

See also   beginRecording, clearFrame, deleteFrame, duplicateFrame, endRecording, the score, the scoreSelection, updateFrame

Menus
Category

These Lingo keywords control the custom menu capabilities of Director movies.

the checkMark of menuItem

MENU ITEM PROPERTY

Syntax   `set the checkMark of menuItem "Bold" of menu "Text" = TRUE`

Usage   *the checkMark of menuItem* is a property that determines if the specified menu item of a custom menu has a checkmark next to it when displayed.

Example   This example from a sprite behavior mirrors a button selection in a corresponding menu by setting *the checkMark of menuItem* property. The menu and menu item associated with the button are specified by the behavior properties *buttonMenu* and *buttonItem*.

```
on mouseUp me
  set the buttonState of me = not (the buttonState of me)
  -- buttonState is a user-defined behavior property
  set the checkMark of menuItem buttonItem ¬
    of menu buttonMenu = the buttonState of me
end
```

Parameters   `the checkmark of menuItem` *integer/string* `of menu` *integer/string*

Value   *boolean*

See also   the enabled of menu, installMenu, menu, the name of menu, the name of menuItem, the number of menuItems, the number of menus, the script of menuItem

the enabled of menuItem

MENU ITEM PROPERTY

Syntax   `set the enabled of menuItem 3 of menu 2 = FALSE`

Usage   *the enabled of menuItem* is a property that determines whether the specified menu item of a custom menu is displayed as active (in black) and can be selected or displayed as inactive (in gray) and cannot be selected.

Example   See the Example for *installMenu* on the following page.

Parameters   `the enabled of menuItem` *integer/string* `of menu` *integer/string*

Value   *boolean*

See also   the checkMark of menu, installMenu, menu, the name of menu, the name of
menuItem, the number of menuItems, the number of menus, the script of
menuItem

installMenu

Syntax   `installMenu 4`

Usage   The *installMenu* command creates a custom menu using data from a field
cast member specified by the parameter. See the *menu* entry for formatting
information.

Examples   A field cast member named "Bezier Menu" contains the following text:

```
menu: Bezier
Create/C
Modify/M
Delete/D
    (-
Extend/E
```

This script, when executed during playback, will create a menu named
"Bezier," with five items: a "Create" item, a "Modify" item, a "Delete" item,
a separating line, and an "Extend" item below the line. It then disables all of
the selectable items except for "Create." Each of the items is assigned a script
to execute when enabled and selected:

```
on installBezierMenu
  installMenu "Bezier Menu"
  set the enabled of menuItem "Modify" ¬
    of menu "Bezier" = FALSE
  set the enabled of menuItem "Delete" ¬
    of menu "Bezier" = FALSE
  set the enabled of menuItem "Extend" ¬
    of menu "Bezier" = FALSE
  set the script of menuItem "Modify" ¬
    of menu "Bezier" = "modifyBezier"
  set the script of menuItem "Delete" ¬
    of menu "Bezier" = "deleteBezier"
  set the script of menuItem "Extend" ¬
    of menu "Bezier" = "extendBezier"
end
```

Parameters   `installMenu` *integer*|*string*

                 `installMenu` *integer*|*string* `of castLib` *integer*|*string*

See also   menu

menu

Syntax   `menu: Bezier`

Usage   The *menu* keyword is used in field cast members to indicate that the text of the cast member will be used to build custom menus and menu items.

     The first line of a field cast member used for a custom menu should always start with the *menu:* keyword, followed by a colon, then the name of the menu as it will appear in the menu bar (this is also used as *the name of menu* property for the menu.

     Additional menus can be created from the same field cast member by using the *menu* keyword again on a subsequent line.

     Each line after the menu keyword can contain data for building the menu, in this format:

```
Extend ( !v<B<I /E | go "Extend"
```

     The word *Extend* represents the name of the menu item. The (character can be used to disable the menu item as an alternative to setting *the enabled of menuItem* property to FALSE. The next items are Macintosh-specific formatting codes, indicating that the menu item should be checked and that the menu item's name should be displayed in a bold italic version of the type used for the menu. The */E* indicates that the Ctrl+E or Command+E key combination will trigger the same action as selecting the menu item. The | symbol separates the name and formatting information for the menu item from its action, which in this case is *go "Extend"*.

     Most of the information in this line can be modified from Lingo as the movie plays.

     The MacOS-specific codes for formatting menu items are:

    !v   checkmark

    <B   bold

    <I   italic

    <U   underline

    <O   outline

    <S   shadow

These codes don't work on most Windows platforms, so don't expect cross-platform support.

Lines to separate groups of menu commands can be inserted by using the characters (-.

> **Tip**
>
> *On MacOS computers, it's possible to create an Apple menu, with access to the control panels and other Apple menu items by using the @ sign for the name of the first menu.*

Example   See the Example for *installMenu*.

See also   installMenu

the name of menuItem MENU ITEM PROPERTY

Syntax
```
set the name of menuItem "Extend" ¬
    of menu "Bezier" = "Extent Path"
```

Usage   *the name of menuItem* is a property that allows you to test and modify the names of menu items during authoring and playback. The name of a menu item is the text displayed in the menu.

While you can change the names of the menu items, you cannot change the names of menus themselves.

Separator lines in menus have a *name of menuItem* value of "".

Example   This example determines the name of the fifth item in the third menu:
```
set whatMenu = the name of menuItem 5 of menu 3
```

Parameters   the name of menuItem *integer|string* of menu *integer|string*

Value   *string*

See also   menu, the name of menu

the number of menuItems

Syntax   `set howMany = the number of menuItems of menu "Bezier"`

Usage   *the numberof menuItems* is a property that determines how many menu items belong to a specific menu. This property cannot be directly modified.

Example   This function returns the total number of menu items, not counting separator lines:

```
on totalMI
  set aCount = 0
  repeat with i = 1 to the number of menus
    repeat with j = 1 to the number of menuItems of menu i
      if not (the name of menuItem j of menu i = "") then
        set aCount = aCount + 1
      end if
    end repeat
    end repeat
  return aCount
end
```

Parameters   `the mnumber of menuItems of menu` *integer|string*

Value   *integer*

See also   the number of menus

the number of menus

Syntax   `set howMany = the number of menus`

Usage   *the number of menus* is a property that contains a value representing the number of user-installed menus in use by the movie. It cannot be directly modified.

Example   See the Example for *the number of menuItems*.

Parameters   `the number of menus`

Value   *`integer`*

See also   installMenu, the number of menuItems

the script of menuItem

MENU ITEM PROPERTY

Syntax   `set the script of menuItem 3 of menu 2 = "attitude"`

Usage   *the script of menuItem* is a property that determines the action to be taken if the menu item is selected with the mouse or its key-command equivalent has been pressed.

Example   See the Example for *installMenu*.

Parameters   `the script of menuItem` *`integer/string`* `of menu` *`integer/string`*

Value   *`string`*

Date and Time Category

These Lingo properties and keywords give you access to time and date information about the computer that the movie is playing on.

abbreviated

Syntax
```
set whatDate = the abbr date
set whatTime = the abbrev time
set whatDate = the abbreviated date
```

Usage
The *abbreviated* keyword is used with *the date* and *the time* properties to return a date or time in the format as shown in the example below. It can be used in three forms: *abbreviated, abbrev,* and *abbr.* All three forms produce the same results.

Examples
This example shows the *abbreviated* keyword used with *the date* property:
```
put the abbreviated date
-- "Mon, Apr 1, 1997"
```
This example shows the *abbreviated* keyword used with *the time* property:
```
put the abbreviated time
-- "11:26 PM"
```

See also
the date, long, short, the time

the date

Syntax
```
set whatDate = the date
```

Usage
the date is a property that contains the current date, according to the computer's system clock. It has three forms: *abbreviated, long,* and *short.* The default is *short.* Beware—non-U.S. systems may have a different date format, such as day/month/year, rather than the U.S. month/day/year format.

Examples
These statements show various values that the *date* function can return (copied from Message window):
```
put the date
-- "9/22/97"
put the short date
-- "9/22/97"
```

```
put the abbr date
-- "Mon, Sep 22, 1997"
put the long date
-- "Monday, September 22, 1987"
```

This function converts *the date* to a standard numerical format for most international date formats by comparing *the short date* to *the abbreviated date*. It builds a list of the values retrieved from the short version, compares that list to data extracted from the abbreviated version, and assigns values in a property list for #day, #month, and #year. To determine the month using this function, set a variable equal to *the month of internationalDate ()*:

```
on internationalDate
  set IDate = [:]
  set aDate = the short date
  set dateLength = the number of chars of aDate
  set sDate = []
  set aNum = ""
  -- the following repeat loop reads the characters of the
  -- short date format, breaking it into individual
  -- numbers and stuffing them into a list
  -- the short date is composed entirely of numbers
  repeat with i = 1 to dateLength
    set aChar = char i of aDate
    set aSCII = charToNum (aChar)
    if (aSCII < 48) or (aSCII > 57) then
      if aNum = "" then nothing
      else
        add sDate, (value (aNum) mod 100)
        set aNum = ""
      end if
    else
      set aNum = aNum & aChar
      if i = dateLength then
        add sDate, (value (aNum) mod 100)
      end if
    end if
  end repeat
  set aDate = the abbreviated date
  set dateLength = the length of aDate
  set abbDate = []
  set aNum = ""
  -- the following repeat loop reads the characters of the
  -- abbreviated date format, breaking it into individual
  -- numbers and stuffing them into a list
  -- the abbreviated date is composed of a year number,
  -- a day number, and strings for the month and
  -- the day of the week
  -- the routine ignores characters other than numbers
```

```
          repeat with i = 1 to dateLength
            set aChar = char i of aDate
            set aSCII = charToNum (aChar)
            if (aSCII < 48) or (aSCII > 57) then
              if aNum = "" then nothing
              else
                add abbDate, (value (aNum) mod 100)
                -- truncates year values to last two numbers
                set aNum = ""
              end if
            else
              set aNum = aNum & aChar
              if i = dateLength then
                add abbDate, (value (aNum) mod 100)
              end if
            end if
          end repeat
          -- at this point, we have two lists, one with three
          -- items (sDate), and one with two (abbDate)
          -- the abbDate list contains numbers only for the
          -- day and year
          -- from here on out, it's a process of elimination
          -- as the day and year are matched up, the remaining
          -- value can only be the month!
          set year = getAt (abbDate, 2)
          set day = getAt (abbDate, 1)
          set whereYear = getOne (sDate, year)
          addProp IDate, #year, value (year)
          deleteAt sDate, whereYear
          set whereDay = getOne (sDate, day)
          addProp IDate, #day, value (day)
          deleteAt sDate, whereDay
          addProp IDate, #month, value (getAt (sDate, 1))
          return Idate
        end
```

Parameters   the date

             the abbr date

             the abbrev date

             the abbreviated date

             the short date

             the long date

Value   *string*

See also   abbreviated, long, short, the time

long

Syntax   `set whatDate = the long date`

Usage   The *long* keyword is used with *the date* and *the time* properties to return a date or time in the format shown in the example below.

Examples   This example shows the *long* keyword used with *the date* property:

```
put the long date
-- "Tuesday, April 1, 1997"
```

This example shows the *long* keyword used with *the time* property:

```
put the long time
-- "10:04:02 AM"
```

See also   abbreviated, the date, short, the time

short

Syntax   `set whatDate = the short date`

Usage   The *short* keyword is used with *the date* and *the time* properties to return a date or time in the format as shown in the examples below.

Examples   This example shows the *short* keyword used with *the date* property:

```
put the short date
-- "4/14/97"
```

This example shows the *short* keyword used with *the time* property:

```
put the short time
-- "10:06 AM"
```

See also   abbreviated, the date, long, time

the ticks

Syntax   `set howLongSinceStarted = the ticks`

Usage   *the ticks* is a property that contains the number of ticks since the computer was started. There are 60 ticks in one second.
   You can use *the ticks* to create any number of custom timers.

Examples   These handlers return the network data rate measured while downloading a remote text file, *myURL,* using the *getNetText* command. We create a custom timer by storing *the ticks* in a global, *gStartTicks,* then we subtract the *gStartTicks* from *the ticks* to calculate elapsed time:

```
on testDataRate myURL
  -- put me in a movie script
  global gStartTicks, gNetID, gTimeFlag
  set gStartTicks = the ticks
  getNetText myURL
  set gNetID = getLatestNetID
  set gTimeFlag = TRUE
end testDataRate

on exitFrame
  -- put me in a frame script

  global gStartTicks, gNetID, gTimeFlag
  if gTimeFlag then
    if netDone(gNetID) then
      set gTimeFlag = FALSE
      if netError(gNetID) = "OK" then
        put "I measured" && ¬
        length(netTextResult(gNetID)) / ¬
        ((the ticks - gStartTicks) / 60) ¬
        && "Bytes Per Second" ¬
        into field "result"
      else
        put "Error:" && netError(gNetID) ¬
        into field "result"
      end if
    end if
  end if
  go to the frame
end exitFrame
```

To use these handlers, put the *exitFrame* handler in a frame script and put the *testDataRate* handler in a movie script. Create a field named "result" and put it on the stage. Make a button with a handler like the following:

```
on mouseUp
  testDataRate("http://www.nnn.com/test.txt")
end mouseUp
```

Then burn the movie into a .dcr and test it in your browser. You can modify this technique in many ways to be able to test the data rate of a user's connection in a behind-the-scenes manner. You can only make this test once per filename without clearing the file cache. If the file is already in the browser's cache, then the measurement will be very inaccurate.

Parameters   the ticks

Value   *integer*

See also   the timer

the time

MOVIE PROPERTY

Syntax   `set whatTime = the time`

Usage   *the time* is a property that contains the current time, according to the computer's system clock. It has three forms: *abbreviated*, *long*, and *short*. The default is *short* and is identical to *abbreviated*.

Examples   These statements show various values that the *time* function can return (copied from Message window):

```
put the time
-- "11:46 PM"
put the short time
-- "11:46 PM"
put the long time
-- "11:46:37 PM"
put the abbr time
-- "11:46 PM"
```

Parameters   the time

Value   *string*

See also   abbreviated, the date, long, short

the timer

Syntax   set howLong = the timer

Usage   *the timer* is a property that contains the number of ticks since the movie started, or since the *startTimer* command was last issued. There are 60 ticks per second. The *startTimer* command sets *the timer* property to 0.

Example   This handler causes a Lingo delay for the specified number of seconds:

```
on wait mySeconds
  startTimer
  repeat while the timer < mySeconds * 60
    nothing
  end repeat
end wait
```

Parameters   the timer

Value   *integer*

See also   startTimer, the ticks

Buttons Category

These Lingo keywords control the operation of button (*#button*) cast members. This is distinct from the custom button type (*#btned*) added in Director 6.

the buttonStyle

MOVIE PROPERTY

Syntax set whatStyle = the buttonStyle

Usage The movie property *the buttonStyle* determines how Director's *#button* members will behave when the user clicks on one button then drags to another button.

If *the buttonStyle* is FALSE, when the user clicks the mouse over a *#button* member then drags to other *#button* members, those other buttons become highlighted. If the user then releases the mouse over a button other than the original, its *mouseUp* handler executes.

If *the buttonStyle* is TRUE, only the first button clicked will be highlighted; subsequent buttons that are dragged over will not highlight, nor do their *mouseUp* handlers execute if the mouse is released over them.

Example This statement sets *the buttonStyle* system property to TRUE. Its default state is FALSE:

set the buttonStyle = TRUE

Parameters the buttonStyle

Value *boolean*

See also the buttonType of member, the checkBoxAccess, the checkBoxType

the buttonType of member

MEMBER PROPERTY

Syntax set the buttonType of member "exit" = #pushButton

Usage The property *the buttonType of member* determines how a *#button* cast member is displayed. The possible values are *#checkBox*, *#pushButton*, and *#radioButton*. You can test or set this property with Lingo.

A standard push button displays as a rounded rectangle with the name of the button displayed inside the rectangle. When highlighted, it reverses. It is typically used for buttons that initiate an action.

A standard check box button displays an empty square box with the name of the button to the right. When highlighted, it displays a cross through the box. It is typically used for multiple-choice selections. Clicking on the button toggles the highlight on and off.

A standard radio button displays an empty circle, with the name of the button to the right. When highlighted, it displays a black circle inside the circle. It is typically used to provide one of a group of mutually exclusive selections. Clicking on the button toggles the highlight on and off.

Example This handler will set *the buttonType* property of a button member, if it is indeed a *#button* cast member:

```
on setButtonType myButtonMember, myType
  if the type of member myButtonMember = ¬
    #button then
    set the buttonType of member ¬
      myButtonMember = myType
  end if
end setButtonType
```

Parameters the buttonType of *member*

Value #checkBox|#pushButton|radioButton

See also the buttonStyle, the checkBoxAccess, the checkBoxType

the checkBoxAccess

MOVIE PROPERTY

Syntax `set the checkBoxAccess = 1`

Usage The movie property *the checkBoxAccess* controls the overall behavior of Director's built-in check boxes and radio buttons. You can test and set this property with Lingo.

If *the checkBoxAccess* is 0 (the default), check boxes and radio buttons behave normally, allowing the user to turn them on and off. When set to 1, the user can turn check boxes and radio buttons on but not off. When set to 2, the user's actions have no effect on check boxes or radio buttons—they can only be changed with Lingo.

Example   This statement sets *the checkBoxAccess* property to 1, allowing the user to turn buttons on but not off:

```
set the checkBoxAccess to 1
```

Parameters   the checkBoxAccess

Value   0|1|2

See also   the checkBoxType, the hilite of member

the checkBoxType

MOVIE PROPERTY

Syntax   `set whatType = the checkBoxType`

Usage   The movie property *the checkBoxType* contains 0, 1, and 2 values that determine how Director's built-in check boxes look when they are selected. You can test and set this property with Lingo.

If *the checkBoxType* is 0 (the default), check boxes have the typical "X" when selected. When this property is set to 1, check boxes have a black box in their center when selected. When set to 2, check boxes are filled with black when selected.

This property does not affect radio buttons.

Example   This statement sets *the checkBoxType* property to determine that check boxes will be filled with black when highlighted:

```
set the checkBoxType to 2
```

Parameters   the checkBoxType

Value   0|1|2

See also   the checkBoxAccess, the hilite of member

the hilite of member

MEMBER PROPERTY

Syntax
```
set isHilighted = the hilite of member "sound"
```

Usage
the hilite of member is a property that is TRUE if the specified check box or radio button member is highlighted. You can test and set this property with Lingo.

Example
This statement will put an X in the checkbox of the button named "has e-mail", indicating that it is highlighted:

```
set the hilite of member "has e-mail" = TRUE
```

Parameters
```
the hilite of member
```

Value
boolean

See also
the checkBoxAccess, the checkBoxType

Shapes Category

These Lingo properties affect cast members of the *#shape* type. These include lines, rectangles, ovals, and rounded rectangles created using the Tool palette. Shapes take up significantly less memory than bitmaps and are resolution-independent. On the other hand, they have no detail.

Most of these properties can be set at the sprite level as well, meaning you can use the same filled rectangle shape cast member as any number of sprites with different fill colors, line widths, and line colors.

the filled of member

Syntax   `set isFilled = the filled of member "disc"`

Usage   *the filled of member* is a property that is TRUE if the specified shape is filled with a pattern, and FALSE if the specified shape is transparent. You can test and set this property with Lingo.

Example   This Lingo function fills the member *myMem* with a pattern, if it really is a *#shape* cast member:

```
on fillMember myMem
  if the type of member myMem = #shape then
    set the filled of member myMem = TRUE
  end if
end fillMember
```

Parameters   `the filled of` *member*

Value   *boolean*

See also   the foreColor of member, the pattern of member

the lineSize of member

Syntax   `set the lineSize of member "ring" = 10`

Usage   *the lineSize of member* is a property that contains the thickness, in pixels, of the line bordering the specified shape cast member. You can test and set this property with Lingo.

     Multiple instances of the same shape cast member may have different line thicknesses set for them, by using *the lineSize of sprite* property.

     The maximum value is 14.

Example This statement sets the line size of the shape member "ball" to 3 points, if it really is a *#shape* member:

```
if the type of member "ball" = #shape then
  set the lineSize of member "ball" = 3
end if
```

Parameters the lineSize of *member*

Value *integer*

See also the lineSize of sprite

the pattern of member

MEMBER PROPERTY

Syntax `set whatpattern = the pattern of member 3 of castLib 2`

Usage *the pattern of member* is a property that contains the index number of the pattern applied to the specified shape cast member. The number corresponds to the patterns available in Director's pattern palette (the pattern palette can be found in the Tools palette and the Paint window). You can test and set this property with Lingo.

Possible *pattern of member* values range from 1 to 64. Two important values to remember are 1 (filled with the color specified by *the foreColor of member* or *the foreColor of sprite* property) and 15 (filled with the color specified by *the backColor of member* or *the backColor of sprite* property). Through value 56, the patterns consist of two-color patterns of black and white. Black pixels are mapped to the foreground color of the cast member; white pixels are mapped to the background color. Patterns in positions 57 through 64 are occupied by user-definable bitmaps, which are tiled.

You can only see the pattern applied to a shape member if its *the filled of member* property is set to TRUE.

Example This Lingo function fills the member *myMem* with a pattern, if it really is a *#shape* cast member:

```
on patternMember myMem, myPat
  if the type of member myMem = #shape then
    set the filled of member myMem = TRUE
    set the pattern of member myMem = myPat
  end if
```

```
        end patternMember
```

Parameters   the pattern of *member*

Value   *integer*

See also   the backColor of member, the filled of member, the foreColor of member

the shapeType of member

MEMBER PROPERTY

Syntax   `set whatShape = the shapeType of member "Jungian"`

Usage   *the shapeType of member* is a property that contains a symbol value indicating which shape the cast member is. The possible shape types are *#line*, *#oval*, *#rect*, and *#roundRect*. You can test and set this property with Lingo.

Example   This code segment creates a new shape cast member and makes it a line:

```
set tNewMember = new(#shape)
set the shapeType of member tNewMember = #line
```

Parameters   the shapeType of *member*

Value   `#line|#oval|#rect|#roundRect`

See also   new, the rect of member, the type of member

External Files Category

31

These Lingo keywords provide access to local files and directories, as well as files on networks. Some of these keywords are not operative in Shockwave; access to local file systems for movies played in a browser is restricted to the use of *getPref* and *setPref*.

@

Syntax

```
sound playfile "@::Witches Brew"

importFileInto member 4, "@/house.jpg"

go movie "@\\shoktest\shoktest.dcr"
```

Usage

The @ symbol, when used as the first character of a string used as a file path, indicates to the movie that it should insert the path to the movie's directory in the string, and to treat colon (:), slash (/), and backslash (\) characters as directory separators, regardless of platform.

With a directory separator, the @ symbol is essentially equivalent to the property *the moviePath*, except that the use of the @ symbol eliminates the need to match director separator characters by platform.

Directories can be traversed by adding the name of a subdirectory to move down the hierarchy ("@/pictures/house.jpg") or two or more separator characters in a row to move up ("@\\\menu.dcr"). Combinations of directory names and multiple separators are possible, to move up a directory tree and back down another branch ("@:::movies:intro.mov").

The @ symbol does not return a value indicating the path it refers to. It can be used in string calculations.

This command works with local file addresses and Shockwave movies. The Shockwave movie path yields its http address rather than the address on the server's hard drive.

Examples

This statement plays a sound file from the directory the movie file is in:

```
sound playFile "@:soundtrack.aif"
```

This handler preloads a Shockwave file from a remote server, waits for the load cycle to finish, then executes a *go movie* command (it assumes that the global *gStarted* has been set to FALSE before the frame is entered). The new movie occupies a directory one level above the current movie:

```
on exitFrame
  global gStarted
  if not gStarted then
    preLoadMovie "@\\navigate.dcr"
    go the frame
  else
    if not netDone () then go the frame
    else go movie "@\\navigate.dcr"
  end if
end
```

Parameters   @:

        @/

        @\

See also   the applicationPath, the moviePath, the pathName, the searchPath, the searchPaths

the applicationPath

MOVIE PROPERTY

Syntax   `set aPath = the applicationPath`

Usage   *the applicationPath* is a property that contains the path to the directory of the application playing the current movie. In cases where the movie is a projector, this will be identical to *the moviePath*. If the movie is playing inside Director, this will be the path to the Director application.

      If the movie has been opened by another Director movie (as in *go to movie, play movie,* or a Movie in a Window), *the applicationPath* is the location of the projector (except when the movie plays in the authoring environment).

      Accessing this property results in an error in Shockwave movies.

Example   This function returns the path to the playback engine of the projector if the movie is playing from a projector. If the movie is playing in authoring mode or as a Shockwave movie, it returns the location of the movie file:

```
on whereMovie
  if the runMode = "Projector" then
    return the applicationPath
  else
    return the moviePath
  end if
end
```

Parameters   `the applicationPath`

Value   *string*

See also   @, the moviePath, the pathName

closeResFile

This MacOS-specific command is obsolete in Director 6. It was used in earlier versions of Director to provide custom cursors and fonts to the movie.

closeXLib

Syntax   closeXLib "IDate"

Usage   The *closeXlib* command closes the XLibrary specified by the parameter. If an XLibrary is not specified, all open external libraries are closed.

Xlibraries are single files containing one or more Xobjects or Xtras, code that extends the capabilities of the Director application, projector, or Shockwave movie.

If the Xlibrary is not in the same directory as a projector (or the Director application, if in authoring mode), a path name to the file must be specified.

In Shockwave, XLibraries must be stored in the Shockwave plug-in support folder.

Example   This handler closes a file opened by the FileIO Xtra, disposes of the instance of FileIO, then closes the Xlibrary.

```
on closeFile
  global gFileObj
  closeFile(gFileObj)
  set gFileObj = 0
  closeXlib "fileio"
end closeFile
```

Parameters   closeXLib *string*

See also   openXlib, showXlib

copyToClipboard

COMMAND

Syntax   `copyToClipBoard member 3 of castLib 2`

Usage   The *copyToClipBoard* command copies a cast member to the clipboard. From there, it can be pasted into other applications.

Example   This statement copies the cast member "waterfall" into the clipboard:

`copyToClipBoard member "waterfall"`

Parameters   `copyToClipBoard` *member*

See also   pasteClipBoardInto

the fileName of castLib

CAST PROPERTY

Syntax   `set whichCast = the fileName of castLib 3`

Usage   *the fileName of castLib* is a property that contains the filename of a specified cast library. If the cast library is internal, it returns EMPTY. If the cast library is external, a string value with the file name is returned.

   In a Shockwave movie, external casts must be located in the plug-in support directory.

   You can test or set this property with Lingo (although modifying the property is only possible for external casts). Changing the property's value changes which file is used to provide cast members for the library. Linking to remote locations with a URL is possible, but downloading the file to a local drive with *downLoadNetThing* before accessing the file with *the fileName of castLib* is recommended due to performance considerations.

   You can include an empty placeholder cast in a Shockwave movie, then link to any external cast with Lingo by setting this property, provided that the external cast is located in the Shockwave plug-in support directory.

Example   This statement sets *the fileName of castLib* property to the file "extLink.cst." If used in a projector, the default location for the file would be the directory where the projector is located. If used in a Shockwave movie, the file would need to be located in the plug-in support directory:

```
set the fileName of castLib "ext" = "extLink.cst"
```

Parameters   `the fileName of castLib` *integer|string*

Value   *string*

See also   the applicationPath, the pathName

the fileName of member

MEMBER PROPERTY

Syntax   `set whatFile = the fileName of member 3 of castLib 2`

Usage   *the fileName of member* is a property that contains the name of the file in use by a linked cast member (one in which the media is stored outside of the cast). You can change the file the cast member is linked to by modifying the value of the property.

It is convenient to change *the fileName of member* with Lingo, to update media "on the fly."

It is possible to use a URL for *the fileName of member* property, but it is recommended that you download the file to a local drive with *downloadNetThing* instead.

For projectors, filenames without directory information assume the file is in the same directory as the projector. In Shockwave movies, the file referred to by filename must be located in the Shockwave plug-in support folder; URLs should not be used.

Example   This statement sets the filename of the digital video member "dv" to "shocker.mov," which is currently located in the Shockwave plug-in support folder:

```
set the fileName of member "dv" = "shocker.mov"
```

Parameters   `the fileName of` *member*

Value   *string*

See also   the applicationPath, the media of member, the pathName, the picture of member

getNthFileNameInFolder

FUNCTION

Syntax

```
set aFile = getNthFileNameInFolder (the applicationPath, 3)
```

Usage

The *getNthFileNameInFolder* function returns a specific item in a directory. The directory you want to search is specified by the first parameter; the position in the folder (alphabetically arranged) is the second parameter.

The function returns just the name of the specified file or folder, with no path information. If there are fewer items in the folder than specified by the second parameter, the returned string will be empty.

The path name can be relative to the current movie's directory or a complete path from the hard drive's main level.

You can retrieve just the folder name from the specified path by using –1 as the second parameter.

Items in the directory include files and other directories. Hidden files and folders are visible to the *getNthFileNameInFolder* function.

> ### Tip
>
> *The @ symbol cannot be used in the path supplied to* getNthFileNameInFolder.

Examples

This example extracts the current movie's directory name from *the moviePath* property:

```
set thisFolder = getNthFileNameInFolder ¬
  (the moviePath, -1)
```

This handler creates a list of .mov (QuickTime movie) files in the directory specified by the *whatDir* parameter:

```
on movieList whatFolder
  set movieList = []
  set aFile = getNthFileNameInFolder (whatFolder, -1)
  --returns name of folder
  repeat while aFile <> ""
    --until all files have been searched
    set aFileLen = length (aFile)
    set aPos = aFile - 3
    if aPos > 1 then  --if not, name's too short
      set anExt = char aPos to char aFileLen of aFile
      if anExt = ".mov" then add movieList, aFile
    end if
  end repeat
  return movieList
end
```

Parameters   `getNthFileNameInFolder (string, integer)`

Value   *string*

See also   @, the applicationPath, the moviePath, the pathName, the searchpath, the searchpaths

getPref

NETWORK/SHOCKWAVE FUNCTION

Syntax   `set aResult = getPref ("preffile")`

Usage   The *getPref* function returns the text contained in a Shockwave preference file written by a *setPref* command.

If the file specified by the parameter doesn't exist, then the *getPref* function returns void.

This powerful Shockwave feature allows you to store user settings that can later be recalled and used in a variety of ways. You can let users store their own ways to view your Shockwave movie, bookmark their current page so they can return later, or even control the look of HTML pages. You can even use this to let multiple Shockwave movies share common data. For Shockwave movies, the preference files are stored in the Shockwave plug-in support folder on the local hard drive. In a projector, the files are stored in a directory called "Prefs," in the same directory as the projector.

Example   This code segment uses *getPref* to retrieve the last frame the user was viewing. The frame must have been stored by the *setPref* command in a previous session:

```
if not(voidP(getPref("lastfram")) then
  go to frame(value(getPref("lastfram")))
end if
```

Parameters   `getPref (string)`

Value   *string*

See also   setPref

importFileInto

Syntax
```
importFileInto member "safari" of castLib "albums", ¬
    "http://www.surftrio.com/albums/safari.gif"
```

Usage
The *importFileInto* command imports the content of a file (specified by the second parameter) into a cast member position (specified by the first parameter). The media from the file then becomes a part of one of the movie's casts.

Typically, this command is used to bring linked content into the cast before delivering a finished project. At run time, use of this command can be problematic, due to memory overhead associated with the command. Setting *the fileName of member* property will give better results at run time.

Director 6 supports the use of URLs for the file name of the cast member, but it is recommended that you use the *downloadNetThing* command to copy the file from its remote location to a local address before using *importFileInto*.

As with all linked media in Shockwave delivery, you must place a file in the plug-in support folder before a Shockwave movie can use *importFileInto*. Any other path to a drive on the local system will be rejected.

Example
This command will import the sound "safari.wav" into the next new cast member:
```
importFileInto new(#sound),"safari.wav"
```

Parameters
```
importFileInto member, string
```

See also
downloadNetThing, the fileName of member, new

the moviePath

Syntax
```
set aMovie = the moviePath
```

Usage
the moviePath is a property that returns the directory location of the current movie.

If the movie is part of a projector, this property contains the location of the projector, and is the same as the *applicationPath* property.

If the movie has been opened from a local volume as a MIAW, with *go to movie* or *play movie*, or if it is playing in the Director authoring environment, *the moviePath* yields the location of the .dir, .dxr, or .dcr file, which may be different than the value of *the applicationPath*. In the authoring environment, if the open movie has not been saved *the moviePath* is an empty string.

If the movie has been opened with a URL, or if it is playing within a Web browser environment, this property contains the full URL path to the movie.

Example   This example determines if the current movie is in the same directory as the projector, and opens a new movie from the same directory if it is:

```
if the runMode = "Projector" then
  if the applicationPath = the moviePath then
    go movie "surfbord.dcr"
  end if
end if
```

Parameters   the moviePath

Value   *string*

See also   the applicationPath, the pathName

open

COMMAND

Syntax   open "C:\PROGRAM FILES\ACROBAT.EXE"

open "Raw Power:Work:background.pict" with ¬
  "Brick by Brick:Photoshop:Adobe Photoshop 3.0"

Usage   The *open* command allows you to start a program or open a document with a program. It does not give you the ability to control the other program's actions once it is started, or to open another document using the same program (although in Windows 95 it is possible to open multiple instances of the same program with different documents in each).

The *open* command with a path name to an application will start the application. If the application performs some task without having an associated document, it will perform the task.

Using the *open...with* format of the command opens the document specified by the first path name with the program specified by the second path name.

Example   This code segment downloads a file from a Web server and saves it to disk, then opens the saved file with the Windows Notepad application:

```
downloadnetthing ¬
    "http://www.surftrio.com/index.html", "surftrio.html"
open "surftrio.html" with "C:\WINDOWS\NOTEPAD.EXE"
```

Parameters   open *string*

open *string* with *string*

See also   openXLib

openResFile

COMMAND

This MacOS-specific command is obsolete in Director 6. It was used in earlier versions of Director to provide custom cursors and fonts to the movie.

openXLib

COMMAND

Syntax   openXLib "Libraries\tbmpg.x32"

Usage   The *openXlib* command opens the specified XLibrary. If the file is already open, *openXlib* does nothing.

Xlibraries are single files containing one or more Xobjects or Xtras, code that extends the capabilities of the Director application, projector, or Shockwave movie.

If the Xlibrary is not in the same directory as a projector (or the Director application, if in authoring mode), a path name must be specified to the file. URLs cannot be used with *openXLib*; the file must be downloaded to the local drive before opening.

In Shockwave, all XLibraries must be stored in the Shockwave plug-in support folder. You cannot include path information in the parameter when opening Xlibraries from Shockwave movies.

Example   This code segment opens the appropriate version of the FileIO Xtra, depending on contents of the platform system property:

```
if the platform contains "32"
  -- 32-bit Windows
  openXlib "fileio.x32"
else if the platform contains "16" then
  openXlib "fileio16.x16"
else if the platform contains "Macintosh" then
  openXlib "FileIO"
end if
```

Parameters   openXLib *string*

See also   closeXlib, showXlib

the pathName

MOVIE PROPERTY

Syntax   `set aMovie = the pathName`

Usage   *the pathName* is a property that returns the directory location of the current movie.

If the movie is part of a projector, this property contains the location of the projector, and is the same as *the applicationPath* property.

If the movie has been opened from a local volume as a MIAW, with *go to movie* or *play movie*, or if it is playing in the Director authoring environment, *the pathName* yields the location of the .dir, .dxr, or .dcr file, which may be different than the value of *the applicationPath*. In the authoring environment, if the open movie has not been saved, *the pathName* is an empty string.

If the movie has been opened with a URL, this property contains the full URL path to the movie.

In a Shockwave movie, this property generates an error.

Example   See the Examples for *the applicationPath* and *the moviePath*.

Parameters   the pathName

Value   *string*

See also   the applicationPath, the moviePath

the *searchCurrentFolder*

MOVIE PROPERTY

Syntax   `set the searchCurrentFolder = FALSE`

Usage   *the searchCurrentFolder* property determines if the folder the currently playing movie occupies is considered the default folder for external files. If TRUE, files without path information are assumed to be in the current folder. If FALSE, they are considered to be elsewhere.

This can be useful for larger projects where, for instance, all movie files are grouped in one directory, all digital video in another, sounds in another, etc. By eliminating the automatic search of the current folder, some time delay may be eliminated.

Example   This handler checks the extension of a file that will be opened, and toggles the *searchCurrentFolder* option on or off, depending on whether the file has the digital video .mov extension:

```
on doSearch aFile
  set fnLen = length ("aFile")
  set cLen = abs (fnLen - 3)
  if cLen > 0 then set exten = char cLen to fnLen of aFile
  else set exten = ""
  if exten = ".mov" then
    set the searchCurrentFolder = TRUE
  else
    set the searchCurrentFolder = FALSE
  end if
end
```

Parameters   `the searchCurrentFolder`

Value   *integer*

See also   the searchPath

the searchPath

MOVIE PROPERTY

Syntax   `set the searchPath = ["RAW Power:", "Brick by Brick:Work:"]`

Usage   *the searchPath* is a property that contains a linear list of one or more alternate directories for the application or projector to search when a file can't be found in the current movie path and no path is specified for the file.

   If *the searchCurrentFolder* property value is FALSE, the directories in the list defined by *the searchPath* are the only folders designated for the search. If a file is not found in the current movie folder or one of the directories in *the searchPath* list, a dialog will appear asking the user to locate the file.

   Paths added to *the searchPath* should be strings containing complete paths, not relative paths, and ending with the appropriate path separator. Neither the @ symbol or URLs can be used as part of a path, although *the applicationPath, the moviePath,* and *the pathName* can be concatenated with other strings to form paths to be searched.

   The property can be set directly or modified using standard commands and functions for linear lists.

   the searchPath property is not functional in Shockwave movies.

   This property is interchangable with *the searchPaths* property. A change to *the searchPath* directly affects *the searchPaths.*

Examples   This example clears all search paths from *the searchPath*:

`set the searchPath = []`

   This statement adds the parent directory of the current movie's directory to *the searchPath* (adding a path separator to a path indicates a move up the directory hierarchy):

`add the searchpath, the moviepath & "\"`

   If a *go movie* command is used to go to a movie in the parent directory in this case, the new *moviePath* property would be of the form:

`put the moviePath`
`--"C:\MOVIES\\"`

   ending in the value contained in the original *moviePath* plus the extra path separator, rather than "C:\".

Parameters   `the searchpath`

Value   *linear list of string*

See also   the applicationPath, the moviePath, the pathName, the searchPaths

the searchPaths

MOVIE PROPERTY

Syntax   `set the searchPaths = ["Surf Trio:Movies:"]`

Usage   *the searchPaths* is a property that is functionally identical to *the searchPath* property (see the preceding entry).

Parameters   `the searchpaths`

Value   *linear list of string*

See also   the applicationPath, the moviePath, the pathName, the searchPath

setCallBack

COMMAND

This command is obsolete in Director 6. It was used in earlier versions to support HyperTalk XCMDs and XFCNs.

setPref

COMMAND

Syntax   `setPref "afile", "datastring"`

Usage   The *setPref* command stores the contents of a string into a file, without the need of the File IO Xtra. For Shockwave movies, the file is stored in the Shockwave plug-in support directory of the local computer. With projectors, the file is saved to a folder called "Prefs," which is created in the same directory as the projector file.

You can retrieve data from preference files created with the *setPref* command by using the *getPref* function.

This feature allows you to store user settings that can later be recalled and used in a variety of ways. You can let users store their own ways to view your movie, bookmark their current position so they can return later, or even control the look of HTML pages with a Shockwave movie. You can also use this to let multiple Shockwave movies share common data.

Example   This code segment uses *setPref* to store the contents of three variables in a preference file named "dugPref":

```
global gName, gStatus, gScore
setPref("dugPref", string(gName) & "," && ¬
    string(gStatus)& "," && string(gScore))
```

Parameters   setPref *string, string*

See also   getPref

showResFile

COMMAND

This MacOS-specific command is obsolete in Director 6. It was used in earlier versions of Director to provide custom cursors and fonts to the movie.

showXLib

COMMAND

Syntax   showXLib

Usage   The *showXlib* command lists all available Xtras and XObjects in the message window. It is only useful in the Director authoring environment.

With an XLibrary file name as a parameter, the list contains only the Xtras and Xobjects in the specified library.

Example | This is an example of the results of typing the *showXlib* command in the message window:

```
-- XLibraries:
--    Xtra: NetLingo
--    Xtra: QTVRXtra
--    Xtra: Mui
--    Xtra: fileio
```

Parameters | showXLib

showXLib *integer*

See also | closeXlib, openXlib

sound playFile

Syntax | sound playFile "soundtrack.aif"

sound playFile 4, "http://www.surftrio.com/soundtrack.wav"

Usage | The *sound playFile* command plays an AIFF or WAV sound file in a sound channel. If no sound channel is specified, the sound plays in sound channel 1. The file path parameter must contain the full name of the file, including any extension.

While it is possible for *sound playFile* to play a sound from a URL address, it is recommended that you download the sound to a local directory before play begins.

This command does not work with internal sound cast members or Shockwave audio files. Use the *puppetSound* command to play internal sounds, and the *play member* command to play SWA files.

Shockwave movies can access external sound files in the plug-in support directory with the *sound playFile* command.

Example | This command plays the file "talk.wav," which is located in the same folder as the movie, or in the plug-in support folder if played from a Shockwave movie. The sound plays in sound channel 1:

sound playFile 1, "talk.wav"

Parameters | sound playfile *string*

sound playfile *integer*, *string*

See also | puppetSound, sound close, sound fadeIn, sound fadeOut, sound stop, soundBusy, soundEnabled, soundLevel, the volume of sound

XFactoryList

Syntax   `set listofXs = XfactoryList ("myLibs")`

Usage   The *xFactoryList* function returns a string with the name of each open Xtra or XObject contained in the specified library. If you use EMPTY for the parameter, *xFactoryList* will return the name of all open Xtras or XObjects that are included in XLibraries.

      If you use an XObject or Xtra in Shockwave, the XLibrary file must be located in the Shockwave plug-in support directory.

Example   This statement sends the name of all open Xtras or XObjects to field "result":

      `put xFactoryList(EMPTY) into field "result"`

Parameters `XfactoryList (EMPTY)`

      `XfactoryList (string)`

Value   *string*

See also   closeXlib, openXlib, showXlib, xtra

Movie in a Window (MIAW) Category

32

These Lingo keywords allow you to create and control multiple Director movies that are running simultaneously. MIAW functions are not available in Shockwave movies.

on activateWindow

Syntax
on activateWindow

Usage
The *activateWindow* message is sent to a window object when it becomes the active, or frontmost, window. This happens if the user clicks on the window or if it is brought to the front by the use of Lingo commands. This handler can be used to activate buttons or perform other actions when the window is activated.

The stage does not receive the *activeWindow* message, and will not execute an *activeWindow* handler. Testing periodically for *the activeWindow* property or sending a message to the stage when a window is deactivated can perform the same function.

Example
This example sets the sprites in channels 10 to 15 to visible when the window is activated:

```
on activateWindow
  repeat with i = 10 to 15
    set the visible of sprite i = TRUE
  end repeat
end
```

Parameters
```
on activateWindow
  statements
end
```

See also
the activeWindow, on closeWindow, on deactivateWindow, the frontWindow, open window

the activeWindow

Syntax   `set whatWindow = the activeWindow`

Usage   *the activeWindow* is a property that indicates the window of the movie executing the command containing *the activeWindow* property. The value of the property is in the special format used by Director to store window references, and looks like this:

`(window "shoktest")`

The string after the keyword *window* is the name or path of the file used as a MIAW. If the property is referenced by the movie playing on the stage, the result will be:

`(the stage)`

This property can be used by a movie to determine the window it is playing in. It cannot be set.

> ### Tip
>
> *The movie in the front window is not necessarily* the activeWindow. *Each movie executing a command with* the activeWindow *property in it will refer to its own window.*

Example   This command tells a MIAW to delete itself from *the windowList* when it is hidden:

```
on closeWindow
  forget the activeWindow
end
```

Parameters   `the activeWindow`

Value   *window*

See also   on activateWindow, the frontWondow, the windowList

close window

Syntax   `close window 3`

Usage   The *close window* command hides but does not delete the specified window.
To delete a window from memory, use the *forget window* command.
The reference to the window can be either by name or by number. A
number indicates a position in the *windowList* property.
The *close window* command sets *the visible of window* property to FALSE.

Example   This example hides the window named "navigate":

`close window "navigate"`

Parameters `close window`

See also   forget window, open window, the windowList

on closeWindow

Syntax   `on closeWindow`

Usage   The *closeWindow* message is sent when a window is hidden. It is now sent
when the window is deleted from *the windowList* by the *forget window*
command.

Example   See the Example for *the activeWindow*.

Parameters `on closeWindow`
`   integer`
`end`

See also   on activateWindow, close window, on deactivateWindow, forget window

on deactivateWindow

HANDLER

Syntax   on deactivateWindow

Usage   The *deactivate* message is sent to a MIAW when another window is brought
to the front. It is not sent when the movie is closed or forgotten.
    This handler can be used to indicate to the user that the MIAW is not
currently active, such as to change the appearance of buttons to indicate that
they are disabled.

Example   This example disables any buttons created with the button editor when a
MIAW is deactivated:

```
on deactivateWindow
  repeat with i = 1 to the number of castLibs
    repeat with j = 1 to the number ¬
      of members of castLib i
      if the type of member j of castLib 1 = #btned then
        set the enabled of member j of castLib i = FALSE
      end if
    end repeat
  end repeat
end
```

Parameters   on deactivateWindow
        integer
    end

See also   on closeWindow, forget window

the drawRect of window

WINDOW PROPERTY

Syntax
```
set the drawRect of window "scroll" = ¬
    rect (0, -200, 296, 200)
```

Usage
the drawRect of window is a property that determines the placement of a Director movie in its window.

Director movies can be scaled and shifted within their windows by setting this property. The background of the window assumes the background color of the movie.

If you assign the property a *rect* that is the same size as the stage of the movie in the window but in a different position than its current one, the movie will be moved to the coordinates of the *rect*.

If the *rect* is a different size than the movie, the entire stage is scaled to fit the position and proportions of the new *rect*. Scaling bitmapped sprites may result in redraw delays and odd colorization (in the case of indexed color sprites). Field cast members on the stage as sprites are scaled, but the text in them is not; rewrapping may occur.

Examples
This handler draws the movie playing on the stage at half its current size, centered on the stage area:

```
on halfSizeMovie
  set stageRect = offset (the rect of the stage, ¬
    - the stageLeft, - the stageTop)
  -- this gives us a rect the size of the stage
  -- with top and left values of 0
  set stageRect = stageRect / 2
  -- creates a rect _ the size of the stage
  set stageRect = offset (stageRect, ¬
    the right of stageRect / 2, ¬
    the bottom of stageRect / 2)
  -- offsets the small rectangle so it is centered
  -- on the stage
  set the drawRect of the stage = stageRect
end
```

This statement draws the movie in the window "viewscreen" so that the left side of the movie is 100 pixels to the left of its current position:

```
set the drawRect of window "viewscreen" = ¬
  the drawRect of window "viewscreen" + ¬
  rect (-100, 0, -100, 0)
```

Parameters   the drawRect of *window*

Value   *rect*

See also   the sourceRect of window

the fileName of window

WINDOW PROPERTY

Syntax   `set the fileName of window "controls" = "hyperspace"`

Usage   *the fileName of window* is a property that allows you to specify the Director movie playing in a window. Setting this property for an already existing window changes the movie appearing in the window.

URL addresses can be used, as well as local drive and local network addresses. It is recommended that a *preLoadNetThing* or *downloadNetThing* command be used before assigning *the fileName of movie* property to a URL address.

the fileName of window property for the stage should not be set.

Example   This example downloads a file from a Web server, then assigns it to the window "promo":

```
on exitFrame
  global gDL  --set to FALSE before this frame
  if not gDL then
    downloadNetThing "http://www.surftrio.com/promo16.dcr"
    set gDL = TRUE
  end if
  if not netDone () then
    go the frame
  else
    set the fileName of window "promo" = ¬
      "http://www.surftrio.com/promo16.dcr"
  end if
end
```

Parameters   the filename of *window*

Value   *string*

See also   open window

forget window

Syntax   `forget window "promo"`

Usage   The *forget window* command closes the specified window and removes it from *the windowList*, freeing up the memory allocated to the MIAW.

No messages are sent to the window when it is forgotten. It is advisable to forget the window only after any necessary housekeeping normally done at the end of the movie has been taken care of.

If more than one global references the window, all globals need to be set to EMPTY before the *forget window* command can be employed.

The stage cannot be forgotten.

Example   See the Example for *the activeWindow*.

Parameters   `forget window`

See also   close window, open window

the frontWindow

Syntax   `set whatWindow = the frontWindow`

Usage   *the frontWindow* is a property that allows you to determine which window is the foremost visible window.

In authoring mode, clicking the mouse on the stage of a Director window (Score, Cast, and so on) deselects any MIAW that is *the frontWindow*. If no MIAW is *the frontWindow* and there are any open Director windows, the value of the property will be VOID. If no Director windows are open, and all MIAWs are deselected, the property will be *(the stage)*.

In a projector, MIAWs do not deselect when the stage is clicked. If any MIAWs are open, the stage will never be *the frontWindow* unless brought to the front with Lingo.

In a Shockwave movie, although the MIAW functions are disabled, the value of *the frontWindow* is always *(the stage)*.

Example This handler does nothing if the movie executing the handler is not the front window. Otherwise, it calls a custom handler that performs standard operations:

```
on exitFrame
  if the activeWindow = the frontWindow then doFrameEvents
  else nothing
end
```

Parameters the frontWindow

Value *window*

See also the activeWindow, moveToBack, moveToFront

the modal of window

WINDOW PROPERTY

Syntax `set isModal = the modal of window 3`

Usage *the modal of window* is a property that determines if the specified window is the only movie that responds to user actions. A window with a *modal* property value of TRUE will be the only movie to respond to clicks within the movie as long as the movie's window is open. Other windows can be brought to the front by clicking on their title bars, but clicking inside the window area will result in an alert sound.

Closing a window allows other windows to respond to keyboard and mouse actions, as well as allowing another window to become a modal window.

Scripts in other windows will still execute, and events such as *on mouseEnter* will still affect sprites on the stage and other windows.

Example These handlers set a window brought to the front to be a modal window:

```
on activateWindow
  set the modal of the activeWindow = TRUE
end
```

Parameters the modal of *window*

Value *boolean*

moveToBack

Syntax   `moveToBack window 3`

Usage   The *moveToBack* command moves the specified window behind all others, including the stage.

Example   This example displays all of the open windows by moving each one to the back in turn (note that this example does not account for invisible windows or any authoring windows):

```
on showAllWindows
  repeat with i = 1 to (count (the windowList) + 1)
  -- the stage does not appear in the windowList
    moveToBack the frontWindow
    starttimer
    repeat while the timer < 60
      updatestage
    end repeat
  end repeat
end
```

Parameters   moveToBack *window*

See also   the frontWindow, moveToFront

moveToFront

Syntax   `moveToFront the stage`

Usage   The *moveToFront* command brings a specified window to the front of all others. If a window has been closed, the *moveToFront* command reopens the window as well as bringing it to the front.

Example   This example brings the window named "messages" to the front:

`moveToFront window "messages"`

Parameters   `moveToFront` *`window`*

See also   moveToFront, open window

on moveWindow

HANDLER

Syntax   `on moveWindow`

Usage   The *moveWindow* message is sent when a movie is moved to a new position by the user who is dragging the window. It is not invoked when the window is moved with Lingo commands.

This handler can be used to make any changes necessary to the MIAW based on position changes of the window caused by the user.

Example   This handler shifts the movie inside the window so that its position relative to the stage remains constant, despite the position of the window itself:

```
on moveWindow
  global gOldWinOffset
  -- point value with former window position
  set winRect = the rect of the activewindow
  set newWinOffset = point (the left of winRect, ¬
    the top of winRect)
  -- establishes the current offset of the MIAW window
  set changeOffset = gOldWinOffset - newWinOffset
  -- vector with change in window position
  set the drawRect of the activewindow = ¬
    offset (the drawRect of the activewindow, ¬
    the locH of changeOffset, the locV of changeOffset)
  set gOldWinOffset = newWinOffset
end
```

Parameters
```
on moveWindow
  integer
end
```

the name of window

Syntax   `set whatWindow = the name of window 2`

Usage   *the name of window* is a property that determines the string used to refer to the window, when referring to the window by name rather than position in *the windowList*.
You cannot rename the stage.

Example   When opening a MIAW from a directory other than the current movie's directory or a directory not in *the searchPaths*, you must use the full path name to the file. Rather than using the entire path to make further references to the MIAW, however, you can simply rename the window:

```
open window "C:\Work\shocktest"
set the name of window "C:\Work\shoktest" = "shoktest"
```

The window can now be referred to simply as *(window "shoktest")*.

Parameters   `the name of` *window*

Value   *string*

See also   the title of window

open window

Syntax   `open window 3`

Usage   The *open window* command can be used to create a new MIAW by specifying a movie to open in the window. It can also be used to bring a window already in *the windowList* to the front, opening it if it has been closed or had its *visible* property set to FALSE.
Movies can be opened from URL addresses as well as local drives, but it is recommended that you use *downLoadNetThing* or *preLoadNetThing* before opening the movie in a window.
This command is not available in Shockwave movies played in the browser environment.

Examples   This example opens a movie named "promo16" in the same directory as the projector. The movie could be a .dir, .dxr, or .dcr file. The window will be added to *the windowList* as *(window "promo16")*:

```
open window "promo16"
```

This example opens a movie named "surftrio" from a directory not in the projector's *searchPath*. The movie could be a .dir, .dxr, or .dcr file. The window will be added to *the windwList* as *(window "American Caeser:LPR:surftrio")*:

```
open window "American Caeser:LPR:surftrio"
```

This example downloads a movie from a Web server, opens the file as a MIAW, and assigns a short name to the window. The movie could be a .dir, .dxr, or .dcr file:

```
set aMovie = "http://www.surftrio.com/albums/safari"
preLoadNetThing aMovie
--a procedure for waiting for the movie to preload
--would go here
open window aMovie
set the name of window aMovie = "safari"
```

Parameters   open *window*

See also   close window, forget window

on openWindow

Syntax   on openWindow

Usage   The *openWIndow* message is sent when a movie's window is opened. This can occur when the window is created or when the window is reopened after being closed.

Example   This example sets a newly opened window to be a modal window (other windows will be inactive):

```
on openWindow
   set the modal of the activeWindow = TRUE
end
```

Parameters   on openWindow
          statements
          end

See also   on closeWindows

the rect of window

Syntax   `set whatRect = the rect of window 4`

Usage   *the rect of window* is a property that is a *rect* value describing the position on the screen of the specified window.

In the authoring mode, this property's value is based on the overall screen coordinates (or the Director window, in Windows): if a 640 x 480 stage is centered on an 800 x 600 monitor, typing **put the rect of the stage** will result in something like *rect(80, 60, 720, 540)*.

In a projector, the coordinates are based entirely on the position of the window created for the stage: typing **put the rect of the stage** for the movie above will always result in *rect(0, 0, 640, 480)*.

the rect of window property can be set for MIAWs but not for the stage.

Example   See the Example for *on moveWindow*.

Parameters   `the rect of `*`window`*

Value   *`rect`*

See also   the drawRect of window

on resizeWindow

Syntax   `on resizeWindow`

Usage   The *resizeWindow* message is sent when a window is resized by the user. Dragging the sides, the grow box, or zooming the window will generate the event. It is not issued when the window is resized with Lingo commands.

This handler can be used to execute tasks necessary to make the movie work at a new size.

Example   This example resizes the sprites in a movie to fit in a newly resized window:

```
on resizeWindow
  set the drawRect of the activeWindow = ¬
    the rect of the activeWindow
end
```

Parameters
```
on resizeWindow
  integer
end
```

See also   on moveWindow, on zoomWindow

the sourceRect of window

Syntax
```
set the rect of window "control" = ¬
  the sourceRect of window "control"
```

Usage   *the sourceRect of window* is a property that is determined by the position and size of the movie in the window as it first appears when opened. It does not change as a result of modifications to the window, and it cannot be modified.

Example   This handler shifts the movie inside the window so that its position relative to the stage remains constant, despite the position of the window itself. It accomplishes essentially the same task as the example for *on moveWindow* but with only one line of code. In this case, however, the position of the movie within the window is restricted to its original opened position:

```
on moveWindow
  set the drawRect of the activewindow = ¬
    the sourceRect of the activeWindow
end
```

Parameters   `the sourceRect of `*window*

Value   *rect*

See also   the drawRect of window, the rect of window

the title of window

Syntax `set the title of window 1 = "OOOPS!"`

Usage *the title of window* is a property that determines what appears in the title bar of the window, if one appears. This is a cosmetic change only; the reference to the window is determined by *the name of member* property.

Example This example changes the title of the window "action" when a button is pressed:

```
on mouseUp
  set the title of window "action" = "Dialing…"
end
```

Parameters `the title of` *window*

Value *string*

See also the titleVisible of window, the windowType of window

the titleVisible of window

Syntax `set the titleVisible of window "Control" = FALSE`

Usage *the titleVisible of window* is a property that controls whether a window displays its title, as determined by *the title of window* property. If TRUE, the title bar is visible; if FALSE, it is not visible.

Example This example hides the title bar if the window is deactivated by the user clicking on another window:

```
on deactivateWindow
  set the titleVisible of the activeWindow = FALSE
end
```

Parameters the titleVisible of *window*

Value *boolean*

See also the title of window

the visible of window

WINDOW PROPERTY

Syntax set the visible of window = TRUE

Usage *the visible of window* is a property that determines if the window is open (TRUE) or closed (FALSE).

Setting *the visible of window* is an alternative to opening or closing windows already in *the windowList*.

It is possible to set *the visible of window* property of the stage to FALSE, but this may cause redraw problems in some situations, particularly in Shockwave movies.

Example It's often preferable to set up a window's properties before it appears on the stage. *the visible of window* property allows you to do that:

```
on makeWindow
  set aWin = window ("control")
  -- this sets up a new window reference
  set the filename of aWin = "C:\Work\conpan.dxr"
  -- assigns a movie file to the window
  set the windowType of aWin = 16
  -- a movable, non-resizable window
  set the rect of aWin = rect (100, 100, 238, 250)
  -- positions the MIAW
  set the title of aWin = "Control Panel"
  set the visible of aWin = TRUE
end
```

Parameters the visible of *window*

Value *boolean*

See also close window, open window

the windowList

Syntax	`set aWin = getAt (the windowList, 1)`
Usage	*the windowList* is a property that contains a reference to all of the MIAWs the movie currently controls. The stage is not a MIAW and does not appear in *the windowList*, although it can be controlled by many of the MIAW commands.
Example	See the Example for *moveToBack*.
Parameters	`the windowList`
Value	*linear list of window*
See also	windowPresent

windowPresent

Syntax	`set isItAWindow = windowPresent ("controls")`
Usage	The *windowPresent* function tests to see if a window with the name specified by the string passed to the function is in *the windowList*.
Example	This statement tests for the "controls" window, opens it if available, and alerts the user if not:

```
if windowPresent ("controls") then
  open window "controls"
else
  alert "Control Panel not available at this time"
end if
```

Parameters	`windowPresent (string)`
Value	*boolean*
See also	the windowList

the windowType of window

WINDOW PROPERTY

Syntax `set whatType = the windowType of window`

Usage *the windowType of window* is a property which contains an integer that determines the attributes and appearance of a MIAW.

The default value is –1, which is a resizable, movable window with a title bar and a close box. Other windows have different borders, may be immovable, include a zoom box, etc.

The windows avaiable on MacOS and Windows machines differ greatly, and you should test the type of window you want before starting a cross-platform project.

This chart details some common *windowType of window* values. For each value, an "M" indicates the feature is enabled on that type of window for the MacOS; a "W" indicates its availability on Windows.

windowType	move	title	close	resize	zoom	minim	thick	shad	float
–1	MW	MW	MW	MW				M	
1							MW		
2									
3								M	
4	MW	W	W				W	M	
5	M	M					M		
6				M					
7				M				M	
8	MW	MW	MW	MW	MW	W	W	M	
12	MW	MW	MW		MW	W	W	M	
16	MW	MW	MW				W		
48	M	M	M	M					M
52	M	M	M						M
56	M	M	M	M	M				M

Example This example sets the window named "apples" to the default window type:

`set the windowtype of window "apples" = –1`

Parameters `the windowType of` *window*

Value *integer*

on zoomWindow

Syntax   on zoomWindow

Usage   The *zoomWindow* message is sent when a user clicks on the zoom box of a window, if one is available. The zoom box will expand the window to fill the entire area of the stage if it doesn't already do so. If the window is already zoomed, it will shrink to its size before it was zoomed.

This handler can be used to rearrange items in the MIAW to take advantage of the larger screen area now available to the movie.

Example   This example resizes the movie in the current window to fill the available area when the *zoomWindow* message is sent to the handler:

```
on zoomWindow
  set the drawRect of the active window = ¬
    the rect of the activeWindow
end
```

Parameters
```
on zoomWindow
    integer
end
```

See also   on moveWindow

Behaviors Category

33

This section covers Lingo that is used to create objects in memory, create parent scripts, and create behaviors in Director 6.

Objects are the most complex and powerful structures in Lingo, and they're also the most difficult to understand—or explain—even though Director is littered with objects: sprites, cast members, MIAWs, and the movie itself.

Parent scripts enable Lingo programmers to create a series of handlers that can operate on a set of data semi-independently. A good parent script keeps track of what's happening and modifies its behavior based on what has happened in the past and what the current state of affairs is.

Parent scripts are useless, however, until they're *instanciated*. An *instance* of a parent script is called an *object*. It is usually a variable or item in a list that refers to a memory position where data (the object's properties) are stored to be acted upon by a parent script. See the *new* function later in this chapter.

Behaviors are new in Director 6. Traditional parent scripts had to be set up with one or more lines of Lingo and were nearly impossible to clearly explain to nonprogrammers. Behaviors are scripts that can be dragged onto a sprite or frame. From a pop-up dialog box, the user can drag the behavior to assign values and actions to an object, with no scripting necessary. While a number of behaviors are built into the Director Behavior Library (see the Xtras menu), you can also write your own.

the actorList

Syntax
```
add the actorList, new (script "Button Parent")
```

Usage
The system property *the actorList* returns a linear list containing all of the child objects added to it. It is a global value, and remains in memory even when a new movie is opened. This can be useful in Shockwave, allowing data (including sprites) to be carried over from one movie to the next.

All child objects in *the actorList* receive a *stepFrame* message each time the playback head moves to a new frame (or loops in the current frame with a *go to the frame* statement). You can capture this message with an *on stepFrame* handler, updating your *actorList* objects in each frame.

Examples
This statement creates a child of the parent script "animator" and adds it to *the actorList*. *the number of member* is a necessary parameter for this parent script.

```
add the actorList, new(script "animator", ¬
    the number of member "green guy")
```

This statement clears all of the objects from *the actorList*. If there are no other variables referring to these objects, they will be removed from memory.

```
set the actorList = []
```

Parameters
```
the actorList
```

Value
linear list of object

See also
add, new, on stepFrame

the ancestor

Syntax
```
set the ancestor = new (script "Inherited")
```

Usage
the ancestor is a property that gives an object access to the handlers of another object.

Ancestors can be strung together in long sequences. When an object receives a message, if it doesn't have a handler for the message, it checks its ancestor object's handlers. If that object doesn't have a handler for the message and it has an ancestor, the message is passed on—and so on, until either a handler is encountered or there are no more ancestors.

Each parent script can have only one ancestor. Handlers in a parent script supersede handlers for the same message in their ancestor. *the ancestor* property is declared at the top of a parent script like any other parent script property (see *property* later in this chapter).

Standard buttons operate in a specific manner: you roll over the button and it changes appearance; you click on the button and it changes again; you roll off of the button with the mouse button held down and it changes; and so on. One very efficient way of creating standard interface objects like buttons has been to use parent scripts. Every button (or other type of object), because it worked the same way as all of the other buttons, used the same parent script to control its operation. It might have different pictures assigned to it, but it did the same things.

If, however, you had a button that was going to be an animation instead of a still picture, you'd need to write some special code to handle the animation. Because the basic function of the button would be the same, however (animation changes while the button is rolled over, when it's pressed, and so on), the parent script that controls the animations can have access to all of the already existing button scripts by setting the animation script's *ancestor* to be the button script, rather than starting from scratch.

Examples   These two script examples are used throughout this section.

The following script goes in a movie script cast member; name it "Adder." This will be the ancestor object of another object:

```
on messageA me, p1, p2
  put "Ancestor message A" && string (p1 + p2)
end

on messageB me, p1, p2
  put "Ancestor message B" && string (p1 + p2)
end

on new me
  return me
end
```

Put the following script into a movie script cast member and name it "Multiplier":

```
property ancestor

on new me
  set ancestor = new (script "Adder")
  return me
end
```

```
on messageA me, p1, p2
  put "Descendent message A" && string (p1 * p2)
end

on messageC me, p1, p2
  put "Descendent message C" && string (p1 * p2)
end
```

When an object is created from the "Multiplier" script (the *new* handler), the object's *ancestor* property is set to the results of another object, this one created from the "Adder" script. An object created from the "Multiplier" script will respond to "messageA" and "messageC" (as a result of the handlers in the "Multiplier" script) as well as "messageB" (because of the handler in the "Adder" ancestor). The "messageA" message is not sent to "Adder" because the handler in "Multiplier" supersedes anything in the ancestor.

In the Message window, create an object from the "Multiplier" script with the following command:

```
set anObject = new (script "Multiplier")
```

This creates a new object from the "Multiplier" script. If you want to see what that object looks like, then type:

```
put anObject
```

The result you get will look something like this:

```
-- <offspring "Multiplier" 2 10d040a>
```

Because the *new* handler for the "Multiplier" object itself contained a *new* function, you actually created two objects with the *set* command. The other object is stored in *the ancestor of anObject*.

```
put the ancestor of anObject
-- <offspring "Adder" 2 10d0446>
```

You can see that *the ancestor of anObject* is another memory location, this time referring to an instance of the "Adder" script.

The object we've created can now respond to three commands. Here's an example from the Message window:

```
messageA anObject, 2, 5
-- "Descendent message A 10"
messageB anObject, 2, 5
-- "Ancestor message B 7"
messageC anObject, 2, 5
-- "Descendent message C 10"
```

As you see, even though the script "Multiplier" doesn't have a "messageB" handler, it can respond to the message because its ancestor does have a handler.

Parameters   ancestor

Value   *object*

See also   actorList, call, callAncestor, new, stepFrame, property

birth

FUNCTION

The *birth* function was used in Director 4 and earlier to create objects. It was replaced in Director 5 by the *new* function (described later in this chapter).

call

COMMAND

Syntax   `call #stopall, soundMgr`

`call #animate, [coffeeCup, pencil], 45`

Usage   The *call* command sends a message and any necessary parameters to one or more scripts or objects.

  This command allows you to target a specific script with a message, if there are multiple scripts with handlers for that message.

  The *call* command lets you send a message to a single behavior attached to a sprite, without invoking handlers for the message in other behaviors attached to the sprite.

  It also allows you to send the same message to a number of scripts or objects.

  The first parameter is a symbol value created from the name of the message to be passed; it can be a variable. The second parameter is the object, script, or list of scripts or objects (again, this can be a variable) the message will be sent to (in the order in which it will be sent). Any parameters to the handler appear as the third, fourth, etc., parameters.

  If a script does not contain a handler for the message, its ancestor will not respond to the message passed by a *call* command, and an error will be generated. If an object does not possess a handler for the message and its ancestor does not respond, an error will be generated

Examples   These examples use the scripts in the *ancestor* example above. All examples below are typed directly into the Message window.

You can *call* a script:

```
call #messageC, script "Multiplier", 2, 5
-- "Descendent message C 10"
```

> **Tip**
>
> *With a single script or object, it may be just as simple to use the following syntax for this example:* messageC script "Multiplier", 2, 5. *However, the* call *function allows you to use variables for the message—something that's not possible with a direct address to the script.*

You can also *call* an object:

```
call #messageA, anObject, 2,5
-- "Descendent message A 10"
```

More important, you can send a message to a list of objects:

```
call #messageA, [anObject, the ancestor of anObject], 2, 5
-- "Descendent message A 10"
-- "Ancestor message A 7"
```

Because both objects' scripts contain handlers for "messageA," each one of the objects responds to the message.

Parameters   `call # message, script/object, value …`

`call # message, [list of script/object], value …`

See also   callAncestor, pass

callAncestor

Syntax   `callAncestor #killAll, soundMgr`

`callAncestor #redraw, [coffeeCup, pencil], -100, -100`

Usage   The *callAncestor* command sends a message and any necessary parameters to the ancestors of one or more objects. In many ways it is similar to the *call* command: its syntax is identical, and you can send the same message to many objects with one command. The *callAncestor* command bypasses scripts in the object being addressed, however, and sends the message directly to the ancestor of the object (if one exists).

Like *call*, *callAncestor* allows you to send the same message to the ancestors of a number of scripts or objects.

The first parameter is a symbol value created from the name of the message to be passed, and it can be a variable. The second parameter is the object, script, or list of scripts or objects (again, this can be a variable) whose ancestors will receive the message (in the order in which it will be sent). Any parameters to the handler appear as the third, fourth, etc., parameters.

If the object has no ancestor, no error is generated.

Example This example uses a script in the *ancestor* example above and can be typed directly into the Message window.

The object created from the "Multiplier" script has a handler for "messageA" in its own script, as well as that of its ancestor. Using the *callAncestor* command bypasses the handler in the "Multiplier" object, sending it directly to the "Adder" ancestor object:

```
call #messageA, anObject, 2,5
-- "Ancestor message A 7"
```

Parameters callAncestor # *message, script/object, value …*

callAncestor # *message, [list of script/object], value …*

See also call, pass

on getBehaviorDescription   HANDLER

Syntax on getBehaviorDescription

Usage The *getBehaviorDescription* handler is a part of the new Director 6 behavior capabilities. It returns a string that displays information about the handler's operation and parameters; it is automatically called by the Behavior Inspector window. When a behavior is highlighted in the upper selection pane of the inspector, the text generated by the *getBehaviorDescription* handler is shown in the lower pane.

Example   This handler returns a description for a behavior that moves a sprite along a
straight line over a period of time (note that this is one long continuous
statement):

```
on getBehaviorDescription
  return "Move sprite along linear path" & RETURN & ¬
    "PARAMETERS:" & RETURN & ¬
    "• Chan: Sprite channel - automatically assigned" ¬
    & RETURN &¬
    "• OriginH: Automatically set by sprite position" ¬
    & RETURN &¬
    "• OriginV: Automatically set by sprite position" ¬
    & RETURN &¬
    "• DestinationH: Horizontal destination value" ¬
    & RETURN &¬
    "• DestinationV: Vertical destination value" ¬
    & RETURN &¬
    "• Period: Number of ticks for movement" ¬
    & RETURN &¬
    "MESSAGES:" & RETURN & ¬
    "• moveDest sprite_number - Starts sprite movement " ¬
    & "toward destination from origin" ¬
    & RETURN & ¬
    "• moveOrig sprite_number - Starts sprite movement " ¬
    & "toward origin from destination" ¬
end
```

Parameters
```
on getBehaviorDescription
  statements
  return string
end
```

See also   getPropertyDescriptionList

on getPropertyDescriptionList

HANDLER

Syntax   on getPropertyDescriptionList

Usage   The *getPropertyDescriptionList* handler is a part of the new Director 6 behavior capabilities. It returns a list that defines the properties of a behavior that
can be edited from the visual parameter interface available to behaviors.

This handler returns a property list defining each parameter that can be edited with the visual behavior interface. This information is used each time the user chooses to edit the user-definable properties of the behavior, by dragging a behavior onto the stage or into the score, by clicking on the Parameters button in the Behavior Inspector window, or by double-clicking on a behavior in the Behavior Inspector.

The property description list is a property list with one or more items; each item includes a property and an associated value. This is an example of a short property description list:

```
[#alternateImage: [ #comment:    "Alternate Image:", ¬
     #format:   #graphic, #default:    memdefault ]]
```

Each property must be a symbol value representing one of the properties defined at the beginning of the behavior script.

The value of each item is itself a property list containing at least three property/value pairs. The required properties are *#comment*, *#format*, and *#default*. An optional fourth property is *#range*.

The *#comment* property's value should be *string* with the text to be displayed in the dialog presented to the behavior's user when they are to make a selection.

The *#format* property's value describes the type of data that the property contains. Possible values are:

#integer	#float	#string	#symbol	#member
#bitmap	#filmloop	#field	#palette	#picture
#sound	#button	#shape	#movie	#digitalvideo
#script	#richtext	#ole	#transition	#xtra
#frame	#marker	#ink	#boolean	#btned
#graphic				

Many of these will cause a pop-up selection menu to be displayed in the Parameters dialog, displaying only the appropriate types of cast members.

The value of the *#default* property is displayed in the selection dialog; it is the one assigned to the property if no other is chosen.

If the *#range* property is used, its value should be a linear list with all possible values that the user can choose. A pop-up selection menu will be displayed with the items of the list.

Only properties modifiable from the behavior parameters interface are described by the property description list; properties that are set by the script should not appear in the list.

Example This handler returns a property list to the behavior interface for the animation behavior described in the preceding *getBehaviorDescription* entry:

```
on getPropertyDescriptionList
  set propDesc = [:]
  addProp propDesc, #DestinationH, ¬
    [#comment: "Horizontal destination coordinate:", ¬
     #format: #integer, ¬
```

```
      #default: the locH of sprite the currentSpriteNum]
  addProp propDesc, #DestinationV, ¬
    [#comment: "Vertical destination coordinate:", ¬
    #format: #integer, ¬
      #default: the locV of sprite the currentSpriteNum]
  addProp propDesc, #Period, ¬
    [#comment: "Time period for movement (in ticks):", ¬
    #format: #integer, #default: 60, ¬
    #range: [15, 30, 45, 60, 90, 120, 180]]
  return propDesc
end
```

If a behavior with this handler is dragged onto a sprite, or if a user clicks the Parameter button in the Behavior Inspector, a dialog box will appear with three fields in it. The first two will allow direct entry of integer values for the *DestinationH* and *DestinationV* property values; the third, because of the *range* property, will display a pop-up selection menu with the seven items from the list in the menu.

Parameters
```
on getPropertyDescriptionList
    statements
  return property list
end
```

See also   getBehaviorDescription

me

Syntax   on new me

Usage   The *me* keyword is used in parent scripts and behaviors to allow an object to refer to itself. Any variable name can be used in its place, but *me* is used by convention.

The most common usage of *me* is in a *new* handler, where it's used as both a parameter for the handler and a value to be returned.

Example   See the Example for the *new handler* that follows.

Parameters   me

Value   *me*

See also   new

new

Syntax `set anObject = new (script "LineAnim", 13, 300, 20, 60)`

Usage The *new* function is used with parent scripts to create a new object in memory from the script. The parameters passed to the function include a reference to the script, as well as any other parameters required by the corresponding script's *new* handler.

There the value returned from the *new* function is the memory position of the newly created object.

Example See the Example for the *new* handler in the following entry.

Parameters `new (script` *string/integer*`)`

`new (script` *string/integer, value …*`)`

See also new

on new

Syntax `on new me`

`on new me, chan, destH, destV, per`

Usage The *new* handler is a user-defined function employed in parent scripts to initialize properties and return a reference to a memory location.

Typically, when a new object is created in memory through the use of a parent script, values are assigned to properties, any other actions necessary to the creation of the object are executed, and then the memory position of the object is passed back to the calling statement by the use of the *return* command.

The *new* command uses the *me* parameter by convention, to refer to the current script. It may have any number of parameters after that, or none at all.

In versions of Director previous to 5, this was known as the *birth* command.

Examples This handler initializes a parent script equivalent to the animation behavior described in the *getBehaviorDescription* and *getPropertyDescriptionList* entries. It moves a sprite from its current location to a new position in a straight line, over a specified period of time. **Note:** this is not the entire parent script, just the initialization routine. The movie script this script occupies is named "LineAnim":

```
-- first we have to define our properties
property chan          -- sprite channel
property origLoc       -- origin
property destLoc       -- destination
property vector        -- movement vector
property period        -- number of ticks for move

on new me, cha, destH, destV, per
  set chan = cha
  set origLoc = the loc of sprite chan
  -- determines location from sprite position in score
  set destLoc = point (destH, destV)
  set vector = destLoc - origLoc
  set period = per
  -- all properties and parameters are accounted for
  return me  -- very important!
end
```

You can see that some of the properties are directly copied from the parameters for the handler (*chan, period*), while others are derived from parameters or other properties (*origLoc, destLoc, vector*).

This statement creates an object from the script above:

```
set animSprite = new (script "LineAnim", 3, 230, 100, 60)
```

If we assume that sprite 3 has a *loc* value of *point (50, 300)*, the parameters passed to the parent script would create an object with the following property values:

chan = 3

origLoc = point (50, 300)

destLoc = point (230, 100)

vector = point (180, -200)

period = 60

Parameters

```
on new me
     statements
  return me
end

on new me, value …
     statements
  return me
end
```

See also   new

objectP

Syntax
```
set isObject = objectP (anObject)
```

Usage
The *objectP* function returns TRUE if the item specified by its parameter is an object created by a parent script, Xtra, or XObject. It returns FALSE otherwise.

Example
This code segment uses the *objectP* function to verify the successful creation of an object with the FileIO Xtra:

```
global gFile
set gFile = new(xtra "fileio")
if not(objectP(gFile)) then
    alert "Problem using FileIO"
else
    openFile(gFile, "temp.txt",1)
    put readFile(gFile) into field "result"
    closeFile(gFile)
    set gFile = 0
end if
```

Parameters
```
objectP (value)
```

Value
boolean

See also
floatP, ilk, integerP, listP, stringP, symbolP, valueP

property

Syntax
```
property chan, origin, destination, period
```

Usage
The *property* keyword declares property variables. Property variables are used in parent scripts, and their contents are stored in each child object created by a parent script.

You can access a property of a child object by using a command like this:

```
put the propertyName of childObject
```

Within a parent script, the property can be referred to as if it was a global variable:

```
set the propertyName = aValue
```

Examples   This parent script declares some properties, and puts data into those properties:

```
----------------------------
property pSprite, pMember
----------------------------

on new me mySprite, myMember
  set pSprite = mySprite
  set pMember = myMember
  return me
end new
----------------------------
```

Then, if you create a child object from this parent script with a code segment like this:

```
global gObject
set gObject = new(script "parent",8, 15)
```

you can get the value of a property in a parent script from outside of that parent script with a statement like this:

```
put the pSprite of gObject
-- 8
```

Parameters   property *value* …

See also   ancestor, new

on runPropertyDialog

HANDLER

Syntax   `on runPropertyDialog me`

Usage   The *runPropertyDialog* handler allows you to set up behaviors using values you have predetermined (or determined through Lingo statements) rather than the dialogs created by the *getPropertyDescriptionList* handler.

Where the values of behavior properties need to be controlled, or where values will be constant, the *runPropertyDialog* handler can specify the proper data.

Example   This segment of a button behavior assigns specific cast members to a button, based on the cast member name of the sprite the behavior is dragged onto:

```
property inactiveButton, rolloverButton
property activeButton, chan

on beginSprite me
  runPropertyDialog me
end

on runPropertyDialog me
  setaProp me,  chan, the spriteNum of me
  setaProp me, inactiveButton, the member of sprite chan
  set aName1 = the name of member inactiveButton
  set aName2 = aName1 & "-rollover"
  setaProp me, rolloverButton, the number of member aName2
  set aName2 = aName1 & "-active"
  setaProp me, activeButton, the number of member aName2
  return me
end
```

Parameters
```
on runPropertyDialog me
  statements
  return me
end
```

See also   getPropertyDescriptionList

the scriptInstanceList of sprite

SPRITE PROPERTY

Syntax   `set whatScripts = the scriptInstanceList of sprite 2`

Usage   *the scriptInstanceList of sprite* is a property that contains a linear list of all of the behaviors attached to a specified sprite. Behaviors can be added and deleted from the list with standard list-manipulation commands.

Example   This movie script handler clears all behaviors from a specified sprite:

```
on misBehavin aSprite
  set the scriptInstanceList of sprite aSprite = []
end
```

Parameters the scriptInstanceList of sprite *integer*

Value *linear list of objects*

See also call, new

the spriteNum of me

OBJECT PROPERTY

Syntax set whatSprite = the spriteNum of me

Usage *the spriteNum of me* is a behavior property that is automatically assigned a value when a behavior is added to a sprite by dragging it onto the sprite. The property does not need to be initialized in a *property* declaration.

This property can be used to determine which sprite a behavior has been assigned to.

No value is assigned to *the spriteNum of me* if the behavior is added to a sprite's *scriptInstanceList* by use of the behavior's *new* handler.

Example This segment of a behavior sets up a list of cast members for an animation sequence. The list is initialized when the playback head reaches the first frame of the sprite's appearance in the score; it uses five consecutive cast members in a cast library, starting with the one currently assigned to the sprite.

```
property animList

on beginSprite me
  set aMember = ¬
    the number of the member of sprite the spriteNum of me
  set animList = [aMember, aMember + 1, aMember + 2, ¬
    aMember + 3, aMember + 4]
end
```

Parameters the spriteNum of me

Value *integer*

See also on beginSprite, currentSprite, on endSprite

on stepFrame

HANDLER

Syntax   on stepFrame

Usage   The *stepframe* message, in Director 6, is sent only to objects in *the actorList*.
The message is sent as the playback head enters a new frame, just before the
prepareFrame message, and is automatically sent to each object of *the actorList*
in the order in which the objects appear in the list.

Example   This handler calls a handler named *animateSprite* every time the playback
head enters a new frame. It will only be effective when the script it is part of
is the parent script of an object in *the actorList*:

```
on stepFrame
  animateSprite
end
```

Parameters   on stepFrame

See also   the actorList

Methods Category

Methods were used in Director prior to Version 5 as a means of communicating with XObjects. Xtras were introduced in Director 5, replacing XObjects as the means to extend the capabilities of Director. While it is possible to use XObjects with Director 6, some may not be fully compatible with the newer program, and it is recommended that whenever possible comparable Xtras be used instead. Although they are functional in Director 6, most of these methods are listed as obsolete in current documentation.

Methods are essentially function and procedure calls to an Xobject. When methods are used, some task is performed or some data is returned.

Not all XObjects respond to every method described in this chapter.

mDescribe

METHOD

Syntax   `put GetDate (mDescribe)`

Usage   The *mDescribe* method is the direct equivalent of the Xtra function *interface* (see Chapter 35). *mDescribe* displays documentation on an XObject's capabilities and the methods it makes available in the Message window. It is only useful in the authoring mode.

Example   These statements open the Xlibrary file "mastrapp.dll" and display its online documentation in the Message window:

```
openXLib the applicationPath & "mastrapp.dll"
put MasterApp (mDescribe)
```

Parameters   *XObject* (mDescribe)

Value   *string*

See also   interface

mDispose

METHOD

Syntax   `printObject (mDispose)`

Usage   The *mDispose* method is a standard XObject command used to delete an instance of the XObject from memory.

Example   This example creates and then disposes of an object created by an XObject:

```
set navApp = MasterApp (mNew)
navApp (mDispose)
```

Parameters   *object* (mDispose)

See also   mNew

mInstanceRespondsTo

Syntax
```
set isResp = GetDate (mInstanceRespondsTo, "printPict")
```

Usage
The *mInstanceRespondsTo* method determines whether an XObject under-stands a particular method. The parameter representing the message you want to check may be a symbol or string value. The XObject returns a value equal to one greater than the number of parameters the method requires if it understands the message, or 0 if it does not.

To determine whether an instance of an XObject (rather than the XObject itself) can respond to a method, use the *mRespondsTo* method.

Example
This code segment determines if an XObject called *MasterApp* understands the method *mLocateExecutable*. If it does, it creates an instance of the XObject then uses the method to find an application that will open an Acrobat PDF file:

```
if MasterApp (mInstanceRespondsTo, ¬
  #mLocateExecutable) then
  set app = MasterApp (mNew)
  set whatApp (mLocateExecutable, "Plants01.pdf")
end if
```

Parameters
XObject (mInstanceRespondsTo, *symbol|string*)

Value
integer

See also
mRespondsTo

mMessageList

Syntax
```
set aMessList = GetDate (mMessageList)
```

Usage
The *mMessageList* message is virtually identical to the *mDescribe* method. It returns the string that describes the specified XObject rather than putting it into the Message window. The string is identical to that returned by the *mDescribe* method, but it may be assigned to a variable rather than simply displayed in the Message window.

Example This statement assigns the message list returned from the XObject *MasterApp* to the variable *messages*:

```
set messages = MasterApp (mMessageList)
```

Parameters *XObject* (mMessageList)

Value *string*

See also interface, mDescribe, mInstanceRespondsTo, mRespondsTo

mName

METHOD

Syntax `set xObjName = GetDate (mName)`

Usage The *mName* method returns a string containing the name of an XObject. Its parameter can be either the XObject or an instance of the XObject.

Example This example sets a variable, *XOName*, to the string value returned by an *mName* method applied to an instance created from an XObject:

```
set XOName = app (mName)
```

Parameters *XObject/object* (mName)

Value *string*

mNew

METHOD

Syntax `set dateObject = GetDate (mNew)`

Usage The *mNew* method creates a new memory object from the specified XObject. Its direct corollary in the world of Xtras is the *new* function (see Chapter 35). Some *mNew* methods may require parameters to be passed to them to create the new object.

Example See the Example for *mDispose* earlier in this chapter.

Parameters *XObject* (mNew)

Value *object*

See also mDispose, new

mPerform

METHOD

Syntax `dateObject (mPerform, "mDispose")`

Usage The *mPerform* method is another way to call a method in an XObject, rather than directly addressing it; this is similar to what the *do* command does for string values containing Lingo statements. A string or symbol representing a message is passed to *mPerform*, along with any parameters the message might require.

Example This example creates a new instance of a file input/output object, using the *mNew* method, called through the *mPerform* method:

```
set fileObject = ¬
   fileio (mPerform, #mNew, "read", "prefs.txt")
```

Parameters *XObject|object* (mPerform, *symbol|string*)

 XObject|object (mPerform, *symbol|string*, *values …*)

mRespondsTo

METHOD

Syntax `set isResp = printObject (mRespondsTo, "printPict")`

Usage The *mRespondsTo* method determines whether an object created from an XObject understands a particular method. The parameter representing the message you want to check may be a symbol or string value. The XObject returns a value equal to one greater than the number of parameters the method requires if it understands the message, or 0 if it does not.

 To determine whether an XObject can respond to a method, use the *mInstanceRespondsTo* method.

Example	See the Example for *mInstanceRespondsTo* earlier in this chapter.
Parameters	*object* (mRespondsTo, *symbol*│*string*)
Value	*integer*
See also	mInstanceRespondsTo

Xtras Category

35

This category covers Lingo commands specific to the use of Xtras (the extensions to Director capabilities introduced in Director 5).

Xtras are automatically available to the authoring application or to a projector, if they are placed in a directory called "Xtras" that is stored in the same folder as the application or projector. They can also be opened using the *openXLib* command from a projector or Director.

Xtras can be used with a Shockwave movie but must be installed in the Shockwave support folder for the browser. Shockwave movies cannot open Xtras with the *openXLib* command.

interface

Syntax   `put interface (xtra "Mui")`

Usage   The *interface* function returns information about the capabilities, functions, and commands available to an object created using the Xtra.
      This function is only useful in authoring mode.

Example   This example puts an Xtra's interface information into the field cast member "Xtra Info":

```
put interface (xtra "PrintOMatic_Lite") into ¬
  member "Xtra Info"
```

Parameters   `interface (xtra integer|string)`

Value   *string*

the name of xtra

Syntax   `set whatXtra = the name of xtra 4`

Usage   *the name of xtra* is a property that allows you to access the names of the Xtras available to the Director application, a projector, or a Shockwave movie.

Example   This example puts the name of all currently installed Xtras into the field cast member "Xtra Display":

```
set XtraList = ""
repeat with i = 1 to the number of xtras
  set XtraList = XtraList & the name of xtra i & REWTURN
end repeat
put XtraList into the text of member "Xtra Display"
```

Parameters   `the name of xtra integer|string`

Value   *string*

See also   xtra

the number of xtras
MOVIE PROPERTY

Syntax	`set numXtras = the number of xtras`
Usage	*the number of xtras* is a property that indicates how many Xtras are currently available to the Director application, projector, or Shockwave movie.
Example	See the Example for *the name of xtra.*
Parameters	`the number of xtras`
Value	*integer*

xtra
KEYWORD

Syntax	`set anXtra = new (xtra "fileio")`
Usage	The *xtra* keyword is used to indicate an Xtra that adds to the capabilities of Director, a projector, or a Shockwave movie, and has a Lingo interface. Not all Xtras are accessible from Lingo; only those that can be controlled with Lingo are counted by *the number of xtras* property.
Example	This example creates an instance of the Macromedia User Interface (MUI) Xtra, and uses its built-in URL entry window to allow the user to enter an Internet address. It then captures what the user has entered and puts it into the variable *anURL*:

```
set anXtra = new (xtra "Mui")
GetUrl anXtra, "", TRUE
-- the GetUrl command is defined by the MUI Xtra, and
-- requires three parameters: the MUI object, a default
-- string value for the URL, and a boolean to determine
-- if the window can be moved
set anURL = the result
-- the URL typed into the window is returned by the result
set anXtra = EMPTY
-- disposes of the object
```

Parameters	`xtra` *integer/string*
See also	the name of xtra, the number of xtras

Lists Category

The List category comprises some of the most powerful objects in Lingo. Lists are not obvious, they're not as flashy as sprites, they don't make a sound, but they're everywhere in Director.

All lists are made up of *items*. Items are separated in lists by commas. There are two types of lists: *linear lists* and *property lists*.

Each item in a linear list consists of a *value*. A value can be something as simple as an integer, or it can be as complex as a child object of a parent script. Strings, symbols, and even other lists are used as values in linear lists. A linear list value is generally referred to by its position in the list. A typical linear list might look like this:

```
["Vancouver", "Seattle", "Portland", "San Francisco"]
```

Each item in a property list consists of a *property* and a *value*, separated by a colon. The value of an item in a property list can be anything that can be used as a value in a linear list. The property itself can be virtually anything as well. An item in a property list can be found not only by its position in the list but also by the property. A simple property list might have the following value:

```
[#brit: "Vancouver", #wash: "Seattle", ¬
    #oreg: "Portland", #cali: "San Francisco"]
```

> **Tip**
>
> *Using a symbol as the property (as in this example) allows you to use the standard property syntax in Lingo. If the example property list was assigned to a variable called gCities, you could refer to the third item in the list as the oreg of gCities.*

[ ]

Syntax `set the actorList = []`

Usage Lingo uses square brackets to signify the beginning and end of a *list* value.
An empty set of brackets is used to initialize a linear list before adding items to it.
A set of brackets separated by a colon is used to initialize a property list before adding items to it.

Examples This statement clears or initializes the linear list *aList*:

`set aList = []`

This statement clears or initializes the property list *aPropList*:

`set aPropList = [:]`

This statement creates a linear list with three integer values as items in the list:

`set aList = [32, 15, 20]`

This statement creates a property list with three properties and associated string values:

```
set aPropList = [#Portland: "Multnomah", ¬
  #Eugene: "Lane", #Yachats: "Lincoln"]
```

This statement creates a linear list with three items, one an integer, one a string, and the last a property list:

```
set aList = ¬
  [106, "Oregon", [10: "Doug Smith", 9: "Darrel Plant"]]
```

Value *list*

add

Syntax   add gCityList, "Springfield"

Usage   The *add* command places a value into a linear list. If the list is not sorted, the value is appended to the end the list. If the list is sorted, the value is added at the appropriate position in the list.

> ### Tip
>
> *You cannot use* add *to place values into a list that doesn't exist yet. You need to initialize the list before you add values to it.*

Example   This code segment adds a new instance of the parent script "SlideMgr" to *gSlideList*:

```
global gSlideList
add gSlideList, new(script "SlideMgr")
```

Parameters   add *list, value*

See also   addAt, addProp, append, count, deleteAt, getAt, getOne, getPos, listP, sort

addAt

Syntax   addAt urlList, 20, "http://www.surftrio.com/"

Usage   The *addAt* command lets you specify a position in a linear list where a value will be added. The value is inserted at the position you specify, increasing the number of items in the list by at least one. If you designate a position in the list that is greater than the number of items currently in the list, the value 0 is inserted in unfilled positions.

Example   This handler returns a linear list populated with unique random numbers, ranging from *myStartValue* to *myEndValue*:

```
on randomList myStartValue, myEndValue

  -- first, make sure end > start
  if myStartValue > myEndValue then
    set tStartValue = myEndValue
    set myEndValue   = myStartValue
    set myStartValue = tStartValue
  end if

  set tReturnedList = []
  repeat with i = 1 to ¨
      (myEndValue - myStartValue + 1)
    addAt tReturnedList, random(i), ¨
        (i + myStartValue - 1)
  end repeat
  return tReturnedList

end randomList
```

Parameters   addAt *list*, *integer*, *value*

Value   *integer*

See also   add, addProp, append, count, deleteAt, getAt, getOne, getPos, listP, sort

addProp

COMMAND

Syntax   addProp gSalmonList, #chinook, 0

Usage   The *addProp* command adds a property and its value to a property list. If the list is not sorted, the property and value are added to the end of the list. If the list is sorted, they are placed in the proper position within the list.

A property can be virtually any type of value itself, from an integer to a string or symbol, even a list.

The *addProp* command only works with property lists. A script error results from attempting to use it with a linear list.

If a property already exists in the propertyList, a new item with the same property is added. Use *setaProp* to replace the value of a property already in existence.

> **Tip**
>
> *You cannot use* addProp *to place values into a list that hasn't been initialized. You need to create the list before you use* addProp *to add values to it.*

Examples   You can maximize the power of property lists by storing a list as the value of a property. In this example, the property list *gControls* contains:

```
[#next: [#sprite:1, #member: "next", ¬
    #rollmember: "nextRoll"], #prev: ¬
    [#sprite:2, #member:"prev", #rollmember:"prevRoll"]]
```

This command adds another button to this list:

```
addProp gControls, #exit, [#sprite:3, ¬
    #member:"exit", #rollmember:"exitRoll"]
```

This is much more efficient than using a large number of individual global variables. In this way, all of the important properties of your controls are stored in one global variable.

Parameters   addProp *list, property, value*

See also   add, addAt, append, count, deleteOne, deleteProp, getaProp, getOne, setaProp, sort

append

COMMAND

Syntax   append chapterList, "Appendix A"

Usage   The *append* command adds a value to the end of a linear list, regardless of whether the list is sorted. If you wish to add a value to a sorted list in its proper order, use the *add* command.

Example   The following statements were entered in the Message window, to illustrate the operation of the *append* command:

```
set gList = [#smiley, #drippy, #boomboom]
sort gList
put gList
-- [#boomboom, #drippy, #smiley]
append gList, #dreeb
put gList
-- [#boomboom, #drippy, #smiley, #dreeb]
```

If the *add* command had been used instead of *append*, the result of the *put* command would have been:

```
-- [#boomboom, #dreeb, #drippy, #smiley]
```

Parameters   append *list*, *value*

See also   add, addAt, addProp, count, deleteAt, deleteOne, deleteProp, getAt, getOne, getPos, listP, sort

count

Syntax   `set howMany = count (countyList)`

Usage   The *count* function returns the number of items in a list. It works with both linear and property lists.

Example   In a scenario where you have created child objects and stored them in a global list variable *gObjects*, this handler would send a custom *mInitialize* message to each of them:

```
on initObjects
  global gObjects
  set tNumOfObjects = count (gObjects)
  repeat with tCurrObj = 1 to tNumOfObjects
    mInitialize (tCurrObj)
  end repeat
end initObjects
```

> **Tip**
>
> *Lingo will execute faster when you assign the result of a count function to a local variable, and use that local variable in a repeat loop. Otherwise, Lingo actually counts the number of entries in the list each time it repeats. On the other hand, if you're adding or deleting items from the list, be sure to update your count!*

Parameters   count (*list*)

Value   *integer*

See also   add, addAt, addProp, append, deleteAt, deleteOne, deleteProp, getAt, getOne, getPos, listP, sort

deleteAt

COMMAND

Syntax	`deleteAt gURLList, 4`
Usage	The *deleteAt* command removes the item at a specific position of a linear or property list. If the specified position is greater than the number of items in the list, Lingo generates an error.
Example	This command removes the string element *"how ya doin'"* from the second position of the list *gList*, which contains: *["hi", "how ya doin'", "just fine"]*:

`deleteAt gList, 2`

The resulting list will now contain:

`["hi", "just fine"]`

Parameters	`deleteAt list, integer`
See also	add, addAt, addProp, append, count, deleteOne, deleteProp, getAt, getOne, getPos, listP, sort

deleteOne

COMMAND

Syntax	`deleteOne gSalmonList, #endangered`
Usage	The *deleteOne* command removes an item with the specified value from a list. If the value appears in the list more than once, only the first occurrence is deleted. If the list is a property list, the property associated with the value is also deleted.
Example	The following statements copied from the Message window demonstrate the operation of the *deleteOne* command:

```
set gList = [#wendy:28, #doug:30, #jeff:31]
deleteOne gList,31
put gList
-- [#wendy: 28, #doug: 30]
```

Parameters	`deleteOne list, integer`
See also	add, addAt, addProp, append, count, deleteAt, deleteProp, getAt, getOne, getPos, listP

deleteProp

Syntax　deleteProp gCityList, #Boise

Usage　The *deleteProp* command removes a property and value pair (specified by property name) from a property list.

Example　This code segment removes the *#loop* property from the property list *gList* which contains:

```
[#name:"groovy", #loop:TRUE]
global gList
deleteProp gList, #loop
```

The *gList* would now contain:

```
[#name:"groovy"]
```

Parameters　deleteProp *list*, *property*

See also　add, addAt, append, count, deleteAt, deleteOne, getaProp, getOne, setaProp, sort

duplicate

Syntax　set listCopy = duplicate (gCityList)

Usage　The *duplicate* function returns an independent copy of a list. Use it if you need to work on a copy of the list without affecting the original list.

Example　This code segment copies the list stored in the global variable *gList* to a global variable named *gCopy*. Then, it sorts the *gCopy* list. The original list is unaffected by the sort and remains independent:

```
global gList, gCopy
set gCopy = duplicate(gList)
sort gCopy
```

After these statements executed, the Message window could return:

```
put gList
-- [9, 5, 7, 2]
put gCopy
```

```
-- [2, 5, 7, 9]
```

Parameters duplicate (*list*)

Value *list*

See also add, addAt, append, count, deleteAt, deleteOne, deleteProp, getaProp, getOne, setaProp,

findPos

FUNCTION

Syntax `set whereProp = findPos (gCityList, #Portland)`

Usage The *findPos* function returns the position in the list occupied by the specified property. If the property is not found in the list, the function returns VOID.

Example The following statements copied from Director's Message window illustrate the operation of the *findPos* function:

```
set gList = [#a:500, #c:200, #b:300]
put gList
-- [#a: 500, #c: 200, #b: 300]
put findPos(gList, #c)
-- 2
```

Parameters findPos (*list*, *property*)

Value *integer*

See also findPosNear, getOne, getPropAt

findPosNear

FUNCTION

Syntax `set whereProp = findPosNear (gCityList, #Gresham)`

Usage The *findPosNear* function returns the position in the property list occupied by the specified property. If the property is not found in the list and the list is sorted, then *findPosNear* returns the position that most closely matches the specified property. If the list is not sorted, *findPosNear* returns a value equal to the number of items in the list, plus one.

Example   The following statements copied from Director's Message window illustrate the operation of the *findPosNear* function:

```
set gList = [#me:"fi", #sa:"wi", #fi:"ea"]
sort gList
put gList
-- [#fi: "ea", #me: "fi", sa: "wi"]
put findPosNear (gList,#m)
-- 2
```

Parameters   findPosNear (*list*, *property*)

Value   *integer*

See also   findPos, getOne, getPropAt

getaProp

FUNCTION

Syntax   `set whatVal = getProp (gCarList, 6)`

Usage   The *getaProp* function returns the value of an item in a linear or property list.

When used with a linear list, *getProp* returns the item specified by the integer value used as the second parameter. If the specified value is not an integer, or if there is no corresponding item in the list, an error is generated.

When used with a property list, *getProp* returns the value of the item specified by the property used in the second parameter. If more than one item with the same property appears in the list, the first item's value is the one to be returned. If no property in the list matches the parameter, VOID is returned.

Example   In this example, each value in the property list *gControls* contains another property list. This strategy can be very powerful. Here is how it would work in the Message window:

```
set gControls = [#next:[#sprite:1, #member:"next", ¬
  #rollmember:"nextRoll"], #prev:[#sprite:2, ¬
  #member:"prev", #rollmember:"prevRoll"], ¬
  #exit: [#sprite:3, #member:"exit", ¬
  #rollmember:"exitRoll"]].
put getProp(gControls, #prev)
-- [#sprite: 2, #member: "prev", #rollmember: "prevRoll"]
```

You can achieve the same result with a different syntax:

```
put the prev of gControls
-- [#sprite: 2, #member: "prev", #rollmember: "prevRoll"]
```

or, even:

```
put the rollmember of (the prev of gControls)
-- "prevRoll"
```

Parameters   getaProp (*linear list*, *integer*)
getaProp (*property list*, *property*)

Value   *value*

See also   add, addAt, addProp, append, count, deleteOne, deleteProp, findPos, findPosNear, getAt, getLast, getProp, getOne, setaProp, sort

getAt

FUNCTION

Syntax   `set todaysFish = getAt (menuList, 4)`

Usage   The *getAt* function returns the value of the item in the specified position of a linear or property list. If the parameter is greater than the number of items in the list, *getAt* returns an alert error.

Example   Here is an example of the use of the *getAt* function in the Message window:

```
set gList = [4,6,9,12]
put getAt(gList, 3)
-- 9
```

Parameters   getAt (*list*, *integer*)

Value   *value*

See also   add, addAt, addProp, append, count, deleteOne, deleteProp, findPos, findPosNear, getaProp, getLast, getProp, getOne, setaProp, sort

getLast

FUNCTION

Syntax   `set saturday = getLast (localizedDayList)`

Usage The *getLast* function returns the value of the last item in a linear or property list. If there are no items in the list, VOID is returned.

Example Here is an example of the use of the *getAt* function in the Message window:

```
set gList = [4,6,9,12]
put getLast(gList)
-- 12
```

Parameters getLast (*list*)

Value *value*

See also add, addAt, addProp, append, count, deleteOne, deleteProp, findPos, findPosNear, getAt, getaProp, getProp, getOne, setaProp, sort

getOne

FUNCTION

Syntax `set whatProp = getOne (gCityList, 1)`

Usage The *getOne* function returns the position or property of an item with the specified value.

   If the list is a linear list, *getOne* returns the position of the first item with the specified value.

   If the list is a property list, *getOne* returns the property of the first item with the specified value.

   If the value is not found in the list, *getOne* returns 0.

Example These statements from the Message window show the behavior of the *getOne* function:

```
set gList = [12,76,34]
put getOne(gList, 76)
-- 2
set gPList = [#fr:"ac",#en:"ls",#do:"oc"]
put getOne(gPList, "ac")
-- #fr
```

Parameters getOne (*list, value*)

Value *integer|property*

See also add, addAt, addProp, append, count, deleteOne, deleteProp, findPos, findPosNear, getAt, getaProp, getLast, getPos, getProp, setaProp, sort

getPos

Syntax   `set whereAt = getPos (gCities, "Vancouver")`

Usage   The *getPos* function returns the position of a value in a list, whether the list is a linear list or a property list. If the value is not found in the list, *getPos* returns 0.

Example   These statements from the Message window show the behavior of the *getPos* function:

```
set gList = [12,76,34]
put getPos(gList, 76)
-- 2
set gPList = [#fr:"ac",#en:"ls",#do:"oc"]
put getPos(gPList, "ac")
-- 1
put getPos(gPList, "dc")
-- 0
```

Parameters   `getPos (list, value)`

Value   *integer*

See also   add, addAt, addProp, append, count, deleteOne, deleteProp, findPos, findPosNear, getAt, getaProp, getLast, getOne, getProp, setaProp, sort

getProp

Syntax   `set whatValue = getProp (myObjects, #button2)`

Usage   The *getProp* function returns the value of an item with the specified property from a property list. This is the same as the *getaProp* function, except *getProp* returns an error dialog box if the property is not found.

Example   These statements from the Message window show the behavior of the *getProp* function:

```
set gPList = [#fr: "ac", #en: "ls", #do: "oc"]
put getProp(gPList, #en)
-- "ls"
```

Parameters   getProp (*list*, *property*)

Value   *value*

See also   add, addAt, addProp, append, count, deleteOne, deleteProp, findPos, findPosNear, getAt, getaProp, getLast, getOne, getPos, getPropAt, setaProp, sort

getPropAt

Syntax   set whatProp (gSalmonList, 4)

Usage   The *getPropAt* function returns the property of the item specified by a position in the list. If the position parameter is greater than the number of items (or if it is less than 1), then *getPropAt* returns an error dialog box.

Example   These statements from the Message window show the behavior of the getPropAt function:

set gPList = [#fr: "ac", #en: "ls", #do: "oc"]
put getPropAt(gPList, 3)
-- #do

Parameters   getPropAt (*list*, *integer*)

Value   *property*

See also   add, addAt, addProp, append, count, deleteOne, deleteProp, findPos, findPosNear, getAt, getaProp, getLast, getOne, getPos, getProp, setaProp, setProp, sort

ilk

Syntax   set whatType = ilk (cityList)
set isPoint = ilk (cityPosition, #point)

Usage   The *ilk* function can be used to determine what type of data a value contains.
    Used with just a value as a parameter, *ilk* returns the value type as a symbol.

> **Tip**
>
> *The* ilk *function is actually much more powerful than the Director documentation would lead you to believe. It will return the type of any* value: #integer, #float, #string, #instance, *even* #void.

The *ilk* function can also be used to test whether a value is of a particular type, returning TRUE or FALSE depending on the value and type specified as the parameters.

This chart shows which types of values return TRUE for different data structures using the *ilk* function:

	Linear List	Property List	Point	Rect
#list	TRUE	TRUE	TRUE	TRUE
#linearlist	TRUE			
#proplist		TRUE		
#point			TRUE	
#rect				TRUE

Example   The following statements from the Message window show the versatility of the *ilk* function:

```
put ilk(500)
-- #integer
put ilk(500.0)
-- #float
put ilk("How are ya?")
-- #string
put ilk(member 11)
-- #member
put ilk(the stage)
-- #window
put ilk(script "pTest")
-- #script
put ilk([1,2,3])
-- #list
put ilk([1,2,3],#linearList)
-- 1
put ilk(the rect of sprite 1)
-- #rect
put ilk(point(1,2),#point)
-- 1
```

Parameters   ilk (*value*)
ilk (*value*, *symbol*)

Value   *symbol*

boolean

list

Syntax   `set newList = list (23, 50, 34)`

Usage   The *list* function creates a linear list filled with the specified values. You can use this function rather than the typical square brackets ([]).

Example   This statement creates a linear list and assigns it to the variable *tList*:

`set tList = list("Bella", "Gellert", "Annie")`

Parameters   `list (value, value, value, …)`

Value   *linear list*

See also   add, addAt, append, count, deleteOne, getAt, getLast, getOne, getPos, listP, sort

listP

Syntax   `set isList = listP (gWhatsit)`

Usage   The *listP* function returns TRUE if the item specified is a linear or property list, a rect, or a point. It returns FALSE otherwise.

Example   This code segment uses the *listP* function as the logical test in an *if* statement:

```
if listP(gTemp) then
   return gTemp
else
   return []
end if
```

Parameters   `listP (value)`

Value   *boolean*

See also   ilk, objectP, stringP, valueP

setaProp

Syntax   setaProp gCities, #wash, "Bellingham"

Usage   The *setaProp* command replaces the value of the item with the specified property. If no item with the property exists, *setaProp* adds an item with the specified property and value to the list.

The *setaProp* command only works with property lists. If you use it with a linear list, you will get a script error.

Examples   In this example, the list *gSoundList* contains:

```
[#song:"http://www.nnn.com/mysong.swa", ¬
 #voice:"http://www.nnn.com/myvoice.swa"]
```

We will change the value of the item with the property *#song* with this statement:

```
setaProp gSoundList, #song, ¬
  "http://www.nnn.com/mynewsong.swa"
```

Parameters setaProp *property list*, *property*, *value*

See also   add, addAt, addProp, append, count, deleteOne, deleteProp, findPos, findPosNear, getAt, getaProp, getOne, getLast, getPos, getProp, getOne, setAt, setProp, sort

setAt

Syntax   setAt rankingList, 2, "Doug"

Usage   The *setAt* command replaces the value of the item in a list. The item is specified by its position in the list.

If the list is a linear list and the position specified is greater than the number of items in the list, intervening positions are filled with the value 0.

If the list is a property list and the position exceeds the number of items in the list, *setAt* returns an error alert.

Example   This code segment shows an application of the *setAt* command in the Message window. A list is created, then we use the *getPos* command to locate the position of the string "cat" in the list, and replace it with "dog":

```
set tList = ["mouse", "hippo", "cat"]
setAt tList, getPos(tList, "cat"), "dog"
put tList
-- ["mouse", "hippo", "dog"]
```

Parameters   setAt *lilst, integer, value*

See also   add, addAt, addProp, append, count, deleteOne, deleteProp, findPos, findPosNear, getAt, getaProp, getOne, getLast, getPos, getProp, getOne, setaProp, setProp, sort

setProp

COMMAND

Syntax   setProp gCities, #oreg, "Yachats"

Usage   The *setProp* command replaces the value of an item associated with an existing property. If an item with the property doesn't already exist, *setProp* displays an error alert. This is different from *setaProp*, which just adds an item with the new property and value.

The *setProp* command only works with property lists. If you try it with a linear list, you will get a script error.

Examples   In this example, the list *gSoundList* contains:

```
[#song:"http://www.nnn.com/mysong.swa", ¬
    #voice:"http://www.nnn.com/myvoice.swa"].
```

If we try to change the *gSoundList* with this statement we will get an error alert:

```
setProp gSoundList, #laugh, ¬
    "http://www.nnn.com/mylaugh.swa"
```

Parameters   setProp *list, property, value*

See also   add, addAt, addProp, append, count, deleteOne, deleteProp, findPos, findPosNear, getAt, getaProp, getOne, getLast, getPos, getProp, getOne, setAt, setaProp, sort

sort

Syntax   `sort gCities`

Usage   The *sort* command puts the items in the list into ascending order. If the list is a linear list, the list is sorted by its values. If it is a property list, the list is sorted by its properties.

> ### Tip
>
> *If you create a list that you intend to sort, you can sort it before you add values to it, and all values added to it will be added in the correct order. It is faster to sort an empty list than a list with many elements.*

Examples   These statements from the Message window show the operation of the sort command:

```
set tLinList = [7,4,9,3,6]
put tLinList
-- [7, 4, 9, 3, 6]
sort tLinList
put tLinList
-- [3, 4, 6, 7, 9]
add tLinList, 5
put tLinList
-- [3, 4, 5, 6, 7, 9]

set tPropList = [#ic:3, #dv:1, #lw:7]
put tPropList
-- [#ic: 3, #dv: 1, #lw: 7]
sort tPropList
put tPropList
-- [#dv: 1, #ic: 3, #lw: 7]
addProp tPropList, #ex, 9
put tPropList
-- [#dv: 1, #ex: 9, #ic: 3, #lw: 7]
```

Parameters   `sort list`

See also   add, addAt, addProp, append, count, deleteOne, deleteProp, findPos, findPosNear, getAt, getaProp, getOne, getLast, getPos, getProp, getOne, setAt, setaProp, setProp

Code Structures & Syntax Category

These Lingo structures are where much of the real work of interactivity is done. Most of the previous sections deal with the control of various media. This section allows you to make decisions.

— —

Syntax   `-- a comment is a good thing to see`

Usage   Two dashes indicate that everything that follows on the line is a comment and is not to be interpreted as part of the Lingo program.

Commenting is extremely useful, even though it's nonfunctional. In a large project, you may write code that you don't look at again for weeks or months. Behaviors you wrote the year before and have used without thinking may need to be modified. You may have gotten so busy that you've had to hire assistants to help with the coding. In any of these cases, uncommented code can get you into trouble.

Comments are stripped out of the code when a projector, protected movie, or Shockwave movie is made, so don't worry about them bloating your file. One small bitmap image will probably be far larger than any comments you're likely to write.

Example   A comment can sit on a line by itself, like this:

`-- this handler does nothing`

or it can be at the end of the line:

`if not netDone (3) then -- stream not finished`

Parameters   `--`

¬

Syntax   `addAt tReturnedList, random(i), ¬`
              `(i + myStartValue - 1)`

Usage   The continuation symbol indicates to the Lingo interpreter that a statement is continued on the next line of the script. There's no need to break long statements, but the continuation symbol is used for clarity.

Programmers often indent the line after the continuation symbol. Again, this is not necessary but is done for clarity.

Example   A statement with a continuation, such as the following:

```
set aCityList = [#brit: "Vancouver", ¬
    #wash: "Seattle"]
```

is the same as if it had been written without a continuation:

```
set aCityList = [#brit: "Vancouver", #wash: "Seattle"]
```

Parameters   ¬

# #

SYMBOL

Syntax   `addProp cityList, #idah, "Boise"`

Usage   The pound character (also called a hash mark) is used to indicate a symbol value in Director.

A symbol is converted to a unique integer value in memory when the Lingo script is compiled for execution. Symbols can be compared against each other. Variables and properties can be assigned symbol values. Symbols can be used as parameters for handlers, etc. The advantage of symbols is that alphanumeric characters can be used in their names, making them easier to read. Also, processing of symbols is much faster than processing of strings.

Symbols are used extensively by Director in properties. A symbol value always begins with a # and a letter, followed by virtually any combination of alphanumeric characters. Symbols are not case-sensitive, and only roman letter characters and numbers are allowed in the symbol name.

Example   This example sets the variable *salmon* equal to the symbol value *#coho*:

```
set salmon = #coho
```

Parameters   #

See also   string, symbol, symbolP

abort

Syntax   abort

Usage   The *abort* command stops the execution of the current Lingo handler as well as any handlers that may have called the current one. If you want to stop the current handler and return to the handler that called it, use the *exit* command.

Example   This handler stops executing under the conditions of the *if* command. In addition, all currently executing handlers would be exited as well.

```
on stopIfWeveWaitedTooLong
  global gLastNetID, gStartTicks
  if the ticks >= gStartTicks + 60*5 AND ¬
  not(netDone(gLastNetID)) then
  netAbort(gLastNetID)
    abort
  end if
end stopIfWeveWaitedTooLong
```

Parameters   abort

See also   exit, halt, netAbort, netDone, quit

on alertHook

Syntax   on alertHook me, err, msg

Usage   The *alertHook* handler is a new Director 6 user-definable function that lets you manage errors generated by your Director movies. The *alertHook* is called whenever an error is encountered while the movie is playing.

The *alertHook* handler needs to be placed in a movie script and initialized by setting the *alertHook* property (see the following entry) to point to the script. This handler uses three parameters:

- The *me* parameter refers to the script object (created by setting the *alertHook* property).

- The *err* parameter (which can be named something else if you wish) contains a string designating what type of error has occurred. Possible values are:

```
"File read error", "File error", "Script syntax error", "Script ¬
    runtime error"
```

- The *msg* parameter (which can also have another name) is a string with specific information about the error. This is typically the same information displayed in an error alert box. A sample message would be:

```
"Handler not defined
    blarg


#blarg
"
```

The *alertHook* handler must return a value using the *return* command. The value it returns determines the action taken by the movie when an alert is encountered:

- In the authoring mode, if a value of 0 is returned, the standard error dialog is displayed when an error is encountered.
- In the authoring mode, if you return the value 1, no alert dialog is generated, and the Debug window is automatically opened.
- In the authoring mode, returning a value of –1 stops the movie, with no alert shown. In the authoring mode, if the *alertHook* handler returns a value of 2, the Script window is automatically opened to the script where the error was encountered.

In projectors and Shockwave movies, returning a value of 1 from the *alertHook* handler prevents an error dialog from appearing. Returning a 0 causes the error dialog to appear, which is the default behavior if no script has been designated as the *alertHook* handler.

Example   This handler determines if the movie generating a run-time error is playing in Director, a projector, or a Shockwave plug-in. If it is playing in Director, the Script window is automatically opened; otherwise, the error is ignored and no alert message is displayed:

```
on alertllook me, err, msg
  if err = "Script runtime error" then return 2
  else return 1
end
```

Parameters   browserName *integer*
```
on alertHook me, err, msg
  statements
  return -1|0|1|2
end
```

See also   the alertHook

the alertHook

Syntax `set the alertHook = script "Alert"`

Usage *the alertHook* property can be set to a movie script containing an *alertHook* handler. If an error is encountered by the movie while playing, the script specified by *the alertHook* property will be called to determine whether an alert window will be shown.

Parameters `the alertHook`

Value *script*

See also on alertHook

case

Syntax
```
case the runMode of
    "Author": set response = "Playing in Director"
    "Projector": set response = "Playing in Projector"
    "Plugin":
      set browser = externalEvent ("whatBrowser")
      set response = "Playing in" && browser
    otherwise
      set response "Player unknown"
end case
```

Usage The *case* keyword begins a multiple-branch decision-making structure. It is similar in function to multiple *if … then … else* statements, but it's more efficient.

    The *case* structure is a very flexible way to accommodate many different possible values that may match the original expression. When Lingo executes the *case* structure, it begins with the first value and tests to see if it matches the expression following the word *case*. If it does, it executes the statement (or statements) following the ":" (colon). If it does not match, Lingo continues looking for a match until it reaches the end of the values. The optional *otherwise* clause can be followed by statements to be carried out if there is no match.

Each value is followed by a colon and one or more Lingo statements. The values must appear on separate lines. If a value is found that matches the expression in the *case* statement, all statements between the colon and the next value (or the *otherwise* clause) are carried out, and no other statements following a value are executed.

Examples   This *case* structure shows how you can test for multiple ranges of values, by placing a logical test in parentheses and letting *case* try to match them against the value TRUE:

```
case TRUE of
   (gValue < 5):doLessThan
   (gValue > 5 AND gValue < 10):doMiddle
   (gValue > 10):doGreaterThan
   otherwise
      set gValue = 0
end case
```

This *case* structure shows how you can easily test to see which sprite the mouse is pointing at with the *rollover* function:

```
case rollover () of
   2:set the memberNum of sprite 2 = "next2"
   3:set the memberNum of sprite 3 = "prev2"
   4:set the memberNum of sprite 4 = "end2"
   5:set the memberNum of sprite 5 = "help2"
end case
```

Parameters   ```
case expression of
   expression: statement
   expression:
      statements
otherwise
   statements
end case
```

**See also**   and, if, not, or
```

clearGlobals

Syntax   `clearGlobals`

Usage   The *clearGlobals* command clears the contents of all user-defined global variables, setting them to VOID. You can use this to start a movie out completely fresh, assuring that all globals are empty before beginning. The *clearGlobals* command does not reset the contents of global system properties like *the actorList* and *the windowList*.

Example   This handler clears all global variables each time the movie is started:

```
on startMovie
  clearGlobals
  -- more init below
end startMovie
```

Parameters   `clearGlobals`

See also   global, showGlobals

exit

Syntax   `exit`

Usage   The *exit* command forces the current handler to stop running and to return to the handler that called the current one. This is in contrast to the *abort* command, which stops all currently executing handlers.

Example   This handler uses the *exit* command to jump out of the handler if the *myValue* argument is not really a value:

```
on square myValue
  if not valueP(myValue) then exit
  return myValue * myValue
end square
```

Parameters   `exit`

See also   abort, halt, netAbort, quit

exit repeat

Syntax   `exit repeat`

Usage   The *exit repeat* command forces Lingo to stop execution of the current *repeat* loop, and to jump the statement immediately following the next *end repeat* statement.

Example   This function picks the first available sprite from *gSpriteList*, which contains [4:TRUE, 5:TRUE, 6:FALSE, 7:FALSE]. The *repeat* loop checks each entry in the list until it finds a FALSE value. It then returns that sprite, after setting its entry in *gSpriteList* to TRUE, indicating that the sprite is now used:

```
on findNextSprite
  global gSpritelist
  set tReturnSprite = 0
  repeat with i = 1 to count(gSpriteList)
    set tProp = getPropAt(gSpriteList, i)
    if getaProp(gSpriteList, tProp) then
      next repeat
    else
      setaProp(gSpriteList, tProp, TRUE)
      set tReturnSprite = tProp
      exit repeat
    end if
  end repeat
  if tReturnSprite > 0 then
    return tReturnSprite
  else
    return #noSprite
  end if
end findNextSprite
```

Then, this statement will send the next available sprite to the Message window:

```
put findNextSprite
-- 6
```

Parameters   `exit repeat`

See also   if, next repeat, repeat while, repeat with

getError

Syntax
```
set whatError = getError (member "soundtrack")
```

Usage   The *getError* function returns the error number of a Shockwave audio cast member. If *getError* returns 0, the streaming process is working with no errors. The *getErrorString* function returns a string describing the error.
The error codes and corresponding strings are:

- 0   "OK"
- 1   "memory"
- 2   "network"
- 3   "playback device"
- 99   "other"

Example   This code segment tests for a streaming error in the cast member "swa", and reports an error if it occurs:
```
if getError(member "swa") <> 0 then
  -- error
  alert getErrorString(member "swa")
end if
```

Parameters   getError (*member*)

Value   0|1|2|3|99

See also   getErrorString, the state of member

getErrorString

Syntax
```
set whatError = getErrorString (member "soundtrack")
```

Usage   The *getErrorString* function returns a string value describing the error state of a Shockwave audio cast member. The *getError* function returns a numeric value representing the error.

The error strings and corresponding codes are:

0 "OK"

1 "memory"

2 "network"

3 "playback device"

99 "other"

Example   See the Example for *getError* in the preceding entry.

Parameters   `getErrorString (member)`

Value   `"OK"| "memory"| "network"| "playback device"| "other"`

See also   getError, the state of member

global

KEYWORD

Syntax   `set`

Usage   The *global* keyword declares the variables that follow as *globals*, which are *variables* that can be used outside the current handler. A variable that is not declared as a global can only be used within the current handler.

Global variables can contain virtually any kind of data that Director can work with, including values, strings, lists, child objects, media, pictures, and sounds. In addition, they remain in memory even when navigating to other movies with commands like *gotoNetMovie*. The data in global variables remains until replaced, set to VOID, or cleared with the *clearGlobals* command.

Global variables may be declared as the first line of each handler they are used in, or at the top of each script in which they appear in any number of handlers.

Example   This code segment declares the global *gNetID*, then assigns the value of the *getLatestNetID* function to it, making that available to any handler in the movie:

```
global gNetID
set gNetID = getLatestNetID
```

Parameters   `global global, ...`

See also   clearGlobals, property, showGlobals, showLocals

if

Syntax

```
if netDone (3) then go "DLcomplete"

if the timer > 30 then
  animateButtons
end if

if the machineType = 256 then doPC
else doMac

if aNum = "" then
  nothing
else
  set aNum = ""
end if
```

Usage

The *if* logical structure performs actions based on an expression evaluating to TRUE or FALSE. If the expression is TRUE, the structure executes a statement or set of statements. If it is FALSE, no action is taken unless the optional *else* clause is present, in which case the statements following the *else* clause are executed.

If the statement or statements executed by the last clause in an *if* structure occupy a different line than the *then* or *else* clause, an *end if* statement is needed to delineate the structure.

Multiple "nested" *if* statements can be constructed, with each *else* clause leading into a new *if* statement. An example:

```
if aNum < 20 then
  set zone = 1
else if aNum < 25 then
  set zone = 2
else if aNum < 32 then
  set zone = 3
else
  set aNum = 4
end if
```

As an example of the use of an *end if* statement, the last clause of the nested *if* structure above could be rewritten like this:

```
else aNum = 4
```

Written on one line, there would be no need for the *end if* statement.

Example This handler uses the *if* structure to wait until the remote data identified by the "1" has finished downloading before going to the next frame. Since the *netDone* function returns either TRUE or FALSE, you don't need to write "*if netDone(1) = TRUE*".

```
on exitFrame
    if netDone(1) then
        go to the frame + 1
    else
        go to the frame
    end if
end exitFrame
```

Parameters
```
if expression then statement
```
```
if expression then
    statements
end if
```
```
if expression then statement
else statement
```
```
if expression then
    statements
else statement
```
```
if expression then statement
else
    statements
end if
```
```
if expression then
    statements
else
    statements
end if
```

See also and, case, FALSE, not, or, TRUE

next repeat

COMMAND

Syntax `next repeat`

Usage The *next repeat* command increments or decrements the counter of a *repeat* loop and forces Lingo to skip to the next *end repeat* statement.

Examples This code segment creates a list of the names of each cast member of the type *myType* in the current cast. It skips all nonbitmap members by using the *next repeat* command:

```
on getMemsOfType myType
   set tList = []
   set tNumOfMems = the number of members
   repeat with tCast = 1 to tNumOfMems
      if the type of member tCast <> ¨
         myType then next repeat

         add tList, the name of member tCast
   end repeat
   return tList
end getMemsOfType
```

Here is an example of how this function could work in the Message window:

```
put getMemsOfType(#bitmap)
-- ["Roll", "George", "Fred", "button1"]
```

Parameters next repeat

See also exit repeat, if, repeat while, repeat with

nothing

Syntax nothing

Usage The *nothing* command does absolutely nothing. It is a useful placeholder for some Lingo structures, to make your code more readable.

Example This handler does nothing for the number of ticks contained in the *myTicks* parameter (a tick is 1/60 of a second). It would work equally well without the *nothing* command:

```
on wait myTicks
   set tTicks = the ticks
   repeat while the ticks < tTicks + myTicks
      nothing
   end repeat
end wait
```

Parameters nothing

repeat while

LOGIC

Syntax
```
repeat while i < count (URLList)
```

Usage
The *repeat while* structure creates a loop that continues to execute the Lingo inside as long as an expression is TRUE, or until an *exit repeat* statement is executed.

Example
This handler halts execution of any Lingo for the number of seconds specified in *mySeconds*:
```
on wait mySeconds
    startTimer
    repeat while the timer < mySeconds * 60
        nothing
    end repeat
end wait
```

Parameters
```
repeat while expression
    statements
end repeat
```

See also
case, exit repeat, if, next repeat, repeat with

repeat with

LOGIC

Syntax
```
repeat with years = 10 to 20
```

Usage
The *repeat with* structure creates a loop using a variable as a counter which is initially set to the value following the "=" (equals) sign. Commands between the *repeat with* statement and the next *end repeat* statement are executed as part of the loop. Each time the accompanying *end repeat* statement is reached, the counter is incremented by 1. Execution of the loop continues until the counter's value exceeds the second value after the "=" sign or until an *exit repeat* command is encountered.

The counter variable may be modified by commands within the *repeat* loop.

Tip

Keep in mind that repeat *loops are* inclusive, *in that they are executed for both of the values passed to the counter as well as those in between. The* repeat with *loop shown in the "Syntax" section above will execute 11 times, not just 10.*

Example   This code segment puppets all 120 sprite channels:

```
repeat with tSprite = 1 to 120
    set the puppet of sprite tSprite = TRUE
end repeat
```

Parameters
```
repeat with variable = integer|float to integer|float
    statements
end repeat
```

See also   case, exit repeat, if then, next repeat, repeat while, repeat with down to, repeat with in

repeat with down to

LOGIC

Syntax   `repeat with countdown = 10 down to 0`

Usage   The *repeat with down to* structure creates a loop using a variable as a counter which is initially set to the value following the "=" (equals) sign. Commands between the *repeat with* statement and the next *end repeat* statement are executed as part of the loop. Each time the accompanying *end repeat* statement is reached, the counter is decremented by 1. Execution of the loop continues until the counter's value is less than the second value after the "=" sign or until an *exit repeat* command is encountered.

The counter variable may be modified by commands within the *repeat* loop.

Tip

Keep in mind that repeat *loops are* inclusive, *in that they are executed for both of the values passed to the counter as well as those in between. The* repeat with *loop shown in the "Syntax" section above will execute 11 times, not just 10.*

Example   This code segment writes a number from 10 to 1 to the field "countDown", pausing for a half-second between each number:

```
repeat with tCounter = 10 down to 1
    put tCounter into field "countDown"
    set tTicks = the ticks
    repeat while the ticks < tTicks + 30
        nothing
    end repeat
end repeat
```

Parameters
```
repeat with variable = integer|float down to integer|float
    statements
end repeat
```

See also   case, exit repeat, if then, next repeat, repeat while, repeat with, repeat with in

repeat with in
LOGIC

Syntax   `repeat with i in [1, 3, 5, 7, 11, 13, 17, 19]`

Usage   This version of the *repeat with* logical structure uses each of the values of a linear list or property list as a value for the counter. The loop is once for each item in the list.

Examples   This code segment puts the items in a property list into the field named "result":

```
set tList = [#name:"Somebody", ¬
             #address:"Somewhere", ¬
             #city:"Nowhere"]
put "" into field "result"
repeat with tItem in tList
    put tItem & "," after field "result"
end repeat
```

Assuming the field "result" was empty before this operation, its contents would be this string:

`"Somebody,Somewhere,Nowhere,"`

Parameters   repeat with *variable* in *list*
          statements
    end repeat

See also   case, exit repeat, if then, next repeat, repeat while, repeat with, repeat with down to

the result

Syntax   set whathappened = the result

Usage   *the result* is a property that contains information about the last command executed.

Example   The *new* command also returns the cast number of the member created. This code segment uses *the result* to retrieve a reference to the new cast number:

```
new #sound
set the name of member (the result) = "loud"
```

Parameters   the result

Value   *value*

return

Syntax   return IDate

Usage   The *return* command exits the current function handler, returning its parameter as a value to the handler that called it.

Example

This function handler returns the value of *pi* squared:

```
on pi2
  return pi * pi
end
```

You can use this handler in a statement like this. Notice that the parentheses are required, even though no parameters are required by this handler:

```
put pi2 ()
```

Parameters `return value`

See also end, exit, on, the result

set

Syntax

```
set whereDay = getOne (sDate, day)
```

```
set whereDay to getOne (sDate, day)
```

Usage

The *set* command assigns a value to the specified variable or property. It can be used either with an "=" (equals) sign separating the variable/property and the value, or with the keyword *to*.

Examples

This command sets the source URL of a Shockwave audio cast member:

```
set the URL of member "swa" = ¬
    "http://www.surftrio.com/wave99.swa"
```

This code segment stores the value of the *getLatestNetID* function in a global variable:

```
global gNetID
set gNetID = getLatestNetID ()
```

Parameters `set variable|property =|to value`

See also global, property, put

showGlobals

Syntax   showGlobals

Usage   The *showGlobals* command displays the names and values of all global variables in the Message window. It is only useful in the Director authoring environment.

Parameters   showGlobals

See also   clearGlobals, global, property, showLocals

showLocals

Syntax   showLocals

Usage   The *showLocals* command shows the names and values of all the current handler's local variables in the Message window. You can only use it from within a handler. It is only useful in the Director authoring environment.

Parameters   showLocals

See also   clearGlobals, global, property, showGlobals

VOID

Syntax   `set blackHole = VOID`

Usage   The *VOID* keyword allows you to set a variable to no value. In Lingo, 0 is
          considered an integer value; setting a variable to VOID means it has no
          assigned value.

Example   This example from the Message window shows a variable being set to VOID,
          the resulting value of the variable, and the results of a test to determine if the
          variable is VOID:

```
put abmap
-- (member 5 of castLib 1)
set abmap = VOID
put abmap
-- <Void>
put voidP (abmap)
-- 1
```

Value   `VOID`

See also voidP

Strings
Category

38

This section covers Lingo related to the manipulation of text strings. Strings comprise one of the most important data types in Director; strings are very flexible and able to be manipulated in more ways than almost any other data type. That said, a string is also the slowest standard data type to manipulate.

Strings can be stored in RAM, as part of a variable, or in a field cast member. They can be read from a disk file or retrieved from a network. Most file input/ output operations require that other types of data be converted to or from strings at some point during the read/write process.

"

Syntax   `set anEmail = "dugsmith@arogos.com"`

Usage   The double quote mark is a delimiter for a string value. Characters appearing between each pair of double quote marks are considered part of the specified string. The string value does not include the double quote marks.
    Two double quote marks together represent an empty string with no characters.

Example   This snippet from the Message window displays information about the string value shown under Syntax, above:

```
put anEmail
-- "dugsmith@arogos.com"
put length (anEmail)
-- 19
-- the " marks are not included
put the number of chars of anEmail
-- 19
-- same information produced by another means
```

See also   EMPTY, QUOTE

&

Syntax   `set aNum = aNum & aChar`

Usage   The ampersand is a Director string *concatenation* operator, joining two expressions end-to-end as a string value. If either or both of the expressions adjoining the & are not already strings, a conversion to a string value is automatically performed.

Examples   This example shows the results of a simple concatenation operation:

```
put "North" & "West"
-- "NorthWest"
```

This example shows the results of a concatenation including a nonstring value as one of the expressions:

```
set street = 14
put street
-- 14
put street & "th Ave."
-- "14th Ave.
```

Parameters   *expression & expression*

Value   *string*

See also   &&

&&

Syntax   `set aName = "Darrel" && "Plant"`

Usage   The double ampersand concatenation operator is identical in operation to the & operator, except that it inserts a space between the two expressions it joins.

Example   This example shows the results of the statement in the Syntax section, above:

```
put aName
-- "Darrel Plant"
```

Parameters   *expression && expression*

Value   *string*

See also   &

alert

Syntax   `alert "Danger, Will Robinson!"`

Usage   The *alert* command displays a dialog box containing a text string and an OK button. The parameter must be a string, or an error will occur. To convert a value to a string, use the *string* function or an operator that automatically converts values to a string (such as *&&*).

     The alert box is only large enough to display a small number of characters, so limit the length of the string accordingly.

Example   This statement shows how the alert command can be used for debugging by displaying variables:

```
alert "The value of gNetID =" && gNetID
```

Parameters   `alert` *string*

See also   string

BACKSPACE

Syntax   `if the key = BACKSPACE then`

Usage   The BACKSPACE character constant represents the backspace key on Windows machines and the Delete key on the Macintosh. It allows testing for those keys being pressed by the user.

     The BACKSPACE character should not generally be included as part of a string value.

     The *charToNum* function returns 8 for BACKSPACE (its ASCII value).

Example   This handler executes the Shockwave command *netAbort* for the first network command if the user presses the backspace or Delete key:

```
on keyDown
  if the key = BACKSPACE then
    netAbort(1)
  end if
end keyDown
```

Value   BACKSPACE

See also charToNum, ENTER, on keyDown, on keyUp, numToChar, QUOTE, RETURN, TAB

char

Syntax
```
set oneChar = char 4 of "abcdefg"

set aCharRange = char 3 to 7 of field 6
```

Usage   The *char* function returns a single character in a string. The *index number* parameter must be an integer.

To extract a range of characters from a string, use the optional *to* keyword and a second index number (which must be equal to or greater than the first index in order to return any value).

You can test and set the value of a section of a string specified by the *char* function by using the *put* command.

Example   This code segment uses the char function to look for the first tag in an HTML file retrieved from the Internet using the *getNetText* function:

```
repeat with i = 1 to length(netTextResult(1))
   if char i of netTextResult(1) = "<" then
      -- we're at the first tag, now what?
   else
      next repeat
   end if
end repeat
```

This excerpt from the Message window shows the process of changing a segment of a string using the *char* function. The segment being replaced is longer than the segment replacing it:

```
set aWord = "Hilighted"
put char 3 to 7 of aWord
-- "light"
put "jack" into char 3 to 7 of aWord
put aWord
-- "Hijacked"
```

Parameters   char *integer* of *string*

char *integer* to *integer* of *string*

Value   *string*

See also   chars, charToNum, contains, delete, item, the last, length, line, the number of chars, the number of items, the number of lines, the number of words, numToChar, offset, starts, stringP, string, value, word

chars

Syntax   `set subString = (aWord, 4, 7)`

Usage   The *chars* function returns a range of characters derived from the specified string, beginning at the first index number and ending at the second. Both index values must be parameters.

The statement above is equivalent to:

`set subString = char 4 to 7 of aWord`

Example   This statement sends the third through sixth characters of the string "Shockwave" to the Message window:

```
put chars ("Shockwave",3,6)
-- "ockw"
```

Parameters   chars (*string, integer, integer*)

Value   *string*

See also   char, charToNum, contains, delete, item, the last, length, line, the number of chars, the number of items, the number of lines, the number of words, numToChar, offset, starts, stringP, string, value, word

charToNum

Syntax
: `set aSCII = charToNum (aChar)`

Usage
: The *charToNum* function returns the ASCII value of a string character. This can be useful when you need to test for characters that are not alphanumeric. It also makes it easy for you to convert uppercase letters to lowercase, by adding 32 to the ASCII value of the uppercase letters (which ranges from 65 to 90).

Example
: This Lingo function returns a lowercase value if you give it an uppercase value:

```
on makeLowerCase myChar
   set tCharNum = charToNum(myChar)
   if tCharNum >= 65 AND tCharNum <= 90 then
      return numToChar(tCharNum + 32)
   else
      return (myChar)
   end if
end makeLowerCase
```

If you use this function in the Message window, this is how it will look:

```
put makeLowerCase("M")
-- "m"
```

Parameters
: `charToNum (char)`

Value
: *integer*

See also
: char, chars, charToNum, contains, delete, item, the key, the keyCode, the last, length, line, the number of chars, the number of items, the number of lines, the number of words, numToChar, offset, starts, stringP, string, value, word

contains

Syntax   `set isItInThere = anURL contains "http://"`

Usage   The *contains* function looks for a string (second parameter) within another string (first string), and returns TRUE if it finds it. It returns FALSE otherwise.

Example   This handler checks some text that was previously retrieved with the *getNetText* command to see if it has an <HTML> tag:

```
on exitFrame
  global gText
  if gText contains "<HTML>" then
    -- gText is an HTML file, deal with it!
  else
    -- gText is not an HTML file, now what?
  end if
end exitFrame
```

Parameters   *string* contains *string*

Value   *boolean*

See also   char, chars, charToNum, delete, item, the key, the keyCode, the last, length, line, the number of chars, the number of items, the number of lines, the number of words, numToChar, offset, starts, stringP, string, value, word

delete

Syntax   `delete word 2 to 4 of aPhrase`

Usage   The *delete* command removes a *chunk* of the specified string variable, field cast member, or *scriptText* of a script cast member. You can use string functions like *char, item, line,* or *word* to specify the portion to be deleted.

Example   This Lingo function uses the delete command with other logic to return a
string that has all HTML tags removed:

```
on stripHTML myString
  set tChar   = 1
  set tTagStart = 0
  repeat while TRUE
    if tChar > length(myString) then exit repeat
    if tTagStart > 0 then
      if char tChar of myString = ">" then
        delete char tTagStart to tChar of myString
        set tChar = tTagStart
        set tTagStart = 0
      else
        set tChar = tChar + 1
        next repeat
      end if
    end if
    if char tChar of myString = "<" then
      set tTagStart = tChar
    end if
    set tChar = tChar + 1
  end repeat
  return myString
end stripHTML
```

Parameters   delete *chunk* of *string*

See also   char, chars, charToNum, contains, item, the key, the keyCode, the last, length,
line, the number of chars, the number of items, the number of lines, the
number of words, numToChar, offset, starts, stringP, string, value, word

do

COMMAND

Syntax   do "set octave = 8"

Usage   The *do* command is among the more powerful commands to use in Director
development. It allows you to execute Lingo statements stored as strings.
You can use the *do* command to completely change the behavior of a movie
by placing Lingo statements in text files stored as field cast members or on
disk and the Internet as text files. Because fields and text files can be modified with Lingo, movie behavior can be modified by the movie itself or
updated periodically by downloading new commands from a Web site.

Example   This code segment uses the *netTextResult* function to retrieve some text already downloaded with *getNetText*. It then executes the first line of the file in Lingo using the *do* command:

```
global gNetID -- the net ID from getNetText
set tText = netTextResult(gNetID)
do(line 1 of tText)
```

If line 1 of the text file that was retrieved from the Internet contains a string like this:

```
set the fileName of member "dv" = "video.mov"
```

then that command would be executed with the *do* command.

Parameters   do *string*

See also   downloadNetThing, getNetText, netTextResult, netDone, netError, getLatestNetID

EMPTY

Syntax   `set field "scores" = EMPTY`

Usage   The EMPTY constant represents an empty string, or one with no characters. It is equal to the string *""*.

> **Tip**
>
> *A field member must have something, if only a space (" "), in order for formatting to be remembered after a movie is saved. So, if you set a field member to EMPTY and then save the movie, the field member will forget all of its formatting such as font, size, color, and so forth.*

Example   This code segment puts "No Data" into field "results" if there was no text returned from the last *getNetText* function:

```
global gLastNetID
-- gLastNetID contains the number returned
-- by getNetText.
```

```
set tNetText = netTextResult(gLastNetID)
if tNetText = EMPTY then
   put "No Data" into field "results"
else
   put tNetText into field "results"
end if
```

Value   EMPTY

See also   ", QUOTE

ENTER

CONSTANT

Syntax   `if the key = ENTER then`

Usage   The ENTER constant represents the Enter key on the numeric keypad of
Windows machines, and represents the Return key on the Macintosh. If you
wish to check for the typical Enter key on a Windows machine or generate a
linefeed in a string, use the RETURN constant.
　　The *charToNum* function returns 3 for ENTER (its ASCII value).

Example   This handler executes the Shockwave command *gotoNetPage* if the user
presses the Enter (or Return) key:

```
on keyDown
   if the key = ENTER OR the key = RETURN then
      gotoNetPage (field "url")
   end if
end keyDown
```

Value   ENTER

See also   BACKSPACE, charToNum, ENTER, the keyCode, on keyDown, the
keyPressed, on keyUp, numToChar, QUOTE, RETURN, TAB

hilite

Syntax   `hilite word 20 of field "annoyed"`

Usage   The *hilite* command selects the specified chunk of a field cast member. It works only with field cast members.

You can use any of the string chunk functions to specify a chunk, such as *char*, *item*, *line*, or *word*.

Examples   This statement selects a range of characters in field "result":

`hilite char 1 to 5 of field "result"`

This Lingo function will search for a word in a field, and highlight the first occurrence of it.

```
on hiliteWord myFieldName, myWord
  if the type of member myFieldName <> ¬
    #field then exit
 set tWords = the number of words ¬
        in field myFieldName
 repeat with tIndex = 1 to tWords
  if word tIndex of field myFieldName = ¬
        myWord then
   hilite word tIndex of field myFieldName
   exit
  end if
 end repeat
end hiliteWord
```

With the above handler in a movie script, you can use a statement like this to select a specific word:

`hiliteWord ("result","frog")`

Parameters   `hilite chunk of field string| integer`

See also   after, before, char, chars, contains, field, item, the last, length, line, member, the number of chars, the number of items, the number of lines, the number of words, offset, starts, stringP, string, value, word

item

FUNCTION

Syntax
```
set address = item 4 of field 3
set names =  item 1 to 3 of bioInfo
```

Usage
The *item* function returns a chunk specified by an index number from a string. String items are separated by the movie property *the itemDelimiter*, which is a comma by default.

Example
These statements from the message window show the operation of the *item* keyword:
```
put the itemDelimiter
-- ","
set tText = "ala carte, frog brain soup, $6.99"
put item 2 of tText
-- " frog brain soup"
set the itemDelimiter = "$"
put item 2 of tText
-- "6.99"
```

Parameters
```
item integer of string
item integer to integer of string
```

Value
```
string
```

See also
after, before, char, chars, contains, field, the itemDelimiter, the last, length, line, member, the number of chars, the number of items, the number of lines, the number of words, offset, starts, stringP, string, value, word

the itemDelimiter

MOVIE PROPERTY

Syntax
```
set the itemDelimiter = ";"
```

Usage
the itemDelimiter property contains the character used by the *item* keyword to separate items. You can test and set this property with Lingo.

Example   This handler will return the filename portion of a full path to a file. It uses *the itemDelimiter* and *the machineType* properties to be compatible with Windows ("\") and Macintosh (":") filename paths:

```
on getFileName myFullPath
   set tSaveDelimiter = the itemDelimiter
   if the machineType = 256 then
      -- I'm a PC
      set the itemDelimiter = "\"
   else
      set the itemDelimiter = ":"
   end if
   set tFile = the last item of myFullPath
   set the itemDelimiter = tSaveDelimiter
   return tFile
end getFileName
```

Parameters   the itemDelimiter

Value   *char*

See also   item

the last

Syntax   set zip = the last item of bioInfo

Usage   *the last* is a property that specifies the final chunk of a string. The chunk can be *char, item, line,* or *word*. The string may be a variable, a field cast member, or any other string or chunk.

The *last* function is the equivalent of chunk expressions like the following:

word (the number of words of aString) of aString

Example These statements from the Message window show how the *last* function works:

```
set tString = "The frog walked, and talked, and danced across the lane."
put the last char of tString
-- "."
put the last word of tString
-- "lane."
put the last item of tString
-- " and danced across the lane."
```

Parameters the last char|word|item|line of *string*

See also after, before, char, chars, contains, field, the itemDelimiter, length, line, member, the number of chars, the number of items, the number of lines, the number of words, offset, starts, stringP, string, value, word

length

FUNCTION

Syntax `set howLong = length (word 4 of bioInfo)`

Usage The *length* function returns the number of characters in a string, including punctuation and special characters. It is functionally equivalent to the property *the number of chars*.

Example This statement sets the variable *tNetTextLength* to the number of characters returned by the last *getNetText* Shockwave function:

```
set tNetTextLength = length(netTextResult ())
```

Parameters length (*string*)

Value *integer*

See also after, before, char, chars, contains, field, the itemDelimiter, the last, line, member, the number of chars, the number of items, the number of lines, the number of words, offset, starts, stringP, string, value, word

line

Syntax	`set city = line 4 of bioInfo`
	`set handler = line 6 to 10 of the scriptText of member 4`
Usage	The *line* function returns a line of text specified by an index number from a string. A line is any number of characters delimited by a RETURN character or the end of the string.
	Used with the keyword *to*, the *line* function will return a range of lines.
	The number of lines of a field cast member is not dependent on the word wrap (determined by the width of the field). Only RETURN characters (or the end of the string) delineate the end of a line.
Example	This statement sets the variable *tNetTextLine* to the contents of the first line retrieved by the last *getNetText* Shockwave function:
	`set tNetTextLine = line 1 of netTextResult ()`
Parameters	`line `*`integer`*` of `*`string`*
	`line `*`integer`*` to `*`integer`*` of `*`string`*
Value	*string*
See also	after, before, char, chars, contains, field, item, the itemDelimiter, the last, length, member, the number of chars, the number of items, the number of lines, the number of words, offset, starts, stringP, string, value, word

the number of chars

Syntax	`set howLong = the number of chars of the text of member 5`
Usage	*the number of chars* is a property that contains the quantity of characters in a string, including punctuation and special characters. It is equivalent to the function *length*.
	This property can use the keywords *of* and *in* interchangeably between the keyword *chars* and the string being evaluated.

Example This statement sets the variable *tTextLength* to the number of characters returned by the last *getNetText* Shockwave function:

```
set tTextLength = the number of chars of netTextResult ()
```

Parameters the number of chars of|in *string*

Value *integer*

See also the number of items, the number of lines, the number of words

the number of items
STRING PROPERTY

Syntax set numItems = the number of items of field 4

Usage *the number of items* is a property that contains the quantity of items in a string, delineated by *the itemDelimiter* property (default is a comma). This will be equal to the number of times the item delimiter character appears in the string, plus 1.

This property can use the keywords *of* and *in* interchangeably between the keyword *items* and the string being evaluated.

Example This statement sets the variable *tTextItems* to the number of items returned by the last *getNetText* Shockwave function:

```
set tTextItems = the number of items of netTextResult ()
```

Parameters the number of items of|in *string*

Value *integer*

See also the number of chars, the number of lines, the number of words

the number of lines

STRING PROPERTY

Syntax   `set numLines = the number of lines of script "tipIndex"`

Usage   *the number of lines* is a property that contains the quantity of lines in a string, with each line delineated by a RETURN or the end of the string.
　　This property can use the keywords *of* and *in* interchangeably between the keyword *lines* and the string being evaluated.

Example   This statement sets the variable *tTextLines* to the number of lines returned by the last *getNetText* Shockwave function:

`set tTextLines = the number of lines of netTextResult ()`

Parameters   the number of lines of|in *string*

Value   *integer*

See also   the number of chars, the number of items, the number of words

the number of words

STRING PROPERTY

Syntax   `set numWords = the number of words of member "Moby Dick"`

Usage   *the number of words* is a property that contains the quantity of words in a string, separated by spaces and other nonvisible characters (including TAB and RETURN).
　　This property can use the keywords *of* and *in* interchangeably between the keyword *words* and the string being evaluated.

Example   This statement sets the variable *tTextWords* to the number of words returned by the last *getNetText* Shockwave function:

`set tTextWords = the number of words of netTextResult ()`

Parameters   the number of words of|in *string*

Value   *integer*

See also   the number of chars, the number of items, the number of lines

numToChar

FUNCTION

Syntax `set aChar = numToChar (95)`

Usage The *numToChar* function converts an integer ranging from 0 to 255 to its equivalent string value. This is the reverse of the *charToNum* function.

Example See the Example for *charToNum* earlier in this chapter.

Parameters `numToChar (integer)`

Value *char*

See also char, charToNum, the keyCode, value

offset

FUNCTION

Syntax `set whereAt = offset ("5", "0123456789")`

Usage The *offset* function finds the first string in the second string, and returns the index position of its first occurrence. If the string isn't found, *offset* returns 0.

Example This statement returns the number 6, since the "<" character is the sixth one in the string given:

```
put offset("<", "Home <B>on the</B> range")
-- 6
```

Parameters `offset (string, string)`

Value *integer*

See also char, contains

put after

Syntax   put "time" after field "time"

Usage   This version of the *put* command inserts a string into a string variable or field cast member.

With no chunk function specified, the string is inserted at the end of the string variable or field.

Chunk functions can be used to specify the position at which the string is inserted. The string is inserted immediately after the last character of the specified chunk. This command is nondestructive; no characters are replaced.

If the position for the insertion does not exist (line 4 of a 1-line field, for instance), then blank characters (SPACE), items (*the itemDelimiter* value), or lines (RETURN) are added to fill empty chunks (words are not added; the string is simply inserted at the end of the target string).

Example   This Message window example inserts a word after the third word of a string variable:

```
set cdTitle = "Ute Lemper: Berlin Songs"
put " Cabaret" after word 3 of cdTitle
put cdTitle
-- "Ute Lemper: Berlin Cabaret Songs"
```

Parameters   put *integer* after *chunk*

See also   put before, put into

put before

Syntax   put "pearls" before field "swine"

Usage   This version of the *put* command inserts a string into a string variable or field cast member.

With no chunk function specified, the string is inserted at the beginning of the string variable or field.

Chunk functions can be used to specify the position at which the string is inserted. The string is inserted immediately before the first character of the specified chunk. This command is nondestructive; no characters are replaced.

If the position for the insertion does not exist (line 4 of a 1-line field, for instance), then blank characters (SPACE), items (*the itemDelimiter* value), or lines (RETURN) are added to fill empty chunks (words are not added; the string is simply inserted at the end of the target string).

Example   This Message window example inserts a word after the third word of a string variable:

```
set cdTitle = "Kurt Weill: Threepenny Opera"
put "The " before word 3 of cdTitle
put cdTitle
-- "Kurt Weill: The Threepenny Opera"
```

Parameters   put *integer* before *chunk*

See also   put after, put into

QUOTE

CONSTANT

Syntax   `set gotd = QUOTE & "Nuts!" & QUOTE`

Usage   The *QUOTE* constant represents a double quotation (") mark in a string. It is useful when you need to put quotes into a variable or field with Lingo. Because this character is used as the literal string delimiter, if you wish to include double quotation marks in a string, you need to use the QUOTE constant.

The *charToNum* function returns 34 for *QUOTE* (its ASCII value).

Example   This statement uses the QUOTE statement to include quotes in a string used in the *alert* command:

```
alert "The variable" && QUOTE & "gVar" & ¬
   QUOTE && "contains" && string(gVar)
```

Value   QUOTE

See also   ", EMPTY, RETURN

RETURN

Syntax   `set bioInfo = name & RETURN & address`

Usage   The *RETURN* constant represents the Return key on Mac and Windows keyboards (labeled as Enter on some Windows keyboards—it's just above the right-hand Shift key). You can use it with *the key* property to determine if the Return key was pressed. You can also use it in string expressions to add a carriage return to a string.

       The *charToNum* function returns 13 for *RETURN* (its ASCII value).

Example   This statement makes a string with two lines:

```
put "this is 1" & RETURN & "this is 2"
-- "this is 1
this is 2"
```

Value   RETURN

See also   BACKSPACE, charToNum, ENTER, on keyDown, on keyUp, numToChar, QUOTE, SPACE, TAB

SPACE

Syntax   `set saying = "To" & SPACE & "Beyond"`

Usage   The *SPACE* constant represents the spacebar. You can use it with *the key* property to determine if the spacebar key was pressed. You can also use it in string expressions (where it may be less confusing than typing " ") to add a space character to a string.

       The *charToNum* function returns 32 for *SPACE* (its ASCII value).

Example   This example inserts a space into a string variable:

```
set composer = "AaronCopland"
put SPACE after char 5 of composer
put composer
-- "Aaron Copland"
```

Value   SPACE

See also   BACKSPACE, charToNum, ENTER, on keyDown, on keyUp, numToChar, RETURN, SPACE, TAB

starts

Syntax   `set isStart = field "amazing" starts "unknown"`

Usage   The *starts* operator returns TRUE if the first characters of the string before the operator are identical to the characters in the string after the operator. Otherwise it returns FALSE.

Example   This handler checks some text that was previously retrieved with the *getNetText* command to see if it starts with "<HTML>":

```
on exitFrame
  set tText = netTextResult()
  if tText starts "<HTML>" then
    -- tText is an HTML file, deal with it!
   parseHTML
  else
    -- tText is not an HTML file, now what?
   showText
  end if
end exitFrame
```

Parameters   *string* starts *string*

Value   *boolean*

See also   contains, offset

string

Syntax   `set aNum = string (42)`

Usage   The *string* function converts an expression to a string, regardless of the expression's original type: integer, float, symbol, or list. It is very useful for preparing data for storage in fields or text files.

Examples This code segment sends the contents of the property list *gList* to the Shockwave preference file "mv1data":

```
global gList
setPref ("mv1data", string (gList))
```

This code segment retrieves the property list from the Shockwave preference file and restores it to a property list:

```
global gList
set gList = value( getPref ("mv1data"))
```

Parameters `string (value)`

Value   *string*

See also   stringP, value

stringP

Syntax   `set isString = stringP (gPort)`

Usage   The *stringP* function tests a value to see if it is a string, returning TRUE if it is, and FALSE otherwise.

Example   This code segment returns TRUE if the variable *gVariable* contains a string:

```
global gVariable
return stringP(gVariable)
```

Parameters   `stringP (value)`

Value   *boolean*

See also   floatP, ilk, listP, integerP, objectP, string, symbolP, value

TAB

Syntax   `set tabDelimited = aFName & TAB & aLName & TAB & anEmail`

Usage   The *TAB* constant represents a tab character in a string, or the Tab key on the keyboard.
        The *charToNum* function returns 9 for TAB (its ASCII value).

Example   This code segment checks for the press of the Tab key:

```
on keyDown
   if the key = TAB then
      go to marker(1)
   end f
end keyDown
```

Value   TAB

See also   BACKSPACE, charToNum, ENTER, on keyDown, on keyUp, numToChar, RETURN

value

Syntax   `set anINT = value ("97")`

Usage   The *value* function converts a string into a Director data value, if possible. If the string contains only numeric characters, an integer or float value is returned. If the string is in the proper format for a list, that list is returned. If the string is a Lingo statement that returns a number, list, or symbol, *value* will return the result of the Lingo statement.

The *value* function can be very useful in situations where you read text data from a file or URL, and need to convert those strings to useable Lingo data, such as numbers, symbols, or lists.

Example
These statements from the Message window show how the *value* function can be used to convert strings to other data types:

```
put value ("[#ac:43,#dc:12]")
-- [#ac: 43, #dc: 12]
put ilk(value("[#ac:43,#dc:12]"))
-- #propList
put value ("5 * 5")
-- 25
put value("#" & "dogByte")
-- #dogByte
put ilk(value("#" & "dogByte"))
-- #symbol
```

Parameters
value (*string*)

Value
value

See also
string, stringP

word

Syntax
```
set lName = word 2 of bioInfo
```
```
set aPhrase = word 6 to 16 of field "quote"
```

Usage
The *word* function returns a specific word of a text string. A word is any number of characters delimited by spaces and other nonvisible characters (including TAB and RETURN). Punctuation marks are considered part of a word.

Used with the keyword *to*, the *word* function will return a range of words.

Example   This statement sets the variable *tNetTextWord* to the contents of the first word retrieved by the most recent *getNetText* function:

```
set tNetTextWord = word 1 of netTextResult ()
```

Parameters   word *integer* of *string*

                 word *integer* to *integer* of *string*

Value   *string*

See also   after, before, char, chars, item, the last, line, the number of words

Math:
Operators Category

These operators transform numeric values of various sorts, including integers, float values, linear lists, property lists, points, and rects. String values use their own set of operators (see Chapter 38).

Operators, in most cases, require two parameters, with the product of the operation being a result of the interaction of the parameters.

It's best not to assume the results of operations performed on mixed value types (multiplying a float value by a point, for instance, results in an apparent point value that is, nonetheless, invalid). In most cases, operations evaluate to an integer if both values are integers, and to a float value if both values are floats or if one value is a float and the other is an integer.

Operations on lists of different types and lengths should be tested to ascertain that the results are the ones that are expected.

Comparison operators can be used with string values as well as numerical values. Strings are compared without regard to their capitalization. Strings are compared on the basis of their alphabetic order; all punctuation marks and numerals have a lower value than letters.

—

Syntax `set stageWidth = the stageRight - the stageLeft`

Usage The *subtraction* operator subtracts the value following the operator from the value preceding the operator.

If used without a preceding value, the value following the operator is treated as a negative value (an assumed subtraction from 0).

Example This example subtracts a point value from another point value, an example of vector mathematics in Director:

`set newLoc = the loc of sprite 4 - point (32, 50)`

Parameters *value - value*

Value *value*

See also +, *, /, mod

( )

Syntax `set startIndex = 2 * (textLen + 1)`

Usage The *parentheses* operators determine precedence in potentially ambiguous situations, or where one operation must be carried out before another operation of higher precedence.

There are five precedence levels for operators in Lingo. In any given expression, operators with the highest precedence are applied before others, regardless of their position within the expression. If two operators are of the same precedence, the first operator encountered in an expression has precedence over the latter, as shown in the table below.

High Precedence				Low Precedence
()	*	+	&	<
– (negative)	mod	– (subtract)	&&	>
sprite within	/			<=
sprite intersects	and			>=
not	or			=
				<>
				contains
				starts

Operators in the first column of the table are always executed first in an expression. A multiplication operator (*) is always evaluated before the addition (+) operator, even if it follows the addition operator in the expression: *2 + 3 * 5,* because parentheses have an even higher precedence than the multiplication operator. However, they can force an addition operation to be evaluated before the multiplication: *(2 + 3) * 5.*

Parentheses are also used by functions to delineate the boundaries of the data they operate on.

Example　This snippet from the Message window shows how parentheses modify values by modifying which operators are evaluated first:

```
put 2 + 2 * 5
-- 12
-- the * has precedence over +
-- parentheses can force the
-- addition operation to evaluate first
put (2 + 2) * 5
-- 20
```

Parameters　*(expression)*

Value　*value*

✱

Syntax `set areaSector = pi () * radius * radius * degrees / 360`

Usage The *multiplication* operator returns the product of two values.

Example This example shows the result of a two-item linear list multiplied by an integer:

```
put [4, 5] * 4
-- [16, 20]
```

Parameters *value* * *value*

Value *value*

See also –, (), /, +, mod

/

Syntax `set secant = 1 / cos (x)`

Usage The *division* operator returns the result of a mathematical division on two values.

Example This example shows the difference in the result of a division operation on two integer values as opposed to a float value and an integer:

```
put 14 / 3
-- 4
put 14.0 / 3
-- 4.6667
```

Parameters *value* / *value*

Value *value*

See also –, (), *, +, mod

+

OPERATOR

Syntax   `set four = 2 + 2`

Usage   The *addition* operator returns the sum of two values.

Example   This example displays the result of an addition operation on two *rect* values:

```
put rect (100, 100, 200, 200) + rect (25, 10, 25, 10)
-- rect(125, 110, 225, 210)
```

Parameters   *value + value*

Value   *value*

See also   –, (), *, /, mod

<

OPERATOR

Syntax   `if year < 1995 then return "pre-Shockwave"`

Usage   The *less than* comparison operator returns a value of TRUE if the value preceding the operator is a lesser value than the value following the operator. Otherwise, it returns FALSE.

Example   This statement sets the variable *entryOK* to TRUE if the value of *age* is less than 11:

```
set entryOK = age < 11
```

Parameters   *value < value*

Value   *boolean*

See also   <=, <>, =, >, >=

<=

Syntax   `repeat while i <= count (myEventList)`

Usage   The *less than or equal to* comparison operator returns a TRUE value when the first parameter is not greater than the second parameter.

Example   This statement returns a value of 1 if the value of the variable *aCode* is not greater than the value of *cNine*:

`if aCode <= cNine then return 1`

Parameters   *value <= value*

Value   *boolean*

See also   <, <>, =, >, >=

##

Syntax   `if aName <> "Bob" then return "not a Bob"`

Usage   The *not equal to* operator returns FALSE only if its two parameters are identical; otherwise it is TRUE.

Example   This example adds the string contained in the variable *aWord* to the linear list *wordList* if the value of *aWord* is not an empty string (EMPTY or ""):

`if aWord <> "" then add wordList, aWord`

Parameters   *value <> value*

Value   *boolean*

See also   <, <=, =, >, >=

=

Syntax   `if aRect = rect (200, 200, 220, 220) then`

Usage   The *equals* operator tests equality for two values, returning TRUE if they are identical and FALSE otherwise.

The equal sign (=) is also used by the *set* and *repeat* commands. The uses should not be confused.

Example   This statement puts the values of the variable *wordCount* and the property *the timer* into the Message window whenever *wordCount* is equal to a multiple of 10:

`if (wordCount mod 10) = 0 then put wordCount, the timer`

Parameters   *value = value*

Value   *boolean*

See also   <, <=, <>, >, >=

>

Syntax   `if x > unknown then`

Usage   The *greater than* operator tests whether the first parameter has a greater value than the second parameter, returning TRUE if so and FALSE otherwise.

Example   This statement tests whether the integer variable *aSCII* is equal to or greater than 58:

`if aSCII > 57 then`

Parameters   *value > value*

Value   *boolean*

See also   <, <=, <>, =, >=

>=

Syntax `if overhill >= 30 then`

Usage The *greater than or equal to* operator tests whether the first parameter is less than the second parameter, returning FALSE if it is or TRUE if it is not.

Example This handler tests *the timer* property, looping in the current frame until the value of *the timer* has reached 300 or more, and going to the marker "showtime" once a *timer* value of 300 or more is detected:

```
on exitFrame
  if the timer >= 300 then go "showtime"
  else go the frame
end
```

Parameters *value >= value*

Value *boolean*

See also <, <=, <>, =, >

mod

Syntax `set remainder = 12 mod 5`

Usage The *mod* operator returns the modulus, or integer remainder, of the preceding value's division by the second value. Both parameters must be integers.
  If the first parameter is a negative integer, the *mod* operation yields a negative value. The sign of the second parameter does not affect the result.
  The absolute value of results derived with the *mod* operator will always range between 0 and 1 less than the absolute value of the second parameter.

Example   This statement adds a number derived from the last two digits of a four-digit year value to the list *sDate*:

```
add sDate, year mod 100
```

If the value of *year* is 1997, a *mod* operation using 100 as the second value yields the number 97.

Parameters   *integer* mod *integer*

Value   *integer*

See also   −, +, *, /

Math:
Functions Category

These mathematical functions provide the basic building blocks of other, more complex functions.

Unlike the math operators, functions will work only with float values and integers.

abs

Syntax set deviation = abs (difference)

Usage The *abs* function returns the absolute value of a number. The result of this function is always a positive value. It is useful for situations where you need to assure that a value will be positive, as in distance calculations.

Examples Both of these statements display the number 3.14 in the Message window:

```
put abs(3.14)
put abs(-3.14)
```

This Lingo function handler returns the horizontal distance between two sprites, which can be used in other handlers:

```
on getLocHDistance mySpriteOne, mySpriteTwo
  -- first, make sure the parameters are
  -- valid sprite numbers
  if mySpriteOne >= 1 AND ¬
    mySpriteOne <= 48 AND mySpriteTwo >= 1 ¬
    AND ySpriteTwo <= 48 then
    set tOneLocH = the locH of sprite mySpriteOne
    set tTwoLocH = the locH of sprite mySpriteTwo
    return(abs(tOneLocH - tTwoLocH))
  end if
end getLocHDistance
```

Parameters abs (*integer*/*float*)

Value *integer*/*float*

atan

Syntax set whatRad = atan (farSide / nearSide)

Usage The *atan* function returns the arctangent (or inverse tangent) of a value. The result is a value in radians from –*pi/2* to *pi/2*.

The arctangent allows you to derive an angle (in radians from the horizontal axis) from the horizontal slope of a line.

Example
This function handler returns the value (in degrees) of the arctangent of a value *slope*:

```
on whatDegree slope
  return atan (slope) / pi * 180
end
```

Parameters
atan (*integer*/*float*)

Value
float

See also
cos, pi, sin, tan

COS

FUNCTION

Syntax
set hypOverNear = cos (pi / 3)

Usage
The *cos* function returns the cosine of an angle specified in radians (180 degrees = pi radians). The cosine of an angle is equal to the length of the near side of a right triangle divided by the hypotenuse.

Examples
This Lingo function returns a point value when given an angle in degrees (*myAngle*) and the radius from a center point (*myRadius*):

```
on polarToRec myAngle, myRadius
  -- myAngle is in degrees, 0-360
  set tAngleInRadians = myAngle*pi*2/360
  set tXLoc = sin(tAngleInRadians)*myRadius
  set tYLoc = cos(tAngleInRadians)*myRadius
  return point(tXLoc, tYLoc)
end polarToRec
```

Then, this statement sets the location of sprite 2 to the location 40 pixels away from sprite 1 at an angle of 180 degrees and centered on sprite 1:

```
set the loc of sprite 2 = ¬
  the loc of sprite 1 + polarToRec(180,40)
```

Parameters
cos (*integer*/*float*)

Value
float

See also
atan, sin, tan

exp

Syntax	`set e2 = exp (2)`

Usage   The exp function returns the value of the natural logarithm (*e*, or 2.7183) raised to the power specified by the parameter.

Example   This statement puts the value of *e* to the power of 9 in the Message window:

```
put exp(9)
-- 8103.0839
```

Parameters   `exp (integer|float)`

Value   `integer|float`

See also   log, power

float

Syntax   `set accurate = float (100)`

Usage   The *float* function changes a numeric expression to a floating-point number. This can be useful when you need to do precise calculations.

> ### Tip
>
> *The* float *function evaluates any values within its parentheses before it converts the value to a floating-point number. The expression* float *(100/33) will result in a value of 3.000, not 3.030, because the expression 100 / 33 is evaluated to the integer value 3 before being converted to a floating-point format.*

Example   These statements copied from the Message window show how the *float* function improves the accuracy of Director's calculations:

```
put 50/100
-- 0
put float(50)/float(100)
-- 0.5
```

Parameters   `float (integer|float)`

Value   `float`

See also   the floatPrecision, floatP, integer, integerP, string, stringP, value

floatP

Syntax   `set`

Usage   The *floatP* function returns TRUE if an expression is a floating-point number, or FALSE if it is not.

Example   These statements from the Message window show how the *floatP* function works:

```
put floatP("frog")
-- 0
put floatP(13)
-- 0
put floatP(.5)
-- 1
```

Parameters   `floatP (value)`

Value   `boolean`

See also   integerP, stringP, symbolP, voidP

integer

FUNCTION

Syntax   `set rounded = integer (taxPayment)`

Usage   The *integer* function returns the value of a numeric expression rounded to the nearest whole integer.

Examples   This statement rounds *pi* to the nearest whole integer:

```
put integer(pi)
-- 3
```

This statement rounds 3.6678 to the nearest whole integer:

```
put integer(3.6678)
-- 4
```

Parameters   `integer (integer/float)`

Value   `integer`

See also   float, the floatPrecision, floatP, integerP, string, stringP, value

integerP

FUNCTION

Syntax   `set`

Usage   The *integerP* function returns TRUE if *expression* is an integer. It returns FALSE otherwise.

Example   This code segment sets the foreground color of sprite 9 to the parameter "sw3", passed by an <EMBED> or <OBJECT> tag to a Shockwave movie. However, it only does this if it is an integer (it also makes sure the value is a positive number between 0 and 255):

```
set tColor = value (externalParamValue ("sw3"))
if integerP(tColor) then
   set the foreColor of sprite 9 = abs (tColor) mod 256
end if
```

Parameters   `integerP (value)`

Value   *boolean*

See also   float, the floatPrecision, floatP, integer, string, stringP, value

log

Syntax   `set log8 = log (8)`

Usage   The *log* function returns the natural logarithm (e) of *number*.

Example   This function handler derives the logarithm of the value *target* for whatever logarithmic base is specified by the *base* parameter:

```
on logConvert base, target
  if not ((integerP (base) or floatP (base)) or ¬
    ((integerP (target) or floatP (target)) then return 0
else
    set base = abs (base)
    set baseLog = log (base)
    set targetlog = log (target)
    return log (target) / log (base)
  end if
end
```

Note that this function determines if the *base* value is actually an integer or float value, returning 0 if it is not.

Parameters   `log (integer|float)`

Value   *float*

See also   exp, power

pi

Syntax   `set circumference = pi * diameter`

Usage   The *pi* function returns the value of pi, which is the ratio of a circle's circumference to its diameter.

Examples   This Lingo function converts a value from degrees to radians, which is useful because all of Director's trig functions expect radians:

```
on degToRad myDeg
    return float (myDeg mod 360) * 2 * pi / 360
end degToRad
```

In the Message window, this function can be used like this to find the cosine of 180 degrees:

```
put cos(degToRad(180))
-- -1.0
```

Parameters   pi

Value   *float*

See also   atan, cos, sin, tan

power

Syntax   `set piSquared = power (pi, 2)`

Usage   The *power* function returns the value of the first parameter raised to the power of the second parameter.

Example   This statement returns the value of 2 to the power of 8, which is 256 (also known as 8 bits):

```
return(power(2,8))
```

Parameters power (*integer*|*float*, *integer*|*float*)

Value *integer*|*float*

See also exp, log, sqrt

sin

Syntax set hypOverFar = sin (pi / 3)

Usage The *sin* function returns the sine of an angle specified in radians (180 degrees = pi radians). The sine of an angle is equal to the length of the far side of a right triangle divided by the hypotenuse.

Example This example displays the sine of a 45-degree angle (pi / 4):

put sin (pi / 4)
-- 0.7071

Parameters sin (*integer*|*float*)

Value *float*

See also atan, cos, tan

sqrt

Syntax set dist = sqrt (dx * dx + dy * dy)

Usage The *sqrt* function returns the square root of a number. If the number is an integer, *sqrt* returns an integer; otherwise, a floating-point value is returned.

Example
These statements send the square root of 15 to the Message window, in two different ways:

```
put sqrt(15)
-- 4
put sqrt(15.0)
-- 3.8730
```

Parameters   sqrt (*integer|float*)

Value   *integer|float*

See also   exp, the floatPrecision, log, power

tan

Syntax   `set whatSlope = tan (pi * 8 / 360)`

Usage
The *tan* function returns the tangent of an angle expressed in radians. The tangent of the angle of a right triangle is the slope of the line described by the angle, or the ratio of the far side to the near side.

Example
Then, you can use a statement like this to get the tangent of an angle—say, 30 degrees:

```
put tanDeg(30)
-- 0.5774
```

Parameters   tan (*integer|float*)

Value   *integer|float*

See also   atan, cos, sin

Logic Category

41

This category covers the elements of Lingo that deal directly with boolean logic, the magical world of TRUE (1) and FALSE (0). In Lingo, any non-0 value can stand in for TRUE.

and

Syntax   `set criteriaMet = (vAge > 20) and (vState = "Oregon")`

Usage   The *and* logical operator returns TRUE if both parameters are true. If one or both of the parameters evaluates to FALSE, the *and* operator returns FALSE. This table shows the possible results of an *and* operation:

	TRUE	FALSE
TRUE	TRUE	FALSE
FALSE	FALSE	FALSE

Example   This handler segment shows an application of the *and* logical operator using Shockwave functions. It waits until both the *netDone* function is TRUE and *the frameLabel* is at the end of a looping animation before it goes to a frame where the text retrieved by *getNetText* will be displayed.

```
if netDone(1) and the frameLabel = "1End" then
  put netTextResult(1) into field "display"
  go to frame "display"
end if
```

Parameters   *boolean* and *boolean*

Value   *boolean*

See also   FALSE, if, not, or, TRUE

FALSE

Syntax   `set verified = FALSE`

Usage   The FALSE constant is one of the two logical constants used in boolean tests. The other logical constant is TRUE.

     The FALSE constant is also represented by the numerical value 0 in situations where a number is required.

Example   This handler keeps the playback head looping in the current frame until the value of *netDone (1)* is no longer FALSE (in other words, it is TRUE):

```
on exitFrame
  if netDone(1) = FALSE then
    go the frame
  else
    go to the frame + 1
  end if
end exitFrame
```

Value   `false`

See also   and, case, if, not, or, TRUE

not

Syntax   `if not (netDone (3)) then`

Usage   The *not* logical operator reverses the value of a boolean expression. It is the logical equivalent of the unary minus sign in front of a number value. As with all boolean operators, there are only two possible results:

> *not TRUE* is equal to *FALSE*
>
> *not FALSE* is equal to *TRUE*

Example   This *mouseUp* handler toggles the visibility of the bitmap graphic in puppeted sprite 8. This works because *the visible of sprite* property contains either TRUE or FALSE:

```
on mouseUp
  set the visible of sprite 8 = ¬
    not (the visible of sprite 8)
end mouseUp
```

Parameters   not *boolean*

Value   *boolean*

See also   and, FALSE, if then, or, TRUE

or

Syntax   `if (bizState = "Oregon") or (homState = "Oregon") then`

Usage   The *or* logical operator returns TRUE if either of its parameters evaluates to TRUE. If both of the parameters are FALSE, the *or* operator returns FALSE, as shown in the table below.

	TRUE	FALSE
TRUE	TRUE	TRUE
FALSE	TRUE	FALSE

Example   This code segment checks for any of three different possible valid responses that the user could enter:

```
set tResponse = the text of field "response"
if tResponse contains "marble" OR ¬
  tResponse contains "granite" OR ¬
  tResponse contains "sandstone" then
  notifyCorrect(tResponse) -- custom handler
else
  notifyIncorrect(tResponse)
end if
```

Parameters   *boolean* or *boolean*

Value   *boolean*

See also   and, FALSE, if then, not, TRUE

TRUE

CONSTANT

Syntax   `set myAim = TRUE`

Usage   The TRUE constant is one of the two logical constants used in boolean tests. The other logical constant is FALSE.

       The TRUE constant is also handled as the numerical value 1 in situations where a number is required.

Example   This handler keeps looping in the current frame until the value of *netDone(1)* is TRUE:

```
on exitFrame
  if netDone(1) = TRUE then
    go the frame + 1
  else
    go the frame
  end if
end exitFrame
```

> **Tip**
>
> *Since the* netDone *function returns only TRUE or FALSE, you can simplify your Lingo by not using the = TRUE; so that* if *statement in the above example would be:*
>
> `if netDone(1) then.`

Value   `true`

See also   and, case, FALSE, if, not, or

Miscellaneous Lingo Category

42

This category covers Lingo keywords that appear on the Miscellaneous Lingo submenu of the Categorized Lingo menu. These entries cover a range of functions: from error handling to Shockwave/browser interaction to testing value types.

on alertHook

Syntax   `on alertHook me, err, msg`

Usage   The *alertHook* handler is a new Director 6 user-definable function that lets
you manage errors generated by your Director movies. The *alertHook* is
called whenever an error is encountered while the movie is playing.

The *alertHook* handler needs to be placed in a movie script, and initialized
by setting *the alertHook* property (see next entry) to point to the script.

This handler uses three parameters:

The *me* parameter refers to the script object (created by setting the
alertHook property).

The *err* parameter (which can be named something else if you wish)
contains a string designating what type of error has occurred. Possible
values are:

"File read error"

"File error"

"Script syntax error"

"Script runtime error"

The *msg* parameter (which can also have another name) is a string with
specific information about the error. This is typically the same information
displayed in an error alert box. A sample message would be:

```
"Handler not defined
    blarg

#blarg
"
```

The *alertHook* handler must return a value using the *return* command. The
value it returns determines the action taken by the movie when an alert is
encountered.

- In the authoring mode, if a value of 0 is returned, the standard error
  dialog is displayed when an error is encountered.

- In the authoring mode, if you return the value 1, no alert dialog is generated, and the Debug window is automatically opened.

- In the authoring mode, returning a value of –1 stops the movie, with no
  alert shown.

- In the authoring mode, if the *alertHook* handler returns a value of 2, the
  Script window is automatically opened to the script where the error was
  encountered.

In projectors and Shockwave movies, returning a value of 1 from the *alertHook* handler prevents an error dialog from appearing. Returning a 0 causes the error dialog to appear, which is the default behavior if no script has been designated as the *alertHook* handler.

Example

This handler determines if the movie generating a run-time error is playing in Director, a projector, or a Shockwave plug-in. If it is playing in Director, the Script window is automatically opened; otherwise, the error is ignored and no alert message is displayed:

```
on alertHook me, err, msg
  if err = "Script runtime error" then return 2
  else return 1
end
```

Parameters

```
browserName integer
on alertHook me, err, msg
  statements
  return -1|0|1|2
end
```

See also   the alertHook

the alertHook

MOVIE PROPERTY

Syntax   `set the alertHook = script "Alert"`

Usage   *the alertHook* is a property that can be set to a movie script containing an *alertHook* handler. If an error is encountered by the movie while playing, the script specified by *the alertHook* property will be called to determine whether an alert window will be shown.

Parameters   the alertHook

Value   *script*

See also   on alertHook

dontPassEvent

This command is obsolete. The *stopEvent* command, which performs the same function but takes behaviors into account, should be used instead.

else

See the entry for *if* in Chapter 37.

on EvalScript

Syntax   on EvalScript scriptPassed

Usage   The *EvalScript* handler is one of the most powerful additions to Shockwave for Director 6. It allows messages and data to be sent as strings from JavaScript or VBScript embedded in an HTML page.

The *EvalScript* handler in the Shockwave movie must be paired with a script function invoking the handler within the HTML page. The handler itself must be placed within a movie script.

You can use a *do* statement inside the *EvalScript* handler to execute any statement you type into a window in the browser. This is both useful and dangerous. Useful, because it allows you to test how your movie will react to certain commands from within the browser environment. Dangerous, because someone else could do the same by looking at the scripts in an HTML document and making educated guesses about how your movie—for instance—sends proprietary information to a server. It's best to allow only specific messages to be evaluated, or only specific data to be passed through the *EvalScript* handler.

Results of operations carried out within a Shockwave movie by the *EvalScript* handler can be returned to the HTML document scripting environment with the *externalEvent* command (see Chapter 3).

Example This simple example shows how a JavaScript in an HTML document can communicate with a Shockwave movie embedded in the page. The user can type their e-mail address into a field on the HTML page and press a button to display the address in the movie.

The movie, *scripdemo.dir*, consists of a single field, named "email". A *go the frame* loop script keeps the movie playing. In a movie script there are two handlers:

```
on startMovie
  externalEvent ("setMovieAlias ()")
  --initializes the reference to the movie for both
  --MSIE and Navigator
end

on evalScript vEmail
  put vEmail into field "email"
end
```

The HTML page the movie is embedded in is somewhat more complex:

```
<HTML>
<HEAD>
<TITLE>EvalScript Demo</TITLE>
<SCRIPT LANGUAGE="JavaScript">
  var scriptDemo;
//global variable declaration for the movie object

  function setMovieAlias() {
//this function is called to set the correct value for the
//scriptDemo variable, which  is referred to as part of
//the document object in Navigator, and directly in MSIE
//it is activated by an externalEvent command in the
//movie's startMovie handler
    if(navigator.appName == "Microsoft Internet Explorer") {
      scriptDemo = evalDemo;
    } else {
      scriptDemo = document.evalDemo;
    }
  }
```

```
function sendAddress() {
//this function is activated by the button on the form
//below being pressed. It then derives the data from the
//text entry field and passes it as a string to the
//Shockwave movie
   var theEmail
   theEmail = document.EvalForm.evalEmail.value;
   scriptDemo.EvalScript(theName);
}

</SCRIPT>

</HEAD>
<BODY>
<CENTER>
<H3>EvalScript Demo</H3>
<HR>

<EMBED WIDTH=320 HEIGHT=100 SRC="scripdemo.dir" NAME="evalDemo">
//the NAME parameter is necessary for the script to
//refer to the movie
<P>

<FORM NAME="EvalForm">
<INPUT TYPE="BUTTON" NAME="EvalScriptBtn"
VALUE="Send Data to Movie" ONCLICK="sendAddress()">
//the ONCLICK parameter calls the "sendAddress"
//function above when the button is pressed

email:<INPUT TYPE="TEXT" SIZE=60
NAME="evalEmail" VALUE="Email">
<P>

<HR>
</FORM>

</CENTER>

</BODY>
</HTML>
```

Parameters

```
on evalScript string
   statements
end
```

See also externalEvent

field

Syntax `put netTextResult () into field 3`

Usage The *field* keyword can be used when referring to a field cast member's *the text of member* property, particularly when carrying out operations on the text contained in the field. This can make Lingo specifically designed for field operations look more readable.

    The *field* keyword can be used as a chunk reference when using string chunk operations.

Example These statements add HTML tags to the beginning and end of a field named "output text":

```
put "<HTML>" before field "output text"
put "</HTML>" after field "output text"
```

Parameters `field integer|string`

Value *chunk*

See also char, item, line, member, the number of chars, the number of items, the number of lines, the number of words, word

halt

Syntax `halt`

Usage The *halt* command causes Lingo to exit the current handler, exit any handler that called it, and stop the movie—if the movie is in the authoring environment or Shockwave. If the movie is being played in a projector, the projector quits.

    When a Shockwave movie is halted, it becomes completely unresponsive to any user input, and essentially dies in the browser until reloaded by the user.

Example   This example halts a movie if the text returned from a *GetNetText* operation indicates an unauthorized usage:

```
if NetTextResult () = "UNAUTHORIZED" then halt
```

Parameters   *halt*

See also   abort, exit, quit

on idle

Syntax   `on idle`

Usage   The *idle* message is generated when no events are occurring. The movie sends *idle* messages as often as possible when *the idleHandlerPeriod* movie property is 0 (its default), or it sends them at user-definable (by setting *the idleHandlerPeriod*) intervals.

   idle handlers are often used to generate messages to parent scripts, update animations, and so on, when the user is not interacting with the movie.

   Numerous complex statements or repeat loops within *idle* handlers may slow the responsiveness of your movie.

Example   This example calls a custom routine that tests the state of various network operations when there are no other events to handle:

```
on idle
  testNetOps
end
```

Parameters
```
on idle
  statements
end
```

See also   the idleHandlerPeriod

max

FUNCTION

Syntax
```
set topScore = max (scoreList)
set topAlpha = max ("Darrel", "Plant, "Doug", "Smith")
```

Usage
The *max* function returns the greatest value in a linear or property list, or from a series of comma-delimited values.
The result of this function would be the last item in a sorted list.

Example
This code segment limits the ability to move sprite 8 beyond the left or right edge of sprite 7, using the *max* and *min* functions:
```
repeat while the stillDown
  set the locH of sprite 8 = ¬
    max(the left of sprite 7, ¬
min(the mouseH, the right of sprite 7))
  updateStage
end repeat
```

Parameters
```
max list
max value, …
```

Value
```
value
```

See also   min

min

FUNCTION

Syntax
```
set loser = min (scoreList)
set bottomAlpha = max ("Darrel", "Plant, "Doug", "Smith")
```

Usage
The *min* function returns the least value in a linear or property list, or from a series of comma-delimited values.
The result of this function would be the first item in a sorted list.

Example   See the Example for *max* in the preceding entry.

Parameters   min *list*

              min *value*, ...

Value   *value*

See also   max

on

Usage   The *on* keyword is used in a script to signify the start of a handler.
              Handlers in Director are statements that are triggered by messages.
              Messages can be events predefined by Director or defined by the user.
              Each *on* keyword must be matched by an *end* keyword, signifying the last
              line of the handler script.

Parameters   on *message value*, ...
                 statements
              end

param

Syntax   set whatVal = param (2)

Usage   The *param* function returns the value of the parameter specified by an index
              number that was passed to the current handler. The index number indicates
              the position of the parameter in the order it was passed to the handler.
              Commas must separate parameters passed to handlers.
                 You can use the *param* function to access an unspecified number of
              parameters passed to a Lingo handler.

Examples   This handler can add the value of an unlimited quantity of numbers and
              return the value. Notice that no parameters are listed after the handler name,
              so any number of parameters can be accepted:

```
on getSum
  set tSum = 0
  repeat with tNum = 1 to the paramCount
    set tSum = tSum + param(tNum)
  end repeat
  return tSum
end getSum
```

Then you can use this function by passing any number of comma-separated numbers to it, like these examples from the message window:

```
put getSum(3,2)
-- 5
put getSum(2,5,7,10,13)
-- 37
```

Parameters   param (*integer*)

Value   *value*

See also   on, the paramCount

the paramCount

Syntax   `set numParams = the paramCount`

Usage   *the paramCount* property contains the number of parameters sent to the current handler. Commas must separate parameters passed to handlers.

Example   If the handler in question looks like this:

```
on doSomething
    return the paramCount
end doSomething
```

and you call the handler with a statement like this:

```
put doSomething("a", "one",[5,6,8])
```

then the value "3" will be displayed in the Message window. In the above example, you can see that a list appears as a single parameter.

Parameters   the paramCount

Value   *integer*

See also   on, param

pass

Syntax   `pass`

Usage   The *pass* command sends the current event message to the next location in
the message hierarchy. If you don't use the *pass* command, event messages
stop at the first place they are intercepted by a handler (except for the
primary event handler).

The typical message hierarchy moves from a sprite script to a cast member script, to a frame script, and then to the movie script.

Example   If you have this handler in the sprite script of a button:

```
on mouseUp
    getNetText "http://mysite.com/myfile.txt"
    pass
end mouseUp
```

and this script in the frame script of the same frame:

```
on mouseUp
    global gNetID, gState
    set gNetID = getLatestNetID
    set gState = #loading
end mouseUp
```

then the second script will execute after the first one sends the *pass* command
to it. Without the *pass* command, the second handler would never execute,
since the mouseUp message would be intercepted by the sprite script and
stopped there.

Parameters `pass`

See also   stopEvent

pictureP

Syntax
```
set isPicture = pictureP (the picture of member 35)
```

Usage
The *pictureP* function returns TRUE if the specified item contains a reference to a picture; otherwise it returns FALSE. The parameter can contain a variable or *the picture of member* property of a bitmap cast member.

Example
See the Example for *the picture of member* (Chapter 13).

Parameters
```
pictureP (value)
```

Value
boolean

See also
floatP, ilk, integerP, listP, objectP, stringP, symbolP, valueP

put

Syntax
```
put count (the actorList)
put the colorDepth, the number of members of castLib 1
```

Usage
In this form, the *put* command displays a value or values in the Message window.

This command can display the results of complex calculations or simple information about variable values or properties. Because the Message window is only visible in the authoring mode, *put* commands are usually commented or deleted before creating final versions of the movie.

Example
This example determines whether the property *the result* currently has no value, and displays the result in the Message window. The value returned appears as a comment, after two hyphens:
```
put voidP (the result)
-- 1
```

Parameters
```
put value
```

See also
put after, put before, put into, set

put into

Syntax `put "Ute Lemper" into item 1 of field "cdInfo"`

Usage The *put into* command is used with strings and chunks of strings to add to and modify part or all of a string value. With *put into*, the string used for the first parameter replaces the chunk specified as the second parameter.

The second parameter can be all or part of a variable or the text of a field cast member.

The text in the chunk specified by the second parameter is replaced by the string value of the first parameter.

Examples This example puts the string value *"Ventana"* into the variable *publisher*. If the variable *publisher* does not exist, this statement will create it:

`put "Ventana" into publisher`

This statement creates a new cast member and puts the value of the variable *bioInfo* into the field:

`put bioInfo into member (new (#field))`

This statement replaces the data in lines 3 through 5 of the string variable *bioInfo* with a single line of text:

`put "39 Overton St." into line 3 to 5 of bioInfo`

In the last example, if the variable does not exist, the new variable appears like this in the Message window:

```
put bioinfo
-- "

39 Overton St."
```

Parameters put *chunk* into *chunk*

See also put after, put before, put

random

Syntax `set diceRoll = random (6) + random (6)`

Usage The *random* function returns a random integer from 1 to the value of the parameter.

Example This handler sends the user to a random URL when they click the button associated with this script:

```
on mouseUp
  global gURLs
  -- this picks one of the URLs from the list
  set tIndex = random (count (gURLs))
  set tURL   = getAt (gURLs, tIndex)
  gotoNetPage tURL
end mouseUp
```

Parameters `random (`*`integer`*`)`

Value *integer*

See also the randomSeed

the randomSeed

Syntax `set the randomSeed = 484950`

Usage *the randomSeed* property contains the seed value used by the *random* function to generate random numbers. You can test and set this property with Lingo.

If you wish to generate the same sequence of random numbers, you can set this to a certain value. The sequence of numbers returned by the *random* function after you set *the randomSeed* will then be the same.

Example   This statement sets *the randomSeed* to 3:

```
set the randomSeed = 3
```

Parameters   the randomSeed

Value   *integer*

See also   random

symbol

Syntax   `set aMessage = symbol ("getAllURLs")`

Usage   The *symbol* function is new in Director 6. It converts string values to a symbol value.

Symbols in Director comprise a special data type that combines fast processing with readability. Symbols begin with a # character (pound sign, or hash mark) and a string of alphanumeric characters beginning with a letter.

Earlier versions of Director can use the *value* command to perform the same function, by attaching a # to the front of a string.

Example   This example from the Message window shows the results of a *symbol* function:

```
put symbol ("returnScores")
-- #returnScores
```

Parameters   symbol (*string*)

Value   *symbol*

See also   value

symbolP

Syntax

```
set isSymbol = symbolP (aState)
```

Usage

The *symbolP* function returns TRUE if the parameter is a *symbol* data type; otherwise it returns FALSE.

Example

This code segment returns TRUE if the variable *gVariable* contains a symbol:

```
global gVariable
return symbolP (gVariable)
```

Parameters

```
symbolP (value)
```

Value

boolean

See also

floatP, ilk, listP, integerP, objectP, string, stringP, value

tell

Syntax

```
tell window (getAt (the windowList, 3)) to animateSprites
tell the stage
  set the stageColor = 34
  go movie "extreme"
end tell
```

Usage

The *tell* command can be used to send a MIAW a command or series of commands for execution within the MIAW.

The *tell to* structure can be used with the stage or a MIAW to send a single command line to a movie. Or, by using the *tell ... end tell* structure, a number of commands can be executed by the other movie.

This makes *tell* very useful for authoring uses, as well as modifying movies.

There are two restrictions with the use of the *tell* command. The first is that the reference to the window should be the full path name of the movie or the movie's position in *the windowList*.

The second is that the script containing the handler invoking the *tell* command should not have a handler called by the *tell* command in the script.

Example This handler, if placed in a movie opened as a MIAW, tells the stage to create a new Shockwave audio cast member, and assigns a URL to the new cast member. The position of the SWA cast member is determined by the value of *the result* property:

```
on newSWA
  tell the stage
    new (#swa)
    set the URL of the result = ¬
      "http://www.surftrio.com/wave99.swa"
  end tell
end
```

Parameters tell *window* to *statement*

```
tell window
  statements
end tell
```

See also cacheSize

voidP

Syntax set isVoid = voidP (the result)

Usage The *voidP* function returns TRUE when the value specified by its parameter contains nothing (represented by *<void>* in the message window), and FALSE otherwise.

Example The Shockwave Lingo function *getPref* returns *<void>* if the preference file is not present. This code segment uses *voidP* to determine whether to use the content retrieved by the *getPref* function:

```
set tLastScore = getPref("lastscor")
if not(voidP(tlastScore)) then
  set the text of field "last score" = ¬
    "Your last score was " & tLastScore
end if
```

Parameters   `voidP (value)`

Value   *boolean*

See also   floatP, ilk, listP, integerP, objectP, string, stringP, symbolP, value

window

Syntax   `set the title of window 1 = "SWA Player"`

Usage   The *window* keyword is used to indicate a particular Movie in a Window (MIAW) object in the movie property *the windowList*.

     MIAWs can be referred to by name or by the index number of their appearance in *the windowList*.

     For more on MIAWs, see Chapter 32.

Example   This example opens a new MIAW, with the movie "wave99.dir" (or .dxr or .dcr) from the same directory as the current movie:

`open window "wave99"`

Parameters   `window` *integer/string*

Value   *window*

See also   close window, forget window, moveToBack, moveToFront, open window, the stage, the windowList

Appendix A
About the Companion CD-ROM

The Companion CD-ROM for *The Lingo Programmer's Reference* book includes the entire contents of the book in hypertext format. It also includes valuable software.

To View the CD-ROM

Macintosh

Double-click on the LAUNCHME icon after opening the CD on your desktop.

Windows 95/NT

If Windows "autorun" is not enabled, double-click on the RUNME_32.EXE file. Or go to START | RUN and type **d:**(where d is the name of your CD-ROM drive) **runme_32.exe** in the space provided.

Windows 3.1x

Double-click on the RUNME_16.EXE file in File Manager, or go to FILE | RUN and type **d:\(where** d is the name of your CD-ROM drive) **runme_16.exe** in the space provided.

   You'll see a menu screen offering several choices. See "Navigating the CD-ROM" below for your options.

Navigating the CD-ROM

Your choices for navigating the CD-ROM appear on the opening screen. You can quit the CD, view the software, browse the book's contents electronically by clicking on The Book, browse the Hot Picks, or learn more about Ventana.

When you click on From the Book, you will be presented with two choices: Locate Browser and Launch Browser. You must click on Locate Browser first and help the program find your Web browser. You will not have to perform this step again, unless you move your Web browser to another directory or another hard drive. You can then click on Launch Browser, and your browser will launch and open up a fully hyperlinked version of the book.

If the viewer does not run properly on your machine, follow the following instructions for optimum performance:

For optimum WINDOWS performance:

1. Copy the RUNME.EXE and RUNME.INI files to the same directory on your hard drive.

2. Open the RUNME.INI file in a text editor such as Notepad.

3. Find the section in the .INI file that reads:

```
[Memory]
;ExtraMemory=400
; Amount of kBytes over and above physical memory for use by a
projector.
```

4. If your computer has enough memory to do so, delete the semicolon from the ExtraMemory line, and change the ExtraMemory setting to a higher number.

5. Save the changes to the RUNME.INI file, and close the text editor.

6. With the CD-ROM still inserted, launch the viewer from the hard drive.

If the viewer still does not run properly on your machine, you can access the material on the CD-ROM directly through File Manager (Windows 3.x) or Windows Explorer (Windows 95).

For optimum MACINTOSH performance:

1. Copy the Launch Me file to your hard drive.

2. Click once on the Launch Me file.

3. Select Get Info from the File menu.

4. If your computer has enough memory to do so, change the amount in the Preferred size field to a higher number.

5. Close the info box.

6. With the CD-ROM still inserted, launch the viewer from the hard drive.

If the viewer still does not run properly on your machine, you can access the files on the CD-ROM directly by double-clicking on its icon on the desktop.

Software Descriptions

Authorware   Demo version of Authorware, the world's leading tool for creating interactive learning solutions. For more information, visit Macromedia's Web site at http://www.macromedia.com.

Director 5   Macromedia's save-disabled version of Director 5, the popular multimedia authoring tool. Director is a multiplatform application, allowing developers to create and exchange files between Macs and PCs. For more information about Director, visit Macromedia's Web site at http://www.macromedia.com.

g/matter Xtras   A collection of g/matter Xtras for Mac and Windows, including Anecdote Xtra, AutoStart, Dialogs Xtra, DropStart, FileUtil Xtra, GetDate XObject , GIFTrader Xtra, Install Xtra, InstalledFonts Xtra, KILLER Transitions, LiveHTML Xtra, MasterApp Xtra, PickFolder Xtra, PopMenu Xtra, PrintOMatic Xtra, ProgressCopy Xtra, Relaunch, ScriptOMatic Lite Xtra, ScrnUtil Xtra, Sound Xtra, StageHand Xtra, Trans-X Xtra, Xtra Draw, XtraNet, and XtraText.

Flash!   With its advanced vector-based technology, Flash! breaks the band-width barrier by enabling you to create interactive Web animations, interfaces, buttons, drawings, cartoons, and more. Please visit Macromedia's Web page to download a copy of Flash 2.0 beta at http://www.macromedia.com on the Web.

FreeHand   This Macromedia demo allows you to explore most of the functionality of FreeHand 7. It includes all of the new user interface enhance-ments such as dockable panels and tear-out tabbed panels. Many new Xtras are included, such as Bend, Roughen, Envelope, and the new Charting tool. Mac and Windows versions.

Highscor   Darrel Plant's HIGHSCOR is a utility that enables the user to save a list of high scores on a Shockwave game, without using CGI scripting. Before using Highscor, please see the vreadme for this program, for more information about the utility, including information about security. There is also more information at http://www.moshplant.com/direct-or/highscor/highscor.html.

The Lingo Timesaver   The Lingo Timesaver, by updateStage, is a CD-ROM library of useful Lingo scripts that you can cut and paste directly into your own movies. The collection contains often-requested functions like rollover, slider, and field-checking handlers and handy utility code that you'll use every day. A script browser, installed under the Director Xtras menus, gives you fast access to the code and documentation for all scripts in the library, and enables you to copy any script into your own movie on the fly. The Lingo Timesaver scripts were written by a team of contract professionals who make their living programming in Lingo. Each script comes with documentation in a consistent format that tells you how to incorporate the code, and a demonstration movie that shows the code in action. Each script has been tested on both the Macintosh and PC platform.

Page Mill 2.0 Tryout for the Mac   Adobe PageMill 1.0 set the standard in ease of use for Web authoring programs. Now, with PageMill 2.0 software's enhanced feature set, it's even easier to create great-looking, information-rich Web pages. From building an entire corporate Web site for use as an Intranet to developing individual home pages, PageMill 2.0 makes it as easy as creating an e-mail message.

xRes   The ultimate in versatility, xRes is tightly integrated with leading graphics programs including FreeHand and Photoshop. The ability to drag and drop between graphics applications on the Macintosh, import Photoshop artwork with layers, and rasterize FreeHand, QuarkXPress, and Illustrator EPS files makes you more creative and productive than ever!

Technical Support

Technical support is available for installation-related problems only. The technical support office is open from 8:00 A.M. to 6:00 P.M. Monday through Friday and can be reached via the following methods:

- Phone: (919) 544-9404 extension 81
- Faxback Answer System: (919) 544-9404 extension 85
- E-mail: help@vmedia.com
- Fax: (919) 544-9472
- World Wide Web: **http://www.vmedia.com/support**
- America Online: keyword *Ventana*

Limits of Liability & Disclaimer of Warranty

The authors and publisher of this book have used their best efforts in preparing the CD-ROM and the programs contained in it. These efforts include the development, research, and testing of the theories and programs to determine their effectiveness. The authors and publisher make no warranty of any kind expressed or implied, with regard to these programs or the documentation contained in this book.

The authors and publisher shall not be liable in the event of incidental or consequential damages in connection with, or arising out of, the furnishing, performance, or use of the programs, associated instructions, and/or claims of productivity gains.

Some of the software on this CD-ROM is shareware; there may be additional charges (owed to the software authors/makers) incurred for their registration and continued use. See individual program's README or VREADME.TXT files for more information.

Appendix B
Error Messages

This reference is a compilation of the common compile and run-time errors in Lingo, with notes on what to look for when they're encountered.

Compile Errors

These errors will appear when the Script window is closed or during a Recompile All Scripts session. They usually indicate syntactical errors in the Lingo scripts. Eradicating compile errors does not guarantee good Lingo, but it's the first step.

Error	Description
Out of memory	Director doesn't have enough memory left to compile the scripts. If possible, save the movie (ignoring compile errors) and quit Director. If possible, allocate more memory to the program.
Name expected	An *on* keyword has been encountered with no handler name following.
Symbol expected Property name expected Chunk expression expected Number expected Expected a variable	These errors all indicate that the wrong data type is being supplied as a parameter.
Handler definition expected	An *on* keyword is missing from a handler.

➡

Error	Description
Comma expected	Check the handler parameter list to determine if all of the parameters are separated by commas.
Variable already defined	The same parameter name is used twice in the handler parameter list.
Command expected	The statement line does not begin with a command.
Right parenthesis expected	Each left parenthesis needs a matching right parenthesis on the same statement line.
Expected TO Expected WHILE or WITH Expected END REPEAT Expected THEN Expected END IF Expected ELSE Expected OF Misplaced END REPEAT Misplaced NEXT REPEAT Expected END TELL Misplaced EXIT TELL Expected OF Expected END CASE Expected CASE clause	A portion of a Lingo control structure is missing or misplaced.
Variable used before assigned a value	A variable name is used in a comparison or an expression before a *set* or *put* expression has assigned it a value, or before it has been used as a parameter.
Expected FIELD	Missing *field* keyword in chunk expression.
String does not end correctly	No closing quote mark on string.
Name already used	Two handlers in the script have the same name.
Expected WITHIN or INTERSECTS	Keyword missing from between two sprite references.
Misplaced Operator	Operator symbol between keywords instead of two values.
Operator expected	Two values together on line without operator between them.
Operand expected	One or more values missing around operator.
Expected end of statement	Items appear after what should be the end of the statement.
Unexpected end of statement	Not enough items appear in the statement.

Run-Time Errors

These error messages appear when the movie is playing. While your Lingo may be syntactically correct, logical errors or mistaken assumptions about how the program will operate can generate a run-time error.

Error	Description
Out of memory for string	String value has exceeded allowable size, or movie has run out of memory.
Handler not defined Handler not found in object	A handler reference has been encountered that does not exist in the movie or object it is addressed to.
Cannot divide by zero	A value that is equal to zero appears on the right side of a divide operator.
Integer expected Number expected Floating point number expected String expected Symbol expected Object expected List expected Rect expected Point expected Cast member expected Cast member name expected Media expected Picture expected Message expected Wrong type Digital video cast member expected Bitmap cast member expected Sound cast member expected Button cast member expected Shape cast member expected Movie cast member expected Script cast member expected Transition cast member expected Label expected Movie name expected Digital video sprite expected Integer or list expected Xtra name expected Xtra handler name expected	These errors indicate that the wrong type of data has been supplied to a command, function, or operator.

Error	Description
Zero parameters expected One parameter expected Two parameters expected Three parameters expected Four parameters expected Too many parameters to an XObject Wrong number of parameters At least 2 parameters expected Too many parameters to Lingo Xtra	An incorrect number of parameters has been supplied to a handler, function, Xtra, or XObject.
Method not defined	An Xobject or Xtra does not contain the method addressed to it.
Command not defined	A statement begins with a command not available to the program.
Function not defined	The function called in a statement is not available to the program.
Cast member not found Digital video cast member not found Bitmap cast member not found Sound cast member not found Button cast member not found Shape cast member not found Movie cast member not found Script cast member not found Window not found Property not found Xtra not found XLib file not found	A cast member name or number has been used that does not exist in any open cast library, or an object is being referred to that does not exist.
Not a text cast member	A command or function specific to text cast members has been used with another type of cast member.
Text style wrong	An attempt has been made to apply a style that does not exist.
Menu not defined Menu item not defined	Reference made to a custom menu or menu item that has not been initialized or does not exist.
Frame not defined	A marker label that does not exist has been referenced.
Sprite number wrong	A number less than one or greater than the maximum number of sprites has been used as a sprite reference.
Index is not positive Index out of range	A negative value, or a value larger than the possible number of items indexed, has been used.

Error	Description
Index too big	An integer value used as an index number is greater than the allowable value for an index number.
Variable not defined	A variable with no value has been used in an expression.
Cannot set this property	The property can only be tested.
Value out of range	An attempt has been made to set a value to a number greater than or less than the allowable range of values.
List must contain integer	Only integer values may be added to the list.
List cannot be empty	List must contain at least one value or property/value pair.
Cast Member not a bitmap or not black and white	An attempt has been made to use a cast member that is not a 1-bit bitmap cast member for a cursor or other operation requiring 1-bit bitmaps.
Property or value missing	An attempt has been made to add an item to a property list, but either the property name or the value is missing.
Movie cast not found	The cast library referred to is not open or available to the movie.
Lingo Xtra handler requires instance	An object needs to be created using the *new* command in order to use the Xtra's functions.
Only field cast members can be used to create menus	An attempt has been made to use a nonfield cast member to create a menu.
Use of unsupported Lingo command	The Lingo used is obsolete.

Director 6 Techniques

This appendix covers the new additions to Lingo in Director 6, in brief.

Shockwave Inside

Shockwave (.dcr) files can be played as MIAWs or by using the *go to movie* or *play movie* command, just like native Director (.dir) and protected (.dxr) files.

Note: Because Shockwave files are compressed, there may be a performance penalty incurred when playing them back, as opposed to uncompressed files. See Chapters 1 and 31.

Browser Scripting

Shockwave movies playing inside browsers can communicate with the scripting language for the browser by using the *EvalScript* handler and the *externalEvent* command.

AppleScript

MacOS users can send messages to the Director application using AppleScript if they have the AppleScript extensions installed on their computer. See the Online Help.

URLs

Most Lingo commands that refer to a file can be used with files on the World Wide Web (WWW) or File Transfer Protocol (FTP) servers. Network Lingo commands can be used inside Director and in projectors.

Note: In some cases, it may be more appropriate to download files to a local drive (*downloadNetThing*) rather than directly linking to remote files. See Chapter 2.

Streaming

Director movies can begin playing before they have completely downloaded. Movies can test for the availability of data being streamed over networks (*the mediaReady of member*) and make decisions based on downloaded files. See Chapter 13.

Cue Points

The new Lingo cue point functions allow you to synchronize your movie with digital video and sounds created with the SoundEdit 16 application. See Chapter 16.

Behaviors

The biggest change to Director 6 Lingo is the addition of a new form of score script, called a *behavior*. A behavior allows programmers to create *object-oriented* scripts that they (or others) can then assign to sprites or frames simply by dragging them onto the stage or into the Score window. Values for the script's properties can be assigned by means of an automatically configured interface, or directly from the script. Multiple frames or sprites may share the same script, each one possessing its own set of parameter values.

Scripts can manage the function of buttons, animations, network operations—virtually anything Lingo can do.

Below is an example of a simple behavior that animates a sprite counterclockwise along the outline of an oval. If you drag this script onto a sprite, you get a dialog box allowing you to enter values for the center of the oval (default is the current position of the sprite) and the width and height of the oval.

```
property ovalWidth, ovalHeight  -- in pixels
property xOrigin, yOrigin
-- horizontal and vertical coordinates of oval center
property chan  -- sprite channel
property axisX, axisY, step, speed, axisX2, axisY2
--used for math routines
```

```
on beginSprite me
  --this handler is called in the first frame the
  --sprite appears in the score

--determines sprite channel
  set chan = the spriteNum of me

  --check valid values for position and size
  set stageWidth = the stageRight - the stageLeft
  set stageHeight = the stageBottom - the stageTop
  if (xOrigin < 0) or (xOrigin > stageWidth) then ¬
    set xOrigin = stageWidth / 2
  if (yOrigin < 0) or (yOrigin > stageWidth) then ¬
    set yOrigin = stageheight / 2
  if (ovalWidth < 1) or (ovalWidth > stageWidth * 2) ¬
    then set ovalWidth = stageWidth
  if (ovalHeight < 1) or (ovalHeight > stageHeight * 2) ¬
    then set ovalHeight = stageHeight

  --set up initial position and values used for animation
  set step = 0  --
  set speed = 20
  set axisX = ovalWidth / 2
  set axisY = ovalHeight / 2
  set axisX2 = float (axisX * axisX)
  set axisY2 = float (axisY * axisY)
  set the loc of sprite chan = ¬
    point (xOrigin - axisX, yOrign
end


on exitFrame me
  --move horizontally
  set step = step + speed
  if step > ovalWidth then
    set step = ovalWidth
    set speed - - speed
  else
    --reverses direction
    if step < 0 then
      set step = 0
      set speed = - speed
    end if
  end if
  set xPos = step - axisX
  --solves ellipse equation for a vertical value
  set yPos = sqrt (axisY2 * (1 - (xPos * xPos / axisX2)))
  --draws upper half of ellipse values as
  --horizontal value decreases
```

```
    if speed < 0 then set yPos = - yPos
    set the loc of sprite chan = ¬
      point (xOrigin + xPos, yOrigin + yPos)
  end


on getPropertyDescriptionList me
  set myProps = [:]

  --calculate the size of the stage:
  set stageWidth = the stageRight - the stageLeft
  set stageHeight = the stageBottom - the stageTop
  set chan = the currentSpriteNum
  set hLoc = the locH of sprite chan
  set vLoc = the locV of sprite chan

  --set the default origin to the sprite location:
  addProp myProps, #xOrigin, [ #comment: "x origin:",
  #format: #integer, #default: hLoc]
  addProp myProps, #yOrigin, [ #comment: "y origin:",
  #format: #integer, #default: vLoc]

  --set the default size to the stage width and height:
  addProp myProps, #ovalWidth, [ #comment: "width:",
  #format: #integer, #default: stageWidth ]
  --set the default radius to 100 pixels:
  addProp myProps, #ovalHeight, [ #comment: "height:",
  #format: #integer, #default: stageHeight ]

  return myProps
end


on getBehaviorDescription me
  return "Move sprite along an oval path. The  default oval center is
  the sprite" && ¬
    "location, maximum values for height and width of the oval are
  twice the stage height" && ¬
    "and width, respectively."
end
```

Appendix D
Shockwave Reference

This Appendix contains information about the use of Director movies within HTML pages, including inserting a movie into the page and communicating with the scripting language supported by the browser.

The EMBED and OBJECT tags are used to insert a Shockwave movie in an HTML page. These tags are similar, but different browsers (and versions of browsers) support each one differently.

Added in the Shockwave plug-in for Director 6 is the ability to send information from the browser scripting language to a Shockwave movie through the *EvalScript* method and handler (see Chapter 42) and the ability to send instructions to the browser from a movie using the *externalEvent* command (see Chapter 3).

The Netscape Navigator and Communicator browsers support the JavaScript scripting language. Microsoft Internet Explorer (MSIE) supports a variant of JavaScript, known as JScript, as well as VBScript, which is based on Microsoft's Visual Basic. This reference describes JavaScript, as it is the most widely supported scripting solution.

EMBED & OBJECT

A Shockwave movie can be added to an HTML document through the use of EMBED and OBJECT tags. In many cases, both tags are used, sometimes with JavaScript filters for various browsers, to ensure cross-browser compatibility. The requirements of your particular situation will determine the method you use to add movies to your own pages.

EMBED

The EMBED tag is really where it all started with Shockwave for Director. Netscape developed the tag to enable the embedding of multimedia objects like Java applets, QuickTime video, and Shockwave movies into an HTML page (rather than opening an external viewer). In its simplest form, an HTML document with a Shockwave movie in it can consist of only one line:

```
<EMBED SRC="http://www.surftrio.com/promo16.dcr" WIDTH=448 HEIGHT=300>
```

The SRC parameter provides a URL (including the HTTP header, or as an absolute or relative address). The WIDTH and HEIGHT parameters determine the area, measured in pixels, reserved for the movie within the page, much as they do for a graphic when used with the IMG tag.

Tip

You can open a Shockwave movie without embedding it in a page as well, simply by typing in the URL address for the movie or opening it from the disk. The movie will open in the upper left corner of the browser window, and you have no control over the background color of the window or the horizontal alignment of the movie.

The EMBED tag has a number of optional, predefined parameters as well:

PALETTE= background | foreground   The default value for this parameter is *background*, indicating that the browser's default palette is used, and that colors in a Shockwave movie will be mapped to that palette. If *foreground* is chosen, custom palette settings in the movie will attempt to override the browser. This can cause irregular results on some machines, and it is not supported at all in the Microsoft Internet Explorer 3.0 browser.

BGCOLOR=#RRGGBB   The default value for this parameter is #FFFFFF, or white. The value following the hash mark (#) is in the same hexadecimal format as other colors in HTML documents, with each two-character segment referring to a component of an RGB color value ranging from 00 (0 in decimal values) to FF (255 in decimal).

PLUGINSPAGE=*URL* The default page for this parameter depends on the browser (if it supports it at all). If the user does not have the correct plug-in installed, an alert will be displayed giving the user the option to go to the page defined by this parameter. The address for the Shockwave download page on the Macromedia site is: *http://www.macromedia.com/shockwave/*.

AUTOSTART=true | false The default value for this parameter is *true*. A movie can be started, stopped, and rewound with scripting commands and the Director 6 plug-in or ActiveX control. This parameter determines whether a movie begins playing as it is loaded, or if it will wait for a command to be sent from a browser script.

NAME=*string* This parameter has no default value. It must be defined in order to use the Shockwave movie with browser scripting. The object that represents the Shockwave movie defined by this parameter is *document.movieName* in Navigator, or *movieName* in MSIE.

Other parameters can be used inside the EMBED tag and accessed with the *externalParamCount*, *externalParamName*, and *externalParamValue* functions in Lingo. Netscape Navigator puts no restrictions on the names assigned to other parameters, but the OBJECT tag used for Microsoft Internet Explorer can only use specified parameter names. Parameters are added to the tag by enclosing them within the tag delimiters. No particular order is necessary.

An example EMBED tag containing the parameters defined above (and two custom tags) appears below:

```
<EMBED SRC="player.dcr" WIDTH=300 HEIGHT=60 PALETTE=background
    BGCOLOR=#000000 PLUGINSPAGE="http://www.macromedia.com/shockwave/"
    TEXTFOCUS=true AUTOSTART=true NAME="ShockwavePlayer" swURL="music/
    curse/wave99.swa" swText="99th Wave">
```

OBJECT

The OBJECT tag was introduced by Microsoft to do much the same task as the EMBED tag, but with some additional capabilities (as well as some restrictions). Since its introduction, the OBJECT tag has been adopted by the W3C governing body into the standards for HTML, and Netscape has announced that the Communicator browser will support the OBJECT tag.

Only specific parameter tags are recognized by the OBJECT tag. Several are mandatory, others are outlined below.

A major advantage of the OBJECT tag is its support by Microsoft's ActiveX technology. When an ActiveX-capable browser encounters an HTML document with an OBJECT tag, it can detect the type of plug-in (called a *control* in ActiveX terms), determine if it is installed, and—if it isn't—download the control, install it, and play the movie, with nothing more than an affirmation by the user.

Another advantage of the OBJECT tag is that it not only identifies if the control is installed, but that it makes sure the correct version is installed; again, it installs the control if the user gives approval. Here's a sample OBJECT tag:

```
<OBJECT CLASSID="clsid:166B1BCA-3F9C-11CF-8075-44455354000"
   CODEBASE="http://active.macromedia.com/director/cabs/
   sw.cab#version=6,0,0,0" WIDTH=448 HEIGHT=300 NAME="Surf">
<PARAM NAME="SRC" VALUE="http://www.surftrio.com/promo16.dcr"
</OBJECT>
```

The main body of the tag contains several required tags and data specific to the Shockwave for Director ActiveX control:

CLASSID="clsid:166B1BCA-3F9C-11CF-8075-44455354000"   The CLASSID tag indicates which control is being used for this object. Its value is a registration number that must exactly match the text in the example.

CODEBASE="http://active.macromedia.com/director/cabs/ sw.cab#version=6,0,0,0"   The CODEBASE tag contains the URL where the control can be found and the version required to play the movie. The data after the word *version* in the example above indicates that the earliest version that should be installed for the movie is Version 6. If an earlier version of the control is installed, the new version will be downloaded and installed. The version number had not been finalized at press time, and you should check Macromedia's site for the latest information as modifications and improvements are made.

WIDTH=*integer* HEIGHT=*integer*   These tags indicate the size of the Shockwave movie in pixels, and should be equal to the size of the movie's stage.

NAME=*string*   This tag is optional, but it is necessary if the movie will be addressed using browser scripting methods. The value of the NAME parameter becomes the name of the Shockwave object (see the JavaScript reference following this section).

The main body of the tag is followed by one or more parameters each with its own set of delimiters (< and >), in this form:

```
<PARAM NAME=paramName VALUE=paramValue>
```

The name of the parameter and its value are string values.

The SRC parameter must be included, to indicate the location of the movie:

```
<PARAM NAME="SRC" VALUE=URL>
```

Unlike the EMBED tag, the OBJECT tag requires a closing tag:

```
</OBJECT>
```

Optional Parameters   There are 23 predefined parameters for the OBJECT tag. They can be used for the EMBED tag as well.

The named parameters are intended to be used for specific types of data (see chart below), but can be used for any purpose. All values assigned to parameters must be strings.

Parameter Name	Purpose
swURL	passing URL value to movie
swText	passing text value to movie
swColor	
swForeColor	
swBackColor	passing color value to movie
swFrame	passing frame target to movie
swName	passing user name to movie
swPassword	passing user password to movie
swBanner	passing text for banner display to movie
swSound	passing sound name to be played
swVolume	passing sound volume to movie
swPreLoadTime	passing Shockwave Audio preLoad time value
swAudio	passing SWA URL to movie
swList	passing list of items to movie
sw1	
sw2	
sw3	
sw4	
sw5	
sw6	
sw7	
sw8	
sw9	undefined

JavaScript (& JScript)

The JavaScript Reference is organized by object, with the methods and properties of each object briefly described in each object. All of the examples focus on the integration of JavaScript in a browser with Shockwave applications. We also show the compatibility of the various objects, methods, and properties within the different Netscape Navigator and Microsoft Internet Explorer (MSIE) browser versions.

In general, when we refer to the Netscape or MSIE browsers in this text, we are referring to Version 2+ of Netscape and Version 3+ of MSIE. All of the JavaScript code contained here works in Netscape 2.0 or above. Most of the commands work in MSIE, except those new to Netscape 3.0 (marked for each entry by the notation NS3+) and above. Known quirks and exceptions are noted.

Tip

Unlike Lingo, JavaScript is case-specific. While you can be a little loose about your typing in Lingo, be extremely careful when reproducing the examples below, or from any JavaScript reference. Be careful, too, when passing data from Shockwave movies to JavaScript via the externalEvent *command.*

Date   OBJECT

The Date object contains all of the methods and properties necessary to work with dates and times within the browser. A date is stored internally as an integer value that is the number of milliseconds since January 1, 1970, at 12:00 am.

Creation   You can create a new Date object with any of the following statements:

```
dateObject = new Date() // empty
dateObject = new Date("m d, y h:m:s")
dateObject = new Date(y, m, d) // m begins with 0
dateObject = new Date(y, m, d, h, m, s)
dateObject = new Date(someObject.itsDateProperty)
```

Then you can use the date methods to work with your new date object.

Methods   **getDate**   This method returns the day of the month contained in the specified date object.

```
dateObject.getDate()
```

getDay   This method returns an integer between 0 and 6 that corresponds to the day of the week contained in the specified date object. Zero corresponds to Sunday, 1 corresponds to Monday, and so on.

```
dateObject.getDay()
```

getHours   This method returns the hours value contained in the specified date object.

```
dateObject.getHours()
```

getMinutes   This method returns the minutes value contained in the specified date object.

```
dateObject.getMinutes()
```

getMonth   This method returns the month value contained in the specified date object. The *integer* value begins with the number 0 (zero) for January, rather than 1.

```
dateObject.getMonth()
```

getSeconds   This method returns the seconds value contained in the specified date object.

```
dateObject.getSeconds()
```

getTime   This method returns the number of milliseconds from January 1, 1970 at 12:00am to the current date/time contained in the specified date object.

```
dateObject.getTime()
```

getTimezoneOffset   This method returns the number of minutes between the time zone in the specified date object and the GMT time zone.

```
dateObject.getTimezoneOffset()
```

getYear   This method returns an integer that corresponds to the current year. If the year is less than 1999, it returns the difference between the current year and 1900, resulting in a two-digit integer. For example, if the year is 1998, then the result of *getYear* will be 98. However, if the year is 2000 or greater, the full four digits of the year are returned. For example, if the year is 2001, then 2001 will be returned by the *getYear* method.

```
dateObject.getYear()
```

parse   This method converts a date/time string into the number of milliseconds from January 1, 1970 at 12:00am to the date/time string supplied to the method. It is a static method of Date, which means that you don't use the typical *dateObject.method()* structure. Rather, you use this:

```
Date.parse(someDateString)
```

setDate   This method replaces the day of the month contained in the specified date object with the *integer* value.

```
dateObject.setDate(integer)
```

setHours   This method replaces the *hours* value contained in the specified date object with the *integer* value.

```
dateObject.setHours(integer)
```

setMinutes   This method replaces the *minutes* value contained in the specified date object with the *integer* value.

```
dateObject.setMinutes(integer)
```

setMonth   This method replaces the *month* value contained in the specified date object with the *integer* value. The *integer* value begins with the number 0 (zero) for January, rather than 1.

```
dateObject.setMonth(integer)
```

setSeconds   This method replaces the *seconds* value contained in the specified date object with the *integer* value.

```
dateObject.setMinutes(integer)
```

setTime   This method replaces the entire date/time value contained in the specified date object with the *integer* value. This value is the number of milliseconds since January 1, 1970 at 12:00am.

```
dateObject.setTime(integer)
```

setYear   This method replaces the year value contained in the specified date object with the *integer* value. The *integer* must be a value greater than 1900.

```
dateObject.setYear(integer)
```

toGMTString   This method converts the date value contained in the specified date object into a GMT string, which is different on the various platforms.

```
dateObject.toGMTString()
```

toLocaleString   This method converts the date value contained in the specified date object into a string, which is different on the various platforms.

```
dateObject.toLocaleString()
```

UTC   This method takes a group of comma-separated values and converts it into a data integer. It is a static method of Date, which means that you don't use the typical *dateObject.method()* structure. Rather, use this:

```
Date.UTC(y, m, d, [h,] [min, ] [s])
```

Where: *y* is a year after 1900

   m is a month between 0-11

   d is a day of the month between 1-31

   h is an hour between 0-23

   min a minute between 0-59

   s a second between 0-59

Tip

The rule stated for the getYear *method is true in Netscape, but MSIE always subtracts the current year from 1900, even for years greater than or equal to 2000. For example, if the year is 2001, getYear returns 2001 in Netscape, and 101 in MSIE.*

The *getTimezoneOffset* method returns a positive number of minutes in Netscape and a negative number of minutes in MSIE. If, for example, you are in the Pacific time zone, the *getTimezoneOffset* method returns 480 (8 hours) in Netscape and –480 in MSIE.

This HTML document contains JavaScript code that displays a nicely formatted date on the page. It takes into account the differences between the Netscape and MSIE browsers in their handling of the *getYear* function.

```
<HTML>
<HEAD>
<TITLE>
JavaScript Date Display
</TITLE>

<SCRIPT LANGUAGE = "JavaScript">

<!-- Hide Script from non-JavaScript browsers

function makeArray() {

// creates an array from a comma-separated list of
// arguments passed to this function.

this.arrayLength = makeArray.arguments.length;
for (var i=0; i<this.arrayLength; i++) {
this[i] = makeArray.arguments[i]
}

}

var gDays   = new makeArray("Sun", "Mon", "Tue", "Wed",
  "Thu", "Fri", "Sat")
```

```
var gMonths = new makeArray("Jan", "Feb", "Mar", "Apr",
  "May", "Jun", "Jul", "Aug",
  "Sep", "Oct", "Nov", "Dec")

function fourDigitYear(myInteger) {

// returns the correct four-digit year
// based on the rules of conduct between the
// two major browser platforms

if(navigator.appName == "Microsoft Internet Explorer")
return myInteger + 1900
else
if(myInteger>1900)
    return myInteger
    else
    return myInteger + 1900

}

// end hiding contents -->

</SCRIPT>

</HEAD>

<BODY BGCOLOR="#FFFFFF">

<SCRIPT LANGUAGE = "JavaScript">
<!-- Hide Me

tDate = new Date(Date.parse(document.lastModified))

document.write("This document was last modified on: " +
    gDays[tDate.getDay()] + ", " +
    gMonths[tDate.getMonth()] + " " +
    tDate.getDate() + ", " +
    fourDigitYear(tDate.getYear()) + "<P>")

// end hiding contents -->

</SCRIPT>

</BODY>
</HTML>
```

This segment of JavaScript code creates an <EMBED> tag for a Shockwave movie, and passes a parameter "sw1" that contains a comma-separated list of the various parts of the current date and time. This can be useful, since the built-in Lingo date and time functions return different values in different countries, but this date information will always be the same regardless of the country or platform. Then, you can use the Lingo command *externalParamValue("sw1")* to get the month and use the other parameter names to get the remaining date information.

```
<SCRIPT LANGUAGE = "JavaScript">
<!-- Hide Me

    tDate = new Date() // current date/time

    document.write("<EMBED SRC=temp.dcr WIDTH=400 " +
      "HEIGHT=240 " +
      "sw1=" + (tDate.getMonth() + 1) + " " +
      "sw2=" + tDate.getDate() + " " +
      "sw3=" + fourDigitYear(tDate.getYear()) +
      + " " + "sw4=" + tDate.getHours() + " " +
      "sw5=" + tDate.getMinutes() + " " +
      "sw6=" + tDate.getSeconds() + ">")

// end hiding contents -->

</SCRIPT>
```

Document

OBJECT

The *document* object contains the methods, properties, and subobjects associated with the HTML document that is inside of a window or frame.

Methods

close This method closes an open document data stream. When you call this method, all of the data sent to the document with the *write* and *writeln* methods is displayed in the document window.

```
document.close()
```

open This method opens a stream to begin receiving data through the *write* and *writeln* methods. You specify the mime type in the *mimeTypeString* argument. When you have finished sending data to the specified document, use the *close* method to close the stream.

```
document.open(mimeTypeString)
```

write   This method displays a dialog box that contains the text you specify in *textMessage* and an OK button. You are not required to specify the *window* keyword when using this method.

```
document.write(textMessage)
```

writeln   This method displays a dialog box with an OK button that contains the text you specify in *textMessage*. You are not required to specify the *window* keyword when using this method.

```
[window.]alert(textMessage)
```

Properties   *alinkColor* reflects the ALINK attribute.

anchors is an array reflecting all the anchors in a document.

bgColor reflects the BGCOLOR attribute.

cookie specifies a cookie.

fgColor reflects the TEXT attribute.

forms is an array reflecting all the forms in a document.

lastModified reflects the date a document was last modified.

linkColor reflects the LINK attribute.

links is an array reflecting all the links in a document.

referrer reflects the URL of the calling document.

title reflects the contents of the <TITLE> tag.

URL reflects the complete URL of a document.

vlinkColor reflects the VLINK attribute.

The following objects are also properties of the *document* object:
anchor
form
history
link

Added Properties   The following properties have been added to the Document object:

Property	Description
applets	An array reflecting all the applets in a document.
embeds	An array reflecting all the plug-ins in a document.
images	An array reflecting all the images in a document.

The following objects are now properties of the Document object:
Applet
Area
Image
Plugin

Shockwave

The Shockwave object is a subobject of the document object in Netscape Navigator and is a directly addressable object in MSIE. The reference to the Shockwave object is determined by the value assigned to the NAME parameter in the EMBED or OBJECT tag.

Creation If the value of the NAME parameter in an EMBED or OBJECT tag is "Surf" a call to the movie's *Rewind* method (see "Rewind" under Shockwave Object Methods below) it would appear like this in Navigator or Communicator:

```
document.Surf.Rewind()
```

and like this in MSIE:

```
Surf.Rewind()
```

Macromedia has developed a movie-aliasing script that determines which browser is playing the movie, and sets a JavaScript alias to the object that can be used throughout the document:

```
var gTheMovie
function setMovieAlias {
  if (navigator.appName == "Microsoft Internet Explorer")
  {
    gTheMovie = movieName;
  } else {
    gTheMovie = document.movieName;
  }
}
```

Replacing the object reference *movieName* in the script above with the value of the NAME parameter in the OBJECT or EMBED tag allows all references in other scripts to use the variable *gTheMovie* to refer to the Shockwave movie, regardless of the browser. The JavaScript function should be called from the Shockwave movie in the *startMovie* or *prepareMovie* handler by an *externalEvent* command:

```
on startMovie
  externalEvent "setMovieAlias()"
end
```

Methods These examples assume that a single reference alias (*movieRef*) has been created for the Shockwave object.

Play If the movie is stopped, the *Play* method starts it up.

```
movieRef.Play()
```

Stop Stops play of the movie, making it unresponsive to interaction until it begins play again.

```
movieRef.Stop()
```

Rewind Stops play of the movie, moves playback head to first frame of the movie.

```
movieRef.Rewind()
```

GetCurrentFrame Determines the current position of the playback head within the movie's score.

```
whatFrame = movieRef.GetCurrentFrame()
```

GotoFrame Tells a movie's playback head to move to the frame specified by the parameter. This method will work with movies that have been stopped.

```
movieRef.GotoFrame(integer)
```

GotoMovie Changes the movie displayed in the Shockwave movie window, having the same effect as the Lingo command *GotoNetMovie*.

```
movieRef.GotoMovie(URL)
```

EvalScript This handler passes a string value from the browser to a Shockwave movie. If the Shockwave movie has an *evalScript* handler, it can interpret the string. For more about the *EvalScript* method and handler, see the entry in Chapter 42, "Miscellaneous Lingo Category."

```
movieRef.EvalScript(string)
```

Window

OBJECT

The *window* object is the highest object in the JavaScript object hierarchy. All *document*, *frame*, and *location* objects are subobjects of the window object.

Creation A new *window* object is created when a page is loaded in the browser, or when you use a JavaScript statement like this:

```
windowObject = window.open(URL, winName [,winFeatures])
```

Then, you can use the methods, properties, objects, and event handlers below to work with your new *window* object.

> **Tip**
>
> *By the way, frames are just another type of* window *object and have all of the properties, methods, and event handlers of any other* window *object.*

Methods **alert** This method displays a dialog box that contains the text you specify in *textMessage* and an OK button. You are not required to specify the *window* keyword when using this method.

```
[window.]alert(textMessage)
```

For example, if you want to display a message that contains "You have Shockwave," use this statement:

```
alert("You have Shockwave")
```

blur (N3+)   This method is used to remove the focus from any object. When you execute the command, the specified window is pushed behind, and the next window behind it becomes the frontmost and active window.

```
windowObject.blur()
```

clearTimeout   This method is used to stop the handler specified by the *setTimeout* method from executing before it is called in the time specified by *setTimeout*. You must refer to the *timerID* returned by *setTimeout* for the timeout to be cleared.

```
clearTimeout(timerID)
```

close   This method closes the specified window. You can use it with or without the *windowObject* reference, unless you are using it from an event handler, where the *windowObject* reference is required. If you use it without the *windowObject* reference, *close()* closes the current window.

```
[windowObject.]close()
```

If you wish to close a window whose object reference is stored in a variable named "carl," you would use:

```
carl.close()
```

confirm   This method displays a dialog box with an OK button and a Cancel button, and the specified message. *Confirm* returns TRUE if the user clicks the OK button, and FALSE otherwise. It can be used within *if* statements to allow the user to make decisions. The *window* keyword is unnecessary, but it can be used to specify a certain window's object reference.

```
[window.]confirm(textMessage)
```

This JavaScript segment sends the user to the specified URL if the user clicks the OK button:

```
<SCRIPT Language = "JavaScript">
function areYouSure(){
        if(confirm("Are you sure?")) {
         window.open("www.url.com", "dug")
         }
}
</SCRIPT>
<BODY>
<A HREF="javascript:areYouSure()">Do you?</A>
</BODY>
```

focus (N3+)   This method makes the specified window object the active window, by bringing it to the front.

```
windowObject.focus()
```

open   This method opens a window. You can specify a URL, a window name, and various window features when you open the new window. You can also assign the window's object reference to a variable so that you can use other window object methods and properties such as *close()*, *focus()*, etc.

```
var=window.open(url[,name][,params])
```

The *var* is a variable that will contain the window object's reference. When you use other window methods or properties, you specify them with *var.method()*.

The *url* parameter must be a valid Internet URL. The *name* parameter is a name that can be used to reference the window in <FORM> and <A> tags.

The *params* parameter specifies the features that the new window will have. It is a string that can contain any of the following, in any order, separated by commas (but *no* spaces):

```
directories[=yes|no|1|0]
location[=yes|no|1|0]
menubar[=yes|no|1|0]
resizable[=yes|no|1|0]
scrollbars[=yes|no|1|0]
status[=yes|no|1|0]
toolbar[=yes|no|1|0]
height=numOfPixels
width=numOfPixels
```

As you can see, you can specify either "yes", "no", "1", or "0" for each of the boolean values. If you omit this parameter entirely, all of the window features will be present in the new window. If you specify an empty string (""), the new window will have none of the possible features.

This function opens a new window with certain window features. It assigns the window object to the variable *gWin*, so that other window commands can be used on the new window, such as *close()* and *focus()*.

```
<SCRIPT Language = "JavaScript">
// opens non-resizable window with
// scrollbars, status box, and fixed size
var gWin = window.open("http://www.nnn.com", "dug",
    "width=500,height=400,scrollbars,status");
</SCRIPT>
```

prompt This method displays a dialog box that contains an OK button and a Cancel button, a specified message, and a text entry field. *Prompt* returns the text the user types in the field if the user clicks the OK button; it returns *null* otherwise. The *window* keyword is unnecessary, but it can be used to specify a certain window's object reference.

The optional *defaultInput* parameter can be used to automatically place some data in the text entry field when it is displayed.

```
[window.]prompt(textMessage [,defaultInput])
```

This JavaScript segment sets the value of the variable *tText* to whatever the user enters in the prompt dialog. It then includes that text as a parameter to the embedded Shockwave movie, which can see that value by using the Lingo *externalParamValue()* function:

```
<SCRIPT Language = "JavaScript">
tText = prompt('What is your name', 'type name')
```

```
document.write("<embed src='temp.dcr' " +
     "width=400 height=240 " +
     "swl='" + tText + "'>")
</SCRIPT>
```

scroll (N3+)   This method scrolls the specified window to the x and y coordinates you specify. The upper left corner of the window is (0,0). (Remember: frames are just another type of window object, so you can use this and the other window object methods on frames too.)

```
windowObject.scroll(xCoord, yCoord)
```

This statement scrolls the frame named *content* to the x and y coordinate specified:

```
<SCRIPT Language = "JavaScript">
parent.content.scroll(0,200)
</SCRIPT>
```

setTimeout   This method executes the specified JavaScript handler after the specified number of milliseconds have elapsed (there are 1,000 milliseconds in one second). It returns a *timerID* value that can be used by the clearTimeout method to stop the previously specified JavaScript handler from executing.

```
timerID = setTimeout(expression, numOfMilliseconds)
```

For example, if you wanted to do a handler called *openHelp()* after five seconds, you would use a statement like:

```
timerID = setTimeout(openHelp(),5000)
```

Quirks   In MSIE, the *window.open()* method requires the "name" parameter, but in Netscape it is optional.

In addition, you can't open a .dcr (Shockwave) file directly in MSIE by passing the .dcr file as the URL in *window.open()* like you can in Netscape. This makes it difficult to create the Movie-In-a-Window (MIAW) type of Shockwave work in MSIE. In Netscape, opening a .dcr file works wonderfully: you can open it and specify no window parameters other than a width and height that is the same as the .dcr file, and have a "virtual" MIAW.

Since MSIE won't open a .dcr file directly, a workaround is to open an HTML file that just contains the <OBJECT> or <EMBED> tag to embed the .dcr file. However, this is not a cross-browser solution, since Netscape includes a generous amount of space around the embedded .dcr—space that is not there when Netscape opens the .dcr file directly.

MSIE displays scroll bars on windows that have content smaller than the visible display area regardless of the setting of the *scrollbar* window feature. Netscape behaves correctly in this regard.

In Netscape, the *alert()*, *confirm()*, and *prompt()* methods bring the specified window to the front and show the appropriate dialog box if a hidden window is specified. However, in MSIE the window remains hidden and the active window becomes unresponsive until you manually switch to the specified window, where you can then respond to the dialog.

Properties **defaultStatus** This property contains the message that is displayed in the window's status bar by default. When you set it, your message overrides the normal behavior of the status bar. This message is only displayed while the mouse pointer is in the window (or frame) specified by the *windowObject* reference.

If you set the *status* property through an event handler (such as *onMouseOver*), it will replace the message set by *defaultStatus*. After the event that is sending the *status* message is no longer occurring, the *defaultStatus* message will again be displayed in the status bar.

You can test and set this property with JavaScript.

This property is not supported in MSIE.

windowObject.defaultStatus(*textMessage*)

The above HTML segment will display a link on a page. When the mouse is not over the link, the *defaultStatus* message will be displayed in the status box.

```
<SCRIPT Language="JavaScript">
  self.defaultStatus = "When you point to a link, it will be described
  here."
</SCRIPT>
<BODY>
<A HREF="http://www.nnn.com" onMouseOver="self.status='Click me to go
  here';return true">Click Me</A>
</BODY>
```

frames This property contains an array with the object reference to each frame in the specified *windowObject*.

Use this syntax to access a certain frame by number (starting with zero):

windowObject.frames[*n*]

Use this syntax to count the total number of frames:

windowObject.frames.length

This JavaScript function will return the names of all of the frames in the topmost window:

```
function showFrameNames() {
  var tFrameCount=top.frames.length
  var tString = ""
  for(var i=0;i<tFrameCount;i++) {
    tString = tString +
            (top.frames[i].name) + "<BR>"
  }

        return tString

}
```

length   This property contains the number of frames in the specified *windowObject*. It returns the same value as *windowObject.frames.length*.

`windowObject.length`

name   This property contains a string that is the name of the specified *windowObject*.

`windowObject.name`

opener (N3+)   This property contains the reference to the window that executed the *open* method that opened the specified window. If the window was not opened by JavaScript, then this property contains *null*.

`windowObject.opener`

parent   This property is a way to refer to the window that contains the <FRAMESET> tag that created the current frame. You can use it anywhere a *windowObject* reference is expected when using a window object method or property.

`parent.methodOrProperty`

This statement writes the text "OK" to the frame named "content," when used from any of the other frames in the current window. You set a frame's name with a parameter like NAME="content" in the <FRAME> tag.

`parent.content.document.write("OK")`

self   This property is a way to refer to the current window or frame. You can use it anywhere a *windowObject* reference is expected when using a window object method or property.

`self.methodOrProperty`

status   This property can be used to send text to the specified window's status box. It is different from the *defaultStatus* property, in that *status* changes the text during the specified event, while *defaultStatus* changes the status box text when no other status-changing event is happening.

If you use the *status* property in an *onMouseOver* event handler, you must return TRUE to make it work correctly.

See the *defaultStatus* property for an example.

`status(textMessage)`

top   This property is used as a way to refer to the topmost window. You can use it anywhere a *windowObject* reference is expected when using a window object method or property.

`top.methodOrProperty`

window   This property is a way to refer to the current window or frame. It is the same as using the *self* property. You can use it anywhere a *windowObject* reference is expected when using a window object method or property.

`window.methodOrProperty`

Objects **document**   The *document* object is a property of the Window object. It contains methods and properties associated with the HTML document that is contained in a window. See the *Document* object methods and properties earlier in this section.

`windowObject.document.methodOrProperty`

frame   The *frame* object is a property of the Window object. A frame is a window object, contained within a window. As a window, a frame has all of the objects, methods, properties, and event handlers of any other window object.

`windowObject.frameName.methodOrProperty`

location   The *location* object contains the URL associated with the specified window object.

`windowObject.location[.property]`

Event Handlers **onBlur (N3+)**   This event handler executes the specified JavaScript code when the focus is removed from the specified window (i.e., when the window is no longer the active one). You specify the onBlur handler in the <BODY> tag of the document that lives in the window you want to use.

`<BODY onBlur=javaScriptCodeHere>`

onError (N3+)   This event handler executes the specified JavaScript code when an error occurs. If you specify an empty string or specify *null*, then all error reporting is suppressed.

`window.onError=javaScriptCodeHere`

onFocus (N3+)   This event handler executes the specified JavaScript code when the specified window becomes the active window. You specify the *onFocus* handler in the <BODY> tag of the document that lives in the window you want to use.

`<BODY onFocus=javaScriptCodeHere>`

onLoad   This event handler executes the specified JavaScript code when the specified window finishes loading its HTML document. You specify the onLoad handler in the <BODY> tag or <FRAMESET> tag of the document that lives in the window you want to use.

`<BODY onLoad=javaScriptCodeHere>`

onUnload   This event handler executes the specified JavaScript code when the user exits the specified window. You specify the onUnload handler in the <BODY> tag or <FRAMESET> tag of the document that lives in the window you want to use.

`<BODY onUnload=javaScriptCodeHere>`

Director Resources Online

Official

Macromedia, Inc.

http://www.macromedia.com/
http://www-euro.macromedia.com/
http://www-asia.macromedia.com/

The place for the latest big news on Director and other Macromedia products. Mirror sites for Europe and Asia.

Macromedia Developer Center

http://www.macromedia.com/support/director/

Links to the official developer support information.

Macromedia Shockzone

http://www.macromedia.com/shockzone/

Shockwave gallery, site of the day, latest plug-ins, and documentation.

Macromedia Director FTP

ftp://ftp.macromedia.com/pub/director/

Macromedia Director files and samples.

Relevant

Ventana's Director Online Companion

`http://www.vmedia.com/director.html`

For the latest information on Director from the publisher of this book.

Moshofsky/Plant

`http://www.moshplant.com/`

Site of Darrel Plant, co-author of *The Lingo Programmer's Reference* and author of *Shockwave! breathe new life into your web pages*.

Arogos Interactive

`http://www.arogos.com/`

Site of Doug Smith, co-author of *The Lingo Programmer's Reference*.

CleverMedia

`http://www.clevermedia.com/`

Site of Gary Rosenzweig, author of *The Director 6 Book* and *The Comprehensive Guide to Lingo*, also from Ventana.

Important

Director Web

`http://www.mcli.dist.maricopa.edu/director/`

The best resource for information on Director programming, examples, way-too-frequently asked questions, explanations of object-oriented programming, links, and access to the DIRECT-L archives.

DirectOregon

`http://www.moshplant.com/direct-or/`

A resource for Director programmers in the Pacific Northwest, home of the Bezier curve demos and the HIGHSCOR server.

breakPoint

`http://www.pixelgeek.com/pg/lingo/`

A monthly Lingo programming challenge from Zachary Belado. A fine way to learn about how to write Lingo.

Director Solutions

http://space.tin.it/internet/gchoo/

Geoff Choo's WEBzine of all sorts of info (including Geoff's MCI command guide) for Director users.

Director Threads

http://ds.dial.pipex.com/andy.white/

Andrew White's experiments and samples of threaded programming strategies in Lingo.

Dirigo Multimedia

http://www.maine.com/shops/gpicher/

The site of Glenn Picher, probably the best known of all independent Xobject and Xtra developers.

g/matter

http://www.gmatter.com/

Distributor of the largest collection of Xobjects, Xtras, and add-ons for Director.

Lingo User's Journal

http://www.penworks.com/LUJ/index.html

Monthly publication, by Tab Julius, of Lingo tips and examples for everyone from beginners to experts.

ObjectShop

http://www.pixelgeek.com/pg/objectS/

A group of Lingo programmers working toward the creation of a standardized OOP structure for Lingo.

SharedCast

ftp://ftp.sharedcast.com/

Marvyn Hortman's long established collection of code, examples, and goodies.

ShockeR

http://www.shocker.com/

Independent site dedicated to the best in Shockwave for Director. Home to the ShockR and FlasheR list servers.

updateStage

http://www.updatestage.com/

Gretchen MacDowell's (author/compiler of *The Lingo Timesaver*) monthly compilation of Director goodies.

Zav's page o stuff

http://www.blacktop.com/zav/

Shockwave godfather Alex Zavatone's *Shockwave Toolkit* lives here, among other things.

Discussion

DIRECT-L

http://tile.net/lists/direct1.html

The largest online community of Director users is an unofficial, unmoderated list server with a couple of thousand subscribers and 150-200 messages a day. Subscribe, set your mail filters, and step back.

DIRECT-L Spanish

http://www.mcli.dist.maricopa.edu/director/direct-1/espanol.html

A Spanish-language list server for Director users.

Director Newsgroup

news:alt.multimedia.director

Unofficial newsgroup for Director discussion.

Macromedia User Forum

http://www.citysites.com/mmuf/

This San Francisco-based group meets at Macromedia's offices on Townsend Street.

ShockeR

http://www.shocker.com/digests/index.html

Active discussion of Shockwave for Director.

UK Director Users Group

http://www.obsolete.com/dug/

Others

Article 19

http://www.article19.com/

Games, custom MIAW info, and the Digital white paper on Networked Interactive Multimedia Training.

donrelyea.com

http://www.donrelyea.com/

Don Relyea's personal site for sample code, some stunning Shockwave movies, and 3D texture maps.

Dreamlight

http://www.dreamlight.com/

Authors of the RAM monitor movie *RAMLight*.

grommett.com

http://www.grommett.com/

Tools and information sponsored by Kirk Keller Productions. Includes a Director Job list server.

Metasys

http://www.metasys.co.jp/

Great examples of Shockwave for Director navigation and use of Shockwave movies querying databases.

Penworks Corporation

http://www.penworks.com/

Creators of the Rollover Toolkit, DateMaster, and Cast Effects Xtras.

Glossary

asynchronous—Describes an action that is executed while other actions are taking place. Most Lingo is *synchronous*, meaning that one task is completed before another task begins. Asynchronous tasks are initiated and continue in the background while other tasks are taking place. Many Network Lingo commands are asynchronous, as are Idle Loading commands.

behavior—A special type of score script, introduced in Director 6, that allows a visual interface to Lingo scripting. Behaviors can be dragged onto sprites and frames, and values for parameters can be set from a visual interface rather than in a script.

branching—When a logical decision is made in a program, the course followed is called a *branch* and the process is sometimes called *branching*. Examples of Lingo constructs that create branching are *if then* and *case*.

cache—In a networked environment, a cache is where files downloaded from a remote location are stored. As the cache fills up during use, older files are deleted from the cache. The Director application and projectors create temporary caches that are cleared after the program quits. Web browsers typically store files until the disk space they occupy is needed.

cast library—A cast library is a collection of individual media items to be used in a Director movie. Since Director 5, movies may have multiple cast libraries, contained within the movie file and external to the movie.

cast member—A cast member is an individual media item to be used in a movie. Different types of cast members include bitmaps, sounds, text, fields, digital videos, scripts, transitions, and so on. The data for each cast member is stored as a part of the cast library or, in some cases, it can be *linked*. Linked cast member data is stored in an external file, and the cast library stores only a reference to the file name and path.

Standard types (identified by the symbol values used in *the type of member* property in Chapter 13) include:

- **#bitmap**   Images created from data that determine the color of individual pixels. File types that may be used as bitmaps include PICT (.PCT), GIF, JPEG (.JPG), BMP, and Photoshop. Bitmaps use from 1 bit to 32 bits of information per pixel to store color data, with 8-bit being the most common color depth used for multimedia. Bitmap cast members can be linked.

- **#btned**   A custom button type first appearing in Director 6. Allows users to create buttons with rollover, active, and disabled states by pasting images into an interface.

- **#button**   A button created using the Button tool from the Tool Palette. Allows for standard interface button types, including check boxes and radio buttons, but provides no automatic rollover function.

- **#digitalvideo**   A reference to a QuickTime (.MOV) or Video for Windows (.AVI) file consisting of digitized video data, sound, or other types of media. A digital video cast member is always linked.

- **#empty**   Indicates a cast member position containing no data and no reference to an external file.

- **#field**   Consists of text data that can be modified by a movie during playback. Field cast members are displayed on the screen with aliased (unsmoothed) text, and if the assigned font is not available on the playback computer, another font will be substituted.

- **#filmloop**   Contains the data copied from one or more cells of the score. Animations of a number of sprites and frames can be encapsulated in a film loop and used as a single sprite channel and frame. Film loops contain references to other cast members, their relative positions, the inks applied, and more.

- **#movie**   Refers to an external Director movie imported as a cast member. These cast members are always linked.

- **#ole**   A cast member created with Microsoft OLE (Object Linking and Embedding). OLE cast members are linked to the original documents from which they were created. This type of cast member is only editable in the Windows 95 and NT operating systems.

- **#palette**   Contains a custom color palette.

- **#picture**   Contains PICT drawing information consisting of shape information; it is similar to the #shape cast member type but is created with a program other than Director, and possibly includes more than one shape. It is smaller than a bitmap but not capable of offering as much detail as bitmaps can. Picture cast members may be linked.

- **#richText**   Text created in Director or as Rich Text Format files. It appears as smooth anti-aliased characters. It is converted to bitmap format when the movie is saved in protected or Shockwave formats.

- **#script**   A cast member containing a score script, a movie script, or a behavior (cast member scripts are part of the cast member).

- **#shape**   A PICT shape created using one of the shape tools from the Director Tool Palette.
- **#sound**   An AIFF (.AIF) or WAVE (.WAV) file imported for use in the sound channels. Sound cast members may be linked.
- **#SWA**   A Shockwave Audio file (a special type of cast member that is always linked to a file compressed using the SWA compression technology developed by Macromedia for Internet delivery of sudio files).
- **#transition**   A cast member created by assigning a transition to a frame in the score.

channel—Each row in the Score window is a channel. There are 120 sprite channels in Director 6, as well as special channels for tempo settings, palettes, transitions, sound, and scripts.

command—Lingo keyword that causes some action to be taken.

cue point—Sound files and digital video files can be marked with cues at specific points in the file. Director 6 can determine whether a particular point in a sound or digital video file has been reached by looking at which cues have been passed during play, and which ones are yet to be reached.

double-byte characters—Languages, such as Japanese, that don't use the roman character set use two bytes for each character of a string instead of one byte.

frame—Each column of the Score window represents a frame of the movie. Each frame represents a position in time within the movie. Frames may have scripts and behaviors attached to them to be executed when the playback head passes through the frame.

function—A function returns a value that may be based on one or more parameter values. An example of a function is *abs*, which returns a value equal to the absolute value of its parameter.

handler—A segment of code in a Lingo script that responds to a particular message. Signified by the keyword *on* and an identifier for the message, a handler contains Lingo statements that are executed when the handler receives the correct message. Handlers can be *procedures* that carry out a series of operations, or they can be *functions* that carry out a series of operations, then return a value to the handler that called them.

keyword—A predefined Lingo word that cannot be used for any purpose other than the one that's already defined.

layer—Sprites appear on the stage in layers, beginning with sprite channel 1 and continuing on to sprite channel 120. In cases where sprites overlap, the highest-numbered sprite always appears on top (direct-to-stage digital video is the only exception).

list—Lingo lists are arrays of items consisting of individual values or property/value pairs.

marker—Individual frames in the score can be tagged with a marker for easy visual identification as well as reference use. Markers can be labeled with text identifiers.

mask—A 1-bit bitmap cast member that can be used to determine how custom cursor images will interact with elements in the stage.

MCI commands—The Windows operating system allows Lingo users to access some types of media files and devices through a series of commands known collectively as the Media Control Interface (MCI). MCI commands can be used to control playback of audio CDs, laser discs, and other types of devices. See the *mci* command in Chapter 9.

Message window—A window in the Director authoring environment that allows commands to be executed and data to be displayed during a movie's development.

MIAW—Acronym for Movie in a Window, a Director movie that has been opened up in a separate window from the movie playing in the authoring environment or a projector. MIAWs are often used for authoring tools.

movie—A Director file containing media and data in the score; it may or may not include interactivity. Not to be confused with a QuickTime or Video for Windows *digital video* file.

movie script—A script whose handlers are available throughout the movie. These scripts are not attached to a specific frame, sprite, or cast member.

object reference—A variable or expression whose value points to a position in RAM that is the location of the child of a parent script, XObject, or Xtra.

palette—In Director, a lookup table with 256 RGB color values, one for each value from 0 to 255.

projector—An application created from a Director movie, capable of being played without the authoring program.

property—The name of a value associated with an object. Director has many properties associated with the movie, cast members, and other predefined objects. Properties can also be created by the user to be associated with objects created from parent scripts and behaviors. Individual items in property lists can be named or identified by properties as well. Most properties can be modified, or *set*, by the user, but some predefined properties are constants and can only be *tested*, not set.

protected—To prevent others from accessing your Lingo scripts and easily accessing the various media elements of your movies, you may choose to protect them, using the Update Movies command in the Xtras menu. Shockwave movies are protected *and* compressed.

proxy server—For security, some organizations have set up a special type of Web server that acts as a buffer between users inside the organization and the outside world. When a user inside the organization makes a request for a document, the request is passed through the proxy server. If the server has recently downloaded the file, it is passed to the user; otherwise, the proxy downloads the file from outside, then passes it on to the user, often after determining whether it may contain known security violations.

puppet—In Director, a puppet is an object normally controlled by the score (sprite, sound, transition, etc.) that is controlled by Lingo. When a sprite or sound has been *puppeted*, it is no longer under the control of the score.

repeat loop—Any type of programming structure that is designed to repeat the same commands over and over, either indefinitely or for a set number of times. A repeat loop can take a number of forms, but the two most common are the *repeat* control structure (which repeats a series of statements until a test value meets specific criteria) and an *on exitFrame go to* loop (where the playback head is sent to the same frame, or an earlier frame, and encounters the same *exitFrame* handler repeatedly).

score—The visual timeline of a Director movie, showing which sprites are on the stage, what sounds are playing, what transitions are taking place, and so on.

script—A cast member that contains programming instructions in Lingo. One or more handlers may be placed into a script. Scripts may also be attached to other types of cast members.

shape cast member—Shapes can be created through the use of Lingo or by the tools in the Tool Palette. They include filled and unfilled rectangles, ovals, and round-edged rectangles, as well as lines. A shape takes up much less memory than a bitmap image but has no ability to display detail.

Shockwave movie—A Director movie that has been protected and compressed, originally solely for use on the Internet but now also for playback by projectors.

significant digits—A mathematical term referring to the number of digits that have any real meaning in a calculation. Generally, the lowest number of digits of any value in a calculation.

sprite—Any cast member that appears on the stage (i.e., it is in the score or has been placed onto the stage through the use of Lingo). Sprites may have scripts and behaviors assigned to them, to control interactivity and/or animation.

sprite channel—One of the 120 numbered rows in the score where cast members are placed so that they will appear on the stage.

sprite property—A named value associated with a sprite object.

OK - DPstage—The visual aspect of a Director movie where sprites appear to the viewer.

statement—An individual unit in a Lingo script, equivalent to a sentence in a language, containing all of the elements necessary to complete a command or control structure.

streaming—The process of displaying or playing part of a file before the entire file has been loaded into memory. This has always been done with digital video in Director: the file is read from the disk and plays as it is read. Shockwave Audio added this capability in Director 5, with the ability to begin play of an audio file from a disk or a Web server while it is still being downloaded. Director 6 extends streaming to the movie files and the casts themselves, with the ability to play movies before the entire file has arrived at its destination.

SWA (Shockwave Audio)—Audio files compressed using Macromedia's compression tools (SoundEdit 16 on the MacOS; the Director Convert WAV to SWA Xtra on Windows) for high-quality, highly compressed sound.

tempo—The speed at which a Director movie plays. Generally rendered in *frames per second* and controlled by settings in the tempo channel or by Lingo.

tick—A tick is roughly $\frac{1}{60}$ of a second. Most Director timing values are rendered in ticks.

track—Digital video can have multiple tracks of data, including the video component, different audio tracks for multiple languages, text overlays, and more.

trails—Normally, when a sprite is moved on the stage, its old position is redrawn so that there is no trace of its having been there. The *trails* property of a sprite controls that redraw, working normally if it is set to FALSE, and leaving the old image of the sprite in place if it is TRUE.

transition—Transitions control how the screen is redrawn between the previous frame and the frame the transition occupies. Director has more than 50 built-in transitions, and others are available as Xtras.

tweening—Borrowed from the world of animation, the process of tweening takes two known values and creates intermediate values *between* them. This is often used to create movement and effects with sprites.

variable—Variables are either *local* or *global*. Local variables can be used only within the handler in which they are defined. Global variables can be used in any handler in the movie by defining the global at the top of the script the handler appears in.

Xtras—Plug-ins that extend the capabilities of Director. Xtras can add new commands to Lingo, new types of transitions, new types of cast members, and many more things.

VENTANA

http://www.vmedia.com

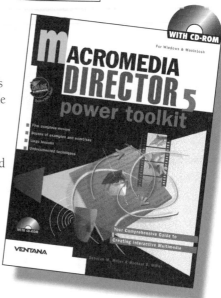

VENTANA

The Director 6 Book

$49.99, 560 pages, part #: 1-56604-658-0

Macintosh, Windows 95/NT
Intermediate to Advanced

Raise your standards—and your stock—as a multimedia specialist by harnessing what's new in Macromedia Director 6. This professional-level guide focuses on key techniques for creating, manipulating and optimizing files. Your projects will look, sound and play back better and more consistently than ever.
Provides:
- Undocumented tricks for Director 6.
- Tips for moving from Director 5 to 6.
- Issues and answers for cross-platform presentations.
- Techniques for integrating Director 6 with JavaScript, CGI and Shockwave audio.

The CD-ROM includes more than 50 sample Director movies with code included, plus Macromedia and gmatter Xtras, shareware and more.

The Lingo Programmer's Reference

$39.99, 500 pages, part #: 1-56604-695-5

Windows 95/NT, Macintosh
Intermediate to Advanced

The Ultimate Resource for Director Professionals! High-level mastery of Lingo is the only route to real Director expertise. This comprehensive reference goes beyond tutorials and simple listings to provide thorough explanations of every aspect of Lingo, supported by practical examples, professional tips and undocumented tricks. Includes:
- What's new in Director 6, property lists for sprites and other objects, and a JavaScript reference for Lingo programmers.
- In-depth discussions, including types of parameters to pass to properties, commands, functions and type of data returned.
- Encyclopedic listing, extensively cross-referenced for easy access to information.

The CD-ROM features a searchable, hyperlinked version of the book.

FreeHand 7 Graphics Studio
The Comprehensive Guide

R. Shamms Mortier
$49.99, 800 pages, illustrated, part #: 679-3

A master class in cutting-edge graphics! Express
your creative powers to the fullest in print, on the
Web, on CD-ROM—anywhere sophisticated imagery
is in demand. Step-by-step exercises help you master
each component—Freehand 7, xRes, Fontographer
and Extreme3D—with professional guidelines for
using them separately, together, and in partnership
with third-party products.
CD-ROM: Sample files, sample web pages, free
Xtras, plug-ins & more!

For Windows, Macintosh • Intermediate to Advanced

Web Publishing With Macromedia Backstage
Internet Studio 2

R. Shamms Mortier, Winston Steward
$49.99, 448 pages, illustrated, part #: 598-3

Farewell to HTML! This overview of all four tiers of
Backstage Internet Studio 2 lets users jump in at
their own level. With the focus on processes as well
as techniques, readers learn everything they need to
create center-stage pages.

CD-ROM: Plug-ins, applets, animations, audio files,
Director xTras and demos.

For Windows, Macintosh • Intermediate to Advanced

VENTANA

Looking Good in Print, Deluxe CD-ROM Edition

$34.99, 416 pages, illustrated, part #: 1-56604-471-5

This completely updated version of the most widely used design companion for desktop publishers features all-new sections on color and printing. Packed with professional tips for creating powerful reports, newsletters, ads, brochures and more. The companion CD-ROM featues Adobe® Acrobat® Reader, author examples, fonts, templates, graphics and more.

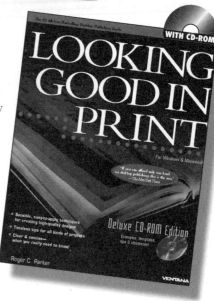

Looking Good Online

$39.99, 384 pages, illustrated, part #: 1-56604-469-3

Create well-designed, organized web sites—incorporating text, graphics, digital photos, backgrounds and forms. Features studies of successful sites and design tips from pros. The companion CD-ROM includes samples from online professionals; buttons, backgrounds, templates and graphics.

Looking Good in 3D

$39.99, 384 pages, illustrated, part #: 1-56604-494-4

Become the da Vinci of the 3D world! Learn the artistic elements involved in 3D design—light, motion, perspective, animation and more—to create effective interactive projects. The CD-ROM includes samples from the book, templates, fonts and graphics.

VENTANA

3D Studio MAX f/x

$49.99, 552 pages, illustrated, part #: 1-56604-427-8

Create Hollywood-style special effects! Plunge into 3D animation with step-by-step instructions for lighting, camera movements, optical effects, texture maps, storyboarding, cinematography, editing and much more. The companion CD-ROM features free plug-ins, all the tutorials from the book, 300+ original texture maps and animations.

Microsoft SoftImage|3D Professional Techniques

$49.99, 524 pages, illustrated, part #: 1-56604-499-5

Create intuitive, visually rich 3D images with this award-winning technology. Follow the structured tutorial to master modeling, animation and rendering, and to increase your 3D productivity. The CD-ROM features tutorials, sample scenes, textures, scripts, shaders, images and animations.

LightWave 3D 5 Character Animation f/x

$49.99, 744 pages, illustrated, part #: 1-56604-532-0

Master the fine—and lucrative—art of 3D character animation. Traditional animators and computer graphic artists alike will discover everything they need to know: lighting, motion, caricature, composition, rendering ... right down to work-flow strategies. The CD-ROM features a collection of the most popular LightWave plug-ins, scripts, storyboards, finished animations, models and much more.

VENTANA

Official Netscape Communicator Book

$39.99, 800 pages
Beginning to Intermediate
Windows Edition: part #: 1-56604-617-3
Macintosh Edition: part #:1-56604-620-3

The sequel to Ventana's blockbuster international bestseller
Official Netscape Navigator Book! Discover the first suite to integrate
key intranet and Internet communications services into a single,
smart interface. From simple e-mail to workgroup collaboration, from
casual browsing to Web publishing, from reading text to receiving
multimedia Netcaster channels—learn to do it all without leaving
Communicator! Covers:

- All Communicator components: Navigator, Netcaster, Messenger,
  Collabra, Composer and Conference.
- Complete, step-by-step instructions for both intranet and Internet
  task.
- Tips on using plug-ins, JavaScript and Java applets.

The CD-ROM includes a fully-supported version of Netscape
Communicator plus hyperlinked listings.

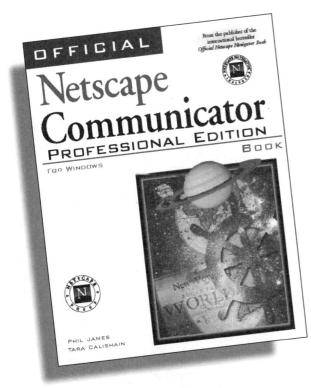

Official Netscape Communicator
Professional Edition Book

$39.99, 608 pages, part #:1-56604-739-0

Windows Edition • Intermediate

**Your Guide to Business Communications Over the
Intranet & the Web!** Unlock the immeasurable potential of
Web technologies for improving and enhancing day-to-day
business tasks. Netscape Communicator and your office
intranet provide the tools and the environment. This easy-to-
use, step-by-step guide opens the door to each key mod-
ule—and its most effective use. Covers:

- Navigator 4, Messenger, Collabra, Conference, Composer,
  Calendar, Netcaster and AutoAdmin.
- Key business tasks: e-mail, workgroups, conferencing and
  Web publishing.
- Step-by-step instructions, tips and guidelines for working
  effectively.

VENTANA

Official Netscape Messenger & Collabra Book

$39.99, 408 pages, part #: 1-56604-685-8

Windows, Macintosh • Intermediate to Advanced

The Power of Web-based Communications—Without a Web Site!
Stay in touch with customers; promote products and services visually; share the latest market trends—with simple Internet dial-up access! This step-by-step guide helps you harness Netscape Communicator's e-mail, newsreader, HTML authoring and real-time conference tools to achieve faster, more powerful business communications—without the effort or expense of a Web site. Learn how to:
• Integrate Messenger, Collabra, Conference and Composer for efficient business communications.
• Distribute eye-catching, HTML-based marketing materials without a Web site.
• Use the Net to gather, organize and share information efficiently.

Official Netscape Composer Book

$39.99, 600 pages, part #: 1-56604-674-2

Windows • Beginning to Intermediate

Forget about tedious tags and cumbersome code! Now you can create sophisticated, interactive Web pages using simple, drag-and-drop techniques. Whether you want to create your personal home page, promote your hobby, or launch your business on the Web, here's everything you need to know to get started:
• Step-by-step instructions for designing sophisticated Web sites with no previous experience.
• JavaScript basics and techniques for adding multimedia, including animation and interactivity.
• Tips for businesses on the Web, including creating forms, ensuring security and promoting a Web site.
The CD-ROM features a wide selection of Web tools for designing Web pages, adding multimedia, creating forms and building image maps.

Official Netscape Plug-in Book, Second Edition

$39.99, 700 pages, part #: 1-56604-612-2

Windows, Macintosh • All Users

Your One-Stop Plug-in Resource & Desktop Reference!
Why waste expensive online time searching the Net for the plug-ins you want? This handy one-stop reference includes in-depth reviews, easy-to-understand instructions and step-by-step tutorials. And you avoid costly download time—the hottest plug-ins are included! Includes:
• In-depth reviews & tutorials for most Netscape plug-ins.
• Professional tips on designing pages with plug-ins.
• Fundamentals of developing your own plug-ins.

The CD-ROM includes all the featured plug-ins available at press time.

VENTANA

Official Online Marketing With Netscape Book

$34.99, 544 pages, illustrated, part #: 1-56604-453-7

The perfect marketing tool for the Internet! Learn how innovative marketers create powerful, effectove electronic newsletters and promotional materials. Step-by-step instructions show you how to plan, deisgn and distribute professional-quality pieces. With this easy-to-follow guide, you'll soon be flexing Netscape Navigator's marketing muscle to eliminate paper and printing costs, automate market research and customer service, and much more.

Official Netscape Guide to Online Investments

$24.99, 528 pages, illustrated, part #: 1-56604-452-9

Gain the Internet investment edge! Here's everything you need to make the Internet a full financial partner. Features an overview of the Net and Navigator; in-depth reviews of stock and bond quote services, analysts, brokerage houses, and mutual fund reports. Plus a full listing of related financial services such as loans, appraisals, low-interest credit cards, venture capital, entrepreneurship, insurance, tax counseling, and more.

Official Netscape Guide to Internet Research

$29.99, 480 pages, illustrated, part #: 1-56604-604-1

Turn the Internet into your primary research tool. More than just a listing of resources, this official guide provides everything you need to know to access, organize, cite and post information on the Net. Includes research strategies, search engines and information management. Plus timesaving techniques for finding the best, most up-to-date data.

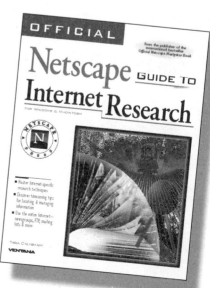

VENTANA

Web Publishing With Adobe PageMill 2

$34.99, 480 pages, illustrated, part #: 1-56604-458-8

Now, creating and designing professional pages on the Web is a simple, drag-and-drop function. Learn to pump up PageMill with tips, tricks and troubleshooting strategies in this step-by-step tutorial for designing professional pages. The CD-ROM features Netscape plug-ins, original textures, graphical and text-editing tools, sample backgrounds, icons, buttons, bars, GIF and JPEG images, Shockwave animations.

Web Publishing With QuarkImmedia

$39.99, 552 pages, illustrated, part #: 1-56604-525-8

Use multimedia to learn multimedia, building on the power of QuarkXPress. Step-by-step instructions introduce basic features and techniques, moving quickly to delivering dynamic documents for the Web and other electronic media. The CD-ROM features an interactive manual and sample movie gallery with displays showing settings and steps. Both are written in QuarkImmedia.

VENTANA

Interactive Web Publishing With Microsoft Tools

$49.99, 848 pages, illustrated, part #: 1-56604-462-6

Take advantage of Microsoft's broad range of development tools to produce powerful web pages, program with VBScript, create virtual 3D worlds, and incorporate the functionality of Office applications with OLE. The CD-ROM features demos/lite versions of third party software, sample code.

Web Publishing With Microsoft FrontPage 97

$34.99, 500 pages, illustrated, part #: 1-56604-478-2

Web page publishing for everyone! Streamline web-site creation and automate maintenance, all without programming! Covers introductory-to-advanced techniques, with hands-on examples. For Internet and intranet developers. The CD-ROM includes all web-site examples from the book, FrontPage add-ons, shareware, clip art and more.

Web Publishing With ActiveX Controls

$39.99, 688 pages, illustrated, part #: 1-56604-647-5

Activate web pages using Microsoft's powerful new ActiveX technology. From HTML basics to layout, find all you need to make web pages come alive, add multimedia punch to pages and streamline work with ActiveX Controls.The CD-ROM features example files from the book, Working Scripts for using Explorer's built-in controls, 3D Viewer, HTML editor, image map editor and more!

The Comprehensive Guide to Corel WEB.GRAPHICS SUITE

$49.99, 696 pages, illustrated, part #: 1-56604-614-9

Create spectacular web pages, incorporating sophisticated graphics and animation! Every component of CorelWEB is highlighted with an introduction, tools, tips and tricks, and a sample project. The Suite features tools for editing web pages, creating animation for web pages, designing 3D worlds and converting word processing files to HTML. Plus an illustration package based on CorelDRAW 5— along with 7,500 Internet-ready clipart images in GIF and JPEG formats. The CD-ROM includes images, textures and shareware for web designers.

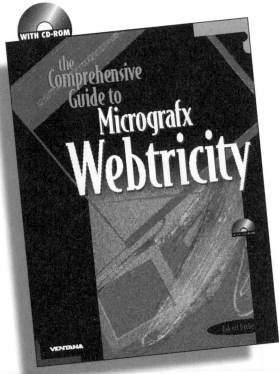

The Comprehensive Guide to Micrografx Webtricity

$49.99, 672 pages, illustrated, part #: 1-56604-607-6

Make your site soar with interactive excitement--and save time and money doing it! Micrografx Webtricity provides the drag-and-drop tool palette--this easy-to-follow, practical guide adds instructions, ideas and professional guidelines. Learn to design sophisticated, eye-catching graphics, optimize your files for the Web, create dazzling 3D effects and animations, catalog the hundreds of graphics files included in Webtricity, and much more. The CD-ROM features in-line viewers for dozens of formats, plus additional web-site utilities and images.

VENTANA

The Comprehensive Guide to VBScript

$39.99, 864 pages, illustrated, part #: 1-56604-470-7

The only complete reference to VBScript and HTML commands and features. Plain-English explanations; A-to-Z listings; real-world, practical examples for plugging directly into programs; ActiveX tutorial. The CD-ROM features a hypertext version of the book, along with all code examples.

The Microsoft Merchant Server Book

$49.99, 600 pages, illustrated, part #: 1-56604-610-6

Open the door to your online store! Now the long-awaited promise of retail sales is closer to fulfillment. From basic hardware considerations to complex technical and management issues, you'll find everything you need to create your site. Features case studies highlighting Microsoft Banner sites and a step-by-step guide to creating a working retail site. The CD-ROM features convenient customizing tools, Internet Information Server, Wallet, ActiveX SDK, Java SDK and more.

Build a Microsoft Intranet

$49.99, 624 pages, illustrated, part #: 1-56604-498-7

Streamline your Intranet design using Microsoft's uniquely integrated tools. Plan, install, configure and manage your Intranet. And use other Microsoft products to author and browse web pages. Includes CD-ROM supporting and reference documents, pointers to Internet resources.

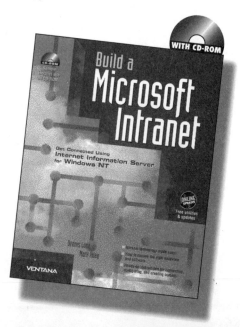

VENTANA

TO ORDER ANY VENTANA TITLE, COMPLETE THIS ORDER FORM AND MAIL OR FAX IT TO US, WITH PAYMENT, FOR QUICK SHIPMENT.

TITLE	PART #	QTY	PRICE	TOTAL

SHIPPING

For orders shipping within the United States, please add $4.95 for the first book, $1.50 for each additional book.
For "two-day air," add $7.95 for the first book, $3.00 for each additional book.
Email: vorders@kdc.com for exact shipping charges.
Note: Please include your local sales tax.

SUBTOTAL = $ _____

SHIPPING = $ _____

TAX = $ _____

TOTAL = $ _____

Mail to: International Thomson Publishing • 7625 Empire Drive • Florence, KY 41042
☎ **US orders 800/332-7450 • fax 606/283-0718**
☎ **International orders 606/282-5786 • Canadian orders 800/268-2222**

Name _____

E-mail _____ Daytime phone _____

Company _____

Address (No PO Box) _____

City _____ State _____ Zip _____

Payment enclosed ___VISA ___MC ___ Acc't # _____ Exp. date _____

Signature _____ Exact name on card _____

Check your local bookstore or software retailer for these and other bestselling titles, or call toll free:

800/332-7450

8:00 am - 6:00 pm EST

New Xtras for THE INTERNET from *g/matter*

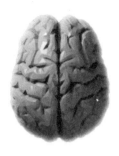

LiveHTML Xtra
Integrated Dynamic Web Browsers for Director

LiveHTML Xtra enables developers to place a custom HTML browser directly into any multimedia interface! The product includes both a built-in HTML renderer and Microsoft's Internet Explorer ActiveX control to display dynamic web pages. Its Server Push features allow remote LiveServers to automatically update content being viewed. (For Director 5 and 6) Developed by *New Alloy, Inc.*

MasterApp Xtra
Comprehensive Control of Web Browsers Within Director and Authorware

MasterApp makes it easy to locate, launch and control other software applications from within any multimedia presentation. Now developers can add Netscape and Internet Explorer web browsers to sales presentations, searchable and printable Adobe Acrobat documents to educational titles, and fully functional product demos to instructional software. (For Director 5 and 6) Developed by *Dirigo Multimedia.*

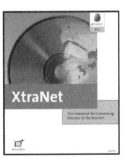

XtraNet
The Standard for Connecting Director to the Internet

XtraNet enables you to add Internet connectivity to any Director-based multimedia production. Now you can merge rich multimedia content found on CD-ROMs and kiosks with the resources and immediacy of the Internet. Best of all, XtraNet works behind the scenes, independent of Web browsers and mail servers. (For Director 5 and 6) Developed by *HumanCode, Inc.*

for more information...

sales@gmatter.com   **1-800-933-6223**   **www.gmatter.com**
(1-415-243-0394)

g/matter: The World's Leading Publisher of Xtras for Macromedia Director and Authorware

Anecdote Xtra	InstalledFonts Xtra	MasterApp Xtra	ProgressCopy Xtra	Trans-X Xtra
Dialogs Xtra	Install Xtra	The MediaBook CD	ScriptOMatic Xtra	XtraDraw
DirectSound Xtra	KILLER Transitions V1	PickFolder Xtra	Sound Xtra	XtraNet
Director ToolBox Pro	LiveHTML Xtra	PrintOMatic Xtra	StageHand Buttons Xtra	XtraText

Xtras for DIRECTOR
from *g/matter*

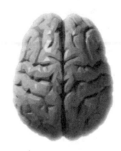

PrintOMatic Xtra
The Best Way to Print from Director
PrintOMatic Xtra enables Director to print just about anything. Now you can easily create kiosks, training programs, reference products and edutainment CDs that allow end users to easily print order forms, datasheets, test results and other material for later use. (For Director 5 and 6) Developed by *Electronic Ink*.

PopMenu Xtra
Creates Instant Pop-up Menus in Director
Easily add single and hierarchical pop-up menus to your Director-based projects with out writing a single line of code. PopMenu Xtra saves development time and enhances the look and feel of your games, reference titles, Shocked web sites and more! (For Director 5 and 6) Developed by *Red Eye Software*.

Sound Xtra
Total Control of Sound Recording and Playback in Director
Sound Xtra enables multimedia developers to create more dynamic children's titles, games, language programs and more by easily adding interactive record and playback sound controls to Director productions. Sound Xtra features a wide variety of recording and playback options to ensure glitch-free audio control. (For Director 5 and 6) Developed by *Red Eye Software*.

---

for more information...

sales@gmatter.com   **1-800-933-6223**   **www.gmatter.com**

(1-415-243-0394)

---

g/matter: **The World's Leading Publisher of Xtras for Macromedia Director and Authorware**

Anecdote Xtra	InstalledFonts Xtra	MasterApp Xtra	ProgressCopy Xtra	Trans-X Xtra
Dialogs Xtra	Install Xtra	The MediaBook CD	ScriptOMatic Xtra	XtraDraw
DirectSound Xtra	KILLER Transitions V1	PickFolder Xtra	Sound Xtra	XtraNet
Director ToolBox Pro	LiveHTML Xtra	PrintOMatic Xtra	StageHand Buttons Xtra	XtraText

MACROMEDIA ®
End-User License Agreement for Shockwave ™ Run-Time Software (*"The Software"*)

PLEASE READ THIS DOCUMENT CAREFULLY BEFORE FIRST USING THE SOFTWARE. THIS DOCUMENT PROVIDES IMPORTANT INFORMATION CONCERNING THE SOFTWARE, PROVIDES YOU WITH A LICENSE TO USE THE SOFTWARE, AND CONTAINS WARRANTY AND LIABILITY INFORMATION. BY FIRST USING THE SOFTWARE, YOU ARE ACCEPTING THE SOFTWARE AND AGREEING TO BECOME BOUND BY THE TERMS OF THIS AGREEMENT. IF YOU DO NOT WISH TO DO SO, DO NOT USE THE SOFTWARE.

1. Important Notice
Shockwave software is a unique addition to Macromedia's Run-Time software library, allowing End-Users to play applications created with Macromedia's authoring software, available on the World Wide Web. The Software is an object code package that is designed to run with and will run only with an Internet browser which is licensed to contain and contains Macromedia Player software. If your browser is not one of these, the Software may not function properly.

2. License
This Agreement allows you to:
    (a) Use the Software on a single computer.
    (b) Make one copy of the Software in machine-readable form for backup purposes.

3. Restrictions
Unless Macromedia has authorized you to distribute the Software, you may not make or distribute copies of the Software or electronically transfer the Software from one computer to another. You may not decompile, reverse engineer, disassemble, or otherwise reduce the Software to a human-perceivable form. You may not modify, rent, resell for profit, distribute or create derivative works based upon the Software.

4. Ownership
This license gives you limited rights to use the Software. You do not own and Macromedia retains ownership of the Software and all copies of it. All rights not specifically granted in this Agreement, including Federal and International copyrights, are reserved by Macromedia.

5. Disclaimer of Warranties and Technical Support
The Software is provided to you free of charge, and on an "AS IS" basis, without any technical support or warranty of any kind from Macromedia, including, without limitation, a warranty of merchantability, fitness for a particular purpose and non-infringement. SOME STATES DO NOT ALLOW THE EXCLUSION OF IMPLIED WARRANTIES, SO THE ABOVE EXCLUSION MAY NOT APPLY TO YOU. YOU MAY ALSO HAVE OTHER LEGAL RIGHTS WHICH VARY FROM STATE TO STATE.

6. Limitation of Damages
MACROMEDIA SHALL NOT BE LIABLE FOR ANY INDIRECT, SPECIAL, INCIDENTAL OR CONSEQUENTIAL DAMAGE OR LOSS (INCLUDING DAMAGES FOR LOSS OF BUSINESS, LOSS OF PROFITS, OR THE LIKE), WHETHER BASED ON BREACH OF CONTRACT, TORT (INCLUDING NEGLIGENCE), PRODUCT LIABILITY OR OTHERWISE, EVEN IF MACROMEDIA OR ITS REPRESENTATIVES HAVE BEEN ADVISED OF THE POSSIBILITY OF SUCH DAMAGES. SOME STATES DO NOT ALLOW THE LIMITATION OR EXCLUSION OF LIABILITY FOR INCIDENTAL OR CONSEQUENTIAL DAMAGES, SO THIS LIMITATION OR EXCLUSION MAY NOT APPLY TO YOU. The limited warranty, exclusive remedies and limited liability set forth above are fundamental elements of the basis of the bargain between Macromedia and you. You agree that Macromedia would not be able to provide the Macromedia Software on an economic basis without such limitations.

7. Government End-Users   RESTRICTED RIGHTS LEGEND
The Software is "Restricted Computer Software." Use, duplication, or disclosure by the Government is subject to restrictions as set forth in subparagraph (c)(1)(ii) of the Rights in Technical Data and Computer Software clause at DFARS 252.227-7013. Manufacturer: Macromedia, Inc., 600 Townsend St., San Francisco, CA, 94103.

8. General
This Agreement shall be governed by the internal laws of the State of California. This Agreement contains the complete agreement between the parties with respect to the subject matter hereof, and supersedes all prior or contemporaneous agreements or understandings, whether oral or written. All questions concerning this Agreement shall be directed to: Macromedia, Inc., 600 Townsend St., San Francisco, CA, 94103, Attention: Chief Financial Officer.

Macromedia is a registered trademark and Shockwave is a trademark of Macromedia, Inc.